Studies in Development Economics and Policy

General Editor: **Finn Tarp**

UNU WORLD INSTITUTE FOR DEVELOPMENT ECONOMICS RESEARCH (UNU-WIDER) was established by the United Nations University as its first research and training centre and started work in Helsinki, Finland, in 1985. The purpose of the Institute is to undertake applied research and policy analysis on structural changes affecting the developing and transitional economies, to provide a forum for the advocacy of policies leading to robust, equitable and environmentally sustainable growth, and to promote capacity strengthening and training in the field of economic and social policy–making. Its work is carried out by staff researchers and visiting scholars in Helsinki and through networks of collaborating scholars and institutions around the world.

UNU World Institute for Development Economics Research (UNU-WIDER)
Katajanokanlaituri 6 B, FIN-00160 Helsinki, Finland

Titles include:

Tony Addison and Alan Roe (*editors*)
FISCAL POLICY FOR DEVELOPMENT
Poverty, Reconstruction and Growth

Tony Addison, Henrik Hansen and Finn Tarp (*editors*)
DEBT RELIEF FOR POOR COUNTRIES

Tony Addison and George Mavrotas (*editors*)
DEVELOPMENT FINANCE IN THE GLOBAL ECONOMY
The Road Ahead

Tony Addison and Tilman Brück (*editors*)
MAKING PEACE WORK
The Challenges of Social and Economic Reconstruction

George G. Borjas and Jeff Crisp (*editors*)
POVERTY, INTERNATIONAL MIGRATION AND ASYLUM

Ricardo Ffrench-Davis and Stephany Griffith-Jones (*editors*)
FROM CAPITAL SURGES TO DROUGHT
Seeking Stability for Emerging Economies

David Fielding (*editor*)
MACROECONOMIC POLICY IN THE FRANC ZONE

Basudeb Guha-Khasnobis and George Mavrotas (*editors*)
FINANCIAL DEVELOPMENTS, INSTITUTIONS, GROWTH AND POVERTY REDUCTION

Basudeb Guha-Khasnobis, Shabd S. Acharya and Benjamin Davis (*editors*)
FOOD INSECURITY, VULNERABILITY AND HUMAN RIGHTS FAILURE

Basudeb Guha-Khasnobis and Ravi Kanbur (*editors*)
INFORMAL LABOUR MARKETS AND DEVELOPMENT

Basudeb Guha-Khasnobis (*editor*)
THE WTO, DEVELOPING COUNTRIES AND THE DOHA DEVELOPMENT AGENDA
Prospects and Challenges for Trade-led Growth

Aiguo Lu and Manuel F. Montes (*editors*)
POVERTY, INCOME DISTRIBUTION AND WELL-BEING IN ASIA DURING THE TRANSITION

George Mavrotas and Anthony Shorrocks (*editors*)
ADVANCING DEVELOPMENT
Core Themes in Global Economics

George Mavrotas and Mark McGillivray (*editors*)
DEVELOPMENT AID
A Fresh Look

George Mavrotas (*editor*)
DOMESTIC RESOURCE MOBILIZATION AND FINANCIAL DEVELOPMENT

Mark McGillivray (*editor*)
ACHIEVING THE MILLENNIUM DEVELOPMENT GOALS

Mark McGillivray (*editor*)
HUMAN WELL-BEING
Concept and Measurement

Mark McGillivray (*editor*)
INEQUALITY, POVERTY AND WELL-BEING

Robert J. McIntyre and Bruno Dallago (*editors*)
SMALL AND MEDIUM ENTERPRISES IN TRANSITIONAL ECONOMIES

Vladimir Mikhalev (*editor*)
INEQUALITY AND SOCIAL STRUCTURE DURING THE TRANSITION

E. Wayne Nafziger and Raimo Väyrynen (*editors*)
THE PREVENTION OF HUMANITARIAN EMERGENCIES

Wim Naudé (*editor*)
ENTREPRENEURSHIP AND ECONOMIC DEVELOPMENT

Machiko Nissanke and Erik Thorbecke (*editors*)
THE IMPACT OF GLOBALIZATION ON THE WORLD'S POOR
Transmission Mechanisms

Machiko Nissanke and Erik Thorbecke (*editors*)
GLOBALIZATION AND THE POOR IN ASIA

Matthew Odedokun (*editor*)
EXTERNAL FINANCE FOR PRIVATE SECTOR DEVELOPMENT
Appraisals and Issues

Amelia U. Santos-Paulino and Guanghua Wan (*editors*)
THE RISE OF CHINA AND INDIA
Impacts, Prospects and Implications

Laixiang Sun (*editor*)
OWNERSHIP AND GOVERNANCE OF ENTERPRISES
Recent Innovative Developments

Guanghua Wan (*editor*)
UNDERSTANDING INEQUALITY AND POVERTY IN CHINA
Methods and Applications

Studies in Development Economics and Policy
Series Standing Order ISBN 978–0333–96424–8 hardcover
Series Standing Order ISBN 978–0230–20041–8 paperback
You can receive future titles in this series as they are published by placing a standing order. Please contact your bookseller or, in case of difficulty, write to us at the address below with your name and address, the title of the series and the ISBNs quoted above.

Customer Services Department, Macmillan Distribution Ltd, Houndmills, Basingstoke, Hampshire RG21 6XS, England

Entrepreneurship and Economic Development

Edited by

Wim Naudé

 in association with the United
Nations University – World Institute
for Development Economics Research

First published 2011 by
PALGRAVE MACMILLAN

Palgrave Macmillan in the UK is an imprint of Macmillan Publishers Limited, registered in England, company number 785998, of Houndmills, Basingstoke, Hampshire RG21 6XS.

Palgrave Macmillan in the US is a division of St Martin's Press LLC, 175 Fifth Avenue, New York, NY 10010.

Palgrave Macmillan is the global academic imprint of the above companies and has companies and representatives throughout the world.

Palgrave® and Macmillan® are registered trademarks in the United States, the United Kingdom, Europe and other countries.

ISBN: 978–0–230–28220–9 hardback

This book is printed on paper suitable for recycling and made from fully managed and sustained forest sources. Logging, pulping and manufacturing processes are expected to conform to the environmental regulations of the country of origin.

A catalogue record for this book is available from the British Library.

Library of Congress Cataloging-in-Publication Data

Entrepreneurship and economic development / edited by Wim Naudé.
    p. cm.—(Studies in development economics and policy)
"In association with the World Institute for Development Economics Research of the United Nations University (UNU-WIDER)."
    ISBN 978–0–230–28220–9 (alk. paper)
    1. Entrepreneurship – Developing countries. 2. Economic development – Developing countries. 3. Development economics. I. Naudé, Wim A.
HB615.E6252 2010
338'.04091724—dc22   2010033964

10 9 8 7 6 5 4 3 2 1
20 19 18 17 16 15 14 13 12 11

Printed and bound in Great Britain by
CPI Antony Rowe, Chippenham and Eastbourne

Contents

Part I   Introduction

Part II   Measuring Entrepreneurship and the Business Environment

Tables

Figures

Abbreviations

AEI	Aggregated Entrepreneurship Index
AU	African Union
CEI	Composite Entrepreneurship Indicator
CI	Composite Indicator
CPCA	Consensus Principal Components Analysis
DB	Doing Business (Indicators)
DEI	Disaggregated Entrepreneurship Index
DNS	Domain Name System
EU	European Union
Eurostat	European Statistical Agency
FDI	Foreign Direct Investment
FIFA	Fédération Internationale de Football Association
GDP	Gross Domestic Product
GEI	Global Entrepreneurship Index
GEM	Global Entrepreneurship Monitor
GLS	Generalized Least Squares
GMM	Generalized Method of Moments
HEA	High-expectation Total Entrepreneurial Activity
HP	Hewlett Packard
IATA	International Air Transport Association
IBRD	International Bank for Reconstruction and Development
ICANN	Internet Corporation for Assigned Names and Numbers
ICAO	International Civil Aviation Organization
ICC	International Criminal Court
ICRC	International Committee of the Red Cross
ICRG	International Country Risk Guide
ICT	Information and Communication Technology
IEG	Independent Evaluation Group
IFC	International Finance Corporation
ILO	International Labour Organisation
IMF	International Monetary Fund
IPO	Initial Public Offering
ISO	International Organization for Standardization
ITU	International Telecommunications Union
IUCN	International Union for the Conservation of Nature
LLCs	Limited Liability Companies

MEI	Multidimensional Entrepreneurship Index
MIT	Massachusetts Institute of Technology
MNC	Multinational Corporation
MNEs	Multinational Enterprises
NECs	Necessity-based Entrepreneurs
NIH	National Institutes of Health
NIPALS	Non-linear Iterative Partial Least Squares
NSE	Non-state Sovereign Entrepreneur
NSO	Non-territorial Sovereign Organisation
OECD	Organization for Economic Co-operation and Development
OEI	Overall Entrepreneurship Index
OLS	Ordinary Least Squares
OPP	Opportunity-based Entrepreneurs
PC	Principal Component
PCA	Principal Components Analysis
PPCA	Probability Principal Components Analysis
PPP	Purchasing Power Parities
PRS	Political Risk Services
R&D	Research and Development
RIS	Regional Innovation Systems
SME	Small and Medium Enterprise
SOE	State-owned Enterprises
TEA	Total Entrepreneurial Activity
TI	Texas Instruments
UNDP	United Nations Development Programme
UNHCR	United Nations High Commissioner for Refugees
UNU	United Nations University
WIDER	World Institute for Development Economics Research
WB	World Bank
WBGES	World Bank Group Entrepreneurship Survey
WGI	Worldwide Governance Indicators
WMD	Weapons of Mass Destruction
WTO	World Trade Organization
WTTC	World Travel and Tourism Council

Acknowledgements

Like a fortunate entrepreneur I was able to edit this book benefiting from an ideal institutional context (provided by UNU-WIDER), supportive networks (of colleagues and scholars) and plenty of 'intellectual' venture capital.

For creating and maintaining an ideal institutional environment I wish to thank my colleagues at UNU-WIDER, in particular Tony Shorrocks, then director of the institute, for championing entrepreneurship in development economics. Thanks are also due to Neha Mehrotra, Luc Christiaensen, and Lorraine Telfer-Taivainen for their help in the publication process and to Lisa Winkler for her overall support to the project, not least editing the final version of the manuscript. I am grateful to Barbara Fagerman for helping to ensure the smooth administrative running of the project, and to Liisa Roponen for copyediting earlier versions of the manuscript.

Outside of UNU-WIDER various scholars appreciated and encouraged this venture. Many of them participated in the UNU-WIDER Workshops on 'Entrepreneurship and Economic Development' and 'Entrepreneurship in Conflict' that were held in Helsinki on 21–23 August 2008 and Londonderry on 20–21 March 2009, respectively. During the meetings most of the chapters in this book were first discussed. I want to thank everyone who contributed to these workshops and to the eventual chapters of this book.

I am grateful also to many colleagues who provided much-needed intellectual 'venture capital' – particularly Zoltan Acs, Erkko Autio, Tilman Brück, Thomas Gries, Enno Masurel, Peter Nijkamp, Roy Thurik, Erik Stam, Adam Szirmai, and Utz Weitzel.

Last but not least, I want to gratefully acknowledge the financial assistance that UNU-WIDER received from the Ministry for Foreign Affairs of Finland to the research project on 'Promoting Entrepreneurial Capacity'. UNU-WIDER also wishes to gratefully acknowledge contributions to its research programmes by the governments of Denmark (Royal Ministry of Foreign Affairs), Finland (Ministry for Foreign Affairs), Norway (Royal Ministry of Foreign Affairs), Sweden (Swedish International Development Cooperation Agency – Sida), and the United Kingdom (Department for International Development DFID).

WIM NAUDÉ
Helsinki, Finland
October 2010

Foreword

When Joseph Alois Schumpeter published his *magnum opus* on entrepreneurship in 1911 he titled it *Theorie der wirtschaftlichen Entwicklung* [The Theory of Economic Development]. Now, almost a century later, his work continues to inspire new generations of economists. In parallel, much progress has been made to further our understanding of the process of development. The World Institute of Development Economics Research (WIDER) was founded 25 years ago as the first research and training centre of the United Nations University (UNU) with this objective in mind. It is therefore both timely and appropriate that UNU-WIDER casts a fresh perspective on the relationship between entrepreneurship and development – and particularly fitting as the centennial year of Schumpeter's pathbreaking work approaches.

A fresh perspective is indeed appropriate. The fields of entrepreneurship and development economics have – despite evolving largely separately since the days of Schumpeter – increasingly started to overlap and cross-fertilize. A fresh perspective is also timely, given the challenges of global development as we stand on the threshold of the second decade of the twenty-first century. These challenges are evident in the triple crisis: finance, food and climate change. Appropriate responses will require innovative entrepreneurship in the fullest sense of the word.

This book, which results from the UNU-WIDER project on 'Promoting Entrepreneurial Capacity', provides a fresh perspective. The increasing interest by entrepreneurship scholars in development, and by development economics scholars in entrepreneurship are reflected in four research themes: (i) the nature of economic development and its relationship with various concepts of entrepreneurship, (ii) improvements in the availability of data on entrepreneurship in developing countries, (iii) the empirical relationship between measures of entrepreneurship and measures of economic development and (iv) the relationship between the state and entrepreneurs. The various chapters in this book address these four themes and provide evidence of a richly dynamic area of research. Scholars are converging on the importance of institutions for understanding how entrepreneurs can play their innovative, Schumpeterian role to the greatest benefit of society.

Understanding institutional–entrepreneurial interactions – even beyond the traditional theatre of the nation-state and the national economy – is a defining challenge for researchers and policy-makers. This book offers an exciting contribution to highlight the state of the art and further stimulate the evolving agenda.

FINN TARP
Director, UNU-WIDER

Contributors

José Ernesto Amorós is Professor at the Universidad del Desarrollo's Center of Entrepreneurship and Innovation in Santiago, Chile and Visiting Professor at the ESADE Business School, Barcelona, Spain.

Diego Avanzini holds a PhD in Economics from the Catholic University of Chile. He has held positions at Auditoría General de la Nación (Argentina), UNDP, and ECLAC (UN), and as a business consultant. Nowadays he is a Visiting Professor at the Information Economy Project, George Mason University School of Law. He also continues working as a private consultant for Chilean and international organizations. His research interests are quantitative and applied economics, entrepreneurship and economic development, and inequality and income distribution.

Mina Baliamoune-Lutz is Professor and Kip Fellow of Economics at the University of North Florida. She is also Associate Editor of Information Technology for Development, the *Journal of Business and Behavioral Sciences*, and the *Journal of African Development*. She holds a PhD from Northeastern University.

Jurgen Brauer is Professor of Economics at the James M. Hull College of Business, Augusta State University, Augusta, GA, USA. He is also co-editor of the *Economics of Peace and Security Journal* and Fellow, Economists for Peace and Security.

Sameeksha Desai is Assistant Professor at the School of Public and Environmental Affairs, Indiana University. She is a graduate of George Mason University.

Chiara Guglielmetti is Post-Doctoral Research Fellow at the School of Local Development and Global Dynamics at the University of Trento, Italy. She has undertaken extensive research and written several articles and book chapters on European integration, private sector development and welfare systems in transforming economies in Central and Eastern Europe. Her research interests include regional economics, economics of inequality, SMEs and entrepreneurship.

Robert Haywood is Executive Director of the One Earth Future Foundation and a Visiting Scholar at the University of Colorado,

Boulder. In 2008 he was an Economic Development Advisor to the British-led Multinational Division in Basra, Iraq. Before that he was the Director of the World Economic Processing Zones Association for 23 years. He graduated with distinction from Harvard Business School in 1977.

Leora Klapper is a Senior Economist in the Finance and Private Sector Research Team of the Development Research Group at the World Bank. She holds a PhD in financial economics from New York University Stern School of Business.

William Lazonick is Professor in the Department of Regional Economic and Social Development at University of Massachusetts Lowell and Director of the UMass Lowell Center for Industrial Competitiveness. Previously, he was Assistant and Associate Professor of Economics at Harvard University (1975–84) and Professor of Economics at Barnard College of Columbia University (1985–93) and Distinguished Research Professor, INSEAD (1996–2007).

Anat Lewin is an Operations Officer with the World Bank's Information and Communication Technologies (ICT) Sector Unit. Prior to joining the World Bank in 2000, she worked for the United Nations Economic Commission for Africa in Ethiopia as an ICT Consultant. Anat holds an MA in International Affairs from Columbia University and a BA in International Relations from the University of Toronto.

Juan Manuel Quesada Delgado has been working for the Development Economics Research Group at the Economic Vice-Presidency of the World Bank since 2005. He holds an MBA from INSEAD in Fontainebleau, France, a Masters in International Law from Washington College of Law, American University and a Juris Doctor from the Alfonso X University in Spain.

Wim Naudé is a Senior Research Fellow at UNU-WIDER, directing its project on entrepreneurship and development. A graduate of the University of Warwick, he is, and has been, member of a number of international networks and advisory bodies, including the International Council for Small Businesses (ICSB), the Club de Madrid and the Households in Conflict Network (HiCN). He has been a Senior Associate Member of St. Anthony's College, Oxford, and has served on the Faculty of Brown University's International Advanced Research Institutes (BIARI) on technology entrepreneurship. He is currently also an associate editor of *Small Business Economics*. Previously he was a professor and research director at North-West University (South Africa) and a lecturer and research officer at the University of Oxford.

Peter Nijkamp is Professor of Regional Economics and Economic Geography at the Vrije Universiteit, Amsterdam, a fellow of the Tinbergen Institute and past President of the Governing Board of the Netherlands Research Council. He is ranked among the best 30 economists in the world according to IDEAS. He is a winner of the Spinozapremie (1996), the European Prize in Regional Science, and the Founder's Medal of the Regional Science Association International.

Gerrit Rooks is Assistant Professor of the Sociology of Innovation, Department of Technology and Policy, Eindhoven University of Technology, The Netherlands. He is a graduate of the Universities of Groningen and Utrecht.

Arthur Sserwanga is Dean of the Faculty of Vocational and Distance Education at Makerere University Business School and a Team Leader of Global Entrepreneurship Monitor, Uganda. He holds a PhD in Entrepreneurship from Makerere University Business School, Kampala, Uganda.

Adam Szirmai is Professorial Fellow at UNU-MERIT and Professor of Development Economics at the Maastricht Graduate School of Governance, Maastricht University. His textbook on development studies, *The Dynamics of Socio-economic Development*, was published by Cambridge University Press in 2005.

Roy Thurik is Professor of Economics and Entrepreneurship at Erasmus University Rotterdam and Professor of Entrepreneurship at the Free University in Amsterdam. He is also Research Professor of Entrepreneurship, Growth and Public Policy at the Max-Planck-Institut für Ökonomik in Jena, Germany. He is associate editor of *Small Business Economics* and *Journal of Small Business Management*.

Part I
Introduction

1
Entrepreneurship and Economic Development: An Introduction

Wim Naudé

Introduction

The intersection of the fields of entrepreneurship and development economics is a challenging and potentially rewarding area of research for social scientists, with important implications for policy-makers, donors, development agencies as well as business owners and managers. It is, however, an area that has been traditionally neglected (Audretsch et al. 2007; Bruton et al. 2008; Naudé 2010). Despite some early contributions, most notably by Leibenstein (1968) and Leff (1979), it was not until almost 40 years later that scholars in economics again started to take notice of the intersection of entrepreneurship and development economics (e.g. Acs et al. 2008a, 2008b; Hausmann and Rodrik 2003; Hwang and Powell 2005; Klapper et al. 2007; Phan et al. 2008). Interest was reignited by the improved availability of relevant cross-country data, by the resurgence of entrepreneurship after the fall of communism and the gradual reforms initiated by China since the late 1970s, by the emerging recognition of the role of institutions in both fields, and by the increasing emphasis on private sector development by donors and international development agencies.

This book takes stock of the body of knowledge on the role of entrepreneurship in economic development, and underscores the challenges that will continue to drive research.

Four main themes

Research on entrepreneurship and its relation to economic development can be grouped into at least four themes. These, providing the framework along which this book is organized, are as follows.

The first theme is concerned with defining the nature of economic development and its relationship with various concepts of entrepreneurship, as outlined in the chapters in Part I of this volume. Here, the fields of development economics and entrepreneurship are defined, the notion of 'economic development' clarified and the question raised of how entrepreneurship (if at all) can advance economic development. The final part of the book (Part V) returns to the latter question in the light of the intervening chapters.

The second theme deals with improvements in the availability of data on entrepreneurship in developing countries. Here, the major data sources for cross-country comparison are those of the Global Entrepreneurship Monitor (GEM) and the World Bank (WB). In addition, data from an increasing number of firm level surveys (some longitudinal, such as the WB's Regional Programme on Enterprise Development) are becoming available and being utilized by researchers to investigate entrepreneurship in developing countries. The growing availability of multiple measures of entrepreneurship and the business environment has led scholars in the field of entrepreneurship to ask whether single summary measures, such as indices, can be compiled in order to assess and compare a country's level of entrepreneurial development (e.g. Acs and Szerb 2009). The theme of measuring entrepreneurship and the business environment in developing countries and constructing indices of entrepreneurial development is addressed in Part II of this book.

The third theme running through recent research by economists in the area of entrepreneurship and economic development is that of the empirical relationship between measures of entrepreneurship and measures of economic development. Part III of this book contains representative work in this regard. The contributions here describe the relationship between economic development and entrepreneurship and explore the relationship between institutional and policy reform and entrepreneurship.

The fourth theme in research interrogates the relationship between the state and entrepreneurs, which is addressed by the chapters in Part IV. This literature is on one hand sceptical that entrepreneurs can prosper unless they are pro-actively supported by the state – and not just measures limiting government red tape or other entry barriers. Pro-active measures, it is argued here, are best implemented on the regional and local level. On the other hand, within this literature there is a broadening of the very scope of entrepreneurship, wherein the limits of 'state entrepreneurship' are now gradually being recognized.

Tantalizingly, entrepreneurship is seen as offering potential solutions to problems that are plaguing the provision of global public goods – such as ensuring peace, addressing climate change, and others.

Concepts and definitions

Before proceeding to survey the individual chapters, it is necessary to define what is meant in this book by entrepreneurship and by economic development (and the field of development economics).

Entrepreneurs and the field of entrepreneurship

The field of entrepreneurship studies the discovery and exploitation of opportunities (Shane and Venkataraman 2000). This is done from the perspective of many different disciplines 'ranging from social anthropology to organizational theory to mathematical economics' (Henrekson 2007: 717). Hence there are many definitions of entrepreneurship (see e.g. Davidsson 2004; Wennekers and Thurik 1999).

Most of the chapters in this book deal with entrepreneurship from an economics perspective. From a definitional point of view, this simplifies matters because as Davidsson (2004: 4) puts it 'some of the variations in entrepreneurship definitions, I believe, are relatively minor and of little import'. Economists tend to define entrepreneurship from an *occupational*, a *behavioural* or an *outcomes* point of view. The chapters in this book generally also define entrepreneurship as such.

From the occupational point of view, entrepreneurs are simply those who are self-employed and/or business owners. Occupational definitions are based on the established economic theory of occupational choice, wherein individuals make the labour market decision whether to be employed, self-employed or remain unemployed. The rate of self-employment differs significantly across countries. According to a sample based on 2001 data put together by Robson (2007) the highest rates of self-employment were in developing countries, for example Sri Lanka (44.8 per cent), Indonesia (44.7 per cent) and Madagascar (43.7 per cent). In contrast, in developed countries the rate is much lower, for instance 6.8 per cent in Norway, 8.8 per cent in Denmark and 8.9 per cent in France.

In measurement, some refine this according to whether the self-employed person employs others or is merely an own-account worker (as by the International Labour Organization) or whether self-employment is a matter of choice (in pursuit of an opportunity) or of necessity (such as unemployment). For instance, the GEM measures both 'opportunity' and 'necessity' entrepreneurship, a distinction that will be used in Chapters 8 and 11 in this book.

Self-employment and business ownership rates are static measures corresponding to the occupation definition of entrepreneurship, whilst measures of the start-up rate of new firms attempt to provide a dynamic perspective.

The occupation definition of entrepreneurship is the most widely used in relation to economic development, as many chapters, especially in Part II and Part III, will attest. In Part II, the chapters will discuss the various ways in which self-employment, business ownership and start-up rates have been measured across countries, and analyse some of the uses and shortcomings of the most widely used international datasets in this regard. In Part III, most of the chapters use an occupational definition of entrepreneurship to empirically study the relationship between entrepreneurship, institutions, policies and economic growth.

Behavioural definitions of entrepreneurship, which describe the entrepreneur according to certain critical functions which he or she is supposed to perform, have abounded since the work of Joseph Schumpeter. In the 'Schumpeterian' behavioural view, entrepreneurship needs to be distinguished from other related activities, such as business ownership, business financing or business management. Others, such as Knight (1921), Kirzner (1973) and Schultz (1975) have emphasized additional functions of an entrepreneur, such as risk-taking and the exploitation of opportunities which lead to arbitrage and a reallocation of resources. More generally today, many entrepreneurship scholars, particularly in economics but also in the fields of management and business studies, would agree that the defining feature of entrepreneurship is innovation through spotting and utilizing opportunities. If one sees or defines innovation as technological progress, and believes that the latter matters for economic growth and a higher quality of life, then it is straightforward to conclude that entrepreneurship will matter for economic development.

While behavioural notions of entrepreneurship are not synonymous with small business start-ups, ownership and management, the study of entrepreneurship has been concerned with small businesses for a variety of reasons. One is that small businesses dominate employment (and self-employment) in both advanced and developing countries. Another is that many leading scholars in entrepreneurship have in recent years described what they call the emergence of an 'entrepreneurial economy', wherein small businesses play an increasingly important role in innovative activities, in the nature of Schumpeter. The chapter by Roy Thurik in Part III of this book discusses in detail the emergence of the 'entrepreneurial economy' and its manifestation in developing countries. Without attention to the entrepreneur, the predominance of small businesses in developing and advanced economies alike cannot be fully explained.

This book is thus largely concerned with entrepreneurs *as opportunity-driven agents who drive economic change through innovative new firms*. It is a view that sees entrepreneurship as a positive quality, resource or process in economic development. Part III of this book in particular asks what determines the extent to which entrepreneurs in developing countries are driven by opportunity (or necessity) and how policies and institutions can affect this.

Economic development and development economics

In this book 'economic development' will refer to sustainable improvements in the material well-being of a society, as measured for instance by GDP per capita, GDP growth, productivity and employment. It is a narrower concept than 'human development', which is understood as the progressive enlargement of human capabilities or positive freedoms (e.g. Sen 2000). The focus here on economic development is justified given that the approach is predominantly an economic one, and given that economic development is a necessary (though not sufficient) requirement for human development.

Development economics is the field within economics that studies the causes and consequences of the economic development of the poorest countries. Addressing the economic dimensions of economic underdevelopment, and explaining its differences across countries, has been the task of development economics since its establishment as a distinctive subdiscipline in economics after the Second World War. It draws on the methods and body of knowledge of economics (and increasingly also on other disciplines such as politics, sociology and anthropology) to explain the causes of economic underdevelopment. Chenery and Srinivasan (1988: xi) noted that these explanations are 'characterized by competing paradigms rather than a dominant orthodoxy' and 'although the core concerns of development economics are clear enough, its outer boundaries are difficult to establish and essentially arbitrary'. This remains a valid assessment.

As such there is, despite many convincing explanations and much progress in conceptualizing and measuring economic development, still no 'unified field theory' of economic development, nor a single, straightforward explanation of the process of economic development and the determinants of poverty and inequality. At present, a fair assessment of the state of the subdiscipline is that it recognizes the importance of context, of history, of path dependency and of the role which good institutions and governance play in the making of good development policies. Indeed, in terms of its emphasis on institutions it has potentially a common area of interest with the rise of institutional thinking in entrepreneurship.

Development economics also has a strong tradition of attempting to formalize its ideas into theoretical constructs based on microeconomic optimization behaviour and of subjecting these ideas to empirically rigorous testing. It has often been remarked that a possible reason for the lack of interest in entrepreneurship in development economics is due to the difficulty of formally modelling a potentially vague concept such as entrepreneurship and due to the lack of adequate and consistent measurement of entrepreneurship. It has also been claimed that development economics' formal models could see no need for entrepreneurship as they assumed perfect information and market clearing. While perhaps true earlier on, this is no longer a strong argument, as development economists have for some time now been assuming imperfect competition and non-market clearing. Indeed, Gries and Naudé (2009, 2010) and the contributions to the January 2010 Special Issue of the journal *Small Business Economics* (devoted to Entrepreneurship and Economic Development), show that entrepreneurship can be usefully incorporated into rigorous economic models with micro-foundations.

Within development economics, 'development' involves both an increase in real output per capita, driven by productivity gains and reflected in the structural transformation of the economy, from being rural- and agricultural-based to mainly urban- and industrial-based (Gries and Naudé 2010). Moreover development economics is concerned that such development should be sustainable, that is that it should be shared (inequality should not increase) and not be environmentally destructive. Hence development is economic growth complemented by qualitative progress. Recently many development economists have also started to subscribe to the notion of development as 'human development', wherein the goal of development is to expand the positive freedoms people enjoy – as described in the capabilities approach associated with Sen (2000) and others. In this respect many development economists tend to adhere to a multidimensional concept of development, perhaps in contrast to those entrepreneurship scholars, who more often than not equate economic development with economic growth, productivity changes or an increase in employment.

Overview of the chapters

In addition to this overview chapter, Part I of the book consists of a chapter (Chapter 2) by William Lazonick, entitled 'Innovative Enterprise and Economic Development'. Lazonick sets the scene for many of the chapters that follow by providing what he calls a theory of innovative enterprise – as opposed to the 'optimising enterprise' that is standard in neoclassical economics. An enterprise is 'innovative' if it manages to generate higher quality and/or lower cost products than were previously available at prevailing factor prices.

Two central questions in this chapter are: what role does entrepreneurship play in the innovation process, and what are the implications for understanding how the entrepreneurial function is performed? Lazonick provides some answers by considering the role of the entrepreneur in the performance of the firm's three generic activities: strategy, organization and finance. He points out that although an entrepreneur is required to start up a new firm, they are often unable or unwilling to manage a complex organization that needs to engage in collective and cumulative learning. As such he concludes that 'policies that place too much stress on entrepreneurship as the key to economic development can undermine the collective and cumulative process of organizational learning required for innovation to occur'.

Contributions from Part II

Part II of this book consists of four chapters focused on measuring entrepreneurship and the business environment in developing countries.

Chapter 3 by Diego B. Avanzini is entitled 'Designing Composite Entrepreneurship Indicators'. It starts out by recalling that it was Joseph Schumpeter himself who stressed the importance of being able to measure entrepreneurship if the concept is to have any value for policy-makers and other 'practical men'.

Avanzini's chapter is an illustration on how to proceed to reconcile theory with the use of robust statistical methods in order to come up with a Composite Entrepreneurship Indicator (CEI) which may be useful to guide policy. Using an 'entrepreneurial scoreboard' and Probability Principal Components Analyses (PPCA) he compiles a CEI that consists of an Overall Entrepreneurship Index (OEI), a Disaggregated Entrepreneurship Index (DEI) and a Multidimensional Entrepreneurship

Index (MEI). The OEI shows that the ranking of developing countries has improved in recent years. The DEI shows that in developing countries necessity-driven entrepreneurship (associated with high unemployment) predominates. The MEI, Avanzini's preferred index, shows that during the 1998 to 2001 period, the top five ranking countries in terms of the index were the United States, Switzerland, Japan, Sweden and China. The index also suggests that lately innovation has become a more important driver of entrepreneurship and that the extent of barriers to entrepreneurship in the business environment had become less. He argues that the MEI offers a useful method for identifying the main reasons for a country's position in the rankings and for identifying the policies that will allow an improvement in outcomes.

Chapter 4 by Sameeksha Desai is on 'Measuring Entrepreneurship in Developing Countries'. Whereas in the previous chapter Avanzini was generally concerned about the need to measure entrepreneurship, and carefully considered many of the most vexing methodological issues, he did point out that the measurement of entrepreneurship is more difficult in developing countries, primarily due to the lack of data. Desai turns the focus more squarely on developing countries. Given the need for standardized measures to compare entrepreneurship across countries and across time, a number of international efforts have been undertaken. Desai critically discusses the most important of these attempts, which include the GEM and the WB Group Entrepreneurship Survey (WBGES). Since both of these data sets will feature prominently in later chapters, this discussion provides a useful introduction and a needed critical perspective.

The next chapter in Part II, Chapter 5, is by Leora Klapper, Anat Lewin and Juan Manuel Quesada Delgado and is entitled 'The Impact of the Business Environment on the Business Creation Process'. Here the WBGES is used by the authors to argue that 'a good regulatory environment can boost entrepreneurial activity in developing countries'.

The WBGES defines and measures 'entrepreneurship' as ownership of formally registered firms. The authors argue that a focus on the formal sector does provide valuable insights into developing country entrepreneurship. They refer to findings in the literature that formal firms tend to be better protected, and have better access to finance, labour and international markets. They also point out that firms that remain informal more often than not stagnate. The WBGES therefore is a useful tool in tracking whether more firms move up into formality as a result of government actions and policies. The authors argue that if developing countries could modernize their business registry office, it would facilitate the entry of firms into the formal economy, with all of its attended benefits.

In Chapter 6, dealing with 'Measuring the Business Environment for Entrepreneurship in Fragile States', Chiara Guglielmetti turns the attention to another major international database that has been increasingly used both by scholars and 'practical men' in the field of entrepreneurship. This is the WB's Doing Business Indicators (DBI) data set, which aims to provide a consistent and comparable set of indicators to reflect the ease or difficulty of doing business in a country. The underlying assumption (which is critiqued by some of the chapters in this book) is that improvements in a country's business environment as reflected in the DBI, will automatically lead to an increase in entrepreneurial activity. In this chapter Guglielmetti asks whether the DBIs are useful in the context of the poorest developing countries, those often described as 'fragile states'.

Focusing on indicators of starting a business, paying taxes, hiring and firing workers and dealing with licences, Gulglielmetti argues that the DBI fail in three aspects: first, in capturing the essentials of the environment through which individuals engage in entrepreneurial activity in fragile states, second, in capturing the central role played by incentives, and last, in taking account of the characteristics and roles of entrepreneurs in fragile states. Guglielmetti's chapter provides a needed reminder that the design of policies to support entrepreneurship is not so obvious in the complex environment characterizing the poorest countries.

Contributions from Part III

There are four chapters in Part III, which deal with 'institutions, policies, growth and entrepreneurship'. The starting Chapter 7 by Roy Thurik is entitled 'From the Managed to the Entrepreneurial Economy: Considerations for Developing and Emerging Economies'. Thurik describes the switch that has taken place from the 'managed' to the 'entrepreneurial' economy. Based on earlier work by Audretsch and Thurik (2001b, 2004), Thurik contrasts the 'managed' to the 'entrepreneurial' economy.

Up until now, the switch from the managed to the entrepreneurial economy has been described and analysed mainly in advanced economies, where it coincided with the rise in the importance of small firms as engines of economic growth. This, however, does not mean that the distinction between the managed and entrepreneurial economies is not relevant for developing and emerging economies. Thurik argues that it is, and that the promotion of entrepreneurship in these economies can greatly benefit from understanding to what extent they are based on various mixes of managed and entrepreneurial economies. Thurik argues that under the managed economy the policy question is 'how can the government withhold firms from abusing their market power?', while under the entrepreneurial model the question is 'how can governments create an environment fostering the success and viability of firms?' He discusses various elements of government policy and their dangers and shortcomings in developing countries. He also considers government support for inputs into the entrepreneurial economy, such as knowledge and know-how to be important and finally argues that decentralized policy-making is most appropriate for supporting the entrepreneurial economy, stating that firms '... tend to be localized in regional clusters'. In this, his chapter anticipates the chapter by Peter Nijkamp (Chapter 13) which focuses on the local and regional dimensions of entrepreneurship.

Chapter 8, by José Ernesto Amorós 'The Impact of Institutions on Entrepreneurship in Developing Countries', provides empirical evidence on the impact of the quality of government and governance on entrepreneurship. Following GEM he makes a distinction between opportunity-based entrepreneurship and necessity-based entrepreneurship. To measure institutional quality, specifically of governance, Amorós uses the WB's Worldwide Governance Indicators (WGI) which measure six aspects of governance, namely voice and accountability, political stability and absence of violence, government effectiveness, regulatory quality, rule of law and control of corruption. As control variables he includes measures of GDP per capita and welfare. Using a random effects estimator (whose applicability is confirmed by a Hausman test), Amorós finds a positive relationship between opportunity-driven entrepreneurship and improvements of corruption control and in political stability. He also finds that improved government effectiveness and rule of law lead to a reduction in necessity-based entrepreneurship.

For Amorós these findings have potentially important policy implications, if one accepts (see Chapter 11 for a further discussion) that opportunity-based entrepreneurship drives economic growth, which means that different aspects of governance affect entrepreneurship differently. Merely improving government effectiveness and upholding the rule of law (key planks in policy reform measures) will not in themselves lead to more productive entrepreneurship. This conclusion is supported by the chapters in Part IV.

Chapter 9, 'Policy and Institutional Reform and Entrepreneurship in Developing Countries' by Mina Baliamoune-Lutz complements and extends the discussion in Chapter 8. First, she provides a survey of the recent literature on entrepreneurship, growth and institutions. In particularly, she discusses the thesis of Iyigun and Rodrik (2004) that 'institutional reform would have negative (positive) effects if preexisting entrepreneurial activity is vibrant (weak)'. The literature overview informs a dynamic panel data model which she then estimates using (unbalanced) panel data covering 44 countries over the period 1990–2002.

Her results are intriguing. They suggest that policy and institutional reforms can alter the way in which entrepreneurship affects economic growth. In particular she finds, counter-intuitively, that trade and financial reform reduce the 'growth-enhancing effects of entrepreneurial activity', when there is an already high level of entrepreneurial activity in a country, but improves it when entrepreneurial activity is lower. She explained this intuitively:

> It is possible, for example, that in settings where entrepreneurial activity is strong, a trade or credit market reform would induce the incumbents to bribe or be part of other rent-seeking activities to access input or output markets or to eliminate possible competition (new entrants), which would have a negative effect on growth.

Chapter 10 by Gerrit Rooks, Adam Szirmai and Arthur Sserwanga, and is about 'Human and Social Capital in Entrepreneurship in Developing Countries'. Their chapter highlights the fact that institutions are not only top-down, nationally based, but bottom-up and locally based. Human and social capital in particular, are important bottom-up and locally formed institutions. The authors ask whether human and social capital are substitutes or complements. To test this and the impact on entrepreneurial performance, they use a sample of over 700 entrepreneurs surveyed in 2008 in Uganda. They measure entrepreneurial performance using data gathered on sales, numbers of customers and profits, innovativeness, gestational activities, firm size and financial resources. A human capital measure is constructed from three indicators: years of education, years of experience as manager and years of experience as an employee. Social capital is measured using indicators of the size of networks and the availability of resources in these networks. Various standard control variables, such as age, gender, marital status, rural location, economic sector and environment context were taken into consideration.

Their results show that entrepreneurial activities in Uganda (echoing findings of many other studies on entrepreneurship in developing countries) are characterized by the dominance of firms that are very small, not dynamic, very young, exhibiting little employment growth. Moreover their results generally fail to support the hypothesis that human and social capital are substitutes in entrepreneurial activity. For some measures of entrepreneurial performance, such as in gestational activities, they found some indications of complementarity. Only in the case of innovativeness did they find evidence of substitution between human and social capital, when the latter is measured as the extent of network resources available.

Contributions from Part IV

The fourth part of the book deals collectively with the topic of entrepreneurship and the state, and does this on various levels, from local to national to global. It advances the basic gist of Parts II and III that basic institutional and policy reform may only be necessary, but not sufficient for entrepreneurial development. In moving developing countries from being predominantly managed to entrepreneurial economies may require a more hands-on, pro-active approach wherein the actions of the state matter greatly. What forms can such actions take? And going beyond the acknowledgement that states influence entrepreneurship, how can entrepreneurship influence states or even usurp state-like (sovereign) functions? These questions are at the cutting edge of entrepreneurship and economic development research. The four chapters in this final part of the book provide glimpses into this tantalizing research area.

In Chapter 11 Wim Naudé introduces some of the main issues by asking 'Is Pro-active State Support Needed for Entrepreneurship in Developing Countries?' He argues that improved governance and lower start-up costs may not be sufficient for encouraging the type of entrepreneurship that matters for economic growth. Using panel data from the GEM and WB's DBI and WGI, he finds that (i) opportunity-based entrepreneurship (as opposed to necessity-based) drives economic growth; (ii) governance and start-up costs are not significant determinants of opportunity entrepreneurship and (iii) better governance does, however, result in higher economic growth.

From this he concludes that better governance can lead to better growth not directly, but indirectly by reducing necessity-based (unproductive) entrepreneurship, even though it does not result in an increase in opportunity-based entrepreneurship. If the interest is in promoting the latter, more pro-active state actions may be required. Particularly, a developmental state may be essential.

In Chapter 12, 'Entrepreneurship and the Developmental State', William Lazonick continues in this vein, and emphasizes the fact that in all of the currently advanced economies, particularly the USA, the developmental state played an important role supporting entrepreneurship in a pro-active manner. Lazonick proceeds to detail these interventions and their outcomes in the UK, Italy, Japan and the USA. Building on the idea of the 'innovating firm' set out in Chapter 2, his chapter provides a useful overview of the important role of innovation in technology-driven growth. The reader will by now understand how relevant the concept of the innovating firm has become in the entrepreneurial economy. Creating innovative firms requires, however, as Lazonick calls, for a development state to subsidize and protect infant firms in infant industries. His chapter opens the debate on industrialization and industrial policy to the field of entrepreneurship.

As Chapter 7 on the differences between the managed and the entrepreneurial economies argues, proper state support for entrepreneurship ought to be primarily local and regional (as opposed to predominantly national and centralist) in approach. Indeed, with the rise of a substantial body of research into national regional innovation systems (RIS) and on the importance of the spatial dimensions of economic growth, the regional and local role of entrepreneurship has been attracting considerable attention (see e.g. Naudé and Gries et al. 2008; Naudé 2009b).

Peter Nijkamp, in Chapter 13, provides the context for examining the local and regional aspects of entrepreneurship. His chapter 'Entrepreneurship, Development and the Spatial Context: Retrospect and Prospects' elaborates the role of entrepreneurship in driving growth on a regional level, how thinking about this has evolved over time, and where future research is likely to take the topic. Nijkamp reminds the reader that 'Entrepreneurship does not take place in a wonderland of no spatial dimensions, but is deeply rooted in supporting geographical conditions.'

These geographical conditions, as discussed in his chapter, include urban agglomerations, human and social capital and networks and have raised the importance in recent years of urban incubation systems, venture capital support mechanisms, management of city diversity, information sharing and learning mechanisms and others as state policies to support entrepreneurship. Nijkamp concludes by stressing that the demand for future research in these areas is substantial, and would increasingly require interdisciplinary approaches to advance our practical knowledge of these.

The last chapter in Part IV is forward-looking. It is not concerned with what the state can do for entrepreneurs or how entrepreneurial performance may be enhanced in developing countries. Neither is it concerned about the role of the state on a local or national level. Rather, the question is asked: how can entrepreneurship contribute to the growing need for global public goods in development or as the authors put it, how can entrepreneurship supplement or supersede the powers of states across the globe?

Thus in Chapter 14 'Non-state Sovereign Entrepreneurs and Non-territorial Sovereign Organizations', Jurgen Brauer and Robert Haywood propose the novel concept of 'Non-State Sovereign Entrepreneurs' (NSE). They distinguish sovereign entrepreneurship from commercial entrepreneurship as well as political and social entrepreneurship. They describe sovereign entrepreneurship as the mix of services and cost a sovereign provides. Traditionally, the concept of a 'sovereign' has been associated with the modern state and its claims to 'sovereignty' which dates back to the 1648 Peace of Westphalia. In our present era of globalization and the rise of the entrepreneurial economy, however, the sovereign state suffers from a number of fundamental weaknesses which inhibit it from playing a more constructive role in meeting the growing demand for global public goods. One is the resolution of violent conflict within and between states (others include addressing climate change, environment degradation and systemic financial crises). To overcome this the authors argue for NSEs. These are actors that have universal reach and assertion of authority but are non-territorial. As such they can impinge on and supplement or supersede the power of sovereign states.

Brauer and Haywood discuss a number of NSEs that already exist, such as the Internet Corporation for Assigned Names and Numbers (ICANN), the International Organization for Standardization (ISO), the International Committee of the Red Cross (ICRC) and even the Fédération Internationale de Football Association (FIFA) and others.

The need for global governance has clearly created opportunities, which require entrepreneurial behaviour beyond the reach of the single state. Many of the world's seemingly most intractable problems may stem from the fact that 'global governance ... is run by distinctly non-global players', as Brauer and Haywood put it. Entrepreneurship may change the very nature of global economic development, just as continuing global economic development is likely to change the nature of entrepreneurship, confirming that the intersection of entrepreneurship and economic development is at the very vanguard of research in these two fields.

Contribution from Part V

Part V of the book contains a concluding chapter (Chapter 15), entitled 'Entrepreneurship and Economic Development: Policy Design' by Wim Naudé. It elaborates and extends some of the policy implications from the preceding chapters, and identifies potentially important areas in the development–entrepreneurship nexus not covered in this book.

Concluding remarks

Joseph Schumpeter was concerned about economic development in his book *The Theory of Economic Development* from the year 1911 (translated in 1934). But he had little direct influence on development economics as a subject as this developed after the Second World War. However, with the world subsequently facing a wide diversity of development experiences, from successful economic structural transformations and mixed success transformations to rapid innovation and growth episodes, but also growth stagnation, collapse and persistent conflict, the interest in innovative entrepreneurship, its relation to the state and its impact on economic development has intensified.

The collection of essays in this book reflects this dynamism and hopes to stimulate further research at the intersection of the fields of entrepreneurship and development economics.

2
Innovative Enterprise and Economic Development
William Lazonick

Introduction

In this chapter I provide the basic outlines of the theory of innovative enterprise with a particular focus on why and how it provides the essential analytical link between entrepreneurship and development. In the theory of the innovating firm, the dynamic interaction of strategy organization and finance will determine whether the transformation of the firm's productive activities eventually results in 'innovation', defined as the generation of higher quality and/or lower cost products than were previously available at prevailing factor prices. This definition of innovation, I argue, is essential for taking us beyond the notion of innovation as a 'new idea', which in and of itself has no economic meaning or even a failed 'new product', which may count as 'entrepreneurship' but not as 'innovation'. Thus defined, innovation provides the foundation for economic development because, adjusted for the quality of services, it makes it possible to get more output from a given amount of input.

Innovation has been central in the study of entrepreneurship, particularly since Joseph Schumpeter's *The Theory of Economic Development*. Schumpeter argued that economic development required the disruption of the general equilibrium of markets by entrepreneurial activity. He defined 'entrepreneurship' as the act of making 'new combinations' out of existing economic resources so that those economic resources yielded a larger amount of valued output for a given value of inputs. He called this productive transformation 'innovation'. Since innovation is essential for economic development, a theory of economic development requires not simply a 'theory of the firm' but a 'theory of the innovating firm'.

Innovating versus optimizing firms

Entrepreneurship and innovative enterprise

In *The Theory of Economic Development*, Schumpeter began his exploration of the development process by focusing on the role of the individual entrepreneur. After several decades of study, however, he came to recognize the centrality of the large-scale business enterprise. As captured in the works of Penrose (1959) and Chandler (1962), by the 1950s the large industrial corporation had come to dominate the US economy and its multinational operations had spread across the globe. For those such as Chandler and Penrose, who studied the role of the business enterprise in economic development, the focus was on how large business enterprises could be managed so that they would continue to grow rather than on how entrepreneurs could be induced to start new firms.

The importance and persistence of the large industrial corporation in the post-Second World War decades led Nelson and Winter (1982) to make Schumpeter's argument concerning the routinization of corporate R&D central to their treatise, *An Evolutionary Theory of Economic Change*. Labelling their economic theory neo-Schumpeterian, Nelson and Winter focused on the need for a theory of the firm that went beyond the optimization principle of neoclassical orthodoxy, and focused on the interrelated concepts of routines and tacit knowledge as basic explanations of the organizational capabilities of firms.

Nelson (1991) articulated the need for a theory of organizational capabilities as a basis for a theory of innovative enterprise:

> I want to put forth the argument that it is organizational differences, especially differences in abilities to generate and gain from innovation, rather than differences in command over particular technologies, that are the source of durable, not easily imitable, differences among firms. Particular technologies are much easier to understand, and imitate, than broader firm dynamic capabilities (ibid.: 72)

He goes on to say that 'the "dynamic capabilities" view of firms being developed by scholars in the strategy field can be seen to be important not only as a guide to management, but also as the basis for a serious theory of the firm in economics' (ibid.: 72).

Teece et al. (1997) see the distinctiveness of firms as opposed to markets as residing in the capabilities in 'organizing and getting things done' in ways that 'cannot be accomplished merely by using the price system to coordinate activity. The very essence of capabilities/competences is that they cannot be readily assembled through markets' (ibid.: 517). 'Organizational processes', they argue, 'often display high levels of coherence, and when they do, replication may be difficult because it requires systemic changes throughout the organization and also among inter-organizational linkages, which may be hard to effectuate.' They liken 'coherence' to Nelson and Winter's notion of 'routines', with the caveat that 'the routines concept is a little too amorphous to properly capture the congruence among processes and between processes and incentives that we have in mind'.

Teece et al. (1997: 520) stress the importance of learning processes that are 'intrinsically social and collective' and argue that the 'concept of dynamic capabilities as a coordinative management process opens the door to the potential for interorganizational learning'. Strategic change is generally incremental, as new capabilities have to build cumulatively on the capabilities previously put in place. From the dynamic capabilities perspective, 'strategy involves choosing among and committing to long term paths or trajectories of competence development' (ibid.: 524–9).

Given the need for long-term paths of competence development, what role does entrepreneurship play in the process? This question can only be answered by means of an analysis of the relation between established corporations and entrepreneurial start-ups in particular industries. For example Pisano (2006) has argued that given the need for collective and cumulative learning over very long periods of time in order to generate a commercializable biotechnology product, the US industry has been afflicted by *too much entrepreneurship*, due to an excess supply of venture capital. He thus raises the important question of when and under which conditions entrepreneurship contributes to innovative enterprise. To answer this question, we need to consider the role of the entrepreneur in what I call the 'innovating firm'.

Key characteristics and activities of the innovating firm

We can derive an understanding of the key characteristics of the innovating firm by comparing it to the 'theory of the optimizing firm' that during the first half of the twentieth century emerged out of the theory of the market economy. Then, given our identification of the activities in which an innovating firm must engage, we can ask what roles 'entrepreneurship' has played in this process. A firm seeks to transform productive resources into goods and services that can be sold to generate revenues. A theory of the firm, therefore, must provide explanations for how this productive transformation occurs and how revenues are obtained. These explanations must focus on three generic activities in which the business enterprise engages: strategy, organization and finance.

Strategy allocates resources to investments in developing human and physical capabilities that, it is hoped, will enable the firm to compete for chosen product markets. *Organization* transforms technologies and accesses markets, and thereby develops and utilizes the value-creating capabilities of these resources to generate products that buyers want at prices that they are willing to pay. *Finance* sustains the process of developing technologies and accessing markets from the time at which investments in productive resources are made to the time at which financial returns are generated through the sale of products.

The neoclassical theory of the optimizing firm trivializes the content of these three generic activities. In neoclassical theory, the rule of profit maximization determines the firm's strategy about the industry in which the firm should compete and the quantity of output that the firm should produce.

Given the industry in which the firm has invested, exogenous production functions and factor prices determine the organization of the firm. Financing the transformation of productive resources into revenue generating products is non-problematic because the theory assumes that the firm can borrow capital at the prevailing market rate and can sell all of the output that maximizes its profits, covering the cost of capital.

While the neoclassical theory of the firm trivializes strategy organization and finance as business activities, the particular formulation of the theory from the 1920s embodied a number of realistic assumptions about the factors that influence the relation between the costs of production and the amount of output produced. These realistic assumptions have made the theory credible as a depiction of the way in which an actual firm operates. Analytically, these assumptions have provided the basis for a reasoned account of why the firm might have a U-shaped cost curve that, through the profit maximization rule, enables it to choose an optimal level of output.

The problem is, however, that the *optimizing* firm of post-Marshallian theory is not an *innovating* firm; indeed it can be characterized as a *non-innovating* firm. In terms of strategy, the theory of the optimizing firm posits that an 'entrepreneur' chooses the industry in which she wants to compete by allocating resources to any industry in which, because of the exogenous appearance of a disequilibrium condition, there are supernormal profits to be made. The disequilibrium condition disappears as entrepreneurs reallocate resources to this particular industry by setting up new firms. As long as equilibrium conditions persist across all industries, there will be no incentive for the entrepreneur to shift resources from one industry to another.

There are two assumptions of the neoclassical theory of the firm that limit its ability to understand innovative enterprise. First, the neoclassical theory assumes that *the entrepreneur plays no role in creating the disequilibrium condition* that triggers the reallocation of resources from one industry to another. In contrast, in the theory of the innovating firm, by investing in 'new combinations', entrepreneurs create new profitable opportunities, and thereby disrupt equilibrium conditions. Second, the neoclassical theory assumes that *the entrepreneur requires no special expertise to compete in one industry rather than another*. All that is required of the entrepreneur is that she follows the principle of profit maximization in the choice of industry in which to compete. In the theory of the innovating firm, in contrast, the entrepreneur's specialized knowledge of the industry in which she chooses to compete is of utmost importance for her firm's ability to be innovative in that industry.

Once the industry has been chosen, the neoclassical theory assumes that there are certain fixed costs, exogenously determined by existing technology and prevailing factor prices, that must be incurred by each and every firm that chooses to compete in the industry. These fixed costs are typically attributed to lumpy investments in plant and equipment, although it is also sometimes recognized that the entrepreneur's salary represents an element of fixed costs. These costs are fixed because they are incurred even if the firm produces no output. As the firm expands its output, the average cost curve slopes downward as fixed costs are spread over a larger volume of output.

The limiting assumption here is that the level of fixed costs is given to any entrepreneur who enters the industry. In the theory of the optimizing firm, *the 'entrepreneur' does not choose the firm's level of fixed costs and the particular productive capabilities embodied in them as part of his firm's investment strategy*. In the theory of the innovating firm, the entrepreneur strategically chooses to make investments that are intended to endow the firm with distinctive productive capabilities compared with its competitors in the industry. These strategic decisions, potentially unique to each entrepreneurial firm, determine the innovating firm's level of fixed costs.

Given the firm's fixed costs, the 'optimizing entrepreneur' (an oxymoronic term) purchases that quantity of complementary variable inputs at prevailing factor prices that are dictated by the technological requirements of the amount of output at which profits are maximized.

Thus variable costs per unit of output are added to the fixed costs per unit of output to yield total unit costs, with the average cost curve mapping these total unit costs for different levels of output. If variable costs were to remain constant as output expands, the average cost curve would slope downwards continuously (although at a declining rate) as fixed costs are spread over more units of output.

At this point, however, the neoclassical theory makes a critical assumption that causes the average cost curve to change direction and slope upwards, thus yielding the well-known U-shaped cost curve. The assumption is that the addition of variable factors of production to the firm's fixed factors of production results in a declining average productivity of these combined factors (that is, the firm's technology, which is also the industry's technology). In deriving the U-shaped cost curve, neoclassical theorists have given two quite plausible reasons for the decline in average productivity as output expands. Both reasons assume that the key variable factor is labour. One reason is that as more variable factors are added to the fixed factors, increasingly crowded factory conditions reduce the productivity of each variable factor as, for example, workers continuously crowd one other. The other reason is that as more workers are added to the production process, the entrepreneur, as the fixed factor whose role it is to organize productive activities, experiences a 'control loss' because of the increasing number of workers whom he has to supervise and monitor.

Hence organization – in this case the relation between the entrepreneur as manager and the workforce that he employs – becomes central to the neoclassical theory of the firm. Within the theory of the optimizing firm, the constraining assumption is that *the so-called entrepreneur passively accepts this condition of increasing costs, and optimizes subject to it as a constraint.* In sharp contrast, in the theory of the innovating firm, the experience of increasing costs provides the firm's strategic decision-makers with an understanding of the limits of the *initial* investment strategy, and with that information they make additional new investments for the strategic purpose of *taking control* of the variable factor that was the source of increasing costs.

The entrepreneur of an innovating firm would not take a condition of overcrowding or control loss that results in increasing costs as a 'given constraint', but rather would make investments in organization and technology to change this condition. In effect, for the sake of improving its capability of developing and utilizing productive resources, the firm makes new *strategic* investments that transform variable costs into fixed costs, in effect transforming external market relations into internal organizational relations. These new strategic investments stack new fixed costs on top of previously incurred fixed costs, thus increasing the challenge that faces the firm of transforming high fixed costs into low unit costs.

The recognition that the firm has fixed costs creates a role for finance in the theory of the optimizing firm. A firm needs to finance fixed cost investments because, by definition, the returns from these investments are generated over time. The theory of the optimizing firm posits that, at any given point in time, the firm can sell all the output that it wants according to a known industry demand schedule. Hence, in theory, there are no risks entailed in the financing of investments over the period of time that it takes to amortize these investments. The cost of capital is built into the firm's cost structure, and simply reflects the market price of finance.

Note that *fixed* costs are not *sunk* costs. Neoclassical theorists have recognized the adjustment problem that faces an industry when there is an exogenous decline in industry demand that results in overcapacity. With market prices depressed, some firms should exit the industry. But given the assumption that all firms in the industry have identical cost structures, there is no reason why some firms would drop out of the industry, leaving other firms to enjoy the restoration of 'normal' profits. Rather all firms in the industry, viewing their fixed costs as sunk costs, continue to produce at the profit maximizing level as long as the market price at least enables them to cover their variable costs. Under such conditions of 'cut-throat competition', firms in effect live off their existing 'sunk cost' investments while they lack the prospective returns to justify the financing of new 'fixed cost' investments.

In the theory of the innovating firm, the uncertainty inherent in fixed costs is central to the analysis rather than, as in the theory of the optimizing firm, an *ad hoc* concession to reality. The theory of the innovating firm assumes that the investments which the firm makes must be developed and utilized over time, as the firm transforms technologies and accesses markets, before returns from those investments can be generated or indeed before the rate of return can even be known. The problem is not, as in the theory of the optimizing firm, whether the prevailing return on investment provided by existing technological and market conditions will continue *in the future*. Since the return on investments depends on the extent of the market that the innovating firm actually attains, a return on investment *does not even prevail in the present*; that is, at the time when the investments in innovation are made.

By definition, investments in innovation are made in the face of uncertainties concerning prospective returns. Any entrepreneur who allocates resources to an innovative strategy faces three types of uncertainty: technological, market and competitive. Technological uncertainty exists because the firm may be incapable of developing the higher quality processes and products envisaged in its innovative investment strategy; if one already knew how to generate a new product or process at the outset of the investment, it would not be innovation. Market uncertainty exists because, even if the firm is successful in its development effort, future reductions in product prices and increases in factor prices may lower the returns that can be generated by the investments. Moreover, the innovative enterprise must access a large enough extent of the product market to transform the fixed costs of developing a new technology into low unit costs. Like transforming technology, accessing the market is an integral part of the innovation process, and, at the time when resources are committed to an innovative strategy, it is impossible to be certain, even probabilistically, about what extent of the market will be accessed. Finally, even if a firm overcomes technological and market uncertainty, it still faces competitive uncertainty: the possibility that an innovative competitor will have invested in a strategy that generates an even higher quality, lower cost product.

The optimizing firm may calculate, on the basis of prior experience, the risk of a deterioration of current market conditions, but it has no way of contemplating, let alone calculating, the uncertainty of returns for conditions of supply and demand that, because innovation is involved, have yet to emerge. The fact, moreover, that the optimizing firm will only finance investments for which an adequate return already exists creates an opportunity for the innovating firm to make innovative investments that, if successful, can enable it to out-compete optimizing firms. Indeed, in the future optimizing firms may find that the cause of the 'poor market conditions' that they face is the result of not an exogenous shift in the industry demand curve but rather competition from innovating firms that have gained competitive advantage while their own managers happily optimized (as indeed the economics textbooks instructed them to do) subject to given technological and market constraints.

The innovation process

The task for a theory of innovative enterprise, therefore, is to explain how, by generating output that is higher quality and/or lower cost, a particular enterprise can differentiate itself from its competitors and over time gain a disproportionate share of the market in its industry. Unlike the optimizing firm, the innovating firm does not take as given the fixed costs of participating in the industry. Rather, given prevailing factor prices, the level of fixed costs that it incurs reflects its innovative strategy. Neither indivisible technology nor the 'entrepreneur' as a fixed factor (typical assumptions in the neoclassical theory of the optimizing firm) dictates this 'fixed cost' strategy. An innovative strategy, with its fixed costs, results from the assessment by the firm's strategic decision-makers of the quality and quantity of productive resources in which the firm must invest to *develop* higher quality processes and products than those previously available or that may be developed by competitors. It is this development of productive resources internal to the enterprise that creates the *potential* for an enterprise that pursues an innovative strategy to gain a sustained advantage over its competitors and emerge as dominant in its industry.

Such development of productive resources, when successful, becomes embodied in products, processes and people with superior productive capabilities to those that had previously existed. But the high fixed costs that such investments entail mean that in and of themselves these investments place the firm at a competitive *disadvantage* until such time that, by developing and utilizing the productive resources in which it has invested, it can transform technologies and access markets to generate sufficient financial returns. An innovative strategy that can enable the firm to develop superior productive capabilities over time may place that firm at a cost disadvantage at a point in time because such strategies tend to entail higher fixed costs than the fixed costs incurred by rivals who choose to optimize subject to given constraints.

For a given level of factor prices, these higher fixed costs derive from the *size* and *duration* of the innovative investment strategy. Innovative strategies will entail higher fixed costs than those incurred by the optimizing firm if the innovation process requires the *simultaneous development* of productive resources across a broader and deeper range of integrated activities than those undertaken by the optimizing firm. But in addition to, and generally independent of, the size of the innovative investment strategy at a point in time, high fixed costs will be incurred because of the duration of time that is required to develop productive resources until they result in products that are sufficiently high quality and low cost to generate returns. If the size of investments in physical capital tends to increase the fixed costs of an innovative strategy, so too does the duration of the investment in an organization of people who can engage in the collective and cumulative – or organizational – learning that is, as I discuss below, the central characteristic of the innovation process.

The high fixed costs of an innovative strategy create the need for the firm to attain a high level of *utilization* of the productive resources that it has developed. As in the neoclassical theory of the optimizing firm, given the productive capabilities that it has developed, the innovating firm may experience increasing costs because of the problem of maintaining the productivity of variable inputs as it employs larger quantities of these inputs in the production process. But rather than, as in the case of the optimizing firm, take increasing costs as a given constraint, the innovating firm will attempt to transform its access to high quality productive resources at high levels of output. To do so, it invests in the *development* of the productive resource, the *utilization* of which as a variable input has become a source of increasing costs.

The development of the productive resource adds to the fixed costs of the innovative strategy. Previously this productive resource was utilized as a variable factor that could be purchased incrementally at the going factor price on the market as extra units of the input were needed to expand output. Having added to its fixed costs in order to overcome the constraint on enterprise expansion posed by increasing variable costs, the innovating firm is then under even more pressure to expand its share of the market in order to transform high fixed costs into low unit costs. As, through the development and utilization of productive resources, the innovating firm succeeds in this transformation, it in effect 'unbends' the U-shaped cost curve that the optimizing firm takes as given.[1] By shaping, and reshaping, the cost curve in this way, the innovating firm creates the possibility of securing sustained competitive advantage over its rivals.

Entrepreneurial functions in the innovating firm

Isolated innovation is rarely the case. What role, then, does entrepreneurship play in the innovation process, and what are the implications for understanding how the entrepreneurial function is performed? In general, the entrepreneur must secure the cooperation of other people who possess specialized labour and sufficient finance in order to transform strategic investment decisions into innovative products. We can illuminate this role by considering the functions of the entrepreneur in the firm's three generic activities: *strategy*, *organization* and *finance*.

The entrepreneur is first and foremost a strategist. She makes strategic investment decisions depending on the particular product market in which she wishes to compete and the particular productive activities that, in her view, will enable her firm to generate competitive products. Investment decisions must be made in the face of technological, market and competitive uncertainty.

While we can expect that an element of inexplicable 'luck' will enter into the success or failure of entrepreneurship, research shows that the successful entrepreneur is a person who confronts uncertainty with considerable career experience in and knowledge of a segment of an industry. Depending on the locus of learning that is relevant to a particular industry as well as the stage of development of that industry, its entrepreneurs may have had prior career experience in established companies, other young companies, research institutes or academia. Studies of 'entrepreneurial spawning' show unequivocally that entrepreneurial activity in high-tech sectors is knowledge-intensive and industry-specific (Gompers et al. 2005). The important point is that the career paths of entrepreneurs who populate an industry are not random, and hence, relative to the general population, their capacity to confront and overcome uncertainty is not simply a matter of luck.

Within a particular industry in a particular time and place, the vast majority of people whose career paths could lead them to engage in entrepreneurship do not aspire to that role. What distinguishes the psychological make-up of the risk-taking entrepreneur from others equally well-placed who do not take up the challenge is probably the most difficult of the determinants of entrepreneurship to document empirically (Shane 2003). Insofar as there is a 'classical' debate in the literature on entrepreneurship, it is whether it is the psychological traits of the entrepreneur or objective conditions, career experience and one's location in time and place that are more important in determining the quantity and quality of entrepreneurship that is forthcoming. In a far-reaching survey of 'the sociology of entrepreneurship', in which entrepreneurship is defined as 'the creation of new organizations', Thornton (1999: 19) argues that 'Until recently, the supply-side perspective, which focuses on the individual traits of entrepreneurs, has been the dominant school of research. Newer work from the demand-side perspective has focused on…the context within which entrepreneurship occurs.'

In a theory of innovative enterprise, the key 'supply side' issue is the capability of the entrepreneur to go beyond the launching of a new venture to contribute to its transformation into a going concern. For a person who makes the strategic decision to become an entrepreneur by founding an innovating firm, the test of her suitability for an ongoing role in the innovation process will come when she tries to build an organization to develop products and processes that will, she hopes, become sources of the firm's innovative success. Unless the new firm is a one-person consultancy, the entrepreneur will find herself playing the role of organizer of other people's labour, and even a very small firm in a knowledge-intensive industry can grow quickly. In the innovating firm, moreover, the organizational challenge is *not* one of keeping easily replaceable employees at work on routine tasks. The innovating firm makes strategic investments in the employment of a significant number of highly capable specialists, who typically have attractive alternative opportunities but whose labour services must be integrated into the firm's collective and cumulative learning process in order to generate innovation.

Some entrepreneurs may have an aptitude for running a learning organization, especially those who have had experience as managers in established companies. In high-tech industries however, it is often the case that the innovating firm will employ professional managers with experience and accomplishments in the industry concerned to run its day-to-day operations. Since the success of organizational learning generally depends on an ongoing process of strategic investment as old problems are solved and new problems are discovered, it is typically necessary for the hired managers to be included, along with the entrepreneur, in the strategic decision-making process. Yet, often reluctant to share strategic control of the firms that they have founded, many entrepreneurs resist employing professional managers, a stance that almost invariably is detrimental to the innovation process.

Also detrimental to the innovation process is the labour market mobility of the specialized labour that the firm employs. Especially in a new venture that, with a relatively small number of people, is striving to integrate the specialized capabilities of highly qualified individuals into a collective and cumulative learning process, the departure of even a few employees can have a devastating impact. The problem of highly mobile labour is particularly the case in US high-tech districts such as Silicon Valley or Boston's Route 128 where, especially in a boom, large numbers of start-ups spring up in close proximity to existing firms in the industry to try to take advantage of the entrepreneurial opportunity.

Yet, while labour market mobility poses a major managerial problem for the new venture, without that mobility the new venture would not have been able to gain access to this specialized labour in the first place. The types of people that a knowledge-intensive start-up wishes to recruit typically have alternative opportunities in established organizations. Relative to the secure employment that these established organizations typically offer, employment at a new venture is inherently insecure.

How then do new ventures attract the quantity and quality of 'talent' that they need to implement their innovative strategies? From the 1960s Silicon Valley high-tech firms began using 'broad-based' employee stock options as the mode of compensation to attract personnel (Glimstedt et al. 2006; Lazonick 2010b). Previously stock options had been a perquisite reserved almost exclusively for top executives of US corporations. They functioned as a tax dodge; with the income from exercising options taxed at the 25 per cent capital gains rate, they avoided the 91 per cent marginal rates of taxation on the highest brackets of personal income in effect in the 1950s. Especially from the 1980s most Silicon Valley high-tech start-ups have offered stock options to virtually all of their employees – hence the term 'broad-based'. A new venture often grants stock options to employees in lieu of a portion of the salary that they could have commanded working for an established organization, and thus conserves cash. Moreover, those individuals who are deemed to be 'stars' can be offered an extra large number of options as a signing bonus without upsetting the firm's normal salary scale or requiring the firm to expend cash up front.

Nevertheless, the point of employee stock options, just as the point of human resource management more generally, is not simply to attract specialized labour or save on salaried compensation. Given the collective and cumulative character of the learning process, once an employee is hired the entrepreneur or her managers has to retain them, and having retained them, continuously motivate them. In a new venture, employee stock options help to perform both the retention and motivation functions.

So that stock options will perform the retention function, it is the practice in US high-tech firms for a block of options granted in any given year to vest in equal proportions at the end of each of the four following years. Once the options have vested, the employee has the right to exercise these options over a period of ten years from the original grant date. Thus the employee must stay with the firm for a period of time to have the prospect of cashing in on her stock options. Furthermore the practice in US high-tech firms is to grant stock options on an *annual* basis, so that the employee always has more options waiting to vest and eligible to be exercised in the pipeline.

Besides attracting and retaining specialized employees, the entrepreneur has to motivate them to engage in an intense process of organizational learning. Established business enterprises can use the realistic promise of promotion within the organization over the course of a career to perform the motivation function. New ventures cannot realistically proffer such an expectation. In a new venture, broad-based stock options can perform this motivation function giving the employees who hold them a strong incentive to contribute to the innovation process. The financial reward for their time and effort will come if and when the new venture has sufficiently developed and utilized its productive resources to do an initial public offering (IPO) or a private sale of the firm to a company that is already listed on the stock market. At that point the new venture's shares, which, not being traded, had previously been difficult to sell after employees exercised their options, now, having become tradable, can become very valuable.

In a new venture, therefore, stock options can serve as a powerful tool for organizational integration. Stock options also serve, however, to dilute the entrepreneur's ownership stake as they are exercised, and as such manifest the collective character of the innovation process. At the same time, the use of this compensation tool creates an almost irresistible pressure for the firm to do an IPO thus tying its performance in the minds of the firm's participants to its prospective stock market valuation. One danger is that in a boom the financial opportunity will overwhelm the productive opportunity, as new ventures that have yet to develop a commercializable product go public and are, as a result, exposed to the demands of financial markets for regular returns.

Another related danger of a premature IPO is that those participants in the firm who hold large ownership stakes can, quite legally, gain incredible wealth from the new venture even though the firm whose stock yields them this wealth have not yet succeeded as a viable business enterprise (Lazonick 2007a). Especially in a speculative environment, the prospect of such gains can in turn attract entrepreneurs into the industry who lack the specialized knowledge of the industry required for innovative strategy, and whose main concern is with cashing in on the new venture whether or not it is a commercial success. Insofar as certain entrepreneurs are able to repeat this process, their 'serial entrepreneurship' may not contribute to innovation in the industry – or industries – in which they are involved.

This financial orientation of the new venture may be reinforced by the way in which it is financed. Although some entrepreneurs may possess sufficient financial resources to launch and sustain a new venture without external funding, such is not generally the case. In the 1960s, in the context of the proliferation of semiconductor start-ups in what became known as Silicon Valley, venture capital became a major force in the financing of new ventures, and in the 1970s this form of finance emerged as an industry in its own right.

Of importance to the success of US venture capital in supporting innovative enterprise has been the fact that many of the leading venture capitalists had themselves followed managerial careers in high-tech industry before becoming purveyors of finance to new high-tech firms. In playing this role, the most successful venture capitalists do more than provide financial commitment. They also participate in the exercise of strategic control, sitting on the boards of the new ventures that they have helped finance, and they are typically the ones who recruit managers to perform the firm's organizational functions instead of the entrepreneur. At the same time, as providers of venture finance, their prime objective is not to build the capabilities of, and reap the returns from, one company for their rest of their careers. Rather their aim is to 'exit' the firm at a propitious time in the not-too-distant future, either by going public with the new ventures in which they have invested or by doing a private sale to an established company. In this context, a well-developed stock market is an institution that permits founder-entrepreneurs and venture capitalists to exit from their investments, quite apart from whether an IPO also raises funds for the firm that has issued its stock. Under these institutional conditions, entrepreneurship may be ephemeral as an input into the innovation process; the entrepreneur disappears as the innovative enterprise lives on.

Concluding remarks

For economic development to occur, it is not enough for entrepreneurs to start new firms; some of those firms must grow over time. Although entrepreneurs launch new ventures, the types of people who are able and willing to engage in this activity may be ill-suited to manage a complex learning organization. The innovation process requires the integration into the organization of professional, technical and administrative personnel who are willing to stay and build companies that they did not found and which they do not own. Policies that place too much stress on entrepreneurship as the key to economic development can undermine the collective and cumulative process of organizational learning required for innovation to occur. Further research is needed to identify the types of employment institutions that support or undermine organizational integration in developing economies.

Note

1. For a more complete theoretical elaboration of this process of sustained innovative transformation, see Lazonick (2010a).

Part II

Measuring Entrepreneurship and the Business Environment

3
Designing Composite Entrepreneurship Indicators

Diego B. Avanzini

Introduction

It was Joseph Schumpeter who recognized the importance of measuring entrepreneurship. He pointed out that:

> ... as long as we are unable to put our arguments into figures, the voice of our science, although occasionally it may help to dispel gross errors, will never be heard by practical men. (Schumpeter 1933: 12)

In light of this recognition, the aim of this chapter is to construct policy useful measures of entrepreneurship, specifically composite entrepreneurship indicators (CEIs). The resulting index, Multidimensional Entrepreneurship Index, can be used for different purposes such as benchmarking and exploratory analysis, helping to disentangle the direction of developments and improvements in policy, and to facilitate communication between the public and decision-makers.

Defining entrepreneurship

Chapters 1 and 2 of this book have defined entrepreneurship. This chapter proceeds on the basis of this recognition that entrepreneurship can, in economics, most usefully be associated with the formation of a new business firm in order to bring an innovative product or service to market. In Chapter 2, William Lazonick discussed the essential characteristics of the innovative firm. Hence, for present purposes we follow Ahmad and Seymour (2008) and define entrepreneurship as the phenomenon associated with the entrepreneurial activity, that is, the enterprising human action in pursuit of the generation of value, through the creation or expansion of economic activity, by identifying and exploiting new products, processes or markets.

Selecting dimensions and indicators

The range of concepts involved in entrepreneurship and the variety of policy goals and the way in which they can be measured, force us not to measure the phenomenon by mean of a lonely indicator but rather a set of them. The chosen practical measure of entrepreneurship will ultimately depend on the nature of the policy objective.[1] Provided there is neither a fully objective way of selecting the relevant subindicators, nor a certain way to group them if it would be necessary, we started designing a *scoreboard,* an idea that has appealed to many managers and policy-makers in recent years[2] and that we adopt here. Our scoreboard uses some ideas that can be found in the *entrepreneurship* (see Ahmad and Hoffmann 2008; Ahmad and Seymour 2008; Behrens 2007; Leitão da Silva Martins 2007; OECD/Eurostat 2009), *innovation* (see Zabala-Iturriagagoitia et al. 2007), and *investment* literature (see Statistics Netherlands 2007).

One of the advantages of the scoreboard is that it is a guide to selecting and collecting available data, and a checklist for not yet available

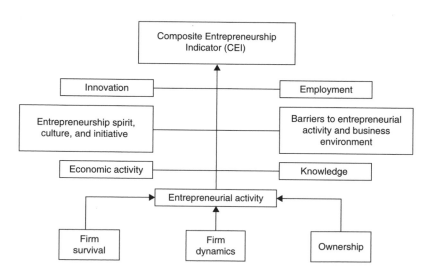

Figure 3.1   The Composite Entrepreneurship Indicator's (CEI) scoreboard
Source: Own elaboration.

data that should be collected. Variables and subindicators have been selected on the basis of their (i) analytical soundness, (ii) measurability, (iii) relevance to the phenomenon being measured, and (iv) relationship to each other (see Freudenberg 2003).

We find it helpful to disaggregate the problem in several dimensions following the way literature have treated those[3] and we propose the following scoreboard as the basis for measuring entrepreneurship. Its basic structure is presented in Figure 3.1. This scoreboard captures the main dimensions of the entrepreneurial activity, facilitating issues and determinants, and its manifestations and impacts.

As indicated in Figure 3.1, we focus our attention in seven dimensions:

1. *Entrepreneurial activity*: this category includes three dimensions, namely (i) firm dynamics, (ii) firm survival and (iii) ownership. The indicators included under firm dynamics and firm survival are the mostly recognized entrepreneurial activity proxies. Ownership is included to avoid confusion between entrepreneurship and management: both concepts are very closely related, given entrepreneurship involves management, but a key difference between them is ownership (that can be translated into a *risk-bearing* activity).

2. *Employment*: describes the impact of entrepreneurship on employment, measured by the number of employees associated with the creation and exit of new enterprises. Employment creation is one of the universally claimed beneficial effects of entrepreneurship and should be an important manifestation of its existence.

3. *Economic activity*: beyond employment, other areas of the economic activity may be reflecting the entrepreneurship development: for instance increasing sales, new SMEs, rising international trade, and an increased number and capitalization of enterprises in the stock market.

4. *Entrepreneurship spirit, culture and initiative*: people engaged in entrepreneurial activities have some particular characteristics that make them unique, for example, entrepreneurial potential and propensity, particular skills, reasons to becoming an entrepreneur, and contact with other entrepreneurs.

5. *Barriers to entrepreneurial activity and business environment*: entrepreneurship arises in a certain time location coordinate and by its nature involves the integration of many aspects that lead it to a successful performance. The pro-entrepreneurship characteristics of the business environment, the available resources and the institutions supporting entrepreneurship play a decisive role in entrepreneurial success.

6. *Knowledge procurement*: following the Schumpeterian association between entrepreneurship and knowledge generation, we attempt to include here those activities oriented to support the knowledge procurement system.
7. *Innovation*: the final outcome of the knowledge procurement system that may show up in a variety of ways: new products, new markets, new processes, and new uses of existing products.

These categories are not exhaustive, and adopting them is in no way a restricting characteristic of our approach because the techniques proposed in this chapter are intended to allow modifications, improvements and widening, to set up better measures. The methodology introduced in this chapter is intended to deal with changes in concepts and dimensions of entrepreneurship, using a flexible, reliable framework.

Data selection and description

We have selected a set of more than 70 variables coming from several sources, for a sample of 69 countries (see Table 3A.1 for a list of countries, and Tables 3A.3 and 3A.7 for a list of variables). The list of variables and its description, separated by source, can be found in Appendix B. These variables present some problems such as periodicity, availability, 'outlying' observations, clumping, truncation and relationship among them that are discussed in what follows.

Dealing with data scarcity

Data availability is an important issue in the design of any indicator. Usually, developing countries are less represented in data sets, biasing the estimation results towards developed countries. Also there is a problem with the periodicity: not all variables are collected on the same time base or they have time gaps, if not for all countries, at least for some of them. Basically, the data sets are unbalanced (different number of observations for each country) but the statistical methods we will implement need balanced data sets.

From a practical perspective, we use a combination of two approaches to deal with data scarcity: the first approach consists of averaging variables for each country over two periods, namely 1998–2001 and 2002–5. In this way we summarize the gathered information in order to obtain more complete data series and to avoid the effects of possible changes in measures and methods – something that often occurs when implementing surveys in their initial stages; such is the case of most of the entrepreneurship surveys. Averaging over a four-year period seems not to cause a large bias in our estimations. We verified that there were not very important changes in scale or growth rate of the variables, and that aggregating information in other periodical base (e.g. three or five years) did not change drastically the outcomes. We found that the separation in these two periods is relatively stable and gave us a more complete data set.

Dealing with missing values

Despite the averaging procedure previously discussed, available statistical series are not complete for all periods and all countries thus plaguing our data set with missing values. Various 'solutions' have been applied in social sciences (Freudenberg 2003) such as: dropping observations (data deletion, as in Cortinovis et al. 1993); replacing missing values with their means (mean substitution, as in Gwatkin et al. 2000, Vyas and Kumaranayake 2006); replacing missing values with estimated or predicted values (i.e. using regressions based on other variables to estimate the missing values); multiple imputation using a large number of sequential regressions with indeterminate outcomes, which are run multiple times and averaged; nearest neighbour imputation, that is, identifying and substituting the most similar case for the one with a missing value; ignoring them and taking the average index of the remaining indicators within the component; and the list goes on.

All of these methods have advantages and disadvantages. The statistical literature has recently centred its attention on the estimation of missing values conditional on available information for the rest of the sample in the context of principal components, such as the Probability Principal Components Analysis (PPCA) developed by Tipping and Bishop (1999). This model suggests that the Principal Components Analysis (PCA) can be considered a linear aggregation of Gaussian processes and that a maximum likelihood approach can be used to estimate its unknowns, namely the set of Principal Components (PCs). Roweis (1998) uses the expectation-maximization algorithm to obtain the PCs, and proposes a simple extension to account for missing data (see the details in Avanzini 2009). This is the statistical approach we adopt in this chapter. Several simulations have been done to test out whether changes in the way the data set is completed has major impact on our CEI. Generally we have found that the outcomes vary little.

Clumping and truncation

As is discussed below, our weighting procedure is based on PCA, and a major challenge for PCA-based weighting is to ensure the range of variables is broad enough to avoid problems such as clumping and truncation. *Clumping* or *clustering* refers to the case in which countries present block behaviour, that is, they behave as if they were put together in small clusters. This data characteristic generates strange behaviours of the variance-covariance matrix that is our basic piece of information.[4] *Truncation* implies that the observations are spread over a narrow range, losing variability and biasing the outcomes towards more even distributions. We can detect these features through a good description of indicators (particularly their ranges) and summary statistics (mean, standard deviation, interquartilic range, maximum and minimum). One way to overcome these pitfalls is to add more variables to the analysis in order to capture full variability through other indicators. This is one of the reasons for using many variables to represent a certain category. Truncation may be very important in the case of developing countries given they are usually under-represented in data sets. In our sample of 69 countries, they constitute about a half of the sample, in order to avoid the oversampling of developed countries.

Compiling the composite indicator

A composite indicator (CI) is the mathematical combination of individual indicators that represent different dimensions of a concept whose description is the objective of the analysis (see Saisana and Tarantola 2002). Composite indicators are appealing due to their usefulness, flexibility and simplicity. They constitute suitable tools for exploring less known phenomena, and for benchmarking performances. Saisana and Tarantola (2002) highlight their usefulness to provide experts, stakeholders and decision-makers with:

- the direction of developments;
- comparison across places, situations and countries;
- assessment of state and trend in relation to goals and targets;
- early warning;
- identification of areas for action;
- anticipation of future conditions and trends; and
- communication channel for general public and decision-makers.

Constructing a CI is a good way to acquire knowledge at a relatively low cost provided CIs are also easily implemented, without requiring deep *a priori* knowledge or assumptions about the studied phenomenon, and generally they are not so computationally expensive. That is why they are extensively used in exploratory analysis or for describing complex structures.

Our CEI shares all these properties and its weighting methodology accommodates a set of eight axioms (see Avanzini 2008).[5] The highest hierarchical level of analysis is the *dimension* and indicates the scope of objectives, individual indicators and variables. Our indicator has seven dimensions as explained. An *objective* indicates the direction of desired change, that is, in what direction (upper or lower values) would an improvement in the indicator be reflected. The *individual indicators* are the basis for evaluation in relation to a given objective (any objective may imply a number of different individual indicators). It is a function that associates each single country with a variable indicating its desirability according to expected consequences related to the same objective. A *variable* is a constructed measure stemming from a process that represents, at a given point in space and time, a shared perception of a real world state of affairs consistent with a given individual indicator. In this context, the composite indicator (or synthetic index) is an aggregate or a function of all dimensions, objectives, individual indicators and variables used. This implies that what formally defines a composite indicator is the set of properties underlying its aggregation convention. The set of axioms ensures that our CEI will behave successfully for benchmarking and exploratory purposes.

Estimating the composite indicator

We are interested in obtaining a weighting procedure with two additional characteristics beyond the axioms: first, we want the technique to be as *independent as possible from the analyst* and second, that the procedure *extracts the maximum information* from available data. Taking into account these two characteristics we begin by discarding *ad hoc* and subjective weightings, and concentrate on statistical and econometrical tools. In the literature many approaches have been used, most of them labelled under multivariate analysis methods, and aimed to extract information from several sort of data under different assumptions.

In what follows we use the PCA[6] to solve the weighting scheme. PCA is a powerful and relatively simple technique for extracting hidden structures from possibly high dimensional data sets. The intuition behind PCA is simple: suppose we have a data set with a high number of variables (i.e. indicators) for various observations. One can think of these indicators as measuring the same object or episode from different perspectives so all of them contain common information about the object. PCA is an orthogonal transformation of the coordinate system in which we describe our data. The new coordinate values by which we represent the data are called *principal components*. It is often the case that a small number of such principal components is enough to account for the most of the structure in the data. These are sometimes called *factors* or *latent variables* of the data.

There are several ways of computing PCA depending on the underlying structure we have assumed. In this chapter, we concentrate on the comparison of the outcomes of four alternative PCA methods: standard PCA, NIPALS-based PCA, multiblock PCA (consensus PCA), and an extension of probabilistic PCA with an EM algorithm for data reconstruction. Each method has particular characteristics that give rise to different sets of weights, and of course, to different CEI. Although our proposed method relies on consensus PCA, we have included standard PCA and NIPALS-based PCA for the sake of comparison given their popularity and availability in statistical and econometric software.

Method I: Overall Entrepreneurship Index (OEI)

It consists of taking the whole set of variables (data set) for each period and computing a standard PCA. There are two well-known variants for obtaining it: using covariance (with standardized indicators) or correlation matrix eigendecomposition (see Jolliffe 2002) or using iterative algorithms such as NIPALS (see Wold et al. 1987). The outcomes of both methods are the same though the eigendecomposition approach is quicker. The square of the eigenvector associated to the first (bigger eigenvalue) principal component gives us the weighting matrix that multiplied by the data set produces the weighted matrix of indicators, that is, the CEI under this approach. We use this index as our benchmark and for the sake of comparability, though inference based on this weighting scheme is not very useful and tends to exacerbate outlying observations.

The indexes obtained with this approach are reported in Table 3A.1 for the period 1998–2001, and in Table 3A.5 for the period 2002–5, and analysed below. The theoretical background can be found in Avanzini (2009).

Method II: Disaggregated Entrepreneurship Index (DEI)

The set of seven indexes per period, one for each dimension, is constructed using standard PCA on each group of standardized indicators. Each index ranks the country performance on the respective dimension, and is a useful tool to get a deeper insight on the driving forces behind entrepreneurship. Nonetheless, as with OEI, it is difficult to assert the degree of entrepreneurship development provided that it is using only the information inside each dimension, so the remaining information is lost for the analysis. To get each index, we squared the eigenvector corresponding to the first principal component (largest eigenvalue) calculated over the set of indicators of each dimension solely, and then we multiply it by the dimensions' block of indicators to get a CEI for each dimension.

The results for each dimension are shown in Table 3A.2 (period 1998–2001) and Table 3A.6 (period 2002–5). Detailed explanations on the mathematical background for the PCA methodology used here can be found in Avanzini (2009).

Method III: Aggregated Entrepreneurship Index (AEI)

Once we get the first principal component of each dimension and the associated index from DEI, a natural extension might be to group the seven principal components (i.e. we accommodate the PCs containing the maximum common information of each dimension) in a single matrix. Each PC represents an important proportion of the information contained in that dimension, so the matrix containing such PCs is our best set of common knowledge about the behaviour of the entrepreneurship dimensions, constrained to use just one PC per dimension. Additionally, PCs are standardized random variables given they are constructed as a weighted sum of standardized random variables. If we then apply standard PCA to this matrix we obtain the AEI. This composite indicator is a summary of the most relevant information of each dimension.

Although we have gathered together all the dimension-related information, much of the interactions among variables of different dimensions are only captured through their impact on the dimensional PCs: indicators that are weak within a dimension, but highly correlated with other indicators in the remaining dimensions, could be underweighted in the aggregate index.[7] Again the explanations related to the mathematical procedure are given in Appendix B, and the indexes are shown in Table 3A.2 (period 1998–2001) and Table 3A.6 (period 2002–5).

Method IV: Multidimensional Entrepreneurship Index (MEI)

Finally, we discuss the key proposal of this chapter. We would like to have a composite indicator capable of accounting for particular intradimensional structures, but also interdimensional relationships, and overall behavioural patterns. The consensus PCA is a method that can account for all these problems and still gives us a consistent, meaningful set of weights.[8] The intuition behind the consensus principal components analysis (CPCA) is explained in Wold et al. (1987) (for details on its computation, see Avanzini 2009).

One of the advantages of CPCA is that it uses all the available information in each iteration: it weights block indicators to get the block scores (in the spirit of DEI), then it uses these scores to construct a super-level block of information and estimates its score (in the spirit of AEI), and finally it re-weights the sub-level indicators with the overall weights (in the spirit of OEI), and iterates this procedure until convergence. Two additional advantages of CPCA are: (i) it has the same objective function as standard PCA, that is, maximization of the variance of the data set and (ii) it automatically adjusts relative variance of different indicators by virtue of its block scaling procedure (Westerhuis et al. 1998). Also notice that the MEI overcomes the drawbacks posed for each of the other methods. First, OEI was not able to focus in certain areas of the correlation matrix, those related with the dimension blocks, and uses all the available information without discriminating. Second, DEI accounted for each dimension behaviour, but was unable to integrate the information remaining. Finally, AEI captured variability at dimensional level, and used the reduced information data set to estimate the relationship among dimensions. However, there was no possibility to capture more complex relationships (possibly represented by higher order principal components). The three drawbacks are elegantly managed in the context of CPCA through the NIPALS algorithm that allows the integration of dimensional (block) and overall information through an iterative procedure.

The set of weights (at dimensional level and at variable/indicator level) are shown in Tables 3A.3 and 3A.7, and indexes are shown in Tables 3A.4 and 3A.8, for the period 1998–2001 and 2002–5, respectively. Avanzini (2009) develops the mathematical background.

Comments on the estimation strategy

Although we have made an effort to rely as much as possible upon statistical methods to construct our CEI, we have been forced to use our own judgement repeatedly. Provided the outcomes of the CEI depend largely on the selected approach, we conducted sensitivity tests to analyse the impact of including or excluding variables, changing the weighting scheme, using different standardization techniques, selecting alternative base years, excluding cases with unreliable data, etc., on the results of the CEI. We used bootstrapping methods to account for these issues, and generally we found no significant (95 per cent confidence level) variations in the outcomes.

The quality of our data set prevents us from doing categorical assertions: averaging over periods makes us lose some of the dynamics of the entrepreneurship process; the methodology we adopt to deal with missing data – though quite reliable – has been forced to deal with many missing values, weakening the outcomes.[9] Although the data set we finally use seems to be quite stable and reliable, we know that countries showing originally more complete data sets are those more developed, with higher per capita income, with better life standards, with higher mean levels of education and so on, while developing countries have more incomplete data sets, so the outcomes referring to developed countries might be more robust than those involving developing countries.

A final comment about dimensions: we have assumed that our indicators can be adequately grouped in nine categories, finally reduced to seven to make robust the estimation of block scores. To determine the number of categories in a more reliable, non-arbitrary way some techniques are available. For example, we can look at the screenplots (available on request), that is, the plot of the eigenvalues, to find out such an 'elbow' as is suggested under this approach. For our data set, such a technique is not helpful because eigenvalues diminish smoothly without showing a sensible break ('elbow') in their values. We can also use estimations of the intrinsic dimensionality (van der Maaten 2007) to determine the number of dimensions: applying this technique we find that, for bootstrapped samples, the dimensions roughly vary among eight and ten. Thus our categorization (as showed in Tables 3A.3 and 3A.7) seems to be a good grouping strategy. Moreover, it seems to be the case that the most significant relationships between indicators are located inside the shaded areas that correspond to the correlation matrixes of each block variables. However, to get more robust results we regroup the first three categories (firm dynamics, firm survival and ownership) in a single category to strengthen block scores estimation. We perform some simulations to evaluate how the results change, and the final distribution of indexes seems to remain unchanged with this procedure.

Analysing entrepreneurship using the CEI

We start the analysis with the simplest index to finally arrive at our key proposal, the MEI. The OEI, our benchmark technique, shows that less developed countries improve their performance in the second period. The indexes are reported in Table 3A.1 for the period 1998–2001, and in Table 3A.5 for the period 2002–5. They are calculated over standardized variables so their means are zeroes, and the standard deviations are about 0.30 for 1998–2001, and 0.22 for 2002–5. The range of the indexes narrows from 1998–2001 to 2002–5 showing that countries are making efforts to improve the entrepreneurial activity. Those efforts narrow entrepreneurial gaps among countries, a conclusion from the observation of actual data where top ranked countries in the first period have maintained their conditions and indicators values. As previously discussed, the weakness of the OEI is that it aggregates all the information without major insight about the different aspects of entrepreneurship that generates the ranking: the way the index weights all the attributes prevents us from using it to infer which are the driving forces behind entrepreneurial development, and in what areas it has major impact. Nevertheless we can still exploit it as a benchmarking tool that gives us some information on the way different countries are performing. But we necessarily need to compare the behaviour of each indicator to know more about the reasons for these behaviours. This index, even though simple, is restrictive for inference purposes, and it is difficult to get more information than the ranking of countries.

The second CEI, the Disaggregated Entrepreneurship Index, explores the behaviour of each of the seven categories. They are reported in Tables 3A.2 and 3A.6 for the periods 1998–2001 and 2002–5, respectively. The behaviour is more erratic at this level of aggregation. Results are difficult to interpret: for example, in 2002–5, the disconnection between knowledge procurement and innovation produces rankings under these categories that are very different.[10] On the issue of the ease of entrepreneurial activity, at the end of the 1990s, Japan and the USA appeared as the most opened economies to this sort of activities. But with Brazil, Paraguay, Bolivia and other developing countries entering the international scene, the classically entrepreneurial countries were relegated to secondary places. Entrepreneurial vocation is stronger in countries such as New Zealand and Australia, but less developed economies like Mexico and Brazil appear to have the necessary intention to get more involved in entrepreneurship development. This is consistent with the evidence that GEM's total entrepreneurial activity (TEA) index shows when it is drawn against GDP per capita: less developed countries are more likely to develop entrepreneurial activities, and are more well disposed towards entrepreneurship than more developed countries. But the driving forces are different for both groups of countries: while less developed countries are performing entrepreneurial activities by *necessity* (generally associated with high rate of unemployment in the formal sector), high income economies focus on *opportunity entrepreneurship*, mostly linked to product innovation, new markets and improved production processes. The *necessity entrepreneurship* is more related to 'economic survival'. Within our data set, Mexico and Brazil are good examples of this situation, as can be inferred from the impact of entrepreneurship in the employment dimension.

When we aggregate the seven dimensions on a single CEI, the AEI (first ranking in Tables 3A.2 and 3A.6), we find that the USA, China and Japan are consolidated as leading entrepreneurial economies. Nonetheless, the indexes are very different between them, with abrupt changes in rankings that are not so convincing. The employment dimension has a strong weight (see the weights on the top of each dimension) and it is dominant in the 2002–5 period. But differences in the range of other less relevant dimensions contribute to generate some important distortions, for example, placing Finland in the 63rd in 2002–5 after being in the 10th position in 1998–2001.

An interesting feature of the AEI, is the way it weights different dimensions:[11] in 1998–2001, the dimensions were weighted in three ranges: less than 5 per cent, between 11 per cent and 13 per cent and beyond 20 per cent. In 2002–5, the dimensions employment and economic activity account for almost 66 per cent of the total variability, being the leading ones. Surprisingly, knowledge procurement and innovation only account for 20 per cent in 2002–5 while in 1998–2001 those dimensions constituted about 55 per cent of the variability. Also the weak role of entrepreneurial activity in 2002–5 is suspicious. With the current data set, this weighting process seems to be very unstable and its outcome is not very sound. However, we have to recognize that during 2002–5 many developing economies presented amazing economic growth rates and improvements in their employment – both phenomena captured by an increased weighting of employment and economic activity dimensions.

Beyond some particular problems arising probably due to data quality, from a methodological perspective, one of the advantages of the composite index obtained in this way is that it is able to capture the areas or dimensions where there is still 'action', in the sense that the highly weighted dimensions are the most relevant differences between countries, and are the areas where major improvements can be done. In this sense, the CEI can help to guide policy-making in order to narrow the gaps with other countries.

Finally, we turn our attention to the MEI that is our starred CEI. Tables 3A.3 and 3A.7 report the relative weighting of variables and dimensions, and Tables 3A.4 and 3A.8 report scores and rankings. The novelty of this index, as was previously discussed, is its capability to capture information inside and outside the specific dimension, through an iterative weighting process that gives us deeper insight on entrepreneurship behaviour. The driving forces in 1998–2001 (Table 3A.3) were related to economic activity (particularly the creation of small and medium enterprises). Entrepreneurship spirit and business environment were almost equally weighted as were knowledge procurement and innovation dimensions. The number of technicians in R&D, and the submission of patent applications and trademarks were relevant aspects of the entrepreneurial development. Also domestic credit played an important role in the strengthening of the entrepreneurial activity.

In 2002–5 (Table 3A.7), countries have improved those dimensions and they have lost their importance. Innovation is now more important and the contribution of entrepreneurial development to employment appears as the major impact. Barriers to entrepreneurship and a suitable environment for business developments have lost their importance given that most of the countries made major reforms and efforts to support entrepreneurial activity. Again the number of technicians in R&D, and the submission of patent applications and trademarks have been important determinants of entrepreneurial performance. The impact on economic activity has been diminished to highlight the employment dimension instead.

This behaviour between periods is consistent with other studies that support the idea that countries evolve through different stages of entrepreneurial development. For example, Acs and Szerb (2009) argue that countries face three different stages: factor-driven, efficiency-driven and innovation-driven stages. Each stage has different characteristics and supports entrepreneurship in a different way, and countries tend to go through the three stages gradually.

In both periods, the dimension reflecting entrepreneurial activity itself has not been important. We find that this is consistent with the fact that information related to firm dynamics and ownership is scarcer as it is less represented in the data set than other information. Perhaps in the future, with improved data sets, this dimension would become more dominant in the determination of the index value. With our current data set, many of the characteristics measured under entrepreneurial activity have been measured under different dimensions with proxies that present a more complete record for the sample.

Developing countries have generally improved their positions in the rankings. Many reforms were conducted at the end of the 1990s and during the first years of this century. Simplified tax schemes, easier business registration and more available financial information (that speed up the credit market) contributed to the generation of a supporting system for entrepreneurial activity. Also the economic prosperity driven by the boom of commodity prices generated a market for new small and medium enterprises that hired new employees. China, Mexico, Brazil, Indonesia and Argentina are good examples of high growth rates that were accompanied by new employment, new small and medium enterprises and technological development. These improvements in the economy and particularly in the entrepreneurial sector in developing countries do not mean that developed countries have worsened their policies: it only means that developing countries have made changes at a quicker rhythm, and the impact of their reforms and economic changes have had major impact on the economy compared to the case in developed countries.

Recall that the most important characteristic of this index is the way it selects the determinants of entrepreneurship, providing us with a closer insight into how policies and efforts should be oriented. And this is the central message of this approach: *the suggested methodology helps us to direct policies towards weak determinants to improve them, and towards strong impacts to ensure they will be maintained or improved.*

Concluding remarks

Much remains for future research. Improving data collection and its reliability is the first step. Continuing to explore robust methodologies to account for variations in entrepreneurship performance is another task that needs more attention. Continuing to improve our understanding of the driving forces behind entrepreneurship and how those relate to economic growth evidently remains an important task for scholars.

Communication is important: it might be very tempting for politicians to show how countries satisfactorily evolve in international benchmarks. However, as was explained here, the way the CEI reports changes makes it less attractive in this regard. This is because when all countries attempt to improve their policies in a certain direction, differences arising from that dimension are not still relevant for the problem, and politicians might feel that being equated to other countries is perhaps not enough to capture voters' attention. We recognize that this can be a pitfall of any CEI.

A CEI like the MEI tells us where we stand in the global economy (benchmarking purpose) and informs us which might be the principal reasons of our situation and how far we are from the best performers (inference purpose), allowing policy-makers to change policy directions to support entrepreneurship (policy purpose). However, weak data sets or careless use of the methodologies may result in misleading interpretations and perverse policies that might block rather than encourage entrepreneurial activity. As always, the art of dealing with an intricate subject such as entrepreneurship is in the hands of the analyst.

Acknowledgements

An earlier version of this chapter was presented at the UNU-WIDER Project Workshop on 'Entrepreneurship and Economic Development: Concepts, Measurements, and Impacts', Helsinki, 21–23 August 2008. I am very grateful to the workshop's assistants, Wim Naudé, and two anonymous referees for their comments, and also to Carolina Serpell for reviewing the original document. As usual, remaining errors are the author's own responsibility.

Appendix

Appendix A: Tables

Table 3A.1 Method I: Overall Entrepreneurship Index (OEI), period 1998–2001

Ranking	Country	Country Code	Index	Ranking	Country	Country Code	Index
1	United States	USA	0.9966	36	Ireland	IRL	−0.0709
2	Switzerland	CHE	0.8925	37	Paraguay	PRY	−0.0724
3	Sweden	SWE	0.8065	38	Syrian Arab Republic	SYR	−0.0779
4	Finland	FIN	0.6078	39	Panama	PAN	−0.0804
5	China	CHN	0.5502	40	El Salvador	SLV	−0.0862
6	Japan	JPN	0.4758	41	Peru	PER	−0.0866
7	Australia	AUS	0.4714	42	Colombia	COL	−0.0896
8	Germany	DEU	0.4062	43	Romania	ROM	−0.0932
9	Korea, Rep.	KOR	0.3362	44	Indonesia	IDN	−0.0980
10	Canada	CAN	0.3223	45	Ecuador	ECU	−0.1004
11	Iceland	ISL	0.2283	46	Denmark	DNK	−0.1033
12	Netherlands	NLD	0.2074	47	Nicaragua	NIC	−0.1054
13	United Kingdom	GBR	0.1608	48	Singapore	SGP	−0.1067
14	France	FRA	0.1577	49	Ukraine	UKR	−0.1073
15	New Zealand	NZL	0.1512	50	Dominican Republic	DOM	−0.1180
16	Malaysia	MYS	0.1235	51	Uruguay	URY	−0.1189
17	Brazil	BRA	0.0727	52	Bulgaria	BGR	−0.1230
18	Hong Kong, China	HKG	0.0688	53	Honduras	HND	−0.1350
19	Lebanon	LBN	0.0455	54	Kazakhstan	KAZ	−0.1433
20	Thailand	THA	0.0417	55	Norway	NOR	−0.1443
21	Egypt, Arab Rep.	EGY	0.0256	56	Venezuela, RB	VEN	−0.1497
22	Argentina	ARG	0.0122	57	Guatemala	GTM	−0.1536
23	Jordan	JOR	0.0006	58	Greece	GRC	−0.1564
24	Italy	ITA	−0.0017	59	Russian Federation	RUS	−0.1685
25	Chile	CHL	−0.0119	60	Estonia	EST	−0.1712
26	India	IND	−0.0169	61	Belgium	BEL	−0.1946
27	Kuwait	KWT	−0.0173	62	Luxembourg	LUX	−0.1986
28	Mexico	MEX	−0.0224	63	Portugal	PRT	−0.3746
29	Israel	ISR	−0.0359	64	Spain	ESP	−0.3796
30	Bolivia	BOL	−0.0388	65	Czech Republic	CZE	−0.4665
31	Saudi Arabia	SAU	−0.0444	66	Slovak Republic	SVK	−0.5015
32	United Arab Emirates	ARE	−0.0447	67	Hungary	HUN	−0.5106
33	Costa Rica	CRI	−0.0612	68	Poland	POL	−0.5590
34	South Africa	ZAF	−0.0678	69	Turkey	TUR	−0.6831
35	Austria	AUT	−0.0696	**Mean**	**0.0000**	**Std. Dev.**	**0.3064**

Source: Own estimations.

Table 3A.2 Methods II and III: Disaggregated (DEI) and Aggregated Entrepreneurship Index (AEI), period 1998–2001

Entrepreneurship Index			Entrepreneurial activity			Employment			Economic activity		
Aggregated			Weight: 13.23%			Weight: 11.54%			Weight: 2.97%		
Ranking	Country	Index	Country	Index	Ranking	Country	Index	Ranking	Country	Index	Ranking
1	CHN	2.7655	CHN	-0.2426	55	CHN	-0.0053	52	CHN	0.5862	2
2	CHE	2.5880	CHE	-0.4952	61	CHE	-0.0054	53	CHE	-0.0011	33
3	JPN	2.4328	JPN	-1.3118	68	JPN	-0.6328	68	JPN	-1.1895	68
4	SWE	2.3246	SWE	-1.0313	66	SWE	-0.0086	57	SWE	-0.0011	32
5	USA	2.2967	USA	-0.3049	57	USA	-0.5338	67	USA	0.4406	3
6	AUS	1.5160	AUS	1.2418	4	AUS	-0.0047	51	AUS	-0.0105	48
7	DEU	1.3168	DEU	-1.0236	65	DEU	-0.3053	64	DEU	-0.5018	64
8	NLD	1.2347	NLD	-0.7329	63	NLD	0.1230	4	NLD	5.3922	1
9	CAN	1.1085	CAN	0.1725	11	CAN	-0.0081	56	CAN	-0.0005	15
10	FIN	0.8221	FIN	-0.3878	59	FIN	1.8165	1	FIN	-1.0218	67
11	ISL	0.7867	ISL	0.2220	9	ISL	-0.0013	48	ISL	-0.0115	52
12	NZL	0.7539	NZL	1.4679	3	NZL	0.0017	16	NZL	-0.0011	30
13	KOR	0.7449	KOR	0.5687	8	KOR	0.0185	7	KOR	0.0009	12
14	DNK	0.5091	DNK	-1.3765	69	DNK	-1.1310	69	DNK	-0.0013	44
15	ITA	0.4738	ITA	1.0614	5	ITA	-0.2793	63	ITA	-1.5118	69
16	GBR	0.4382	GBR	-0.6784	62	GBR	0.3997	3	GBR	-0.6187	65
17	ISR	0.2171	ISR	-0.0706	50	ISR	-0.0069	55	ISR	-0.0012	39
18	EGY	0.1939	EGY	-0.0218	48	EGY	-0.0004	47	EGY	0.0516	7
19	MYS	0.1659	MYS	0.0002	33	MYS	0.0004	36	MYS	0.0046	11
20	LBN	0.1081	LBN	0.0000	43	LBN	0.0004	35	LBN	-0.0007	23
21	ARG	0.0975	ARG	-0.0263	49	ARG	0.0006	24	ARG	-0.0131	53
22	HKG	0.0928	HKG	0.0002	32	HKG	0.0004	30	HKG	-0.0011	29

#											
23	FRA	0.0401	FRA	-0.2228	54	FRA	1.2753	2	FRA	-0.8527	66
24	JOR	0.0245	JOR	0.0000	41	JOR	0.0004	32	JOR	-0.0006	17
25	THA	0.0208	THA	0.0002	35	THA	0.0004	44	THA	-0.0010	28
26	BRA	-0.0785	BRA	0.1908	10	BRA	0.0184	9	BRA	-0.0095	46
27	CHL	-0.1075	CHL	0.0001	36	CHL	0.0045	12	CHL	-0.0007	20
28	SGP	-0.1506	SGP	-0.2532	56	SGP	0.0004	41	SGP	-0.0011	31
29	BEL	-0.1528	BEL	-0.3950	60	BEL	-0.4487	66	BEL	0.0856	5
30	SYR	-0.1633	SYR	0.0000	45	SYR	0.0004	43	SYR	0.0075	10
31	ZAF	-0.1843	ZAF	-0.1503	52	ZAF	0.0004	42	ZAF	-0.0006	18
32	ARE	-0.1925	ARE	0.0000	46	ARE	0.0004	46	ARE	-0.0007	27
33	NOR	-0.2187	NOR	-0.9834	64	NOR	-0.0113	59	NOR	-0.0012	40
34	SAU	-0.2245	SAU	0.0001	38	SAU	0.0004	40	SAU	-0.0007	26
35	IRL	-0.2326	IRL	0.6255	7	IRL	-0.3356	65	IRL	0.0288	8
36	COL	-0.2353	COL	0.0003	25	COL	0.0004	27	COL	-0.0012	35
37	KWT	-0.2427	KWT	0.0000	42	KWT	0.0004	34	KWT	-0.0007	22
38	AUT	-0.2636	AUT	-0.3817	58	AUT	-0.0056	54	AUT	-0.0012	34
39	RUS	-0.2667	RUS	-0.1556	53	RUS	-0.0129	62	RUS	0.0931	4
40	PRY	-0.2895	PRY	0.0000	44	PRY	0.0004	37	PRY	-0.0007	25
41	PER	-0.2979	PER	0.0002	34	PER	0.0004	38	PER	-0.0012	41
42	LUX	-0.3018	LUX	-1.2080	67	LUX	-0.0115	61	LUX	-0.0007	24
43	SLV	-0.3289	SLV	0.0196	23	SLV	0.0012	23	SLV	-0.0362	54
44	BOL	-0.3406	BOL	0.0000	39	BOL	0.0004	25	BOL	-0.0007	19
45	BGR	-0.3428	BGR	0.0003	24	BGR	0.0004	26	BGR	-0.0112	50
46	EST	-0.3638	EST	0.0003	26	EST	-0.0103	58	EST	-0.0013	45
47	CRI	-0.3773	CRI	0.0000	40	CRI	0.0004	28	CRI	-0.0007	21
48	IDN	-0.3781	IDN	0.0001	37	IDN	0.0004	31	IDN	-0.0005	16
49	PAN	-0.4174	PAN	0.0342	16	PAN	0.0018	14	PAN	-0.0928	61
50	ROM	-0.4217	ROM	0.0003	28	ROM	0.0004	39	ROM	-0.0004	14
51	ECU	-0.4253	ECU	-0.0007	47	ECU	0.0004	29	ECU	0.0161	9
52	KAZ	-0.4526	KAZ	0.0003	27	KAZ	0.0004	33	KAZ	-0.0100	47

Continued

Table 3A.2 Continued

Entrepreneurship Index Aggregated			Entrepreneurial activity Weight: 13.23%			Employment Weight: 11.54%			Economic activity Weight: 2.97%		
Ranking	Country	Index	Country	Index	Ranking	Country	Index	Ranking	Country	Index	Ranking
53	IND	-0.4535	IND	0.0857	13	IND	0.0014	21	IND	-0.0746	57
54	UKR	-0.4565	UKR	0.0003	30	UKR	0.0004	45	UKR	-0.0112	51
55	VEN	-0.4610	VEN	0.0352	15	VEN	0.0018	15	VEN	-0.0949	62
56	NIC	-0.5199	NIC	0.0301	18	NIC	0.0016	18	NIC	-0.0736	56
57	DOM	-0.5835	DOM	0.0233	22	DOM	0.0013	22	DOM	-0.2804	63
58	GRC	-0.5878	GRC	2.6899	1	GRC	0.0232	6	GRC	-0.0012	37
59	GTM	-0.6048	GTM	0.0296	19	GTM	0.0016	17	GTM	-0.0821	60
60	HND	-0.6419	HND	0.0267	21	HND	0.0015	20	HND	-0.0624	55
61	URY	-0.6893	URY	0.0306	17	URY	0.0016	19	URY	-0.0761	58
62	MEX	-0.7708	MEX	0.8363	6	MEX	0.0185	8	MEX	-0.0107	49
63	ESP	-1.0695	ESP	0.1338	12	ESP	0.0020	13	ESP	0.0005	13
64	CZE	-1.1104	CZE	0.0002	31	CZE	-0.0042	50	CZE	-0.0012	36
65	SVK	-1.1773	SVK	0.0003	29	SVK	-0.0113	60	SVK	-0.0012	43
66	POL	-1.3587	POL	-0.0953	51	POL	0.0049	11	POL	0.0568	6
67	HUN	-1.4186	HUN	0.0767	14	HUN	-0.0035	49	HUN	-0.0012	38
68	PRT	-1.5399	PRT	1.9154	2	PRT	0.0082	10	PRT	-0.0012	42
69	TUR	-2.1782	TUR	0.0283	20	TUR	0.0397	5	TUR	-0.0773	59
	Mean: 0.0000		Mean: 0.0000			Mean: 0.0000			Mean: 0.0000		
	Std.Dev.: 0.9507		Std.Dev.: 0.6356			Std.Dev.: 0.3333			Std.Dev.: 0.7263		

Source: Own estimations.

Table 3A.2 Methods II and III: Disaggregated (DEI) and Aggregated Entrepreneurship Index (AEI), period 1998–2001 (continued)

Entrepreneurship spirit, Culture, and initiative			Barriers to entrepreneurial Activity and business Environment			Knowledge procurement			Innovation		
Weight: 4.25%			Weight: 13.65%			Weight: 23.52%			Weight: 30.85%		
Country	Index	Ranking	Country	Index	Ranking	Country	Index	Ranking	Country	Index	Ranking
CHN	0.7783	5	CHN	0.6640	5	CHN	0.6574	9	CHN	1.5801	3
CHE	0.0826	15	CHE	0.7311	4	CHE	2.4029	2	CHE	0.7605	7
JPN	-2.0847	69	JPN	1.5337	1	JPN	0.1323	17	JPN	2.9160	2
SWE	-0.5603	60	SWE	0.0794	28	SWE	2.6067	1	SWE	1.1185	4
USA	1.7076	4	USA	1.0509	2	USA	0.2199	15	USA	3.7077	1
AUS	1.7431	3	AUS	0.2141	21	AUS	0.9074	6	AUS	0.3030	13
DEU	-0.4915	59	DEU	0.5066	8	DEU	0.6418	10	DEU	0.8660	6
NLD	-1.2943	65	NLD	0.6034	6	NLD	0.8810	7	NLD	0.1586	16
CAN	0.7016	7	CAN	0.5097	7	CAN	0.3934	13	CAN	0.4988	8
FIN	-0.1957	56	FIN	-0.1147	39	FIN	1.6879	3	FIN	0.4052	10
ISL	-0.0008	42	ISL	0.1188	24	ISL	1.2599	4	ISL	-0.2214	46
NZL	3.3628	1	NZL	0.0976	26	NZL	0.3445	14	NZL	-0.6954	62
KOR	0.5427	10	KOR	0.0937	27	KOR	-0.5672	58	KOR	0.8786	5
DNK	-0.4890	58	DNK	0.3156	13	DNK	0.9709	5	DNK	-0.1727	42
ITA	0.5382	11	ITA	0.1221	23	ITA	-0.8790	61	ITA	-0.6018	61
GBR	-0.6214	61	GBR	0.3345	11	GBR	0.6046	11	GBR	0.4126	9
ISR	-1.5185	68	ISR	0.2736	17	ISR	0.4106	12	ISR	-0.1578	40
EGY	0.0700	16	EGY	0.0375	29	EGY	0.0586	19	EGY	0.0282	19
MYS	-0.0005	32	MYS	0.7505	3	MYS	-0.0490	43	MYS	-0.0325	30
LBN	0.0001	27	LBN	0.2751	16	LBN	0.0021	20	LBN	0.0016	21
ARG	0.2334	12	ARG	-0.3392	53	ARG	-0.0303	34	ARG	0.2074	14

Continued

Table 3A.2 Continued

Entrepreneurship spirit, Culture, and initiative			Barriers to entrepreneurial Activity and business Environment			Knowledge procurement			Innovation		
Weight: 4.25%			Weight: 13.65%			Weight: 23.52%			Weight: 30.85%		
Country	Index	Ranking	Country	Index	Ranking	Country	Index	Ranking	Country	Index	Ranking
HKG	-0.0005	34	HKG	0.2787	15	HKG	-0.0311	35	HKG	0.0476	17
FRA	-1.2407	64	FRA	0.1506	22	FRA	0.7281	8	FRA	0.3386	12
JOR	0.0001	22	JOR	-0.0038	31	JOR	0.0013	21	JOR	0.0016	22
THA	-0.0003	31	THA	0.4020	10	THA	-0.0468	40	THA	-0.0786	35
BRA	0.7186	6	BRA	-0.3533	55	BRA	-0.1263	53	BRA	0.4033	11
CHL	0.0001	24	CHL	-0.0069	32	CHL	-0.0298	33	CHL	-0.0751	34
SGP	-1.3167	66	SGP	0.1101	25	SGP	-0.0251	32	SGP	0.0358	18
BEL	-1.4930	67	BEL	0.4118	9	BEL	-0.0194	30	BEL	-0.1380	38
SYR	0.0001	20	SYR	-0.4436	64	SYR	-0.0071	26	SYR	-0.0310	29
ZAF	-0.1601	55	ZAF	-0.0014	30	ZAF	-0.1532	54	ZAF	0.0016	28
ARE	0.0001	29	ARE	-0.4977	67	ARE	-0.0039	23	ARE	0.0016	23
NOR	-0.2493	57	NOR	-0.0140	34	NOR	0.0805	18	NOR	0.0154	20
SAU	0.0000	30	SAU	-0.3057	50	SAU	-0.0071	25	SAU	-0.0903	36
IRL	0.6047	8	IRL	0.2791	14	IRL	-1.0816	65	IRL	-0.2753	49
COL	-0.0006	35	COL	-0.2015	44	COL	-0.0472	41	COL	-0.1800	44
KWT	0.0001	26	KWT	-0.4185	61	KWT	-0.0421	39	KWT	0.0016	26
AUT	-0.0019	43	AUT	0.3198	12	AUT	-0.2170	56	AUT	-0.2859	51
RUS	-1.0988	63	RUS	-0.0676	37	RUS	-0.0947	49	RUS	-0.0356	31
PRY	0.0001	28	PRY	-0.4817	66	PRY	-0.0412	37	PRY	0.0016	25
PER	-0.0006	36	PER	-0.1942	43	PER	-0.0087	28	PER	-0.1800	43
LUX	-0.0005	33	LUX	0.2215	20	LUX	0.2113	16	LUX	-0.2951	53

SLV	-0.0625	44	SLV	-0.3359	52	SLV	-0.0635	44	SLV	-0.1286	37
BOL	0.0001	23	BOL	-0.0636	36	BOL	-0.0475	42	BOL	0.0016	27
BGR	0.0285	17	BGR	-0.3679	56	BGR	-0.0056	24	BGR	-0.2981	54
EST	-0.0008	40	EST	-0.3458	54	EST	-0.1727	55	EST	-0.3020	56
CRI	0.0001	25	CRI	-0.3810	57	CRI	-0.0074	27	CRI	0.0016	24
IDN	0.0001	21	IDN	-0.5866	68	IDN	-0.0131	29	IDN	-0.0656	32
PAN	-0.1096	52	PAN	-0.0725	38	PAN	-0.1117	52	PAN	-0.2340	47
ROM	-0.0007	38	ROM	-0.3869	58	ROM	-0.0221	31	ROM	-0.2934	52
ECU	0.0023	18	ECU	-0.4092	59	ECU	-0.0413	38	ECU	-0.2146	45
KAZ	-0.0008	41	KAZ	-0.4694	65	KAZ	-0.0336	36	KAZ	-0.3123	57
IND	-0.6466	62	IND	-0.2518	46	IND	-0.2639	57	IND	-0.0695	33
UKR	-0.0006	37	UKR	-0.1264	40	UKR	0.0001	22	UKR	-0.2604	48
VEN	-0.1127	54	VEN	-0.4338	63	VEN	-0.1045	50	VEN	-0.1636	41
NIC	-0.0963	50	NIC	-0.2226	45	NIC	-0.0883	47	NIC	-0.3308	59
DOM	-0.0744	45	DOM	-0.6439	69	DOM	-0.0708	45	DOM	-0.1533	39
GRC	0.0014	19	GRC	-0.0115	33	GRC	-0.7801	59	GRC	-1.0697	67
GTM	-0.0946	49	GTM	-0.4306	62	GTM	-0.0935	48	GTM	-0.3009	55
HND	-0.0852	47	HND	-0.4184	60	HND	-0.0868	46	HND	-0.3219	58
URY	-0.0981	51	URY	-0.1772	41	URY	-0.1050	51	URY	-0.2832	50
MEX	2.5684	2	MEX	-0.3019	49	MEX	-2.1465	69	MEX	0.1873	15
ESP	-0.1097	53	ESP	0.2519	19	ESP	-0.9515	63	ESP	-0.5867	60
CZE	-0.0816	46	CZE	-0.1804	42	CZE	-0.9281	62	CZE	-0.7243	63
SVK	-0.0007	39	SVK	-0.0359	35	SVK	-0.9738	64	SVK	-0.8481	64
POL	0.0850	14	POL	-0.2884	47	POL	-0.8728	60	POL	-0.9977	66
HUN	0.5808	9	HUN	-0.3283	51	HUN	-1.0941	66	HUN	-0.9470	65
PRT	0.1336	13	PRT	0.2646	18	PRT	-1.3079	67	PRT	-1.3002	69
TUR	-0.0905	48	TUR	-0.2885	48	TUR	-1.3088	68	TUR	-1.1293	68
Mean: 0.0000			**Mean: 0.0000**			**Mean: 0.0000**			**Mean: 0.0000**		
Std.Dev.: 0.8018			**Std.Dev.: 0.4086**			**Std.Dev.: 0.7447**			**Std.Dev.: 0.7577**		

Source: Own estimations.

Table 3A.3 Method IV: Multidimensional Entrepreneurship Index (MEI)
Distribution of weights among indicators and dimensions, period 1998–2001

Dimension	Dimension's weight	Indicators	Indicator's weight (intra-area)	Indicator's weight (overall)
1. Entrepreneurial activity	0.48%	1.1. Firm dynamics		
		1 Bankruptcy rate (%)	0.08	0.00
		2 Entry rate (%)	10.96	0.05
		3 Exit rate (%)	0.00	0.00
		4 Share of bankruptcies in firm exits (%)	43.97	0.21
		1.2. Firm survival		
		5 Young firm entrepreneurial activity index (Index) (%)	14.55	0.07
		6 Total entrepreneurial activity index (Index) (%)	30.43	0.15
		1.3. Ownership		
		7 Business ownership rate (agriculture, hunting, forestry and fishing, rate) (%)	0.00	0.00
		8 Business ownership rate (private sector excluding agriculture, hunting, forestry and fishing, rate) (%)	0.00	0.00
		9 Business ownership rate (total private sector, rate) (%)	0.00	0.00
2. Employment	2.50%	10 Average size of firm entries (number) (%)	0.04	0.00
		11 Share of entries in employment (%)	0.00	0.00
		12 Share of exits in employment (%)	0.00	0.00
		13 Aver. number workers for fast growers; last year period (x 1) (%)	12.47	0.31
		14 Aver. number workers for all enterpr.; growth rate period (%)	7.68	0.19
		15 Aver. number workers for all enterpr.; last year period (x 1) (%)	1.44	0.04
		16 Aver. number workers for fast growers; growth rate period (%)	0.17	0.00
		17 Aver. number workers for not-fast growers; growth rate period (%)	7.62	0.19
		18 Self-employment rates: total, as a percentage of total civilian employment (%)	70.57	1.77

		#			
3. Economic activity	33.02%	19	Average sales for all enterprises; growth rate period (%)	0.00	0.00
		20	Average sales for all enterprises; last year period (x € 1000) (%)	0.00	0.00
		21	Average sales for fast growers; growth rate period (%)	0.00	0.00
		22	Average sales for fast growers; last year period (x € 1000) (%)	0.00	0.00
		23	Average sales for not-fast growers; growth rate period (%)	0.00	0.00
		24	Average sales for not-fast growers; last year period (x € 1000) (%)	0.00	0.00
		25	Listed domestic companies, total (%)	0.00	0.00
		26	Micro, small and medium enterprises (number) (%)	100.00	33.02
		27	Micro, small and medium enterprises (per 1,000 people) (%)	0.00	0.00
		28	Taxes on exports (% of tax revenue) (%)	0.00	0.00
4. Entrepreneurship spirit, culture, and iniciative	18.13%	29	Female total entrepreneurial activity index (Index) (%)	0.63	0.11
		30	Necessity entrepreneurial activity index (Index) (%)	0.55	0.10
		31	Opportunity entrepreneurial activity index (Index) (%)	0.11	0.02
		32	Potential entrepreneur index (Index) (%)	0.00	0.00
		33	Highskilled self-employment rates (%)	0.00	0.00
		34	Fear of failure index (Index) (%)	0.00	0.00
		35	Know entrepreneur index (Index) (%)	0.00	0.00
		36	Latent entrepreneurship (%)	98.69	17.89
		37	Informal investors index (Index) (%)	0.00	0.00
		38	Nascent entrepreneurial activity index (Index) (%)	0.02	0.00
5. Barriers to entrepreneurial activity and business environment	14.79%	39	Domestic credit provided by banking sector (% of GDP)	51.90	7.68
		40	Domestic credit to private sector (% of GDP)	36.31	5.37
		41	Highest marginal tax rate, corporate rate (%)	0.07	0.01
		42	Highest marginal tax rate, individual rate (%)	0.78	0.12
		43	Interest rate spread (lending rate minus deposit rate) (%)	0.14	0.02
		44	Labour force with primary education (% of total)	5.08	0.75
		45	Labour force with secondary education (% of total)	4.78	0.71
		46	Labour force with tertiary education (% of total)	0.93	0.14
6. Knowledge procurement	17.53%	47	R&D performed by the non-business sector as a percentage of GDP (%)	0.00	0.00
		48	Non-business researchers per10 000 labour force (%)	0.00	0.00

Continued

Dimension	Dimension's weight		Indicators	Indicator's weight (intra-area)	Indicator's weight (overall)
		49	Basic research as a percentage of GDP (%)	0.00	0.00
		50	PhD graduation rates in science, engineering and health (%)	0.00	0.00
		51	Scientific and technical articles per million population (%)	0.98	0.17
		52	Business-financed R&D performed by government or higher education as a percentage of GDP	0.00	0.00
		53	Scientific papers cited in US-issued patents (%)	0.00	0.00
			Publications in the 19 most industry-relevant scientific disciplines per million		
		54	Population (%)	0.00	0.00
		55	Gross domestic expenditure on R&D (% of GDP)	0.00	0.00
		56	Physicians (per 1,000 people) (%)	0.00	0.00
		57	Technicians in R&D (per million people) (%)	99.01	17.36
7. Innovation	13.55%	58	BERD as a percentage of GDP (%)	0.00	0.00
		59	Business researchers per10 000 labour force (%)	0.00	0.00
		60	Number of patents in 'triadic' patent families per million population (%)	0.00	0.00
		61	Share of firms with new or technologically improved products or processes (%)	0.00	0.00
		62	Patent applications, non-residents (%)	7.51	1.02
		63	Patent applications, residents (%)	31.16	4.22
		64	Trademarks, non-residents (%)	0.83	0.11
		65	Trademarks, residents (%)	60.49	8.20

Source: Own estimations.

Table 3A.4 Method IV: Multidimensional Entrepreneurship Index (MEI), period 1998–2001

Multidimensional Entrepreneurship Index			Entrepreneurial Activity Weight: 10.27%			Employment Weight: 13.29%			Economic activity Weight: 9.00%		
Ranking	Country	Index	Country	Index	Ranking	Country	Index	Ranking	Country	Index	Ranking
1	USA	1.1863	USA	-0.4686	57	USA	-0.7708	67	USA	-0.2723	68
2	CHE	0.7991	CHE	-0.5596	58	CHE	-0.0400	54	CHE	-0.0440	32
3	JPN	0.7424	JPN	-1.0700	63	JPN	-0.7865	68	JPN	-3.9166	69
4	SWE	0.7317	SWE	-1.1976	66	SWE	-0.0634	58	SWE	-0.0405	30
5	CHN	0.6296	CHN	-0.2885	54	CHN	0.1955	6	CHN	0.3660	9
6	FIN	0.5787	FIN	-0.6626	61	FIN	1.4805	1	FIN	0.6992	3
7	DEU	0.4533	DEU	-1.1608	65	DEU	-0.0716	59	DEU	0.4983	7
8	AUS	0.3864	AUS	1.3924	5	AUS	-0.0347	53	AUS	0.0380	16
9	KOR	0.3720	KOR	0.6208	8	KOR	0.1368	8	KOR	0.0671	15
10	CAN	0.3370	CAN	0.1908	11	CAN	-0.0597	57	CAN	0.0824	13
11	NLD	0.2197	NLD	-0.5976	59	NLD	-0.3572	66	NLD	0.9220	2
12	FRA	0.2135	FRA	-1.3029	67	FRA	0.6684	2	FRA	0.6424	4
13	GBR	0.1978	GBR	-0.6103	60	GBR	0.2165	5	GBR	0.1143	12
14	MYS	0.1554	MYS	0.0003	32	MYS	0.0030	34	MYS	0.0310	18
15	ISL	0.1530	ISL	0.2561	9	ISL	-0.0095	40	ISL	-0.0946	62
16	HKG	0.0916	HKG	0.0003	31	HKG	0.0030	33	HKG	0.0128	20
17	LBN	0.0569	LBN	0.0000	45	LBN	0.0032	25	LBN	-0.0696	55
18	THA	0.0541	THA	0.0002	36	THA	0.0031	29	THA	-0.0277	26
19	BRA	0.0477	BRA	0.2406	10	BRA	0.1362	10	BRA	-0.0485	36
20	EGY	0.0237	EGY	-0.0259	49	EGY	0.0178	14	EGY	0.0706	14
21	NZL	0.0144	NZL	1.6932	3	NZL	0.0122	16	NZL	-0.0564	41
22	ITA	0.0131	ITA	1.6128	4	ITA	0.3635	3	ITA	1.5982	1

Continued

Table 3A.4 Continued

Multidimensional Entrepreneurship Index			Entrepreneurial Activity Weight: 10.27%			Employment Weight: 13.29%			Economic activity Weight: 9.00%		
Ranking	Country	Index	Country	Index	Ranking	Country	Index	Ranking	Country	Index	Ranking
23	JOR	0.0007	JOR	0.0000	43	JOR	0.0032	23	JOR	-0.0537	39
24	ARG	-0.0062	ARG	0.0114	24	ARG	0.0002	39	ARG	-0.0642	47
25	KWT	-0.0153	KWT	0.0000	44	KWT	0.0032	24	KWT	-0.0627	45
26	CHL	-0.0157	CHL	0.0001	37	CHL	0.0333	13	CHL	-0.0412	31
27	ISR	-0.0182	ISR	-0.1804	52	ISR	-0.0509	56	ISR	0.0000	21
28	IND	-0.0232	IND	0.1211	13	IND	-0.0138	44	IND	0.5237	6
29	MEX	-0.0246	MEX	1.0125	7	MEX	0.1362	9	MEX	-0.0811	57
30	BOL	-0.0413	BOL	0.0000	41	BOL	0.0032	21	BOL	-0.0685	53
31	IRL	-0.0483	IRL	1.0184	6	IRL	-0.0119	42	IRL	-0.0863	58
32	ZAF	-0.0495	ZAF	-0.1409	51	ZAF	0.0032	28	ZAF	-0.0002	22
33	ARE	-0.0538	ARE	0.0000	47	ARE	0.0032	27	ARE	-0.0664	51
34	SGP	-0.0543	SGP	-0.3090	55	SGP	0.0030	38	SGP	-0.0304	27
35	SAU	-0.0564	SAU	0.0001	39	SAU	0.0032	19	SAU	-0.0628	46
36	AUT	-0.0723	AUT	-0.4273	56	AUT	-0.0413	55	AUT	-0.0601	44
37	CRI	-0.0736	CRI	0.0000	42	CRI	0.0032	22	CRI	-0.0665	52
38	PRY	-0.0842	PRY	0.0000	46	PRY	0.0032	26	PRY	-0.0648	49
39	PAN	-0.0883	PAN	0.0407	16	PAN	-0.0198	49	PAN	-0.1282	67
40	SYR	-0.0963	SYR	0.0001	40	SYR	0.0032	20	SYR	0.0239	19
41	SLV	-0.1011	SLV	0.0233	23	SLV	-0.0099	41	SLV	-0.0867	60
42	COL	-0.1109	COL	0.0003	29	COL	0.0030	32	COL	-0.0559	40
43	PER	-0.1132	PER	0.0003	33	PER	0.0030	35	PER	-0.0454	33
44	IDN	-0.1170	IDN	0.0001	38	IDN	0.0032	18	IDN	-0.0380	28

45	NOR	-0.1178	64	NOR	-1.1163	62	NOR	-0.0834	37	NOR	-0.0496
46	ROM	-0.1242	34	ROM	0.0003	36	ROM	0.0030	5	ROM	0.5434
47	ECU	-0.1257	48	ECU	-0.0008	17	ECU	0.0036	42	ECU	-0.0583
48	NIC	-0.1270	18	NIC	0.0358	47	NIC	-0.0170	34	NIC	-0.0460
49	RUS	-0.1317	53	RUS	-0.2166	64	RUS	-0.0950	10	RUS	0.2327
50	BEL	-0.1361	62	BEL	-0.8412	65	BEL	-0.3173	8	BEL	0.3816
51	URY	-0.1396	17	URY	0.0364	48	URY	-0.0174	65	URY	-0.1214
52	UKR	-0.1407	35	UKR	0.0003	37	UKR	0.0030	59	UKR	-0.0866
53	DOM	-0.1418	22	DOM	0.0277	43	DOM	-0.0124	11	DOM	0.1731
54	DNK	-0.1475	68	DNK	-1.3693	69	DNK	-0.7974	35	DNK	-0.0462
55	BGR	-0.1599	28	BGR	0.0003	31	BGR	0.0030	25	BGR	-0.0258
56	HND	-0.1648	21	HND	0.0317	45	HND	-0.0147	63	HND	-0.0974
57	VEN	-0.1731	15	VEN	0.0419	50	VEN	-0.0205	64	VEN	-0.1140
58	KAZ	-0.1814	26	KAZ	0.0004	30	KAZ	0.0030	61	KAZ	-0.0945
59	GTM	-0.1850	19	GTM	0.0352	46	GTM	-0.0167	66	GTM	-0.1267
60	EST	-0.1866	25	EST	0.0004	60	EST	-0.0764	54	EST	-0.0688
61	GRC	-0.1927	1	GRC	3.0711	7	GRC	0.1708	29	GRC	-0.0384
62	LUX	-0.2021	69	LUX	-1.3727	63	LUX	-0.0844	50	LUX	-0.0654
63	ESP	-0.3231	12	ESP	0.1472	15	ESP	0.0154	17	ESP	0.0311
64	PRT	-0.3732	2	PRT	2.1947	11	PRT	0.0601	43	PRT	-0.0584
65	CZE	-0.4584	30	CZE	0.0003	52	CZE	-0.0314	38	CZE	-0.0533
66	SVK	-0.4880	27	SVK	0.0004	61	SVK	-0.0833	23	SVK	-0.0074
67	HUN	-0.5258	14	HUN	0.1071	51	HUN	-0.0262	48	HUN	-0.0647
68	POL	-0.5777	50	POL	-0.0820	12	POL	0.0574	24	POL	-0.0150
69	TUR	-0.6705	20	TUR	0.0337	4	TUR	0.2652	56	TUR	-0.0806

Mean: 0.0000
Std.Dev.: 0.3200

Mean: 0.0000
Std.Dev.: 0.7459

Mean: 0.0000
Std.Dev.: 0.2754

Mean: 0.0000
Std.Dev.: 0.5577

Source: Own estimations.

Table 3A.4 Method IV: Multidimensional Entrepreneurship Index (MEI), period 1998–2001 (continued)

Entrepreneurship spirit, culture, and initiative			Barriers to entrepreneurial Activity and business Environment			Knowledge procurement			Innovation		
Weight: 4.81%			Weight: 15.74%			Weight: 13.27%			Weight: 33.61%		
Country	Index	Ranking	Country	Index	Ranking	Country	Index	Ranking	Country	Index	Ranking
USA	0.6239	10	USA	1.3105	2	USA	0.5016	12	USA	3.1493	1
CHE	0.0009	31	CHE	0.8463	4	CHE	2.4588	2	CHE	1.2093	5
JPN	-1.3624	66	JPN	2.0233	1	JPN	0.4489	14	JPN	2.9665	2
SWE	-0.9661	63	SWE	0.1532	25	SWE	2.6915	1	SWE	1.5829	3
CHN	-0.7849	58	CHN	0.5819	8	CHN	0.6333	11	CHN	1.3760	4
FIN	-0.8201	60	FIN	-0.1375	37	FIN	1.6415	3	FIN	0.6853	8
DEU	-0.5437	56	DEU	0.5034	10	DEU	0.8943	6	DEU	1.0874	6
AUS	1.2646	4	AUS	0.1841	24	AUS	0.7479	10	AUS	0.1651	14
KOR	1.1513	6	KOR	0.1517	26	KOR	-0.2523	55	KOR	0.7087	7
CAN	0.5373	11	CAN	0.7652	5	CAN	0.4016	15	CAN	0.3522	10
NLD	-1.5393	67	NLD	0.6449	6	NLD	0.8079	7	NLD	0.3302	11
FRA	-0.8849	62	FRA	0.2049	22	FRA	0.7993	8	FRA	0.3123	12
GBR	-0.7262	57	GBR	0.4340	11	GBR	0.4554	13	GBR	0.3797	9
MYS	0.0008	35	MYS	1.0847	3	MYS	-0.0580	42	MYS	-0.0324	31
ISL	0.0011	27	ISL	0.1960	23	ISL	1.1194	4	ISL	-0.1276	41
HKG	0.0008	36	HKG	0.6284	7	HKG	-0.0438	36	HKG	-0.0093	28
LBN	0.0002	49	LBN	0.4004	12	LBN	-0.0044	22	LBN	0.0010	20
THA	0.0007	38	THA	0.5555	9	THA	-0.0526	38	THA	-0.0722	35
BRA	1.4255	3	BRA	-0.7055	69	BRA	-0.2198	54	BRA	0.2404	13
EGY	-0.0703	54	EGY	0.0172	33	EGY	0.0574	18	EGY	0.0319	18
NZL	2.2213	2	NZL	0.1455	27	NZL	0.0274	19	NZL	-0.8615	63

ITA	0.3483	12	ITA	0.0414	31	ITA	-0.8512	59	ITA	-0.7590	61
JOR	0.0002	43	JOR	0.0280	32	JOR	0.0027	20	JOR	0.0010	19
ARG	0.9796	7	ARG	-0.4565	57	ARG	-0.0429	35	ARG	0.0856	16
KWT	0.0002	44	KWT	-0.0203	35	KWT	-0.0543	40	KWT	0.0010	24
CHL	0.0003	40	CHL	0.0615	28	CHL	-0.0345	34	CHL	-0.0640	34
ISR	-2.0353	69	ISR	0.2720	19	ISR	0.7623	9	ISR	-0.1155	40
IND	1.2097	5	IND	-0.3731	48	IND	-0.4067	58	IND	-0.0790	37
MEX	3.2419	1	MEX	-0.4226	54	MEX	-1.9749	69	MEX	0.0982	15
BOL	0.0002	48	BOL	-0.1779	40	BOL	-0.0598	44	BOL	0.0010	25
IRL	0.3166	13	IRL	0.3307	16	IRL	-1.0116	62	IRL	-0.2279	54
ZAF	0.0535	23	ZAF	-0.0009	34	ZAF	-0.2884	56	ZAF	0.0010	26
ARE	0.0002	46	ARE	-0.3052	44	ARE	-0.0044	23	ARE	0.0010	21
SGP	-1.2501	65	SGP	0.3205	17	SGP	-0.0299	33	SGP	-0.0195	29
SAU	0.0003	41	SAU	-0.1618	38	SAU	-0.0045	26	SAU	-0.0749	36
AUT	-0.0072	53	AUT	0.2167	20	AUT	-0.0154	30	AUT	-0.1463	45
CRI	0.0002	47	CRI	-0.4308	55	CRI	-0.0044	24	CRI	0.0010	22
PRY	0.0002	45	PRY	-0.4604	58	PRY	-0.0506	37	PRY	0.0010	23
PAN	0.1109	15	PAN	0.0441	30	PAN	-0.1124	51	PAN	-0.2252	53
SYR	0.0002	42	SYR	-0.5557	62	SYR	-0.0044	25	SYR	-0.0324	30
SLV	0.0634	22	SLV	-0.3275	46	SLV	-0.0598	45	SLV	-0.1128	39
COL	0.0009	33	COL	-0.3419	47	COL	-0.0582	43	COL	-0.1332	42
PER	0.0009	32	PER	-0.4067	52	PER	-0.0050	28	PER	-0.1337	43
IDN	0.0003	39	IDN	-0.5986	64	IDN	-0.0045	27	IDN	-0.0572	33
NOR	-0.7864	59	NOR	0.0507	29	NOR	0.1084	17	NOR	0.0832	17
ROM	0.0010	28	ROM	-0.6754	67	ROM	-0.0285	32	ROM	-0.1891	49
ECU	-0.0020	50	ECU	-0.4006	50	ECU	-0.0534	39	ECU	-0.1507	46
NIC	0.0975	17	NIC	-0.1763	39	NIC	-0.0897	49	NIC	-0.2658	58
RUS	-1.2350	64	RUS	0.1982	41	RUS	-0.1939	53	RUS	-0.0042	27
BEL	-1.5505	68	BEL	0.3960	14	BEL	0.0024	21	BEL	-0.0887	38
URY	0.0992	16	URY	-0.2387	43	URY	-0.1225	52	URY	-0.2411	55

Continued

Table 3A.4 Continued

Entrepreneurship spirit, culture, and initiative			Barriers to entrepreneurial Activity and business Environment			Knowledge procurement			Innovation		
Weight: 4.81%			Weight: 15.74%			Weight: 13.27%			Weight: 33.61%		
Country	Index	Ranking	Country	Index	Ranking	Country	Index	Ranking	Country	Index	Ranking
UKR	0.0009	34	UKR	-0.4926	59	UKR	-0.0051	29	UKR	-0.1643	47
DOM	0.0754	21	DOM	-0.6848	68	DOM	-0.0703	46	DOM	-0.1343	44
DNK	-0.8588	61	DNK	0.2157	21	DNK	0.9232	5	DNK	-0.0351	32
BGR	0.0010	30	BGR	-0.5790	63	BGR	-0.0160	31	BGR	-0.1929	50
HND	0.0863	20	HND	-0.4145	53	HND	-0.0799	47	HND	-0.2549	57
VEN	0.1140	14	VEN	-0.6045	65	VEN	-0.1042	50	VEN	-0.1813	48
KAZ	0.0011	26	KAZ	-0.6270	66	KAZ	-0.0545	41	KAZ	-0.2008	52
GTM	0.0958	18	GTM	-0.5382	60	GTM	-0.0882	48	GTM	-0.2476	56
EST	0.0011	25	EST	-0.3829	49	EST	-0.3305	57	EST	-0.1971	51
GRC	0.0132	24	GRC	-0.0788	36	GRC	-0.9207	60	GRC	-1.1709	67
LUX	-0.0029	51	LUX	0.2894	18	LUX	0.2957	16	LUX	-0.3824	59
ESP	-0.3051	55	ESP	0.3768	15	ESP	-1.0345	64	ESP	-0.7451	60
PRT	-0.0055	52	PRT	0.3977	13	PRT	-1.1715	67	PRT	-1.5122	69
CZE	0.0008	37	CZE	-0.4065	51	CZE	-0.9526	61	CZE	-0.7708	62
SVK	0.0010	29	SVK	-0.2040	42	SVK	-1.0900	65	SVK	-0.8915	64
HUN	0.7544	8	HUN	-0.4348	56	HUN	-1.1384	66	HUN	-1.0243	65
POL	0.7461	9	POL	-0.5454	61	POL	-1.0280	63	POL	-1.1579	66
TUR	0.0917	19	TUR	-0.3072	45	TUR	-1.4996	68	TUR	-1.3658	68
Mean: 0.0000			Mean: 0.0000			Mean: 0.0000			Mean: 0.0000		
Std.Dev.: 0.8051			Std.Dev.: 0.5154			Std.Dev.: 0.7563			Std.Dev.: 0.7611		

Source: Own estimations.

Table 3A.5 Method I: Overall Entrepreneurship Index (OEI), period 2002–5

Ranking	Country	Country code	Index	Ranking	Country	Country code	Index
1	Indonesia	IDN	0.9061	36	Panama	PAN	-0.0325
2	United States	USA	0.7928	37	Ukraine	UKR	-0.0364
3	China	CHN	0.5728	38	Kuwait	KWT	-0.0430
4	Finland	FIN	0.4601	39	Kazakhstan	KAZ	-0.0491
5	Korea, Rep.	KOR	0.4162	40	Guatemala	GTM	-0.0524
6	Mexico	MEX	0.2943	41	Spain	ESP	-0.0528
7	Brazil	BRA	0.2800	42	Thailand	THA	-0.0534
8	United Kingdom	GBR	0.2322	43	Japan	JPN	-0.0554
9	India	IND	0.2014	44	Jordan	JOR	-0.0601
10	Argentina	ARG	0.1387	45	Turkey	TUR	-0.0679
11	Greece	GRC	0.1031	46	Czech Republic	CZE	-0.0720
12	New Zealand	NZL	0.0864	47	Luxembourg	LUX	-0.0728
13	Australia	AUS	0.0576	48	Costa Rica	CRI	-0.0768
14	Venezuela, RB	VEN	0.0572	49	Uruguay	URY	-0.0771
15	Israel	ISR	0.0534	50	Chile	CHL	-0.0957
16	Russian Federation	RUS	0.0244	51	Bulgaria	BGR	-0.0980
17	Dominican Republic	DOM	0.0171	52	Austria	AUT	-0.1025
18	Bolivia	BOL	0.0164	53	Hong Kong, China	HKG	-0.1056
19	Canada	CAN	0.0084	54	Malaysia	MYS	-0.1083
20	Switzerland	CHE	0.0064	55	Hungary	HUN	-0.1121

Continued

Table 3A.5 Continued

Ranking	Country	Country code	Index	Ranking	Country	Country code	Index
21	Egypt, Arab Rep.	EGY	0.0056	56	Colombia	COL	-0.1180
22	Syrian Arab Republic	SYR	0.0045	57	South Africa	ZAF	-0.1282
23	El Salvador	SLV	0.0043	58	Romania	ROM	-0.1356
24	Lebanon	LBN	0.0026	59	Estonia	EST	-0.1359
25	United Arab Emirates	ARE	0.0007	60	Norway	NOR	-0.1456
26	Paraguay	PRY	-0.0055	61	Poland	POL	-0.1468
27	Ireland	IRL	-0.0157	62	France	FRA	-0.1595
28	Iceland	ISL	-0.0202	63	Slovak Republic	SVK	-0.1662
29	Saudi Arabia	SAU	-0.0203	64	Singapore	SGP	-0.2136
30	Ecuador	ECU	-0.0234	65	Italy	ITA	-0.2558
31	Sweden	SWE	-0.0234	66	Belgium	BEL	-0.2705
32	Nicaragua	NIC	-0.0268	67	Denmark	DNK	-0.3477
33	Peru	PER	-0.0296	68	Netherlands	NLD	-0.3921
34	Portugal	PRT	-0.0304	69	Germany	DEU	-0.4761
35	Honduras	HND	-0.0319	**Mean**	**0.0000**	**Std. Dev.**	**0.2248**

Source: Own estimations.

Table 3A.6 Methods II and III: Disaggregated (DEI) and Aggregated Entrepreneurship Index (AEI), period 2002–5

Entrepreneurship Index (Aggregated)			Entrepreneurial activity (Weight: 0.12%)			Employment (Weight: 42.29%)			Economic activity (Weight: 23.54%)		
Ranking	country	Index	Country	Index	Ranking	Country	Index	Ranking	Country	Index	Ranking
1	USA	7.8874	USA	-0.3104	57	USA	1.6598	1	USA	1.7692	2
2	IDN	6.8605	IDN	-0.0632	53	IDN	1.0445	3	IDN	-0.4881	67
3	NLD	1.9445	NLD	-0.4881	58	NLD	-0.4944	65	NLD	2.5107	1
4	KOR	1.6307	KOR	0.0613	13	KOR	0.0596	9	KOR	0.0112	22
5	JPN	1.4976	JPN	-1.1484	67	JPN	-0.0871	64	JPN	-0.4730	66
6	CHN	1.2288	CHN	-0.0008	20	CHN	0.0401	11	CHN	0.0132	16
7	IND	0.9924	IND	0.0749	12	IND	0.0014	17	IND	0.1050	6
8	BRA	0.9634	BRA	0.2742	9	BRA	0.0900	7	BRA	-0.0408	61
9	MEX	0.9109	MEX	-0.0507	51	MEX	0.0608	8	MEX	-0.0212	60
10	RUS	0.5227	RUS	-0.1542	56	RUS	0.1053	6	RUS	-0.0684	62
11	ARG	0.4167	ARG	0.2223	10	ARG	0.0014	16	ARG	-0.0151	47
12	CAN	0.0833	CAN	0.1651	11	CAN	-0.0179	36	CAN	0.0699	7
13	VEN	0.0706	VEN	-0.0020	31	VEN	0.0014	24	VEN	-0.0161	50
14	TUR	0.0594	TUR	-0.0014	22	TUR	0.0561	10	TUR	-0.0105	44
15	SYR	0.0543	SYR	-0.0079	45	SYR	0.0013	34	SYR	-0.0011	40
16	DOM	0.0473	DOM	-0.0020	23	DOM	0.0014	18	DOM	-0.0012	41
17	ARE	0.0277	ARE	-0.0020	30	ARE	0.0014	23	ARE	-0.0164	53
18	BOL	0.0261	BOL	-0.0077	43	BOL	0.0014	26	BOL	-0.0166	54
19	EGY	0.0136	EGY	-0.0070	39	EGY	0.0013	31	EGY	0.0041	37
20	GTM	-0.0029	GTM	-0.0075	40	GTM	0.0013	32	GTM	-0.0173	59
21	SLV	-0.0073	SLV	-0.0077	44	SLV	0.0014	27	SLV	-0.0166	55
22	LBN	-0.0105	LBN	-0.0076	42	LBN	0.0014	25	LBN	-0.0171	58

Continued

Table 3A.6 Continued

Entrepreneurship Index			Entrepreneurial activity			Employment			Economic activity		
Aggregated			Weight: 0.12%			Weight: 42.29%			Weight: 23.54%		
Ranking	country	Index	Country	Index	Ranking	Country	Index	Ranking	Country	Index	Ranking
23	NZL	-0.0149	NZL	1.4651	4	NZL	-0.0439	43	NZL	0.0107	23
24	AUS	-0.0233	AUS	1.2544	5	AUS	-0.0328	38	AUS	0.0304	10
25	PAN	-0.0250	PAN	-0.0020	28	PAN	0.0014	21	PAN	-0.0169	57
26	KWT	-0.0351	KWT	-0.0020	26	KWT	0.0014	19	KWT	-0.0149	46
27	NIC	-0.0368	NIC	-0.0020	27	NIC	0.0014	20	NIC	-0.0012	42
28	SAU	-0.0495	SAU	-0.0020	29	SAU	0.0014	22	SAU	-0.0157	48
29	ECU	-0.0511	ECU	-0.0020	24	ECU	0.0013	29	ECU	-0.0167	56
30	HND	-0.0645	HND	-0.0020	25	HND	0.0013	30	HND	-0.0011	39
31	GRC	-0.0778	GRC	3.3792	1	GRC	0.0072	14	GRC	0.0095	30
32	ESP	-0.1117	ESP	0.5267	6	ESP	0.0276	12	ESP	0.0476	8
33	CZE	-0.1130	CZE	-0.0050	37	CZE	0.0030	15	CZE	-0.0160	49
34	KAZ	-0.1371	KAZ	-0.0076	41	KAZ	0.0013	33	KAZ	-0.0162	51
35	ZAF	-0.2074	ZAF	-0.1042	55	ZAF	0.0014	28	ZAF	-0.0012	43
36	ISR	-0.2252	ISR	-0.0490	50	ISR	-0.0546	52	ISR	0.0192	13
37	POL	-0.2314	POL	-0.0392	49	POL	0.0104	13	POL	-0.0121	45
38	PRY	-0.2811	PRY	0.0001	19	PRY	-0.0456	45	PRY	0.0061	35
39	HUN	-0.2838	HUN	-0.0821	54	HUN	-0.0063	35	HUN	-0.0163	52
40	THA	-0.2896	THA	0.0076	14	THA	-0.0377	40	THA	0.0106	25
41	PER	-0.3104	PER	-0.0030	33	PER	-0.0426	42	PER	0.0072	33
42	CHL	-0.3143	CHL	-0.0138	47	CHL	-0.0329	39	CHL	0.0080	32
43	ROM	-0.3471	ROM	0.0019	15	ROM	-0.0497	47	ROM	0.1066	5
44	CHE	-0.3572	CHE	-1.0149	65	CHE	-0.0579	56	CHE	0.0131	18
45	PRT	-0.3589	PRT	1.9048	3	PRT	-0.0231	37	PRT	0.0039	38

46	-0.3689	CRI	21	-0.0009	CRI	57	-0.0591	CRI	27	0.0104	CRI
47	-0.3705	URY	16	0.0006	URY	55	-0.0569	URY	31	0.0095	URY
48	-0.3737	UKR	32	-0.0025	UKR	48	-0.0510	UKR	28	0.0103	UKR
49	-0.3820	JOR	35	-0.0042	JOR	53	-0.0564	JOR	17	0.0131	JOR
50	-0.3839	HKG	48	-0.0245	HKG	50	-0.0532	HKG	9	0.0323	HKG
51	-0.4233	MYS	18	0.0001	MYS	46	-0.0464	MYS	11	0.0262	MYS
52	-0.4382	COL	38	-0.0054	COL	41	-0.0425	COL	36	0.0050	COL
53	-0.4390	BGR	17	0.0005	BGR	51	-0.0544	BGR	15	0.0161	BGR
54	-0.4413	LUX	69	-1.8056	LUX	63	-0.0840	LUX	20	0.0117	LUX
55	-0.4461	ISL	8	0.2952	ISL	58	-0.0604	ISL	19	0.0121	ISL
56	-0.5054	AUT	60	-0.5260	AUT	59	-0.0661	AUT	29	0.0098	AUT
57	-0.6061	SGP	52	-0.0604	SGP	54	-0.0566	SGP	12	0.0226	SGP
58	-0.6254	SWE	64	-0.9282	SWE	49	-0.0525	SWE	34	0.0067	SWE
59	-0.6261	SVK	36	-0.0042	SVK	61	-0.0724	SVK	14	0.0162	SVK
60	-0.6367	EST	34	-0.0039	EST	60	-0.0689	EST	26	0.0105	EST
61	-0.6800	NOR	66	-1.1469	NOR	62	-0.0761	NOR	21	0.0114	NOR
62	-0.7468	IRL	7	0.3249	IRL	44	-0.0444	IRL	24	0.0107	IRL
63	-1.0192	FIN	62	-0.6487	FIN	2	1.5529	FIN	65	-0.3295	FIN
64	-1.0539	BEL	46	-0.0112	BEL	66	-0.5219	BEL	3	0.6534	BEL
65	-1.2425	GBR	61	-0.5261	GBR	4	0.4168	GBR	4	0.3324	GBR
66	-1.9344	FRA	59	-0.4946	FRA	5	0.1498	FRA	68	-1.3418	FRA
67	-2.0395	DEU	63	-0.8650	DEU	67	-0.7481	DEU	69	-2.3139	DEU
68	-2.4353	DNK	68	-1.3891	DNK	68	-0.8729	DNK	64	-0.3291	DNK
69	-3.0526	ITA	2	2.0882	ITA	69	-1.1391	ITA	63	-0.3145	ITA
Mean: 0.0000			**Mean: 0.0000**			**Mean: 0.0000**			**Mean: 0.0000**		
Std.Dev.: 1.5100			**Std.Dev.: 0.7259**			**Std.Dev.: 0.3779**			**Std.Dev.: 0.5138**		

Source: Own estimations.

Table 3A.6 Methods II and III: Disaggregated (DEI) and Aggregated Entrepreneurship Index (AEI), period 2002–5 (continued)

Entrepreneurship spirit, culture, and initiative			Barriers to entrepreneurial activity and business Environment			Knowledge procurement			Innovation		
Weight: 11.95%			Weight: 2.47%			Weight: 5.50%			Weight: 14.13%		
Country	Index	Ranking	Country	Index	Ranking	Country	Index	Ranking	Country	Index	Ranking
USA	0.6180	8	USA	−0.2231	47	USA	−0.2415	46	USA	3.6191	1
IDN	0.9700	7	IDN	0.7444	5	IDN	−2.8648	69	IDN	2.6597	3
NLD	−1.0821	67	NLD	−0.2256	48	NLD	0.9697	7	NLD	−0.2998	45
KOR	3.3733	1	KOR	−0.0896	39	KOR	−0.4076	54	KOR	0.9922	5
JPN	−1.3118	69	JPN	0.3978	12	JPN	0.3681	16	JPN	2.2289	4
CHN	0.3975	9	CHN	0.3968	13	CHN	−0.4932	57	CHN	3.5254	2
IND	2.8769	2	IND	0.6269	7	IND	−0.9805	65	IND	−0.0832	28
BRA	1.0304	6	BRA	1.3663	1	BRA	−0.5106	58	BRA	0.2814	8
MEX	2.0041	3	MEX	−0.1545	42	MEX	−1.1073	67	MEX	0.3333	7
RUS	−0.4093	56	RUS	−0.1987	46	RUS	0.3341	17	RUS	−0.0993	29
ARG	1.1262	5	ARG	0.0732	29	ARG	−0.2036	43	ARG	0.2312	10
CAN	−0.0855	49	CAN	−0.4281	58	CAN	0.4467	14	CAN	0.5375	6
VEN	−0.0002	19	VEN	0.7066	6	VEN	0.0185	33	VEN	−0.0264	16
TUR	−0.0002	16	TUR	−0.0313	35	TUR	−1.1392	68	TUR	−0.3595	50
SYR	−0.0003	24	SYR	0.2314	19	SYR	0.0187	32	SYR	−0.0266	22
DOM	−0.0002	14	DOM	0.1625	24	DOM	0.0185	34	DOM	−0.0264	17
ARE	−0.0002	20	ARE	−0.0621	37	ARE	0.1160	24	ARE	−0.0264	15
BOL	−0.0003	27	BOL	0.8189	3	BOL	−0.3958	51	BOL	−0.0266	24
EGY	−0.0003	22	EGY	0.7646	4	EGY	−0.0069	36	EGY	−0.1913	34
GTM	−0.0003	31	GTM	0.3053	17	GTM	0.0187	31	GTM	−0.1978	36
SLV	−0.0003	28	SLV	0.4072	10	SLV	−0.3994	53	SLV	−0.0266	25

LBN	−0.0003	30	LBN	0.3987	11	LBN	−0.0300	37	LBN	−0.0266	23
NZL	1.2958	4	NZL	−0.6073	64	NZL	−0.1903	42	NZL	−0.1700	31
AUS	0.3602	10	AUS	−0.6624	66	AUS	0.0738	25	AUS	0.2809	9
PAN	−0.0002	21	PAN	0.1033	26	PAN	−0.1628	39	PAN	−0.0264	18
KWT	−0.0002	17	KWT	0.0945	27	KWT	−0.5781	59	KWT	−0.0264	20
NIC	−0.0002	15	NIC	−0.0231	34	NIC	−0.6865	60	NIC	−0.0264	21
SAU	−0.0002	18	SAU	0.0758	28	SAU	−0.2577	47	SAU	−0.1942	35
ECU	−0.0003	29	ECU	0.5186	8	ECU	0.0188	29	ECU	−0.4303	54
HND	−0.0003	23	HND	0.3425	15	HND	0.0188	30	HND	−0.4631	56
GRC	−0.0384	32	GRC	0.3706	14	GRC	0.4820	12	GRC	−0.4606	55
ESP	−0.8357	62	ESP	0.0256	31	ESP	0.0663	26	ESP	−0.2868	42
CZE	−0.0003	25	CZE	−0.4263	57	CZE	0.3811	15	CZE	−0.4727	57
KAZ	−0.0003	26	KAZ	−0.1444	41	KAZ	0.0173	35	KAZ	−0.5282	66
ZAF	−0.5552	57	ZAF	0.0006	33	ZAF	−0.2939	49	ZAF	−0.0264	19
ISR	0.1183	13	ISR	−0.2598	51	ISR	1.5969	4	ISR	−0.3182	48
POL	−0.2423	54	POL	−0.0698	38	POL	−0.7460	62	POL	−0.4179	53
PRY	−0.0439	35	PRY	0.8567	2	PRY	−0.7543	63	PRY	−0.1718	32
HUN	−0.1973	53	HUN	−0.4368	59	HUN	−0.1652	40	HUN	−0.4877	58
THA	0.1521	12	THA	−0.3559	53	THA	−0.2134	45	THA	−0.1598	30
PER	−0.0412	34	PER	0.1858	23	PER	0.1389	23	PER	−0.3272	49
CHL	0.3162	11	CHL	−0.1828	44	CHL	−1.0480	66	CHL	−0.2883	43
ROM	−0.0478	37	ROM	−0.2398	49	ROM	−0.3961	52	ROM	−0.4963	59
CHE	−0.1361	50	CHE	−0.2594	50	CHE	1.8851	2	CHE	−0.2856	41
PRT	−0.0403	33	PRT	0.2276	20	PRT	−0.2850	48	PRT	−0.5114	62
CRI	−0.0565	45	CRI	0.2273	21	CRI	0.1841	22	CRI	−0.2137	38
URY	−0.0544	42	URY	0.2865	18	URY	0.0527	27	URY	−0.3012	46
UKR	−0.0490	38	UKR	0.3096	16	UKR	0.2716	20	UKR	−0.4171	52
JOR	−0.0540	41	JOR	0.4313	9	JOR	0.0319	28	JOR	−0.2054	37
HKG	−0.0612	48	HKG	−0.4982	62	HKG	−0.1231	38	HKG	0.0223	14
MYS	−0.0446	36	MYS	0.0142	32	MYS	−0.9184	64	MYS	−0.0806	26

Continued

Table 3A.6 Continued

Entrepreneurship spirit, culture, and initiative			Barriers to entrepreneurial activity and business Environment			Knowledge procurement			Innovation		
Weight: 11.95%			Weight: 2.47%			Weight: 5.50%			Weight: 14.13%		
Country	Index	Ranking	Country	Index	Ranking	Country	Index	Ranking	Country	Index	Ranking
COL	-0.1576	52	COL	0.2190	22	COL	-0.7031	61	COL	-0.3169	47
BGR	-0.0521	40	BGR	-0.1167	40	BGR	0.2831	19	BGR	-0.5155	64
LUX	-0.0569	46	LUX	0.0716	30	LUX	1.9303	1	LUX	-0.3650	51
ISL	-0.0589	47	ISL	-0.4386	60	ISL	1.6774	3	ISL	-0.5495	69
AUT	-0.0513	39	AUT	-0.1957	45	AUT	0.9364	8	AUT	-0.5014	60
SGP	-0.6563	58	SGP	-0.5411	63	SGP	-0.4533	56	SGP	0.1487	12
SWE	-1.0648	66	SWE	-0.7530	68	SWE	1.1575	5	SWE	-0.2221	39
SVK	-0.0558	43	SVK	-0.3669	55	SVK	-0.3468	50	SVK	-0.5123	63
EST	-0.0559	44	EST	-0.6325	65	EST	-0.4116	55	EST	-0.5320	68
NOR	-0.3896	55	NOR	-0.8423	69	NOR	0.2594	21	NOR	-0.2908	44
IRL	-0.1568	51	IRL	-0.4534	61	IRL	-0.1677	41	IRL	-0.5033	61
FIN	-0.8767	63	FIN	-0.7136	67	FIN	0.7915	10	FIN	-0.5293	67
BEL	-1.2049	68	BEL	-0.2785	52	BEL	1.0510	6	BEL	-0.2242	40
GBR	-0.8011	59	GBR	-0.3873	56	GBR	-0.2127	44	GBR	-0.0821	27
FRA	-1.0282	65	FRA	-0.1819	43	FRA	0.4779	13	FRA	-0.1848	33
DEU	-0.8088	60	DEU	-0.0609	36	DEU	0.8524	9	DEU	0.0438	13
DNK	-0.8332	61	DNK	-0.3577	54	DNK	0.6503	11	DNK	-0.5183	65
ITA	-0.9391	64	ITA	0.1375	25	ITA	0.2989	18	ITA	0.1536	11
Mean: 0.0000			Mean: 0.0000			Mean: 0.0000			Mean: 0.0000		
Std.Dev.: 0.7819			Std.Dev.: 0.4350			Std.Dev.: 0.7513			Std.Dev.: 0.8146		

Source: Own estimations.

Table 3A.7 Method IV: Multidimensional Entrepreneurship Index (MEI)
Distribution of weights among indicators and dimensions, period 2002–5

Dimension	Dimension's weight	Indicators	Indicator's weight (intra-dim)	Indicator's weight (overall)
1. Entrepreneurial activity	6.01%	**1.1 Firm dynamics**		
		1 Bankruptcy rate (%)	5.21	0.31
		2 Entry rate (%)	20.95	1.26
		3 Exit rate (%)	1.03	0.06
		4 Share of bankruptcies in firm exits (%)	9.82	0.59
		5 New businesses registered (number) (%)	11.11	0.67
		1.2 Firm survival		
		6 Young firm entrepreneurial activity index (Index) (%)	2.18	0.13
		7 Total entrepreneurial activity index (Index) (%)	0.38	0.02
		8 Established businesses activity index (Index) (%)	20.43	1.23
		1.3 Ownership		
		9 Business ownership rate (agriculture, hunting, forestry and fishing, rate) (%)	18.27	1.10
		10 Business ownership rate (private sector excluding agriculture, hunting, forestry and fishing, rate) (%)	10.43	0.63
		11 Business ownership rate (total private sector, rate) (%)	0.12	0.01
		12 Non-agricultural business ownership rate (%)	0.07	0.00
2. Employment	22.01%	13 Average size of firm entries (number) (%)	9.22	2.03
		14 Share of entries in employment (%)	1.95	0.43
		15 Share of exits in employment (%)	0.50	0.11
		16 Aver. number workers for fast growers; last year period (x 1) (%)	17.87	3.93
		17 Aver. number workers for all enterpr.; growth rate period (%)	18.13	3.99
		18 Aver. number workers for all enterpr.; last year period (x 1) (%)	13.44	2.96

Continued

Table 3A.7 Continued

Dimension	Dimension's weight		Indicators	Indicator's weight (intra-dim)	Indicator's weight (overall)
		19	Aver. number workers for fast growers; growth rate period (%)	0.81	0.18
		20	Aver. number workers for not-fast growers; growth rate period (%)	17.53	3.86
		21	Aver. number workers for not-fast growers; last year period (x 1) (%)	11.82	2.60
		22	Non-agricultural self-employment rate (%)	3.01	0.66
		23	Self-employment rates: total, as a percentage of total civilian employment (%)	5.73	1.26
3. Economic activity	13.21%	24	Average sales for all enterprises; growth rate period (%)	5.64	0.74
		25	Average sales for all enterprises; last year period (x € 1000) (%)	6.83	0.90
		26	Average sales for fast growers; growth rate period (%)	13.80	1.82
		27	Average sales for fast growers; last year period (x € 1000) (%)	2.13	0.28
		28	Average sales for not-fast growers; growth rate period (%)	21.82	2.88
		29	Average sales for not-fast growers; last year period (x € 1000) (%)	6.08	0.80
		30	Listed domestic companies, total (%)	5.70	0.75
		31	Micro, small and medium enterprises (number) (%)	29.90	3.95
		32	Micro, small and medium enterprises (per 1,000 people) (%)	7.34	0.97
		33	Taxes on exports (% of tax revenue)	0.75	0.10

4. Entrepreneurship spirit, culture, and iniciative	12.42%	34	Female total entrepreneurial activity index (Index) (%)	7.71	0.96
		35	Necessity entrepreneurial activity index (Index) (%)	17.72	2.20
		36	Opportunity entrepreneurial activity index (Index) (%)	1.16	0.14
		37	Potential entrepreneur index (Index) (%)	4.11	0.51
		38	Fear of failure index (Index) (%)	2.33	0.29
		39	Know entrepreneur index (Index) (%)	19.54	2.43
		40	Innovative entrepreneurship (%)	20.24	2.51
		41	Future entrepreneur index (Index) (%)	10.44	1.30
		42	Informal investors index (Index) (%)	15.84	1.97
		43	Nascent entrepreneurial activity index (Index) (%)	0.91	0.11
5. Barriers to entrepreneurial activity and business environment	3.05%	44	Cost of business start-up procedures (% of GNI per capita)	10.64	0.32
		45	Domestic credit provided by banking sector (% of GDP)	2.25	0.07
		46	Domestic credit to private sector (% of GDP)	0.50	0.02
		47	Ease of doing business index (1=most business-friendly regulations) (%)	9.30	0.28
		48	Highest marginal tax rate, corporate rate (%)	0.77	0.02
		49	Highest marginal tax rate, individual rate (%)	0.75	0.02
		50	Interest rate spread (lending rate minus deposit rate) (%)	0.30	0.01
		51	Labour force with primary education (% of total)	4.17	0.13
		52	Labour force with secondary education (% of total)	8.50	0.26
		53	Labour force with tertiary education (% of total)	27.23	0.83
		54	Management time dealing with officials (% of management time)	2.12	0.06

Continued

Table 3A.7 Continued

Dimension	Dimension's weight		Indicators	Indicator's weight (intra-dim)	Indicator's weight (overall)
		55	Procedures to enforce a contract (number) (%)	3.01	0.09
		56	Procedures to register property (number) (%)	1.14	0.03
		57	Start-up procedures to register a business (number) (%)	8.21	0.25
		58	Time required to start a business (days) (%)	21.11	0.64
6.- Knowledge procurement	15.86%	59	Gross domestic expenditure on R&D (% of GDP)	24.54	3.89
		60	Physicians (per 1,000 people) (%)	40.39	6.41
		61	Technicians in R&D (per million people) (%)	35.08	5.56
7.- Innovation	27.44%	62	Patent applications, non-residents (%)	16.19	4.44
		63	Patent applications, residents (%)	9.01	2.47
		64	Trademarks, non-residents (%)	36.63	10.05
		65	Trademarks, residents (%)	38.17	10.47

Source: Own estimations.

Table 3A.8 Method IV: Multidimensional Entrepreneurship Index (MEI), period 2002–5

Multidimensional Entrepreneurship Index			Entrepreneurial activity Weight: 6.01%			Employment Weight: 22.01%			Economic activity Weight: 13.21%		
Ranking	Country	Index	Country	Index	Ranking	Country	Index	Ranking	Country	Index	Ranking
1	CHN	1.1502	CHN	0.0183	27	CHN	0.1987	9	CHN	0.0013	17
2	USA	1.1075	USA	0.8171	5	USA	0.8428	2	USA	0.5900	4
3	IDN	1.0372	IDN	-2.8137	69	IDN	0.5433	3	IDN	2.3330	1
4	KOR	0.4491	KOR	-0.1754	57	KOR	0.1991	8	KOR	0.1111	11
5	JPN	0.2922	JPN	-1.4612	68	JPN	-0.2422	64	JPN	-0.4417	68
6	FIN	0.2584	FIN	0.3017	11	FIN	1.3675	1	FIN	0.2695	5
7	BRA	0.2314	BRA	0.2151	12	BRA	0.1374	10	BRA	0.0516	12
8	MEX	0.1970	MEX	-0.1193	51	MEX	0.2177	6	MEX	-0.0568	44
9	CHE	0.1790	CHE	-0.0176	38	CHE	-0.0642	56	CHE	-0.1268	49
10	ISR	0.1567	ISR	-0.1319	54	ISR	-0.0627	55	ISR	-0.0478	43
11	CAN	0.1473	CAN	-0.0225	39	CAN	-0.0883	58	CAN	0.1939	10
12	ARG	0.1380	ARG	0.5140	7	ARG	-0.0007	19	ARG	-0.0104	24
13	AUS	0.1099	AUS	0.4573	9	AUS	-0.0486	54	AUS	0.0223	14
14	LUX	0.0978	LUX	-0.3630	65	LUX	-0.1502	63	LUX	-0.1349	50
15	GBR	0.0897	GBR	0.6083	6	GBR	0.3952	4	GBR	1.0758	2
16	GRC	0.0786	GRC	1.0899	1	GRC	0.2041	7	GRC	-0.0384	41
17	SWE	0.0700	SWE	-0.1640	56	SWE	-0.1000	61	SWE	0.0471	13
18	ISL	0.0699	ISL	0.5028	8	ISL	-0.0391	53	ISL	-0.0458	42
19	RUS	0.0643	RUS	-0.3029	61	RUS	-0.0350	51	RUS	0.2503	7
20	IND	0.0226	IND	-0.1215	53	IND	-0.0007	27	IND	0.2114	9
21	NZL	0.0194	NZL	0.8933	4	NZL	0.0060	17	NZL	-0.0363	39
22	VEN	0.0172	VEN	0.0042	37	VEN	-0.0007	26	VEN	-0.0312	29
23	DOM	0.0014	DOM	0.0042	32	DOM	-0.0007	21	DOM	-0.0039	22

Continued

Table 3A.8 Continued

Multidimensional Entrepreneurship Index			Entrepreneurial activity Weight: 6.01%			Employment Weight: 22.01%			Economic activity Weight: 13.21%		
Ranking	Country	Index	Country	Index	Ranking	Country	Index	Ranking	Country	Index	Ranking
24	SYR	-0.0045	SYR	-0.0670	48	SYR	-0.0008	37	SYR	-0.0008	20
25	ARE	-0.0147	ARE	0.0042	36	ARE	-0.0007	25	ARE	-0.0316	31
26	LBN	-0.0172	LBN	-0.0637	45	LBN	-0.0008	34	LBN	-0.0334	37
27	EGY	-0.0302	EGY	-0.0564	41	EGY	-0.0008	31	EGY	0.0056	16
28	PAN	-0.0462	PAN	0.0042	35	PAN	-0.0007	24	PAN	-0.0327	36
29	BOL	-0.0542	BOL	-0.0654	47	BOL	-0.0008	36	BOL	-0.0324	34
30	GTM	-0.0565	GTM	-0.0628	43	GTM	-0.0008	32	GTM	-0.0379	40
31	AUT	-0.0570	AUT	0.0495	26	AUT	-0.0890	59	AUT	-0.1847	58
32	HKG	-0.0635	HKG	-0.2073	59	HKG	-0.0292	45	HKG	-0.1157	47
33	ITA	-0.0659	ITA	-0.4162	66	ITA	-0.6724	68	ITA	0.6419	3
34	FRA	-0.0773	FRA	-0.2004	58	FRA	0.1315	11	FRA	-0.2523	66
35	THA	-0.0784	THA	0.2141	13	THA	-0.0211	38	THA	-0.1898	59
36	PER	-0.0786	PER	0.0800	24	PER	-0.0237	40	PER	-0.1772	55
37	ESP	-0.0796	ESP	0.3554	10	ESP	0.0244	15	ESP	0.2274	8
38	CZE	-0.0821	CZE	-0.0323	40	CZE	0.0046	18	CZE	-0.0313	30
39	SLV	-0.0826	SLV	-0.0651	46	SLV	-0.0008	35	SLV	-0.0324	33
40	BEL	-0.0834	BEL	-0.5443	67	BEL	-0.4337	65	BEL	0.2621	6
41	URY	-0.0867	URY	0.1519	15	URY	-0.0311	49	URY	-0.1794	56
42	SAU	-0.0876	SAU	0.0043	31	SAU	-0.0007	20	SAU	-0.0304	28
43	CRI	-0.0881	CRI	0.1378	17	CRI	-0.0323	50	CRI	-0.2579	67
44	UKR	-0.0944	UKR	0.1023	20	UKR	-0.0281	44	UKR	-0.2446	65
45	JOR	-0.1032	JOR	0.0923	23	JOR	-0.0309	47	JOR	-0.1977	60

#			#			#			#		
46	ECU	-0.1099	29	ECU	0.0045	29	ECU	-0.0008	35	ECU	-0.0326
47	KWT	-0.1144	33	KWT	0.0042	22	KWT	-0.0007	27	KWT	-0.0286
48	HND	-0.1202	30	HND	0.0045	30	HND	-0.0008	21	HND	-0.0009
49	ZAF	-0.1261	63	ZAF	-0.3505	28	ZAF	-0.0007	19	ZAF	-0.0007
50	BGR	-0.1290	16	BGR	0.1457	46	BGR	-0.0299	57	BGR	-0.1833
51	NOR	-0.1293	50	NOR	-0.0828	62	NOR	-0.1455	46	NOR	-0.0730
52	KAZ	-0.1334	44	KAZ	-0.0637	33	KAZ	-0.0008	38	KAZ	-0.0350
53	PRT	-0.1442	2	PRT	0.9650	12	PRT	0.0675	45	PRT	-0.0655
54	NIC	-0.1445	34	NIC	0.0042	23	NIC	-0.0007	18	NIC	-0.0007
55	IRL	-0.1573	3	IRL	0.9128	14	IRL	0.0260	62	IRL	-0.2126
56	SGP	-0.1744	52	SGP	-0.1196	48	SGP	-0.0310	53	SGP	-0.1637
57	PRY	-0.1763	19	PRY	0.1233	41	PRY	-0.0252	15	PRY	0.0165
58	HUN	-0.1824	60	HUN	-0.2430	52	HUN	-0.0390	32	HUN	-0.0319
59	NLD	-0.2241	62	NLD	-0.3361	66	NLD	-0.5924	63	NLD	-0.2314
60	MYS	-0.2302	18	MYS	0.1253	42	MYS	-0.0256	52	MYS	-0.1621
61	DEU	-0.2329	55	DEU	-0.1581	67	DEU	-0.6513	69	DEU	-1.1256
62	TUR	-0.2370	28	TUR	0.0118	5	TUR	0.2718	25	TUR	-0.0198
63	ROM	-0.2413	14	ROM	0.1533	43	ROM	-0.0274	23	ROM	-0.0088
64	CHL	-0.2423	49	CHL	-0.0744	16	CHL	0.0223	48	CHL	-0.1200
65	COL	-0.2507	25	COL	0.0499	39	COL	-0.0236	61	COL	-0.2067
66	SVK	-0.2508	22	SVK	0.0962	60	SVK	-0.1000	64	SVK	-0.2341
67	EST	-0.2570	21	EST	0.0998	57	EST	-0.0871	51	EST	-0.1488
68	POL	-0.2675	64	POL	-0.3627	13	POL	0.0490	26	POL	-0.0234
69	DNK	-0.2778	42	DNK	-0.0580	69	DNK	-0.6950	54	DNK	-0.1652
Mean: 0.0000			**Mean: 0.0000**			**Mean: 0.0000**			**Mean: 0.0000**		
Std.Dev.: 0.2783			**Std.Dev.: 0.5064**			**Std.Dev.: 0.2815**			**Std.Dev.: 0.3829**		

Source: Own estimations.

Table 3A.8 Method IV: Multidimensional Entrepreneurship Index (MEI), period 2002–5 (continued)

Entrepreneurship spirit, culture, and initiative			Barriers to entrepreneurial activity and business environment			Knowledge procurement			Innovation		
Weight: 12.42%			Weight: 3.05%			Weight: 15.86%			Weight: 27.44%		
Country	Index	Ranking	Country	Index	Ranking	Country	Index	Ranking	Country	Index	Ranking
CHN	0.3405	8	CHN	0.2912	16	CHN	-0.5541	58	CHN	4.1623	1
USA	0.0194	17	USA	0.1758	24	USA	-0.2401	49	USA	3.0082	3
IDN	1.3196	4	IDN	1.9728	1	IDN	-2.8290	69	IDN	3.6560	2
KOR	1.9456	1	KOR	-0.1731	38	KOR	-0.4912	55	KOR	0.8845	5
JPN	0.2234	11	JPN	0.2472	18	JPN	0.2224	21	JPN	1.5346	4
FIN	-0.2580	57	FIN	-0.3836	53	FIN	0.6670	11	FIN	-0.5775	68
BRA	0.8841	5	BRA	1.0635	2	BRA	-0.4592	54	BRA	0.4081	8
MEX	1.7476	2	MEX	-0.1378	37	MEX	-1.0901	65	MEX	0.4511	7
CHE	0.0669	14	CHE	-0.3810	52	CHE	1.8064	1	CHE	-0.2636	41
ISR	0.3290	9	ISR	0.0703	28	ISR	1.5118	4	ISR	-0.3575	51
CAN	-0.4364	61	CAN	-0.0585	32	CAN	0.3434	18	CAN	0.5248	6
ARG	0.4350	7	ARG	0.0825	27	ARG	-0.1870	43	ARG	0.2982	9
AUS	0.1421	12	AUS	-0.5572	66	AUS	0.0627	27	AUS	0.2900	10
LUX	-0.0830	49	LUX	-0.1166	36	LUX	1.7802	2	LUX	-0.3573	50
GBR	-0.7312	64	GBR	-0.4462	59	GBR	-0.2351	47	GBR	-0.1247	28
GRC	-0.1662	54	GRC	0.0477	29	GRC	0.7880	10	GRC	-0.4830	55
SWE	-0.0667	40	SWE	-0.5173	64	SWE	1.0701	6	SWE	-0.1826	37
ISL	-0.1783	55	ISL	-0.5038	62	ISL	1.6193	3	ISL	-0.6014	69
RUS	0.0432	16	RUS	0.2152	22	RUS	0.5357	13	RUS	-0.1452	33
IND	1.4216	3	IND	0.5702	9	IND	-1.0944	66	IND	-0.0665	26
NZL	0.4841	6	NZL	-0.5911	67	NZL	-0.1988	45	NZL	-0.1508	34

VEN	-0.0055	23	VEN	0.9587	3	VEN	32	0.0155	VEN	-0.0359	15
DOM	-0.0055	19	DOM	0.3249	13	DOM	33	0.0155	DOM	-0.0359	16
SYR	-0.0056	27	SYR	0.2602	17	SYR	30	0.0157	SYR	-0.0361	22
ARE	-0.0055	24	ARE	0.1604	25	ARE	36	-0.0314	ARE	-0.0359	17
LBN	-0.0056	31	LBN	0.3020	15	LBN	38	-0.0469	LBN	-0.0361	23
EGY	-0.0056	26	EGY	0.4000	11	EGY	35	-0.0172	EGY	-0.1317	30
PAN	-0.0055	25	PAN	-0.2514	43	PAN	42	-0.1498	PAN	-0.0359	18
BOL	-0.0056	29	BOL	0.7279	6	BOL	52	-0.3622	BOL	-0.0361	24
GTM	-0.0056	32	GTM	-0.3981	57	GTM	31	0.0157	GTM	-0.1356	32
AUT	-0.0204	36	AUT	-0.4271	58	AUT	8	0.9349	AUT	-0.5422	61
HKG	-0.0837	50	HKG	-0.6540	69	HKG	39	-0.1029	HKG	0.0632	13
ITA	-0.7552	65	ITA	-0.5000	61	ITA	15	0.5043	ITA	0.1874	12
FRA	-0.6933	63	FRA	-0.3281	49	FRA	14	0.5204	FRA	-0.1723	35
THA	0.1086	13	THA	-0.3469	50	THA	44	-0.1882	THA	-0.1263	29
PER	-0.0615	37	PER	0.5960	8	PER	26	0.1339	PER	-0.3155	48
ESP	-0.7879	66	ESP	0.1966	23	ESP	24	0.1548	ESP	-0.2515	39
CZE	-0.0057	34	CZE	-0.3885	54	CZE	16	0.4827	CZE	-0.5141	57
SLV	-0.0056	28	SLV	0.6272	7	SLV	56	-0.5214	SLV	-0.0361	25
BEL	-0.9405	69	BEL	-0.0847	34	BEL	5	1.1201	BEL	-0.1753	36
URY	-0.0796	45	URY	-0.2450	42	URY	22	0.1830	URY	-0.2806	44
SAU	-0.0055	22	SAU	0.2437	19	SAU	51	-0.3393	SAU	-0.1333	31
CRI	-0.0824	48	CRI	0.0121	30	CRI	23	0.1783	CRI	-0.2682	42
UKR	-0.0722	42	UKR	0.8071	4	UKR	20	0.2968	UKR	-0.4548	53
JOR	-0.0790	44	JOR	0.2346	21	JOR	34	-0.0150	JOR	-0.2579	40
ECU	-0.0056	30	ECU	0.4835	10	ECU	29	0.0157	ECU	-0.4455	52
KWT	-0.0055	21	KWT	-0.0839	33	KWT	59	-0.6154	KWT	-0.0359	20
HND	-0.0057	33	HND	0.3826	12	HND	28	0.0158	HND	-0.4871	56
ZAF	-0.4567	62	ZAF	-0.0086	31	ZAF	48	-0.2393	ZAF	-0.0359	19
BGR	-0.0765	43	BGR	-0.1891	39	BGR	17	0.3824	BGR	-0.5555	63
NOR	-0.3021	59	NOR	-0.3925	55	NOR	19	0.3100	NOR	-0.3001	47

Continued

Table 3A.8 Continued

Entrepreneurship spirit, culture, and initiative			Barriers to entrepreneurial activity and business environment			Knowledge procurement			Innovation		
Weight: 12.42%			Weight: 3.05%			Weight: 15.86%			Weight: 27.44%		
Country	Index	Ranking	Country	Index	Ranking	Country	Index	Ranking	Country	Index	Ranking
KAZ	-0.0057	35	KAZ	0.3154	14	KAZ	0.1504	25	KAZ	-0.5744	66
PRT	-0.2202	56	PRT	-0.3701	51	PRT	-0.1246	40	PRT	-0.5464	62
NIC	-0.0055	18	NIC	0.2359	20	NIC	-0.8902	63	NIC	-0.0359	21
IRL	-0.1082	52	IRL	-0.2670	46	IRL	-0.1258	41	IRL	-0.5403	59
SGP	-0.8102	67	SGP	-0.4827	60	SGP	-0.5428	57	SGP	0.2284	11
PRY	-0.0652	38	PRY	0.7921	5	PRY	-0.8643	62	PRY	-0.2162	38
HUN	0.0594	15	HUN	-0.2560	45	HUN	-0.0397	37	HUN	-0.5406	60
NLD	-0.8766	68	NLD	-0.3954	56	NLD	0.9778	7	NLD	-0.2809	45
MYS	-0.0662	39	MYS	-0.1960	40	MYS	-1.0633	64	MYS	-0.1013	27
DEU	-0.4034	60	DEU	-0.2010	41	DEU	0.8491	9	DEU	-0.0357	14
TUR	-0.0055	20	TUR	-0.5465	65	TUR	-1.1458	68	TUR	-0.3490	49
ROM	-0.0705	41	ROM	-0.6269	68	ROM	-0.4404	53	ROM	-0.5307	58
CHL	0.2495	10	CHL	-0.2819	47	CHL	-1.0961	67	CHL	-0.2748	43
COL	-0.1626	53	COL	0.1568	26	COL	-0.7879	61	COL	-0.2943	46
SVK	-0.0814	46	SVK	-0.2954	48	SVK	-0.2022	46	SVK	-0.5556	64
EST	-0.0816	47	EST	-0.1126	35	EST	-0.3294	50	EST	-0.5770	67
POL	-0.0947	51	POL	-0.2517	44	POL	-0.6711	60	POL	-0.4647	54
DNK	-0.2676	58	DNK	-0.5070	63	DNK	0.6515	12	DNK	-0.5618	65
Mean: 0.0000			Mean: 0.0000			Mean: 0.0000			Mean: 0.0000		
Std.Dev.: 0.5106			Std.Dev.: 0.4793			Std.Dev.: 0.7549			Std.Dev.: 0.8605		

Source: Own estimations.

Appendix B: Data sources and variables description

Following is a list of the used indicators and variables.

From COMPENDIA

COMPENDIA (Comparative Entrepreneurship Data for International Analysis) is an across-countries and -time comparable data set for 23 developed countries covering information from 1970 onwards. The data series taken from this database enter Table 4 as indicators 7–9, and Table 10 as indicators 9–11. The indicators are:

Business Ownership Rates: This is the number of business owners divided by total labour force. Only persons who are self-employed as their main occupation are included in the figures. The owners are classified depending on the sector they develop their entrepreneurial activity: private or public sector, and in the private sector, agricultural and non-agricultural subsectors.

From GEM

The GEM data set contains annual harmonized data on early stage entrepreneurial activity for 43 countries since 1998. The abbreviation GEM stands for Global Entrepreneurship Monitor and is the common name for this international survey. The data series taken from this database enter Table 4 with indicators 5, 6, 29–32, 34, 35, 37, and 38, and Table 10 with indicators 6–8, 34–39, and 41–43. All the indicators are taken relative to the adult population 18–64 years. The selected indicators are:

TEA Index: number of people currently setting up a business or owning/managing a business existing up to 3, 5 years.

Necessity Entrepreneurial Activity Index: number of people involved in entrepreneurial activity out of necessity.

Opportunity Entrepreneurial Activity Index: Measures the number of people involved in entrepreneurial activity out of opportunity.

Female Total Entrepreneurial Activity Index: Measures the number of women involved in entrepreneurial activity.

Nascent Entrepreneurial Activity Index: Measures the number of people currently setting up a business.

Young Firm Entrepreneurial Activity Index: Measures the number of people owning/managing a business that exists up to 3, 5 years.

Established Businesses Activity Index: Measures the number of people owning/managing a business which exists over 3, 5 years.

Future Entrepreneur Index: Share of people expecting to start a business within three years.

Known Entrepreneur Index: Share of people that personally know someone who started a business in the past two years.

Potential Entrepreneur Index: Share of people indicating to have the required skills and knowledge for setting up a business themselves.

Fear of Failure Index: Share of people that would abstain from setting up a business when they sense a fear of failure.

Informal Investors Index: Measures the number of people investing own money to start-ups.

From EIM

The data set International Benchmark of Entrepreneurs from Entrepreneurship International Monitor (EIM) contains data about firm entries, firm exits and bankruptcies. Therefore, 9 countries from the EU and additionally the USA and Japan, are included in this set. The figures in this set are comparable across countries and over time. Additionally, the set has data of fast growing firms with a high employment growth and/or a high sales growth, measured for periods of three years. The performances of these companies are compared to companies with an 'average growth pattern'. The indicators and are based on the following:

Entry rate: number of new 'activities' started by entrepreneurs, divided by the total number of companies in a certain country.

Exit rate: number of 'activities' that finished their activities, divided by the total number of companies in a certain country.

Average size of firm entries: average number of workers in the new 'activities'.

Share of entries in employment: number of new 'activities', divided by the total number of workers in a certain country.

Share of exits in employment: number of companies that stopped their activities, divided by the total number of workers in a certain country.

Bankruptcy rate: number of bankruptcies, divided by the total number of companies in a certain country.

Share of bankruptcies in firm exits: number of bankruptcies, divided by the total number of companies that stopped their activities.

Average sales for all enterprises – last year of period: for a certain 3-year period, average sales (in regard to companies) for the last year.

Average sales for all enterprises – growth rate over whole period: for a certain 3-year period, growth rate of the average sales over the whole period.

Average sales for not-fast growing enterprises – last year of period: for a certain 3-year period, average sales (in regard to not-fast growing companies) for the last year.

Average sales for not-fast growing enterprises – growth rate over whole period: for a certain 3-year period, growth rate of the average sales over the whole period (not-fast growing companies).

Average sales for fast growing enterprises – last year of period: for a certain 3-year period, average sales (fast growing companies) for the last year.

Average sales for fast growing enterprises – growth rate over whole period: for a certain 3-year period, growth rate of the average sales over the whole period (fast growing companies).

Average number of workers for all enterprises – last year of period: for a certain 3-year period, average number of employees (in regard to companies) for the last year.

Average number of workers for all enterprises – growth rate over whole period: for a certain 3-year period, growth rate of the number of employees over the whole period.

Average number of workers for not-fast growing enterprises – last year of period: for a certain 3-year period, average number of employees (not-fast growing companies) for the last year.

Average number of workers for not-fast growing enterprises – growth rate over whole period: for a certain 3-year period, growth rate of the average number of employees over the whole period (not-fast growing companies).

Average number of workers for fast growing enterprises – last year of period: for a certain 3-year period, average number of employees (fast growing companies) for the last year.

Average number of workers for fast growing enterprises – growth rate over whole period: for a certain 3-year period, growth rate of the average number of employees over the whole period (fast growing companies).

From Freudenberg (2003)

The data set covers innovation and knowledge procurement-related indicators for the last years of the 1990s. Their description follows:

R&D performed by the non-business sector as a percentage of GDP: is a proxy for a country's relative efforts to create new knowledge, though it should be noted that new knowledge can also originate in firms or in partnership with firms. Public R&D activities also disseminate new knowledge and exploit existing knowledge bases in the public sector. It is reported as a ratio for 1995–99.

Number of non-business researchers per 10,000 labour force: (self-explanatory).

Expenditures on basic research as a percentage of GDP: basic research is experimental or theoretical work undertaken primarily to acquire new knowledge of the underlying foundation of phenomena and observable facts, without any particular application or use in view.

Ratio of science, engineering and health PhDs per population aged 25 to 34 years: this age group was chosen because it is the only one for which there are internationally comparable data.

Number of scientific and technical articles per million population: article counts of scientific research are based on scientific and engineering articles published in approximately 5,000 of the world's leading scientific and technical journals.

Business financed R&D performed by government or higher education as a percentage of GDP: R&D expenditure financed by industry but performed by public research institutions or universities.

Number of scientific papers cited in US-issued patents per million population: this indicator is based on US patent data and may favour English-speaking countries.

Ratio of publications in the 19 most industry-relevant scientific disciplines per million population: between 1980 and 1995.

Business enterprise R&D (BERD) as a percentage of GDP: between 1996 and 1999. This covers R&D activities carried out in the business sector regardless of the origin of funding. R&D data are often underestimated, especially in small and medium-sized enterprises (SMEs) and in service industries.

Number of business researchers per 10,000 labour force in 1999: researchers are defined as professionals engaged in the conception and creation of new knowledge, products, processes, methods and systems and are directly involved in the management of projects.

Number of patents in 'triadic' patent families per million population: patent families, as opposed to patents, are a set of patents taken in various countries for protecting a single invention.

Share of firms having introduced at least one new or improved product or process on the market over a given period of time: is an indicator of the output of innovative activities. This indicator is taken from the Community Innovation Survey (CIS2) managed by Eurostat. It is weighted here by number of employees in order not to underestimate the weight of large firms (unweighted results would give an unduly large weight to the mass of small firms). Data are available only for 21 OECD countries.

From the World Bank's WDI

The WB's World Development Indicators are a huge database covering country level annual indicators for more that 180 countries and aggregates, since 1960. The indicators are numbered 25–28, 39–46, 55–57, and 62–65 and 5, 30–33, and 44–65. Their descriptions are as follows:

Cost of business start-up procedures (per cent of GNI per capita): cost to register a business is normalized by presenting it as a percentage of gross national income (GNI) per capita.

Domestic credit provided by banking sector (per cent of GDP): domestic credit provided by the banking sector (monetary authorities, deposit money banks and other banking institutions) includes all credit to various sectors on a gross basis, except the central government.

Domestic credit to private sector (per cent of GDP): refers to financial resources provided to the private sector, such as through loans, purchases of non-equity securities, and trade credits and other accounts receivable that establish a claim for repayment.

Highest marginal tax rate, corporate rate (per cent): highest rate shown on the schedule of tax rates applied to the taxable income of corporations.

Highest marginal tax rate, individual (on income exceeding, US$): highest rate shown on the schedule of tax rates applied to the taxable income of individuals.

Interest rate spread (lending rate minus deposit rate): (self-explanatory).

Labour force with primary/secondary/tertiary education (per cent of total labour force): (self-explanatory).

Management time dealing with officials (per cent of weekly management time): time dealing with requirements imposed by government regulations (taxes, customs, labour regulations, licensing and registration).

Patent applications, non-residents/residents: applications filed with a national patent office for exclusive rights for an invention.

Procedures to enforce a contract (number): number of independent actions, mandated by law or courts that demand interaction between the parties of a contract or between them and the judge or court officer.

Procedures to register property (number): number of procedures required for a businesses to secure rights to property.

Physicians (per 1,000 people): physicians are defined as graduates of any facility or school of medicine who are working in the country in any medical field (practice, teaching, research).

Start-up procedures to register a business (number): number of required actions to start a business, including interactions to obtain necessary permits and licences and to complete all inscriptions, verifications and notifications to start operations.

Time required starting a business (days): number of calendar days needed to complete the procedures to legally operate a business.

Technicians in R&D (per million people): technicians in R&D and equivalent staff are people whose main tasks require technical knowledge and experience in engineering, physical and life sciences (technicians), or social sciences and humanities (equivalent staff). They participate in R&D by performing scientific and technical tasks involving the application of concepts and operational methods, normally under the supervision of researchers.

Trademarks, non-residents/residents: applications for registration of a trademark with a national or regional trademark office.

Taxes on exports (per cent of tax revenue): (self-explanatory).

Micro, small and medium enterprises (number): (self-explanatory).

Listed domestic companies, total: domestically incorporated companies listed on the country's stock exchanges at the end of the year.

Notes

1. For example, if policy-makers are interested in employment creation, they may focus on a measure that seems more directly linked to jobs, such as self-employment or new firm creation, no matter what the size or growth rate of the firm. If the policy objective is competitiveness or productivity growth,

however, a measure of entrepreneurship that distinguishes high growth or innovative firms may be preferred.

2. See Kaplan and Norton (1992, 1993) for managerial applications.

3. The approach is not new: Leitão da Silva Martins (2007) proposes a score-board for measuring entrepreneurship that defines six categories: enterprises, human resources, innovation, social economy, initiative and knowledge. The OECD's Entrepreneurship Indicator Programme (EIP) is another example of multilevel categorization in such a scoreboard layout (see Davis 2007). Acs and Szerb (2009) use 14 pillars (or sets of indicators) in order to reflect three aspects of entrepreneurship: attitudes, activity and aspirations.

4. As will be discussed below, we are working on the implementation of multilevel multiblock PCA that might improve the estimation of weights in the presence of data clumping.

5. The weighting rule is built in order to incorporate the following axioms: rationality, weak Pareto rule, non-dictatorship, unrestricted domain, independence of irrelevant alternatives, neutrality, monotonicity and reinforcement. These axioms cannot be accomplished together (Arrow's impossibility theorem) though they are statistically weighted to obtain an optimal measure, the weights given by the PCA.

6. The origins of the method can be found in Pearson (1901), who coined the name and the mathematical principles, Hotelling (1933), who studied its properties, and Karhunen (1946). Recent literature reviews are contained in Diamantaras and Kung (1996) and Jolliffe (2002).

7. We may be violating the reinforcement axiom. See Avanzini (2008) on this point.

8. Borrowed from chemical and batch processes monitoring, this method is based in non-linear iterative partial least squares (NIPALS) and was introduced by Wold et al. (1987). As was previously discussed, NIPALS is one of the alternatives to estimate PCs by means of an iterative weighting algorithm. This weighting algorithm allows the differentiation of multiple layers of information aggregation through successive re-weighting of indicators under a hierarchical categorization.

9. Roweis (1998) tested out the algorithm with a data set that has one missing dimension on each observation, and he considered the algorithm performed successfully under that constraint. Here, we are forcing it to deal with many missing indicators for every observation.

10. As an example: Indonesia is assigned the third place under the Innovation dimension, and the last place under the Knowledge Procurement dimension.

11. Each dimension's weight can be found in the top of the dimension's disaggregate index. These weights correspond to the importance each dimension has in the aggregate index.

4
Measuring Entrepreneurship in Developing Countries
Sameeksha Desai

Introduction

The role of entrepreneurship in economic development is the subject of much interest to academic and policy circles alike. Entrepreneurship is often credited with many positive changes in developing countries. At the very least, it is associated with job creation, wealth creation, innovation and related welfare effects. A strong small business sector and entrepreneurship are usually linked to a strong economy (Beck et al. 2005). Across developed and developing countries, entrepreneurship has become a critical part of economic development strategies – even goals.

The theoretical justifications for the role of entrepreneurship in economic development are relatively well discussed in both the economics and management literature. Entrepreneurship achieves important functions related to efficiency, competition, product innovation, pricing and industry survival by acting either to disequilibrate (Schumpeter 1911/1934), to equilibrate (Kirzner 1997) or to do both (Hall 2007) in the market. However, the nuances of entrepreneurship are not easily generalized and complicate policy-focused interpretations related to level and role of economic development.

As many economic development interventions failed through the 1980s, policy-makers and researchers began to search for other answers. Although entrepreneurship was not a new phenomenon, it was also not a popular approach when goals were aligned with structural adjustment, large-scale infrastructure development and macroeconomic change. However, entrepreneurship offered many things that other economic development interventions did not. First, most other strategies were expected to be top-down but most did not, in fact, reach all the way down. Entrepreneurship is a local and regional level activity, and new firms can immediately begin benefiting their host locations (see also the discussion in Chapter 13 by Nijkamp). For this reason, the idea of entrepreneurship was a perfect complement to an increasing focus on community-based economic development. Second, economic development interventions focused on building hard infrastructure – bridges, roads, transportation networks – and often neglected to consider how the infrastructures would be used. The previously popular mentality, 'build bridges and they will come', failed to consider what might come *with* them and *how* they might produce and exchange their goods. Entrepreneurship can work without a perfect system of hard infrastructure (or, at least, can begin to work) and often with minimal other resources. In many countries, entrepreneurship has gained popularity because it cuts across a range of priorities. It can truly be a low cost, high impact approach to economic development, through self-employment for example. At the same time, entrepreneurs who expand and innovate can fuel major changes leading to growth. Subsistence entrepreneurs and large companies can provide different classes of effects on their communities. Third, although economic development interventions were designed to support long-term change and build infrastructure, they were still unable to address immediate and short-term problems. Entrepreneurship can address individual level needs related to income and employment. At the very least, entrepreneurship creates one job for the entrepreneur as well as income. At best, it generates additional jobs and (financial or non-financial) compensation for other people.

The explosion of interest in entrepreneurship has been sudden, and has demanded significant investigation to uncover its true relationship with economic development. This is urgent for developing countries, where entrepreneurship has become a popular component of economic development policies, and where ironically its dynamics are perhaps the least clear. The relationship between entrepreneurship and economic development appears to be at least bi-directional. In fact, many empirical studies have provided contradictory findings, leaving larger public policy questions unanswered.

Documenting, measuring and therefore *understanding* entrepreneurship is a difficult task because of the characteristics and dynamics involved (Bygrave and Hofer 1991). One important contributor to this difficulty is that 'available indicators relating to entrepreneurship measure everything from personal attributes of the entrepreneurs like gender to outcome of the entrepreneurial process like start-up rates' (Hoffmann et al. 2006: 10). For this reason, the context of entrepreneurship is important. The purpose of this chapter is to address how 'entrepreneurship' is usually conceived and characterized in developing countries.

I will first describe three common dichotomies used to describe entrepreneurship as well as several measures. I will present two important implications that result from considering so many types and measures of entrepreneurship: that these measures can only be useful when tied to context, and that these types of entrepreneurship exist and are not mutually exclusive in any given context.

Types of entrepreneurship

Entrepreneurship is a complex subject of study and its characteristics, dynamics, determinants and manifestations differ across countries. The overall level of economic development is an important contextual distinction for the research on entrepreneurship, as it can take very different forms. Much of the research on entrepreneurship in developing countries indirectly or directly categorizes activities within several frequently discussed dichotomies. These are (i) formal/informal, (ii) legal/illegal and (iii) necessity/opportunity.

Formal and informal entrepreneurship

The distinction between formal and informal entrepreneurship is determined by registration status. If a firm has been registered with the appropriate government agency, then it is a formal entity that is authorized to do business. The classification of a firm as 'formal' or 'informal' does not therefore relate to the nature of its activities, but rather to its presence within the formal (taxable) sector or the informal sector. The formality (or not) of firms does not provide any indication of the legality (or not) of their business activities. For example, entrepreneurs that operate outside the market can broadly be categorized as informal. The size of the informal labour force can vary, but can reach more than 50 per cent in some countries (ILO 2007). In many developing countries, the incentives for entrepreneurs to participate in the formal sector may be weak and few, particularly if they operate on a small scale. Entering the formal sector can be a deliberate decision based on the tradeoff between regulatory disadvantage (such as taxes) and formalization advantages (such as better access to export markets) (Schneider and Enste 2000).

Legal and illegal entrepreneurship

A source of confusion in the research on entrepreneurship arises from the study and separation of activities that are legal and illegal. This dichotomy is often used interchangeably with the formal/informal dichotomy, though they are not the same. Legal firms are engaged in legal activities. Entrepreneurs engaged in illegal activities (for example, mining in prohibited areas) are illegal entrepreneurs. In fact, the nature of informal entrepreneurship in developing countries necessitates that informal and illegal are not equivalent. *Illegal* applies to the nature of the selected activity, and depends on the explicit legal code and regulatory frameworks in the country. *Legal* entrepreneurship applies to activities that are permitted by law.

There are two ways to approach this dichotomy. First, entrepreneurship itself may be illegal, such as in pre-transition Lithuania (Aidis and van Praag 2004). If this is the case, then all entrepreneurial activities would be classified as illegal. This is becoming less common as more developing countries have undergone transition in recent decades and continue to accept some level of capitalist orientation. Second, entrepreneurship may be legal and carried out by registered firms, but the activities undertaken may be illegal. For example, firms authorized to operate in certain sectors in developing countries may still be engaged in illegal activities. Anecdotal evidence suggests this to be the case in the timber industry in the Philippines and Indonesia in the 1990s.

These classifications of entrepreneurship as formal/informal and legal/illegal are not mutually exclusive, which can lead to confusion.[1] Firms operating without business registration, permits and licences are by nature informal, but they are illegal if their activities are so. For example, Aidis and van Praag (2004) examine *illegal entrepreneurship experience* in pre-transition Lithuania. Although it may initially appear that their study treats illegal entrepreneurship experience simply as informal entrepreneurship experience, it is consistent with the separation of illegal as *not legal*, given the political regime of the country. Prior to transition, Lithuania hosted 'an environment in which the very act of private entrepreneurship is illegal regardless of business activity' (ibid.: 285). Examples are provided in Table 4.1 to demonstrate the overlap between formal/informal and legal/illegal entrepreneurship.

Necessity and opportunity entrepreneurship

The distinction between necessity and opportunity entrepreneurship is largely reliant upon the motivation for activity, as Naudé also pointed out in Chapter 1. Necessity entrepreneurs engage in entrepreneurship

Table 4.1   Formal, informal, legal and illegal entrepreneurship

	Formal	Informal
Legal	Registered firm that is engaged in legal activities. Example: Registered manufacturing firm producing plastic packaging for medical supplies, in compliance with national health, safety, environmental and factory regulations.	Unregistered firm that is engaged in legal activities. Example: Unregistered private cars, operating as corporate drivers and tourist taxis.
Illegal	Registered firm that is engaged in illegal activities. Example: Registered foreign law firms in a country, operating outside authorized areas of expertise as explicitly defined by local government legal code.*	Unregistered firm that is engaged in illegal activities. Example: Loan sharking that occurs in many slum areas in Mumbai; unregistered entrepreneur lending money at above market interest rates to borrowers without access to the formal, official banking system.

Note: * See Lin (2006) and Shanghai Bar Association (2006).

to avoid unemployment, whereas opportunity entrepreneurs pursue a recognized opportunity for profit (Reynolds et al. 2002).[2] Necessity entrepreneurs are an important force in developing countries, and are relatively less common in developed countries. For example, rates of necessity entrepreneurship for Brazil, Argentina, India and Chile ranged between 6.5 per cent and 7.5 per cent in 2002, compared to 0.33 per cent and 0.43 per cent in Denmark and Finland, respectively (Cowling and Bygrave 2002).

The breakdown of necessity/opportunity entrepreneurship is closely connected to formal/informal status. One reason for high rates of necessity entrepreneurship in developing countries is the size of the informal sector. Workers that become entrepreneurs to avoid unemployment will likely be starting small-scale, subsistence activities. For this reason, they may lack incentives to formalize (Chaudhuri et al. 2006).

Opportunity entrepreneurs in developing countries can be both formal and informal. Rapidly developing countries often experience significant shifts in domestic markets and their conditions, creating opportunities for new entrants. The political and regulatory systems in these countries can lag behind economic expansion, as it takes time for behaviour and everyday interactions to align with changes enacted into law. This lag may lead to (at least temporarily) a larger informal sector. Many opportunity entrepreneurs may begin informally, and may formalize once they perceive significant benefits from doing so.

Measures of entrepreneurship

The policy relevance of entrepreneurship places a great deal of importance on the effectiveness of measurement and interpretation. Given the range of dichotomies discussed in the previous section, it is clear that different kinds of entrepreneurial activities exist regardless of sector and industry. Each kind of entrepreneurship calls for different policies, depending on the purpose of policy intervention. For example, there are policies aimed at formalizing existing informal sector business as well as policies aimed at creating new business. Other policies are focused on preventing illegal entrepreneurship. In order to design effective policies that are relevant to the nature and context of entrepreneurship in a given country, it is important first to examine its entrepreneurial activities.

This requires a deliberate degree of segmentation because any one measure does not capture all entrepreneurs in any country, let alone for comparison consistently across countries, and because only some types of entrepreneurship are of interest for study (Davis 2006).

Multiple measures of 'entrepreneurship' exist and reflect different types of activities. Self-employment has often been used as to measure entrepreneurship (Storey 1991), but may not adequately reflect the context in developing countries. Self-employment may be measured from official self-reported employment data and would likely leave out unreported (informal) respondents (Storey 1991).

Although self-employment data can be used across countries when collected from standardized sources, it may also not be an accurate measure of (actual) formal entrepreneurship in the developing country context. The overlap between self-employment and necessity entrepreneurship in developing countries leads to a very different meaning of self-employment than in developed countries. Rather, it is a good proxy for entrepreneurial activity (Thurik et al. 2008) and can be interpreted to some extent as a measure of *entrepreneurial potential*.

The Global Entrepreneurship Monitor (GEM) project is an effort to produce data that can be comparable across countries.[3] GEM collects data on *early-stage entrepreneurship*, which comprises two measures.

Start-up activity is measured as *nascent entrepreneurship*, and is counted as the proportion of the adult population[4] that is currently engaged in the process of creating a business. New firm activity is measured as *baby entrepreneurship*, and is counted as the proportion of the adult population that is currently involved in operating a business of less than 42 months.

Definition and the data collection process are consistent and therefore comparable across countries for the GEM data. Data are likely to overestimate early-stage entrepreneurship activities because current nascency does not immediately translate into actual firm formation. For example, respondents may be considered nascent entrepreneurs if they have taken steps to form a business, but this may not materialize for several years – or it may never do so. Taking steps to form a business does not mean the business has met (or will meet) all official regulatory criteria. Unlike the GEM data, measures of entrepreneurship derived from official sources can underestimate actual entrepreneurship activities.

The World Bank Group Entrepreneurship Survey (WBGES) is also designed to be comparable across countries, and measures formal sector entrepreneurship as the number of new officially registered limited liability corporations (LLCs). By definition, WBGES does not include the informal sector, counting only *economic units of the formal sector incorporated as a legal entity and registered in a public registry, which is capable, in its own right, of incurring liabilities and of engaging in economic activities and transactions with other entities.*[5]

This approach explicitly seeks to provide data that can be compared across countries, and counting LLCs maintains a high level of comparability across countries despite different political systems and legal origins. The WBGES offers cross-country comparability but cannot be applied to two types of entrepreneurship. First, the informal sector is an important and often large component of economic activity in many developing countries. Second, LLCs are not the only kind of 'economic unit' operated by entrepreneurs, though the most common in many countries.

Other approaches to measuring entrepreneurship include a focus on dynamics. For example, until a single (stand-alone) measure of entrepreneurship can be developed, the approach of the OECD has been to identify key indicators that 'paint part of the overall picture' (Davis 2006) while being standardized enough to allow for cross-country research. This approach is substantially broader than other approaches. To support this goal, a core list of indicators reflects different types of entrepreneurs, as measured by individual variables for number of business owners (including self-employment), firm formation in general and for specific types of firms (e.g. gazelles and high growth firms).[6] This core list allows researchers to isolate specific types of entrepreneurs for study. This approach includes the development of a framework with entrepreneurial performance conditions and larger institutional measures. Entrepreneurs are taken as (business owners) 'who seek to generate value, through the creation or expansion of economic activity, by identifying and exploiting new products, processes or markets' (Ahmad and Seymour 2008: 14). The OECD Entrepreneurship Indicators Project presents a framework with determinants, outputs and manifestations of entrepreneurship (ibid.: 14). This broader approach offers a more comprehensive view of entrepreneurship than other approaches, but it may lose some of the refinement in analysis that more narrowly defined data sets can provide. On the one hand, this approach presents a strong synthesis of institutions and the relationship with entrepreneurship; on the other hand, conditions and manifestations may be hard to separate.

These commonly used measures of entrepreneurship tend to reflect specific types of entrepreneurship or even entrepreneurs at different parts of the process. For example, a nascent entrepreneur may not be reflected in the formal data for a given year, but may be counted in the formal data five years later, after incorporation and registration.

Implications: Entrepreneurship and institutions

Understanding and measuring entrepreneurship in developing countries is complicated by institutional environment and context. With respect to analysis, it is important to maintain clarity about both the quality of measurement and what exactly is being examined. For example, a formal measure of business registration represents entrepreneurship in the formal sector only, and would not be an accurate reflection of actual entrepreneurial activity in a country hosting a significant informal labour force.

At the level of interpretation, there are two general implications. First, it is important to acknowledge the relationship between the selected measure and the economic development context of the country. This requires interpretation of the relationship between *institutions, entrepreneurship* and *economic development* as it relates to the time and level of economic development. Countries can target the type of entrepreneurship they wish to encourage, depending on current economic context. Some countries undergoing or planning reforms may be best served by focusing on policies of formalization, where they seek to redirect what may already be substantial informal entrepreneurship into the formal sector. Other countries may be better served by policies to boost economic participation of certain demographics, which often equates to necessity entrepreneurship as at least a first step. Still other countries can pursue policies focused on high growth entrepreneurship (Davis 2006). The appropriate policies to serve these purposes can be vastly different, ranging from supporting the proliferation of microfinance institutions to venture capital funds.

The effect of institutions on entrepreneurship has been the subject of much study. The findings of research, particularly cross-country studies, are often different for the same variables, depending on the measures being used. For example, van Stel et al. (2007) and Klapper et al. (2007) report different results on the relationship between entrepreneurship and some administrative barriers to starting a business. Van Stel et al. (2007) use GEM data whereas Klapper et al. (2007) use WBGES data. A possible explanation for this discrepancy is that nascent entrepreneurs (GEM) do not necessarily face administrative barriers, since they do not have to be formal in order to be counted in the data. However, the WBGES data set measures registered LLC businesses, so all respondents will have faced administrative barriers in order to register their businesses. In other words, the entrepreneurs in the GEM data set may not be reporting on administrative barriers simply because they have not encountered them, not because they are not a problem.

Klapper et al. (2006) find a significant relationship between business registration in 35 European countries (including developing countries) and barriers to entry. Similarly, Djankov et al. (2002) find that higher regulations can hinder the establishment of new firms. Licensing procedures and permit requirements were reported as the greatest barriers to operations by Polish business owners in 1997 (Balcerowicz et al. 1999; World Bank 2000). Barriers to entry include the cost of registration and regulation, as well as access to credit. Acs et al. (2008b) use many of the same institutional variables in an analysis of GEM and WBGES data and find that access to credit does not have an important effect on entrepreneurship. Such differences can be explained at least partly by differences in the data. GEM data used to include informal entrepreneurs, who may rely out of necessity on channels for credit outside the formal banking system. Figures for nascent entrepreneurship, baby entrepreneurship and corporate entrepreneurship are reported in Table 4.2 as averages for 2003, 2004 and 2005. Nascent and baby entrepreneurship are captured in the GEM data, and corporate entrepreneurship is measured as new

LLC registrations in the WBGES data. In general, developing countries report higher levels in the GEM data and developed countries report higher levels in the WBGES data. This is consistent with larger proportions of the informal sector in the developing countries.

The spreads calculated in Acs et al. (2008b) between nascent-corporate and baby-corporate entrepreneurship are also reported in Table 4.2 (again as averages for 2003, 2004 and 2005). The spread between measures exists because they capture fundamentally different manifestations of entrepreneurship. In other words, 'firm formation does not necessarily mean firm registration' (ibid.: 266). The GEM data reflect entrepreneurial intent whereas the WBGES data reflect formal entry of LLC entities. An interesting interpretation[7] of the spread between nascent-corporate entrepreneurship is to treat it as *entrepreneurship potential*. There are two important implications of this interpretation. First, this reflects the spread between potential formal sector entrepreneurs and existing formal sector entrepreneurs. Second, this does not indicate accurately what proportion of these potential formal sector entrepreneurs are working as informal entrepreneurs versus formal or informal wage workers.

The second implication related to interpretation is the relevance of multiple types of entrepreneurship in developing countries. These categories of entrepreneurship are not mutually exclusive and can overlap or be present in some degree in most countries. Countries can host multiple types of entrepreneurship in a different 'mix' determined by context – legal and illegal, formal and informal, necessity and opportunity. The biotechnology sector in Bangalore is host to many high growth new firms, while the manufacturing sector in Mumbai is host to many informal new firms. Many of these firms may start informally but reach a point where formalization is necessary to maintain growth and access larger markets. The allocation of entrepreneurship is therefore dynamic and responsive to context.

For example, domestic economic development policies in Peru in the 1990s included an initiative to increase formal sector participation by lowering the burdens of registration across several different government agencies. These efforts led to the formalization of more than 671,000 businesses between 1991 and 1997 (Zuin 2004). These policies were enacted after decades of growth of the informal sector, driven largely by increased taxation and regulation in the 1960s (de Soto 1989). Although formal entry has been on the rise since policy reforms in the 1990s, the scope of entrepreneurship in Peru remains overwhelmingly informal. This is connected at least in part to a lack of formal sector employment,

Table 4.2 Nascent entrepreneurship (GEM), baby entrepreneurship (GEM), corporate entrepreneurship (World Bank), nascent-corporate spread, baby-corporate spread

Country	Nascent	Baby	Corporate	Nascent-corporate spread	Baby-corporate spread
Argentina	9.17	5.65	1.67	7.50	3.98
Australia	7.32	5.58	6.70	0.61	–1.12
Austria	3.02	2.37	3.10	–0.08	–0.73
Belgium	2.64	1.25	4.83	–2.19	–3.58
Canada	5.88	3.66	6.35	–0.47	–2.69
Chile	8.49	6.23	1.58	6.91	4.65
Croatia	2.84	1.49	3.60	–0.76	–2.11
Czech Republic	6.41	1.98	3.77	2.64	–1.79
Denmark	2.68	2.86	6.04	–3.36	–3.18
Finland	3.29	2.26	3.24	0.05	–0.98
France	3.47	1.02	3.00	0.47	–1.98
Germany	3.16	2.31	0.84	2.34	1.27
Greece	3.92	2.54	0.43	3.49	2.10
Hong Kong	1.61	1.58	10.29	–8.68	–8.71
Hungary	2.96	2.28	3.35	–0.40	–1.07
Iceland	7.83	4.46	11.64	–3.81	–7.18
India	5.42	5.31	0.10	5.32	5.21
Indonesia	9.63	11.51	0.18	9.45	11.33
Ireland	5.05	4.03	5.56	–0.51	–1.53
Israel	4.32	2.53	8.59	–4.27	–6.06
Italy	2.49	1.90	4.37	–1.87	–2.47
Japan	0.96	1.21	3.02	–2.06	–1.81
Jordan	10.38	8.26	2.94	7.44	5.32
Latvia	4.17	2.77	12.33	–8.16	–9.56
Mexico	4.59	1.36	6.54	–1.95	–5.18
Netherlands	2.43	2.01	8.96	–6.53	–6.94
New Zealand	9.02	7.82	12.73	–3.71	–4.92
Norway	4.14	4.11	9.69	–5.55	–5.58
Peru	31.36	12.93	3.05	16.00	9.88
Poland	3.92	5.20	1.85	2.07	3.35
Russia	3.46	1.71	4.69	–1.23	–2.98
Singapore	3.33	2.98	3.03	0.02	–0.39
Slovenia	2.62	1.08	2.64	–0.02	–1.56
South Africa	3.40	1.79	1.86	1.54	–0.07
Spain	2.95	2.97	6.90	–3.95	–3.93
Sweden	1.81	2.37	5.02	–3.21	–2.64
Switzerland	3.49	3.71	2.71	0.78	1.00
Turkey	2.20	4.01	1.25	0.95	2.76
Uganda	16.01	18.02	0.66	15.35	13.00
United Kingdom	3.41	3.07	5.01	–1.60	–1.94
United States	8.12	4.98	2.55	5.57	2.43

Note: Numbers provided are the averages for 2003, 2004 and 2005.

Source: Acs et al. (2008b).

and is evidenced by the high number of necessity entrepreneurs in the country (Serida et al. 2006).

An important consideration arises from the allocation of entrepreneurship among productive, unproductive and destructive forms (Baumol 1990). This perspective differs from the dichotomies discussed earlier because the dichotomies are defined based on the entrepreneur, process or activity selected. However, the impact or outcome of the activity is more relevant to the allocation of entrepreneurship and its associated tradeoffs.

In different papers that end with similar implications, Baumol (1990) and Murphy et al. (1991) argue that the allocation of entrepreneurship is driven by the overall structure of institutions or rewards. Entrepreneurs are not driven by the possible or expected effects of their activities on society – rather, they act in ingenious and creative ways to increase wealth, power and prestige (Baumol 1990). Activities are chosen based on perceived profit and can include activities of questionable value to society (Baumol 1990), arguably because entrepreneurial talent 'goes into activities with the highest private returns, which need not have the highest social returns' (Murphy et al. 1991: 506). The allocation of entrepreneurship represents a tradeoff between several possible choices and is reflective of the state and quality of incentives and institutions in the society. Increasing the relative size of productive entrepreneurship is a goal for economic development because it translates into higher GDP growth. However, it is not the only step for many developing countries, given the role played by necessity entrepreneurship and informal entrepreneurship.

One country undergoing systemic change or multiple countries with similar systems may still see vastly different manifestations of entrepreneurship. A key problem for developing countries is the incidence of productive, unproductive and destructive manifestations of entrepreneurship *under the same policy regime.* The relationship between changes in the structure of entrepreneurship over time, especially within one country, is not straightforward and is a promising area for further research. For example, why and how does the share of productive entrepreneurship change from on year to another? Can one type of entrepreneurship act as a springboard for another? Earle and Sakova (1999, 2000) examine six transition countries[8] and find that owning a side business before transition increases the probability of owning a private business later. This supports an understudied connection between the informal sector and future private sector participation, an important question given the size and strength of the unofficial sector in transition economies (for more on this subject, see Johnson et al. 1997). Aidis and van Praag (2004) find limited support for the role of illegal entrepreneurship experience in future private enterprise, only among younger and highly educated entrepreneurs. In general, however, prior illegal entrepreneurship experience did not enhance future business ownership. This suggests that skills and knowledge acquired in one system are not easily transferred to another system (Aidis and van Praag 2004), and bringing informal or illegal entrepreneurs into the formal or legal sectors is a difficult task.

Concluding remarks

Improving our understanding of entrepreneurship in developing countries is an important prerequisite to appropriate public policy planning. The existence of multiple types and measures of entrepreneurship means great care is necessary when they are applied and interpreted. Generalizing research findings can lead to potentially costly mistakes, particularly when they are carried over from different country contexts. For example, findings from cross-country research on OECD are not generalizable for developing countries in Asia.

The current research on entrepreneurship is driven by three trends related to measurement. First, there is a push to develop and validate a measure of entrepreneurship that can be used reliably and consistently across countries. Second, there is increasing interest in segmenting and differentiating among types of entrepreneurship being measured. Third, the relationship between economic development, institutions and entrepreneurship necessitates a comprehensive research approach.

Acknowledgements

The author thanks Zoltan Acs, David Audretsch, William Baumol, Johan Eklund, Leora Klapper, Wim Naudé and Roger Stough for insight on various topics included in this chapter.

Notes

1. All informal firms are not necessarily illegal; all formal firms are not necessarily legal.
2. See also Storey (1994) for a similar discussion of push/pull factors of entrepreneurship.

3. For more on GEM data, see Reynolds et al. (2005).
4. Defined as between 18 and 64 years of age.
5. For more on WBGES data, see Klapper et al. (2007).
6. For more on the development of this approach, see Davis (2006).
7. For more on interpreting this spread, see Acs et al. (2008b) and Ardagna and Lusardi (2008).
8. Bulgaria, Czech Republic, Hungary, Poland, Russia and Slovakia.

5
The Impact of the Business Environment on the Business Creation Process

Leora Klapper, Anat Lewin and Juan Manuel Quesada Delgado

Introduction

Following the G20 summit on 15 November 2008, the leaders of the world's largest economies issued a statement explaining how they intended to restructure the world's economic architecture. On the very first page of this statement, they articulate (quoted in *The Canadian Press* 2008: 15):

> Our work will be guided by a shared belief that market principles, open trade and investment regimes, and effectively regulated financial markets foster the dynamism, innovation, and entrepreneurship that are essential for economic growth, employment, and poverty reduction.

This statement highlights the relevance of entrepreneurship as a force behind economic development. It is therefore critical that governments be able to measure and understand the entrepreneurial activity of their countries. However, the mere concept of entrepreneurship, and the way to measure it, still lack a common language among scholars and academia.

The World Bank Group Entrepreneurship Survey (WBGES) was conceived to answer the demand of scholars and governments for a reliable and internationally comparable indicator to measure entrepreneurial activity. In its third year, data for 100 countries have been collected directly from registrars of companies around the world on the number of total and newly registered corporations over an eight-year period (2000–7).

The WBGES database continues to show that a good regulatory environment can boost entrepreneurial activity in developing countries. After controlling for economic development (GDP per capita), higher entrepreneurial activity is significantly associated with cheaper, more efficient business registration procedures (IBRD and WB 2008b) and better governance (Kaufmann and Mastruzzi 2008).

The WBGES 2008 includes new data on the impact of modernization of business registries on business creation. It gathers extensive data on the functioning and structure of business registries in 71 countries from the registrars of companies. The data show that registry modernization is associated with shorter incorporation time and markedly lower cost of entry, thus reducing barriers to formal business formation and entrepreneurial activity, and relatively higher business entry rates. While the degree of progress in the modernization of business registries varies greatly, countries usually have a common goal to evolve from a paper-based business registry to a one-stop, automated, web-enabled registry capable of delivering products and services online via transactions involving authenticated users and documents. Our tests show that business registry modernization (often a component of broader private sector reforms) has a positive impact not only on the ease of creating a business, but also on new business registration. Overall, the data show that a quick, efficient and cost-effective business registration process is critical to fostering formal sector entrepreneurship.

Methodology overview

The WBGES aims to understand the dynamics of private enterprises around the world through the collection of data on business creation at the international level that can be compared across heterogeneous legal, economic and political systems. In order to make data comparable, the WBGES strives to define a unit of measurement, source of information, and concept of entrepreneurship applicable and available among the diverse countries surveyed. The definition of entrepreneurship used in the survey limits findings to the formal sector.

We exclude firms that operate informally because we are unable to measure the size of the informal economy across countries, although this sector is important for both job and enterprise creation in many developing economies. However, our analysis focuses on the role of entrepreneurship for macroeconomic development and growth, which is likely to be driven by formally registered firms. For example, in Côte d'Ivoire there are only about 4,000 registered firms – relative to the estimated 100,000 plus informal firms – yet the formal sector accounts for more than 60 per cent of GDP and 90 per cent of value added. Moreover, previous literature highlights the potential advantages of formal sector participation, including police and judicial protection (and less vulnerability to corruption and the demand for bribes), access to formal credit institutions, the ability to use formal labour contracts, and greater access to foreign markets. We argue that firms that choose to stay informal might be unable to realize their full growth potential and that 'high growth' entrepreneurship is most likely to happen through formally registered firms.

The WBGES database on formal business creation permits the study of regulatory, political and macroeconomic institutional changes on entrepreneurship. The data also facilitate the analysis of the growth of the formal private sector relative to the informal sector, and the identification of factors that encourage firms to begin operations in or transition to the formal sector.

While there are numerous established definitions for entrepreneurship, the concept still lacks a common language. Furthermore, many of the current definitions focus disproportionately on industrialized countries, highlighting the assumption of risks, innovation and high growth as necessary characteristics of entrepreneurial activity. These characteristics are typical of entrepreneurship in industrialized countries, but might be difficult to measure in developing countries. Therefore, to make the data comparable across a large number of countries, the specific type of business measured is simply the number of limited liability corporations or its equivalent in other legal systems.

The main sources of information for this study are the national business registries.[1] In a limited number of cases where the business registry was unable to provide the data – usually because they do not keep business registrations digitalized – the WBGES uses alternatives sources, such as statistical agencies, tax and labour agencies, chambers of commerce and private vendors (such as Dun and Bradstreet). Given that business registration is the first step to entering the formal sector, the WBGES also gathered information on the registries' functioning and structure to better understand their role in the business creation process.

The collection process involved telephone interviews and email/ fax correspondence with business registries in over 120 countries; 112 countries responded to the survey in 2008 and data from 101 countries were considered accurate and comparable according to the WBGES methodology.

The WBGES aims to provide an indicator of entrepreneurship based on an objective measure of business creation. Its nature makes the WBGES an appropriate indicator to measure the impact of regulatory, political and macroeconomic institutional changes on the private sector, therefore becoming a valuable tool for policy-making.

In itself, the data only provide a snapshot of the countries' business demographics, and cannot by themselves explain the factors that affect the business creation circle. However, when the WBGES is combined with other data such as the World Bank's *Doing Business* report, Investment Climate Assessments, OECD Entrepreneurship Indicators or the Global Entrepreneurship Monitor (GEM), researchers and policy-makers can better understand the variables that affect the business creation process.

Despite efforts to minimize disparities and make the data comparable across countries, certain limitations preclude a completely systematic analysis of entrepreneurial development. The following represent the most frequently faced problems in the process of gathering and processing the data:

– *Data availability*: several countries are only able to provide data on newly registered companies – and not able to provide data on total registered companies – since recent registration information is stored electronically, but historical data have not been digitalized. Some countries were excluded from this survey because they lacked tools or resources to measure business registration. For instance, some countries have decentralized business registries that make aggregation at the national level extremely difficult. In other cases, the data are archived only in paper format.

– *Limitations regarding data on firm closures*: although approximately 80 per cent of surveyed countries require businesses to report closures, only a few are actually able to report the number of business closures. The reasons differ from country to country, but are mainly due to the fact that the registrars generally have no enforcement mechanisms to compel businesses to report closures. In other cases, the number of closed businesses reported may be imprecise because of the low percentage of reporting businesses. Although the number of closed companies is essential to paint a clear picture of the economic and entrepreneurial activities of a country, it is not yet feasible to obtain comparable data.

In this regard, while information on 'active' companies – excluding closed or inoperative businesses – is sometimes available from national tax agencies and labour ministries, the research shows that only a low number of countries can actually provide these data. Therefore, it was decided to focus on the business registries. Yet, this is an important indicator of private sector activity for business registrars to measure.

– *Shell corporations*: shell companies are defined as companies that are registered for tax purposes, but are not active businesses. These corporations do not fit into the methodology of our study, since they do not correspond to the category of 'entrepreneurship' or to that of a 'business'. Therefore, we also exclude some countries that are internationally recognized tax havens (e.g. Gibraltar).

– *Diverse methodologies*: some of the data collected by the WBGES 2008 might differ from official data published by individual countries. The reason for this is that local statistical agencies might use a different methodology. For instance, the European Statistical Agency (Eurostat) methodology is based on the minimum number of employees to measure entrepreneurship. As a result, in some instances the data published by Eurostat and the WBGES, while accurate in all cases, can differ.

Data on new firm creation

The WBGES 2008 gathered data on the number of new and total businesses for 101 countries for the time period 2000 to 2008. In order to make these data comparable across countries, three different indicators were used, each displaying a different dimension of entrepreneurship (Figure 5.1):

– *Entry density rate*: this is the indicator used to measure new firms (those that were registered in the current year) as a percentage of working age population (ages 18–65). The data collected for 101 countries show significant disparities across regions, ranging from 0.05 per cent in Africa and the Middle East to 0.58 per cent in industrialized countries.

– *Business density*: this is the indicator used to measure the number of businesses per capita. It is calculated as the number of total businesses (those that existed at the beginning of the given year) as a percentage of working age population (ages 18–65). Similar to the entry rate density, this indicator shows a remarkable gap between industrialized countries, with an average of 5.48 per cent, and developing countries, with an average of 1.39 per cent.

– *Entry rate*: this indicator is used to measure the number of new businesses as a proportion of existing businesses. It is calculated as newly registered firms as a percentage of total registered firms. The data collected show that this indicator presents fewer disparities across regions, ranging from 6.6 per cent to 10 per cent.

Our two measures of new firm creation – entry density and entry rates – are correlated at over 40 per cent at 1 per cent significance (over 80 countries are correlated at more than 85 per cent). The main difference is that entry rates are sensitive to the recorded number of total registered firms, which as discussed above, might be inflated if firms do not report closures to the registry; for instance, the correlation in Zambia is very low, and indeed, the number of total registered firms does not vary much over time (to correct for firm closures). However, all results are robust to the inclusion of either estimate.

In addition to these indicators, the WBGES 2008 provides enough historical data to establish the trends in the number of new and total businesses in 100 countries during the nine-year period, 2000–8. In this regard, it is interesting to note that developing countries have a higher trend in both the number of total and new businesses, with some of the countries doubling their numbers during the period, whereas industrialized countries show little variation during the same period (Figure 5.2).

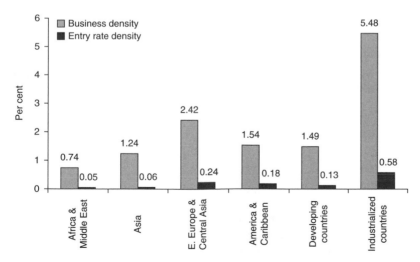

Figure 5.1 Entrepreneurship around the world
Source: WBGES (2008).

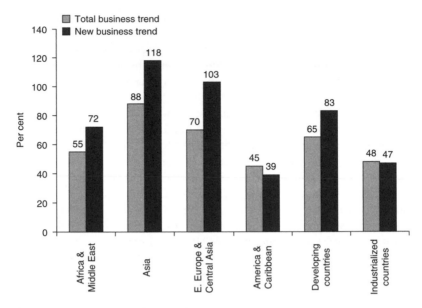

Figure 5.2   Entrepreneurship trends
Source: WBGES (2008).

Interestingly, the majority of the surveyed countries with a negative business growth were those that suffered a war, civil unrest or remarkable political instability during the nine-year period.[2]

The impact of the regulatory and legal environment

The WBGES data were merged with other variables measuring governance, political stability, the business environment and the ease of registering a business. The data reveal interesting correlations, providing further evidence of the relevance of the regulatory and political environment in fostering entrepreneurship.

Governance

The WBGES 2008 data suggest that good governance and political stability constitute the first prerequisites to setting up a favourable business environment. The information collected reveals an inverse relationship between political risk and business creation, with countries with lower political risk having significant higher business entry rates.

For instance, using the average of the six Kaufmann governance indicators (voice and accountability, political stability, government

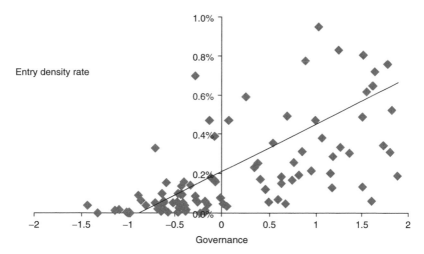

Figure 5.3 Relationship between governance and entrepreneurship
Source: WBGES (2008) and Kauffman et al. (2008).

effectiveness, regulatory quality, rule of law and control of corruption) to measure good governance, the data also show a strong and significant relationship between higher business entry rates and better governance (Figure 5.3).

What is more, the majority of the surveyed countries with a negative business growth were those that suffered a war, civil unrest or remarkable political instability during the nine-year period (e.g. Lebanon, Bosnia and Herzegovina and Haiti).

'Red-tape' reduction

The indicator used to measure the bureaucratic and legal hurdles an entrepreneur must overcome to incorporate and register a new firm is the 'ease of starting a business' indicator from World Bank (2009). Unsurprisingly, the data show a strong relation between a cheap and fast incorporation process as measured by the 'ease of starting a business' ranking, and the number of new businesses per capita (Figure 5.4).[3]

Empirical tests show that the World Bank (2009) and governance indicators significantly predict new business creation (Table 5.1). Our dependent variable is entry density rates, averaged over 2004–7. Ordinary least square regressions show a significantly positive relationship between economic development (as measured by GDP per capita) and new business creation. Even after controlling for economic

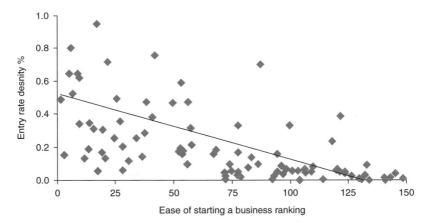

Figure 5.4 Relationship between the business environment and entrepreneurship
Source: WBGES (2008) and World Bank (2009).

Table 5.1 The relationship between the business environment and entrepreneurship

	(1)	(2)	(3)	(4)	(5)
Log GDP per capita	0.0017*** [0.000]	0.0010*** [0.000]	0.0014*** [0.000]	0.0009*** [0.000]	0.0005 [0.186]
Log 'starting a business' ranking	–	–0.0013*** [0.000]	–	–	–
Cost of starting a business	–	–	–0.0008* [0.093]	–	–
Log number of procedures to start a business	–	–	–	–0.0029*** [0.009]	–
Governance index	–	–	–	–	0.0018*** [0.004]
Constant	–0.0122*** [0.000]	–0.0013 [0.633]	–0.0100*** [0.000]	0.0003 [0.933]	–0.0019 [0.525]
Observations	99	97	97	97	99
R-squared	0.308	0.473	0.332	0.453	0.368

Notes: The dependent variable in all regressions is average new density for 2004–7; p-values are shown in parentheses; and *significant at 10% level, ** significant at 5% level, *** significant at 1% level.

Source: GDP per capita and one-year GDP growth rates are from World Bank WDI statistics (n.d.).

development, we find a significantly positive negative relationship between the World Bank (2009) 'ease of starting a business' indicator (where 1 is the highest ranking), the number of procedures and cost of doing business, and average density rates. Furthermore, we find a significantly positive relationship between better governance (as measured by Kauffman et al. 2008) and entry density rates. These results provide strong evidence of the relationship between better governance and business regulations and private sector development.

The 'starting a business' index (a lower number is a higher ranking), and the cost and number of procedures to start a business are from World Bank (2009). The governance index is from Kauffman et al. (2008).

Box 5.1   Georgia: The impact of reforms

The impact of regulatory reforms can be further assessed by studying Georgia, a top *Doing Business* reformer in 2007. For instance, beginning in 2004, Georgia undertook a series of dramatic regulatory reforms aimed to alleviate the excessive financial and administrative burden placed on entrepreneurs. The most important reforms included an unparalleled gradual elimination by 2006 of the minimum capital required to start a new business, as well as a reduction in the number of registration procedures from nine in 2004 to five in 2006 and a reduction in the number of days required to register a business from 25 days in 2004 to 11 days in 2006. In addition, Georgia created 'one-stop registration' by delegating certain formalities such as tax and statistical registration to the company registrar. The impact of these progressive reforms – in combination with the significant simplification of the licensing regime and strengthening of investor protection laws – led to an

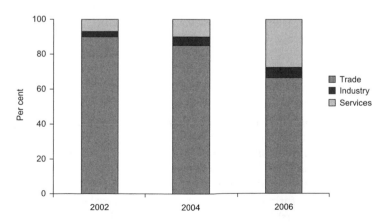

Figure 5.5   Sectoral distribution, Georgia
Source: WBGES (2008).

increase in business activity, as evidenced by the growth in the number of new businesses per capita.

Furthermore, as shown in Figure 5.5, a sectoral analysis of the dynamics of business registration indicates that this reform encouraged greater registration of companies working in the service sector. The large increase in the number of service-oriented firms, relative to trade and manufacturing firms, might indicate that this reform led not only to a larger absolute number of newly registered service-sector firms (from 103 in 2002 to 1,432 in 2006), but also encouraged informally operating service firms to transition to the formal sector.

Legal reform

In an effort to better understand the legal forms favoured by entrepreneurs and their impact on the creation of new businesses, the WBGES collected data on the main characteristics of the three prevalent legal forms per country. However, given that legal forms cannot be accurately translated across different legal systems, each legal form was dissected according to the following characteristics: registration requirements, legal entity, minimum and maximum number of shareholders, liability, transferability of shares, possibility of 'going public', taxation and minimum capital requirements.

The data collected in 59 countries revealed that entrepreneurs tend to choose the simplest legal form available, usually one that requires only one shareholder and has low capital requirements. Yet, while these simplified legal forms might be adequate for single employee establishments, they may not be suitable for the future growth of the business as they generally impose restrictions in the transferability of shares and cannot be publicly traded. Moreover, the data suggest that those countries that have more flexible legal business forms enjoy a higher entry rate density, with an average of 0.36 per cent, than those that impose more requirements, such as limitations in the number of shareholders, with an average entry density of 0.15 per cent.

It is also notable that the equivalents of joint stock companies (more rigid and usually associated with bigger businesses) prevail in developing countries, while limited liability corporations (LLCs) and sole proprietorships (more flexible and generally used by small and micro-enterprises) dominate in industrialized countries. This fact does not entail that the average size of the businesses in developing countries is bigger, but rather that only the bigger businesses in these countries transition to the formal economy, while the equivalents of the LLCs and sole proprietorships (small and micro-enterprises) in these countries tend to remain unregistered and in the informal sector.

An analysis of the variety of legal business forms across countries suggests that industrialized countries have a rather homogeneous business regulation that shares equivalent legal forms, as opposed to developing countries, where endemic business legal forms that do not have equivalents in other countries abound. Although we cannot rule out reverse causality – that greater private sector activity and higher levels of new firm creation lead to legal reform – the evidence suggests that more flexible legal regime encourages greater formal sector participation.

Data on business registry modernization

The first step for entrepreneurs joining or transitioning to the formal sector is to register their business at the registrar of companies. A modernized, quick, efficient and cost-effective business registry is therefore critical to enable entrepreneurial activity and its business environment. Creating such a modernized business registry entails reforming inefficient or ineffective processes and automating the reformed registry.

The WBGES 2008 includes new data on the impact of modernization of business registries on business creation. The WBGES gathers extensive data on the functioning and structure of business registries in 71 countries directly from the registrars of companies. First, data were collected on the types of information firms are required to report to the registry, such as annual financial filings. Second, in order to asses the different degrees of automation of business registries, the survey collected information on the availability of electronic registration, which broadly includes the computerization of local registrars, the ability to register over the Internet, and electronic distribution of data via the Internet.

The findings show that while almost 80 per cent of high and upper middle income countries require firms to file annual financial statements, only about half of lower middle and low income countries require their firms to do so. Moreover, while most countries have regulations compelling a business to notify the business registry if the business ceases operations, few countries have mechanisms to enforce such an obligation. As a result, most developing countries do not have accurate records on businesses that have ceased to exist. Correcting such ineffective functions and automating a reformed business registry remain important tasks of business registry modernization in many developing countries.

The benefits are multifold. Both businesses and governments can see reduced transaction time and costs through proper streamlining of registry processes and removal of the hurdles of in-person visits. These efficiencies include the extension of service availability to 24 hours, seven days a week through online transactions rather than travelling to a physical location and waiting in line; improving data quality and accuracy through reduction of human error; providing real time access to registry updates; automatic verification of identities and roles; as well as facilitating anti-corruption efforts where needed by removing middle persons and providing full transparency of information. In Latvia, for example, reforming and automating the business registry reduced processing time of typical transactions from weeks to (with a rush-charge) four hours. In Bologna (Italy), the electronic business registry reduced the average time for correcting errors ('suspended registrations') from ten days to a half day. The benefits of business registry reforms implemented during the last decade have led to web-based overtaking paper-based transactions in developed countries such as Italy (2003) and Denmark (2004). Advanced electronic business registries can also aggregate and analyse data, which can provide an important tool for market surveillance and business monitoring, such as for attracting FDI.

While the degree of progress in the modernization of business registries varies greatly, countries usually have a common goal to evolve from a paper-based business registry to a one-stop, automated, web-enabled registry capable of delivering products and services online via transactions involving authenticated users and documents. The implementation of such an electronic business registry has a positive impact not only on the ease of creating a business, but also on other aspects of the business cycle (Table 5.2).

Table 5.2   Potential uses of an electronic business registry

Potential users of an e-BR	Potential use of e-BR services
A business owner	registers a new business, lists the board of directors of his/her firm, makes changes to the business's contact details, or files annual financial statements.
A loan approval officer at a financial institution	confirms the financial health and history of a potential borrowing firm and owners.
A potential customer	confirms information on the operations and management of the firm.
A potential supplier	confirms the financial health of a potential buyer in making trade credit decisions.
A lawyer or notary	signs in to validate information.
A government official (e.g. a tax, customs, pension, VAT or social security authority official)	verifies a firm's active business status.

The data collected by the WBGES 2008 suggest a relation between the implementation of electronic registration and an increase in the number of new businesses registered. Countries like Slovenia, Guatemala, Azerbaijan, Jordan, Oman and Sri Lanka had increases of more than 30 per cent in new density rates after the full implementation of electronic registries (Figure 5.6). These increases cannot be attributed solely to improvements in the countries' business registries, but it can be stated that the modernization of their business registries was the culmination of a successful implementation of regulatory reforms, which when taken together, produced a significant and positive impact in the ease of doing business in these countries.

The data also show that the percentage of countries beginning the automation process (electronic data storage) is similar regardless of their stage of economic development (Figure 5.7). The differences begin to rise gradually in the next steps of the automatization process, resulting in a wide gap between industrialized and developing countries in the latter steps. For example, none of the low income countries in the survey has implemented remote or Internet registration, in comparison to 50 per cent of high income countries.

Multiple elements can achieve this goal. For example, registries in developing countries might start by offering entrepreneurs the ability to retreive information on a website (such as laws and regulations), download registration forms (but not necessarily to submit them online), and check available firm names. Governments may need to provide a centralized interface for a regional system, such as by merging local courts' business registries into a central registry database. Countries

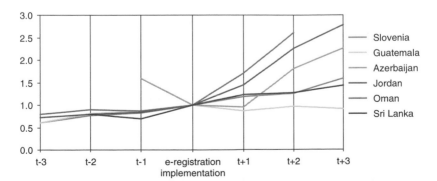

Figure 5.6 Impact of e-registration implementation
Source: WBGES (2008).

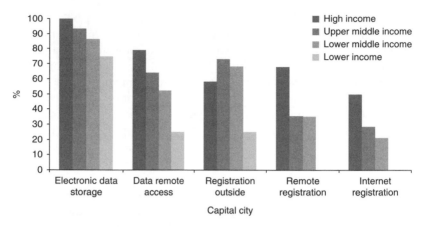

Figure 5.7 Business registration modernization
Source: WBGES (2008).

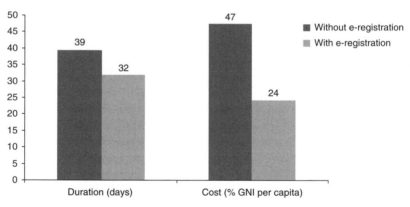

Figure 5.8 Impact of business registration modernization
Source: WBGES (2008) and World Bank (2009).

that already have a centralized registry but are still paper-based need to digitize historical and automate new data entries by using networked computers and online forms. Registries that are already automated need to implement secure, legal authentication methods, such as digital signatures, to remove the last vestiges of in-person or in-paper requirements. Registries that aim to benefit from further time and cost savings would interlink the electronic business with other e-government services, such as e-tax, e-customs or e-procurement applications, for additonal cost and time efficiencies for governments.

It is difficult to isolate the causality between the implementation of electronic registration, improvements in the business environment, and the creation of new businesses. Nevertheless, the data collected by the WBGES 2008 suggest that business registry modernization provides a more favourable business environment for starting a business and facilitates the business creation process. On average, countries with remote registration (including Internet, phone and kiosks) require over 30 per cent less time to start a business, and that costs are reduced by 50 per cent, as measured by the *Doing Business* report (Figure 5.8).

Concluding remarks

With new topics and broader coverage of developing countries, the WBGES 2008 and future surveys will continue to support a deeper and more comprehensive understanding of conditions that can encourage entrepreneurship, as a policy tool to measure the impact of policy reforms to create new firms and stimulate economic growth.

The WBGES findings show that those countries with highest business entry rates provide entrepreneurs with a stable political climate, good governance, modernized business registries, reduced red tape and simplified business legal forms. Therefore, policy-makers and governments should take these variables into account to better design, implement, monitor and evaluate their policies and programmes aimed to develop their private sector.

Acknowledgements

We thank the Ewing Marion Kauffman Foundation, the Development Research Group at the World Bank and the International Finance Corporation for financial support. This chapter was prepared with outstanding assistance from Anna Cusnir and Ana Ribeiro. Thanks to Maxwell Aitken, Laurence Carter, Asli Demirguc-Kunt, Andrei Mikhnev, Raphael Amit and Mauro Guillén for valuable comments. This chapter's findings, interpretations and conclusions are entirely those of the authors and do not necessarily represent the views of the World Bank.

Notes

1. The complete database and list of sources are available at: http://econ.worldbank.org/ research/entrepreneurship.
2. Such as Lebanon, Bosnia and Herzegovina and Haiti.
3. For an additional discussion, see Klapper et al. (2008).

6
Measuring the Business Environment for Entrepreneurship in Fragile States
Chiara Guglielmetti

Introduction

More than a billion people live in around 50 developing countries that have been described as 'fragile states' (Naudé and Santos-Paulino et al. 2008). According to Binzel and Brück (2007: 5) fragility refers to 'the existence of persistent, systematic, significant and interrelated social, political and economic uncertainties'. Fragile and post-conflict state policy priorities may differ from those of non-conflict affected countries because the necessities *per se* are different, but also because problems are atypically severe and they are atypically sensitive to specific reform processes (Collier and Hoeffler 2002).

Increasingly, donors and international development agencies are turning to private sector development where state capacity is lacking. Promoting entrepreneurship in fragile states has therefore assumed high importance in strategies dealing with fragile states (Addison and Brück 2009; Anand 2009; Naudé 2009a, 2009b).

This chapter aims to contribute to a better understanding of entrepreneurship in fragile states. Despite the practical interest and relevance, this topic has been neglected. The aim is to address this neglect by scrutinizing the World Bank's (WB) *Doing Business* (DB) indicators and investigating whether they can capture entrepreneurial dynamics in a fragile country. Because many fragile states are either in conflict or emerging from conflict, particular reference will be made to the context of conflict.

There is wide recognition that 'the level and quality of entrepreneurship make a difference in the economic vitality of communities, regions, industries and the nation as a whole' (Hart 2003: 4; Baumol 2009; Kanniainen and Keuschnigg 2005, Malecki 1994). Nevertheless, in the literature awareness is growing about the strong need of empirical evidence on the direction and the interaction between entrepreneurs, policy, institutions and context, instead of taking for granted the positive effect of entrepreneurship – the latter is often employed as an 'umbrella' concept – on development and prosperity (Shane 2008), leaving apart, for example, impacts on the environment and the ambiguous role of entrepreneurship in conflict dynamics.

The DB indicators measure different kinds of inputs of entrepreneurship development and ranks countries according to ten dimensions. These dimensions are starting a business, dealing with construction permits, employing workers, registering property, getting credit, protecting investors, paying taxes, trading across borders, enforcing contracts and closing a business. The premise of DB approach is that:

> ... a vibrant private sector – with firms making investments, creating jobs, and improving productivity – promotes growth and expands opportunities for poor people and that in many countries...entrepreneurial activity remains limited, poverty high, and growth stagnant...(IBRD and WB 2004: viii)

DB reports are based on the thesis that although macro-policies are unquestionably important, the quality of business regulation is a major determinant of development. The relevance of DB is thus twofold: both positive and normative. The principal aim is 'to guide reform of the scope and efficiency of government regulation' in order to foster entrepreneurship and thus promote economic, social and human development (IBRD and WB 2004).

The outreach of DB indicators to fragile states has been eased by their wide geographical coverage (183 countries in DB 2010). The DB indicators represent a precious, and often unique, access to information, in particular in countries which lack adequate and reliable data on business environment and performance.

About one-third of the countries reviewed by DB can be considered fragile and in conflict. This notwithstanding, the DB does not explicitly deal with the relationship between state fragility and entrepreneurship. As far as a mere linguistic analysis is concerned, the terms 'conflict' and 'post-conflict' appear once in DB 2009 for the first time in all the DB report series. Even in regional or national reports, DB does not consider any context variable.

As underlined by Naudé (2009b), the scarce availability of data on entrepreneurship in fragile states places a significant constraint on both research and policy design. Yet, paradoxically, DB indicators tend to acquire more attention in fragile or conflict prone countries. This chapter shares the critical statements made in this volume about the danger of applying 'the most readily available statistics' (Avanzini, Chapter 3, this volume) with scant concern for how the data are built and the understanding of entrepreneurship in a specific context (Desai, Chapter 4, this volume). It is worth noting that the WB has been using DB data in establishing conditions towards its debtors and that the International Development Association has set business regulatory environment as one of the criteria in the country policy and institutional assessment. Moreover, the Millennium Challenge Corporation also relies on DB data to build its six governance indicators for the eligibility of assistance programmes and for the Millennium Challenge Account selection criteria.

The criticism of the DB advanced in this chapter is twofold. First, the development process is traced by the interaction between forces that are meant to generate a progressive convergence. DB upholds a strategy of development which neither contextualizes information nor interprets it accordingly, disregarding the role of historical, institutional and cultural heritage, which is often only anecdotally evoked. The context in which economic agents act varies in terms of opportunities, constraints and incentives, and exerts a strong influence on individual behaviour. Second, through an interplay of simplification, measurement and convergence, DB risks becoming a race-to-the-bottom – the country which reforms the most gets the higher score[1] – in various crucial institutional and political features in which the pivotal role of pro-active public policies in entrepreneurship development is disregarded (Lazonick, Chapter 12, this volume; Naudé 2009a and Chapter 11, this volume).

In particular, DB indicators give a partial picture of the nexus between institutional context, policy reforms, entrepreneurship and economic development and fail in addressing pivotal aspects as the process through which individuals become entrepreneurs, the ambiguous role of entrepreneurship in fragile states, the relationships between enterprises, both inter-sectoral and across different sectors of the economy, and the characteristics of workers employed in enterprises. In doing so, DB fails to capture firm internal and external contexts, and thus does not trace innovation. Consequently, DB policy recommendations often end in a focus on short-term horizons and on the relative ease in implementing the reforms.

Critical assessment

General assessment

Two general issues can be addressed at the outset: what do the DB indicators really measure? Entrepreneurship or business? The first issue relates to the normative approach of DB.

Concerning the second, the entrepreneur is not assigned a distinct, specific role in DB: entrepreneur, manager and owner of an ongoing business are often regarded as synonymous. Even though they often appear to partially overlap in practice, they are nevertheless functionally and theoretically distinct (Baumol 1968). The choice of focusing on the number of registered enterprises partly depends upon the availability of comparable statistical data. The implications are nevertheless important as far as DB explanatory power is concerned, especially in post-conflict dynamics. Data concerning business death rates, business churn, net business population growth and survival rates seem pivotal in connecting the act of DB with entrepreneurial function and in assessing development potential and sustainability of the private sector, along with its potential to influence the welfare and growth of a disrupted country.

Concerning the first, it needs to be pointed out that on the premise that 'what gets measured gets done' to clarify what is actually measured, acquires a normative value. The problem is acknowledged by the Independent Evaluation Group (IEG), a unit within the WB in charge of the assessment of the International Finance Corporation (IFC) work towards the private sector:

> DB assesses the burden of regulation on firms without aiming to capture the social or economy-wide benefits that regulations yield, such as safety, environmental protection, worker protection or transparency. (IEG 2008: xi)

Yet, the explicit normative function given to the DB since the very beginning seems to sharply contrast with the statement that 'the context and perspective on what DB really measures or addresses are crucial for policymakers and practitioners to keep in mind' (IEG 2008: xi).

Indeed, DB data are meant to be transparent and, therefore, objective, showing empirical evidence on business regulation which justify an *ex post* adherence to theoretical positions. Consequently, a number of key concepts are regarded as unquestionable and automatically interacting with each other. DB adopts a one-size-can-fit-all (IBRD and WB 2004) development strategy, which is made up of a number of predefined steps. The assumption is that improvements in a business environment occur through a precise set of *de novo* reforms. This perspective, whose failure has been emphasized (Acs et al. 2008a; Easterly 2001), becomes even more dangerous in fragile states.

The rather centralized view of policy-making is complemented by the focus only on firms based in capital cities. This does not fully take into account the fact that local and regional conditions exert a deep influence on entrepreneurial development and that the role played by decentralized policy-making is thus crucial, as pointed out in this volume by Thurik (Chapter 7) and Nijkamp (Chapter 13). This shortcoming has been partly recognized by DB. Subnational analyses for 17 countries have been recently released and, at the time of writing, another five are planned. However, subnational reports consider only a few indicators and are not released on a regular basis.

Finally, the DB approach has a number of general shortcomings which limit its ability to inform entrepreneurship policy in fragile states. A full discussion of these falls outside the scope of this chapter, but the following may be mentioned. First, the theme of security of property is pivotal in the DB approach, of which the Coase theorem seems to be one of the pillars. But, if the reports keep stressing the fundamental role of well-defined property rights, they disregard transaction costs. Yet, conflict dynamics and the insecurity inherent in fragile states increase transaction costs, bringing about social fragmentation and jeopardizing transactions (Collier 1994). For example, the starting a business indicator only takes into consideration compulsory costs and not the time needed to acquire information. The DB entrepreneur is a standard economic agent. His or her choices are predictable because they are guided by an individualistic view, according to which the main purposes are to maximize profit and to optimize the choice between regular or irregular economy. The DB approach seems therefore to follow the approach to entrepreneurship of neoclassical microeconomics. Yet, the assumption of complete and perfect information leads to a biased comparison among fragile and non-fragile states.

Second, the role of formal and informal institutions has to be emphasized. Post-conflict countries are in particular need of a comprehensive public effort to recover war-damaged infrastructures and to provide a larger amount of public goods, in order to recreate an environment able to convey dispersed resources.

Third, the implications of an unpredictable and unstable environment for economic and non-economic incentives to become an entrepreneur are manifold. The types of barriers which individuals face in fragile states are harsher and more diversified. The indicators, on the one side, lack any concern about the qualitative characteristics of entrepreneurs and businesses (Smallbone and Welter 2001) and, on the other side, focus on a partial consideration of the economic incentives to entrepreneurship. The issue of a productive allocation of entrepreneurial resources, which is important in any economic system, acquires a specific relevance in post-conflict environments (Naudé 2007). Indeed, state fragility offers remarkable possibilities for profits and rents. As a matter of fact, post-conflict economic recovery implies restructuring the basis of a competitive market as well as the reallocation or the repression of misallocated resources. Moreover, as to portfolio decisions, there is a high risk of adverse selection behaviours by private agents, which can lead to a sub-optimal amount of those investments that foster sustainable growth (Alesina et al. 1992; Alesina and Perotti 1993; Collier and Gunning 1995). A crucial aspect to be considered is the individual necessity to adapt to a changing environment, recalibrating knowledge, personal endowments and capabilities (Audretsch and Thurik 2004; Kauffman Foundation 2007; Naudé 2007). Furthermore, in fragile states the need to create, recreate and strengthen social ties and economic networks is particularly high (Cusmano et al. 2008; Fagerberg and Godinho 2005; Mazzoleni and Nelson 2007; Mytelka 2004; Niosi 2008; Smallbone and Welter 2001). Yet, in a fractured environment, in which social relations and networks among economic agents, both individuals and enterprises, have been abruptly interrupted, missing institutions are 'substituted' by long-term relations between economic actors (McMillan and Woodruff, 1999a, 1999b, 2002; Stiglitz 2006). The role of firms' networks is also crucial in fostering innovation, whilst DB seems rather focused on a static and traditional manufacturing economic system (Mazzoleni and Nelson 2007; Mytelka 2004; Niosi 2008).

Social mobility acquires a particular relevance. The same can be said for entrepreneurs in diaspora and for return migration; recent literature (McCormick and Wahba 2000; Taylor 2006) has considered the role of the latter on the development of skilled entrepreneurship in their country of origin. A DB entrepreneur is assumed to be national, a strong assumption that acquires more relevance in post-conflict dynamics. The role of (ethnic or religious) minority and immigrant entrepreneurs (Naudé 2007) must be analysed. Moreover, addressing the economic potentialities of women is of major importance. Despite the declared intention (IBRD and WB 2008a), the role of women is remarkably disregarded by DB (Hampel-Milagrosa 2008).

The current DB indicators therefore face a number of serious limitations as indicative tools for entrepreneurship policy in the poorest countries.

Assessment of the 'starting a business' indicator

Starting a business ranks the countries according to four subindicators, the weighted average of which forms the indicator: the number of procedures, time, cost and paid-in minimum capital necessary to start and legally run a business. Fewer procedures, and less time, cost and capital, increase the score a country acquires (Table 6.1).

The outcomes of easier and faster procedures to starting up a business are, in the DB approach, more start-ups, less informal economy, with consequently more protection of employees and higher productivity caused by increased entry pressure, which in turn lead to more competitiveness between enterprises.

In post-conflict countries start-ups play an important role for a number of reasons. First, as Naudé (2009c) highlights, they are likely to have fewer legacies with conflict dynamics. A major task that must be dealt with is the necessity to reallocate into peace and productive activities entrepreneurs who have been active during the conflict. The question is, on one side, to convey entrepreneurial resources which need to adapt to a new environment. On the other side, during the first post-conflict period, societies are particularly unstable and the possibility of a relapse into conflict remains extremely high (Collier 2006). A major issue that must be tackled is dealing with those entrepreneurs that have gained economic and political power because of the conflict and therefore represent a force prone to increase instability and social, political and economic fragmentation. Even though the dynamics among forces in a fragile area tend to reproduce themselves, it can be stated that, according to McMillan and Woodruff's (2002) analysis of the role of small and medium enterprises (SMEs) in transition economies, new SMEs can contribute to create a business environment more conducive to a productive allocation of entrepreneurship.

Second, even though the evidence of a better performance of *de novo* companies in respect to the private sector as a whole is not uncontroversial (McMillan and Woodruff 2002) recent literature has emphasized the positive effect of start-ups on employment and growth (Audretsch and Keilbach 2003; Audretsch et al. 2002, 2006).

Therefore, in this perspective, DB's focus on start-ups seems to properly address the specificity of post-conflict countries. Nevertheless, there are two aspects which need to be considered. First, the question

Table 6.1 The starting a business indicator

Indicator	Background paper	Subindicators	Assumption on the business
Starting a business	*The Regulation of Entry* Djankov et al. (2002)	Number of procedures (any interaction of the company founders with external parties).	Limited liability company (if more than one, the most popular form).
			Operates in the economy's largest business city.
		Caveat: procedures that the company undergoes to connect electricity, water, gas and waste disposal services are not included.	100% domestically owned (five owners, none of whom is a legal entity).
			Start-up capital of 10 times income per capita at the end of 2007, paid in cash.
		Time (days).	General industrial or commercial activities, not foreign trade activities and not products subject to a special tax regime. No heavily polluting production processes..
		Cost (% of income per capita).	
		Caveat: time spent on gathering information is ignored.	Leases the commercial plant, no real estate.
		Paid-in minimum capital (% of income per capita).	No investment incentives or any special benefits.
			Between 10 and 50 national employees one month after the commencement of operations.
			Turnover of at least 100 times income per capita.
			Company deed 10 pages long.
			The entrepreneur is aware of all entry regulations and their sequence from the beginning but has had no prior contact with any officials.

that must be coped with in post-conflict countries is not the lack of entrepreneurial resources, but their productive allocation (Naudé 2009c). This issue will be analysed in the next section. Second, procedures for starting up a business are equated to entry barriers which obstruct entrepreneurship and private investment. This statement is drawn from public choice theory on regulation and from the hypothesis that two procedures are 'sufficient for business registration: notification of existence and tax and social security registration' (IBRD and WB 2004: 17 and 21; IBRD and WB 2005: 19).[2] As noted by Arruñada (2007: 2):

> ... [the] use of this simile [between procedure for starting up a business and entry barriers] leads to omission of the fact that, by incurring certain formalisation costs today, transaction costs in the future will be reduced, whereas conventional entry barriers do not generate this kind of positive effect.

The perspective adopts a company's short-term private point of view, mainly considering private costs while the social and long-term private benefits of regulation are often disregarded. Regulation of entry is analysed merely from an entrepreneur's perspective, taking into account only quantity and not quality and therefore disregarding the costs borne by other agents, namely public administration and courts (to whom registration formalization provides necessary information) and other companies (due diligence) in the case of poor quality registration services. DB firmly upholds the elimination of minimum capital requirements and reliance on private contracts between creditors and debtors, which would substitute capital rules. This position is in line with an approach that mainly relies on the market as a source of efficiency, besides highlighting an element that supports the efficiency of common law.

The basic hypothesis on which the reports are implicitly built is Baumol's thesis of the fundamental role of institutions in influencing the allocation of entrepreneurship resources. According to this thesis, what varies most among countries is not the number of entrepreneurs or 'the nature of their objectives', but the relative payoffs society offers (Baumol 1990) to entrepreneurial activities. It is therefore possible and desirable to modify the reward structure in the economic system in order to enhance a productive allocation of entrepreneurial resources. So, what is the role of regulation in a DB perspective? The background study (Djankov et al. 2002) on which the starting a business indicator is methodologically and theoretically based, in accordance with de Soto's work (de Soto 2000) provides evidence that:

>...the countries with more open access to political power, greater constraints on the executive, and greater political rights have less burdensome regulation of entry...than do the countries with less representative, less limited, and less free governments. (Djankov et al. 2002: 5)

This statement is presented as an *ex post* and evidence-based adherence to public choice theory. Entry regulation is set up in order to benefit regulators, who seek to gain rents exerting unjustified control on private entrepreneurs, according to the tollbooth strand of public choice theory developed by de Soto (2000), McChesney (1987) and others. No efficiency or public interest reasons justify the majority of entry regulations, no empirical evidence supports Pigou's public interest theory of regulation in the pilot research carried out by groups of researchers headed by Simeon Djankov.[3]

From our standpoint, two aspects are relevant here. First, the role played by the state in resetting the rules of the game, in coordinating different economic actors, and in facilitating economic exchanges and development, is undervalued. As a matter of fact, DB's theoretical premise and Baumol's theory greatly diverge on the nature of entrepreneurship. Baumol's central message is that 'the exercise of entrepreneurship can sometimes be unproductive or even destructive' (Baumol 1990: 898–9), and that the role of the rules of the game in the economic system is to induce a productive allocation of entrepreneurial resources. Entrepreneurship can be productive, innovative, with a positive economic and social role or rent-seeking, parasitic or criminal. Therefore, supporting existing SMEs does not necessarily imply supporting productive entrepreneurship, and adopting the point of view of the entrepreneur does not necessarily imply assuming a socially and economically sustainable perspective. This statement is pivotal in addressing post-conflict strategies aimed at fostering productive entrepreneurship. As Cooper (2006) notes, economic war systems often do not reflect a specific and alternative system of profit, being rather deeply rooted both in pre- and post-conflict economic structures.

Second, the 'Manichean' view (Arruñada 2007) which supports the DB theoretical framework represents the influence between business environment and entrepreneurial behaviour as a uni-directional relationship between two homogeneous parties, preventing DB from investigating more complex dynamics. The relationship between 'the institutions of the market place and the spectrum of entrepreneurial behaviour it engenders and supports' (Metcalfe 2004: 35) is widely recognized, both politically and academically. At the same time, it is important to take into account the influence that a particular social and cultural *milieu*, in which entrepreneurship behaviour develops, may exert on political and institutional processes. Moreover, the dualistic vision of institution and politics on one side and entrepreneurs on the other, does not take into account the spectrum of the heterogeneous forces involved. The response to the regulation of economic agents varies widely and does not often confirm the simplistic dualism of regulation versus the free market. This is particularly true as far as post-conflict dynamics are concerned. Moreover, the serious need for public intervention requires an assessment of the government level of corruption, effectiveness, and capability to define a long-term strategy, all aspects disregarded by DB conceptualization, representing public intervention *per se* as a shortcoming in the economic system.

Assessment of the 'paying taxes' indicator

The paying taxes indicator measures amount, procedural and time requirements of taxes and government mandatory contributions a SME is required to pay in a fiscal year. The indicator is made up of tax payments for a manufacturing company, time required to comply with three major taxes and total tax rate.

The rationale of the indicator is that corporate taxes and social and labour contributions lessen the economic incentives to engage in an entrepreneurial venture, having consequently negative effects on aggregate investments, FDI and entrepreneurship activities and leading to slower economic growth, more reliance on debt than on equity and more irregular economy. In the DB analysis, burdensome regulation causes economic agents to give up their economic activities regularly carried out (or even not to engage in a regular economic activity) and force them to choose the unregulated alternative, which DB reports define as 'informal economy' and estimate as the percentage of activity that is unofficial or not registered (Djankov et al. 2008a). The concept of informal economy in the DB reports seems to identify economic activities carried out against the rules posed by a system – that is, irregular economy (Dallago 1990) – not activity of self-consumption, criminal activity or simply unrecorded activity. Thus it is worth noting that the method of calculation chosen overlaps two conceptually and logically distinct phenomena, and that the reports do not clarify their definition of informal economy, a controversial concept which encompasses a number of different actors and aspects.

Several caveats are necessary as far as post-conflict countries are concerned. Collier (1994) highlights the decay of institutions and conventions of civil society – the private sector has learned how to evade the state – and, consequently, the inadequacy of the state to effectively manage the tax-gathering system and to increase revenue without intensifying arbitrary actions. Moreover, Collier states the necessity of setting low taxation on transactions in order to help the market recover. Nevertheless, returning to market implies a comprehensive effort aimed at restructuring the fundamental institutions, the formal and informal rules of the game, which can hardly be done by the interaction of private economic agents. A tradeoff comes, in this perspective, between low taxes and a government budget capable of restoring and activating virtuous market mechanisms.

The DB approach conceives of underdevelopment as being the result of private under-utilized socio-economic potential, as a waste of opportunity due to institutional frameworks which inhibit economic agents. The roadmap to development therefore means freeing the private sector from bureaucratic and political ties which hinder growth. Yet, the role of public intervention in post-conflict dynamics seems pivotal for at least five reasons, which represent increased sources of public expenditure. First, there is room for substantial state intervention to help war-damaged infrastructures recover, which is necessary to foster market processes (Anand 2009). These kinds of public interventions can have a rapid and positive influence on the indicator trading across borders, which records procedural requirements for exporting and importing goods by ocean transport.

Second, the state needs to ensure security in an environment where micro-insecurity is considerably high. Post-conflict dynamics exert a remarkable influence on individuals' portfolio choices, which, as mentioned above, are more liquid than normal, and on entrepreneurs, who are likely to prefer reversible and short-term investments. Therefore, lower taxes, which decrease government budgets, are likely to produce more individual savings rather than foster private investments. Thus, public interventions which lessen micro-instability and ease market exchange are important.

Third, the role of the state as a facilitator of knowledge creation and sharing, investments and spillovers seems pivotal. Research that sustains the effects of policy – specifically corporate-income tax rates, minimum wages and bankruptcy law – on entrepreneurship across the

US has been presented (Garrett and Wall 2006). Nevertheless, what Schramm (2004) stresses is the necessity of taking into account the whole system that supports entrepreneurship.

Fourth, there are many conduits to entrepreneurial development which post-conflict countries are likely to be particularly short of: investments in R&D, the general level of knowledge, networks and relations among firms, highskilled employees who can detect and exploit opportunities and social services, which can support and sustain entrepreneurial ventures by reducing the individuals' exposure to social risks. At the same time, post-conflict countries can be unusually responsive, with unexploited human resources and capabilities which can be very productively harnessed. Therefore, what seems necessary for private sector development are broadly based institutional interventions that are

> ... aimed at supplying common goods such as training, technological capabilities and quality assurance... There is the need for regulative interventions encouraging larger local and foreign enterprises to adopt more socially inclusive patterns of sourcing and subcontracting. (Schulpen and Gibbon 2002: 6)

Finally, the redistributive role of the state seems to be important in the phase of transition. Market disruption brings about a less competitive environment in which profit margins widen and there are more opportunities for rent positions; at the same time, opportunities for profits and rents, which would have been illegitimate in a non-conflict situation, arise (Collier 1994; Collier and Gunning 1995; Keen 1994). Thus, post-conflict societies are likely to be characterized by high income inequality and weak social protection. Two consequences are relevant here: first, high income inequality increases vulnerability and internal conflicts, and makes the restoration of normal conditions difficult. Second, higher income inequality implies a market characterized by weaker demand and lower individual capability to engage in entrepreneurial ventures.

Another element which is worth noting about the paying taxes indicator is that social contribution and labour taxes are encompassed in order to measure all 'imposed charges that affect business accounts' (IBRD and WB 2009). The construction of the indicator is in line with the DB approach towards the dynamics between entrepreneurs and workers, focusing on two desired policy outcomes: increasing flexibility of labour regulation and decreasing costs.

Assessment of the 'employing workers' indicator

The indicator measures the regulation of employment, specifically how it affects the hiring and firing of workers and the rigidity of working hours (IBRD and WB 2009), and is made up of five subindicators: difficulty of hiring, rigidity of hours, difficulty of firing, rigidity of employment and firing cost (Table 6.2).

In the background paper of the indicator, Botero et al. (2004) present the results of a comparative empirical study on regulation of the labour market (employment, collective relations and social security laws) in 85 countries. The paper shows how higher regulation is associated with higher levels of unemployment and a larger irregular economy, and is therefore harsher on the weaker part of the workforce, that is, women and young people, thus causing a *de facto* weakening of the system of social protection. The risk is to increase unemployment and to force individuals towards an irregular economy whilst trying to protect workers. If, in the DB vision, public institutions often fail, reliance on the market leads to efficiency even in the labour market: DB 2004 states that 'if business does not provide its workers with adequate conditions of employment, other companies will attract the workers' (IBRD and WB 2004: 93). DB therefore adopts a neoclassical approach to the labour market, in which real wages determine equilibrium, similar to what happens in any other market. DB 2009 highlights how overly rigid labour regulation brings about difficulties in adjusting to demand, limits firm size and discourages both incumbent and possible entrepreneurship, increasing firm costs and decreasing economic incentives to become an entrepreneur.

The following remarks are necessary. Positive externalities of labour market regulation and of a well-funded social security system are disregarded: minimum wages, restriction of working hours, employment protection and restriction on the use of fixed-term contracts are considered barriers and sources of delay for business, in spite of a controversial debate on these issues (e.g. Berg and Cazes 2007; Eyraut and Saget 2005; Fox 2006; Lee and McCann 2007). The less a country regulates, the better the score the indicator assigns. Criticisms have been made that it is possible to change a DB ranking without improving business (Channel 2008). Moreover, empirical research on labour markets has shown that it is possible to improve the DB ranking but make, at the same time, business and quality of life worse. It seems relevant that DB 2008 highlights that 'it is now possible for an economy to receive the highest score on the ease of employing workers – indicating the most flexible labour regulation – and comply with all 187 ILO conventions'

Table 6.2 The employing workers indicator

Indicator	Background paper	Assumptions		Subindicators
		Business	Worker	
Employing workers (until DB 2006, *Hiring and firing workers*)	*The regulation of Labour* (Botero et al. 2004)	Limited liability company in the country's most populous city	42 year old, non-executive, full-time, male employee	**Rigidity of employment index**
		100% domestically owned	Has worked at the same company for 20 years	**Difficulty of hiring index** — Fixed term contracts for permanent tasks
		Operates in the manufacturing sector	Salary plus benefits equal to the country's average wage during the entire period of his employment	Max. cumulative duration of fixed term contracts
		60 employees (201 until DB 2009)		Ratio of minimum wage for a trainee or first employee to the average value added per worker
				Rigidity of hours index — Night work unrestricted
				Weekend work unrestricted
				Workweek can consist of 5.5 days
				Workweek can extend to 50 hours (for seasonal increase in production, 2 months a year)
				Paid annual vacation 21 working days or fewer

Term	Definition
Subject to collective bargaining agreements in countries where such agreements cover more than half the manufacturing sector and apply even to firms not party to them	
Abides by every law and regulation but does not grant workers more benefits than mandated by law, regulation or (if applicable) collective bargaining agreement	
Lawful citizen, same race and religion of the majority of the country's population	
Resides in the country most populous city	
Not a member of a labour union, unless membership is mandatory	

Term	Definition
Difficulty of firing index	Redundancy disallowed as basis for terminating workers
	Notify a third party to terminate one redundant worker
	Notify a third party to terminate a group of 25 redundant workers
	Approval from a third party to terminate one redundant worker
	Approval from a third party to terminate a group of 25 redundant workers
	Reassignment or retraining options before redundancy termination
	Priority rules apply for redundancies
	Priority rules apply for reemployment
Non-wage labour cost	All social security payments and payroll taxes associated with hiring an employee (% of the worker's salary)
Firing cost	Cost of advance notice requirements, severance payments and penalties due when terminating a redundant worker

(IBRD and WB 2008b). For the first time DB 2009 recognizes the necessity of a good balance between worker protection and labour market flexibility and lists the countries that have ratified the four ILO conventions which are considered relevant for the indicator. This aspect, in any case, is not included in the assessment of the policy of a country. Consequently, not only does DB not value the compliance with ILO regulations, but also it does not establish any minimum regulation standards to be met.

The indicator does not consider any interaction between regulation in different areas. For example, flexibility in labour market and taxes to finance passive and active labour market policies, are necessarily connected in flexicurity systems, which are 'economically and socially superior to flexibility systems' (Auer 2007; see also Berg and Cazes 2007). Moreover, by stating that 'Denmark, Hong Kong (China), New Zealand, Sweden and the United States are among the countries with the most flexible labour regulation overall' (IBRD and WB 2004: 83), the DB report decontextualizes labour regulations from the overall institutional and political framework of a country, disregarding how welfare systems vary among the countries quoted.

A further shortcoming of the indicator is the narrow focus on flexibility of the labour force. Critical for an entrepreneurial economy is the quality of the workers: the Kauffman Foundation (2007: 2) stresses that 'entrepreneurs tell us that perhaps the most significant constraint on their future growth, and on the growth of future entrepreneurs, is the difficulty finding and attracting "talent" – highly skilled, entrepreneurial workers'. In post-conflict dynamics, the above-mentioned aspect is critically intertwined with the necessity to resettle displaced workforces and to recreate an environment conducive to entrepreneurial development. It is worth noting that civil war creates an exodus of the most skilled human capital (Collier 1994); displaced communities need to be reintegrated and to find income-earning opportunities, while demobilized soldiers are likely to be unemployed. Notwithstanding the context-specific nature of the situation, it is also plausible to hypothesize a substantial number of demobilized soldiers who are unskilled or at least poorly skilled outside the military sphere (see Collier 1994 for the cases of Uganda and Ethiopia) and seriously needing to adapt their competencies to a new environment.

The position of working women in a post-conflict environment presents particular aspects to consider. During conflicts, women are likely to have been widely employed in order to sustain the war economy. It must also be considered that a substantial number of families are likely to rely on working women in a post-conflict period. Given that an economy has to be shifted into peaceful activity, that women are typically vulnerable economic agents and that social services are likely to be weak in post-conflict countries, it is very important to assess the relative position of women in the labour market and their possibility of being productively reallocated.

Finally, the possible tradeoff between a highly flexible labour market and the development of workers' skills and competencies (Antonelli 2009) is disregarded not only by the indicator here considered but also by the academic literature. The relevance of this tradeoff seems particularly severe in a fragmented environment in which the reconstruction of social and labour ties and the strengthening of individual skills are pivotal.

Assessment of the 'dealing with construction permits' indicator

DB policy recommendations on dealing with construction permits – named dealing with licences until DB 2007 – focus on simplification of procedures, limitation of regulators' rent-seeking and corruption and on efficiency. The recommendations are: to give builders a step-by-step specific chart and not to mandate use of specific materials (IBRD and WB 2006), to discard obsolete licensing regulations every decade (IBRD and WB 2007), to make information easily available, to introduce online licence applications and consolidate project clearances (IBRD and WB 2006, 2008), to reduce licensing requirements and 'curb inspections' (IBRD and WB 2008), to update zoning maps periodically (IBRD and WB 2006), to adjust licences and inspections to the size and nature of the project, and to involve the private sector (IBRD and WB 2007). The greater the number of licences issued, the cheaper and faster the procedures, and the better the score. The necessity of cutting the red tape of a burdensome administration represents a goal worth pursuing. But the risks of prioritizing policy reforms in accordance with this maxim are serious. From this perspective regulation of licensing, as well as labour regulation, being a barrier to business, is seen as a source of costs, delays and rigidity. The problem that the DB perspective brings about is twofold: first, the automatic connection between less regulation of business and development is presented as evidence-based and therefore often regarded as unquestionable; second, DB does not establish minimum regulation standards to be met.

DB analyses procedures, time and cost of building a warehouse. The choice seems peculiar. The explicit rationale of this choice seems even more peculiar:

> ...because warehouses do not house people, there are fewer safety concerns than with construction of offices and homes. At worst, a company's goods could be destroyed by fire, collapse or flooding. What would it take to build such a warehouse legally? (IBRD and WB 2006: 15)

The case study adopted leads to avoiding valuing any security, health or environmental regulation, omitting to deal with pivotal features of the phenomena analysed and compromising seriously the analysis. A common remark is that DB is likely to be beset by poor understanding, which can lead to misuse (Arndt and Oman 2006; Bakvis 2006; Channel 2008). The remark seems to miss the point, ignoring that the ranking system and the normative approach *de facto* tends to undermine the role of regulation in areas such as security, health and environmental protection. The recommendation of 'don't mandate use of specific materials' (IBRD and WB 2006) in order to avoid the problem of not up-to-date buildings codes, seems particularly relevant here. Recent important literature (Kuesel et al. 2008) has highlighted the critical role of environmental concern in social and economic development. Moreover, the perspective adopted seems unable to cope with the problems and needs of a post-conflict environment: strong commitment in reconstruction of war-damaged buildings and infrastructures (Anand 2009); the presence of an uneven playing field having the market become less competitive during war time (Collier 1994) and the necessity of a comprehensive effort of town and infrastructure planning.

Concluding remarks

There are three pivotal aspects of entrepreneurship development which need to be considered in fragile and post-conflict states that are currently disregarded by the DB indicators.

The first is the ambiguous and ubiquitous role of entrepreneurship, which is neither positive nor negative in essence. The second is the complex and intertwined legacies between pre-conflict, conflict and post-conflict economic systems in fragile states. The third is the consequently central role played by incentives in economic systems, which cannot be reduced to lessen regulation and room for public intervention.

As far as the descriptive power of DB is concerned, three kinds of problems have been identified in this chapter. The first is about what the indicators are really measuring. The DB reports, as well as the background papers on which the indicators are constructed, lack definition of the phenomena analysed. A second issue concerns the short-term, private perspective adopted by the indicators. On the one hand, the indicators seem to measure aspects of business environment often linked to a short-term view of the business activity, disregarding a more sustainable perspective. This approach disregards the sources and the role of innovation, which is the essence of an entrepreneurial economy (see Chapter 2 by Lazonick and Chapter 13 by Nijkamp, this volume). Third, the risks of adopting only a private perspective are serious. Private and social benefits do not always converge and the role of the state, as discussed in this volume by Naudé (Chapter 11) and Lazonick (Chapter 12), may need to be more pro-active.

Notes

1. Reforms Simulator on DB website, which shows how a country's ranking would change if it reformed, and the agonistic terminology often employed (see, for example, WB and IFC 2008) are interesting examples of this approach.
2. DB considers environmental permits, statistical and health benefits registrations as socially desirable practices (DB 2004: 21). Any other procedure for starting up a business not only can limit competition, but also has dubious purposes and negative social outcomes, preventing 'people from getting out of poverty' (DB 2008a: 9).
3. Three studies by Djankov, Ganser, McLiesh; seven by Ramalho and Shleifer, four by Hart and La Porta, four by Lopez-de-Silanes, Freund, Pham and Botero (see also Djankov et al. 2002, 2003, 2007, 2008a, 2008b, 2008c, 2008d).

Part III
Policies, Institutions and Entrepreneurship

7
From the Managed to the Entrepreneurial Economy: Considerations for Developing and Emerging Economies
Roy Thurik

Introduction

Capital and labour are the essential input factors of large-scale production that dominated the business world in modern developed economies until the late 1980s. The increasing level of transaction costs (Coase 1937) incurred in large-scale production dictated increasing firm size over time. Indeed, statistical evidence points towards an increasing role of large enterprises in the economy in this period (Brock and Evans 1989; Caves 1982; Teece 1993). This development towards large-scale activity was visible in most modern developed economies. In this same period, the importance of self-employment and small business seemed to be waning. More recently, with knowledge[1] being recognized as a vital factor in endogenous growth models many scholars further predicted that this would render self-employment and small firms even more futile. How could they generate the means and insights to exploit R&D activities, to employ highly trained knowledge workers and to bring their efforts to the patent or even the commercial stage? Basically, scholars conclude that with the arrival of knowledge as a production factor the world of business becomes dominated by exporting giant firms.[2] This is the world of global markets, global products and global players. Small firms were thought to be at a disadvantage *vis-à-vis* larger firms because of the fixed costs of learning about foreign environments, communicating at long distances and negotiating with national governments. Consolidation seems to have become a law of nature, while the number of global players declines continuously.

Despite these forces, small and young firms have returned as the engine of economic and social development in highly developed economies. This return required a dramatic economic switch. Audretsch and Thurik (2001b, 2004) call this the switch from the managed economy to the entrepreneurial economy. The model of the *managed economy* is the political, social and economic response to an economy dictated by the forces of large-scale production, reflecting the predominance of the production factors of capital and (mostly unskilled) labour as the sources of competitive advantage. By contrast, the model of the *entrepreneurial economy* is the political, social and economic response to an economy increasingly dominated by knowledge as the production factor, but also by a different, yet complementary, factor that had been overlooked: entrepreneurship capital or the capacity to engage in and generate entrepreneurial activity. Without new and young firms it is not straightforward that knowledge or R&D always spills over to an environment where it leads to tangible products.[3]

This distinction between the models of the managed and entrepreneurial economy applies to both advanced and emerging economies although it has been set up to better understand the role of entrepreneurship, its drivers, its consequences and its policy requirements in the framework of advanced economies (Thurik 2009). In developing and emerging economies matters are complicated because both elements of the managed and entrepreneurial economies are often found side by side. The role of entrepreneurship in the mixed managed-entrepreneurial model of emerging economies is an under-researched phenomenon (Naudé 2010), not only because the role of entrepreneurship for economic development is complex and in a mixed economy even more so, but also because a typical model of mixed emerging economies does not exist. Emergence or non-emergence has many faces like that of success (East Asia, Eastern Europe) and that of failed or fragile states (Africa).

The purpose of this chapter is to present the distinction between the models of the managed and entrepreneurial economies and to explain why the model of the entrepreneurial economy is a better frame of reference than the model of the managed economy when explaining the role of entrepreneurship in contemporary, advanced (Thurik 2009) and emerging economies.

The managed economy

Until the late 1980s the large enterprise was the dominant form of business organization (Chandler 1990; Schumpeter 1942). The decrease in the role of small business in developed countries after the Second World War is well documented. This was the era of mass production where economies of scale became the decisive factor in dictating efficiency. In this era Galbraith (1956) proposed his idea of countervailing power, where the power of 'big business' is balanced by that of 'big labour' and 'big government'. There was no mention of 'small businesses'. The corporatist organization of societies goes very well together with the managed economy. Chandler (1977), Piore and Sabel (1984), Whyte (1960) and many others show that stability, continuity and homogeneity are the cornerstones of the managed economy. Large firms dominated this economy while Taylorism, Fordism and Keynesianism were central concepts. One of the best descriptions of the large enterprise and its domination of the managed economy is given in *The Economist* (22 December 2001: 76):

> They were hierarchical and bureaucratic organizations that were in the business of making long runs of standardized products. They introduced new and improved varieties with predictable regularity; they provided workers with life-time employment; and enjoyed fairly good relations with the giant trade unions.

Also until late in the 1980s small firms were viewed as a luxury, as something Western countries needed to ensure the infrastructure and safety of inner cities, to absorb part-time and low skilled labour, to help decentralization of decision-making and to safeguard the oldest of all business models, the family firm. One took for granted that they survived only at the cost of efficiency. It is not surprising that many scholars from many academic disciplines have sought to create insight into the issues surrounding this perceived tradeoff between economic efficiency and political and economic decentralization (Williamson 1975).[4] The alleged success of the communist, centrally led economies played a huge role in the prevailing way of thinking of that era. These economies thrived on uniform, stable mass production. It was straightforward that entrepreneurship was viewed as behaviour hostile to the communist system and declared criminal. How ironic that these economies broke down in the late 1980s due to a total lack of decentralized, experimental, free, risky and small-scale economic activities.

The emergence of the entrepreneurial economy

While business schools thrived training young people for jobs in large-scale operations, these same schools housed researchers establishing a revival of small-scale operations. In the late 1980s and early 1990s, fascinating data were published: the share of smallness varied in modern economies, but increased everywhere.[5] In the United States the average real GDP per firm increased by nearly two-thirds between 1947 and 1989 – from US$150,000 to US$245,000 – reflecting a trend towards larger enterprises and a decreasing importance of small firms. However, within the subsequent seven years it had fallen by about 14 per cent to US$210,000, reflecting a sharp reversal of this trend and the re-emergence of small business (Brock and Evans 1989). Similarly, small firms accounted for one-fifth of manufacturing sales in the United States in 1976, but by 1986 the sales share of small firms had risen to over one-quarter (Acs and Audretsch 1993).

Such a U-shaped relation between number of firms and time or inverse U-shaped relation between average firm size and time, seems to be ubiquitous. There is much debate about its meaning, but two things seem evident: the trough or the summit is not determined by the calendar year but by the level of economic development of a country. It is as if the trough or the summit marks a regime switch. The first can be best illustrated using the material of the Global Entrepreneurship Monitor (GEM). The second is documented by Audretsch and Thurik (2001b, 2004) distinguishing between the managed and the entrepreneurial economy.

Table 7.1 shows the results of a linear regression estimation where the total entrepreneurial activity (TEA) index is 'explained' using the level of economic development of countries. The TEA index is the number of 'nascent' and new entrepreneurs as a percentage of the population between 18 and 65 years of age.[6] Following Wennekers et al. (2005), two measures of the level of economic development are used: per capita income (in PPP) and the innovation index as computed by the authoritative World Economic Forum (WEF 2007).[7] We test for the presence of a U-curved relation by including the 'squared' level of economic development. Using the 2007 observations from 42 countries we observe that the results are similar to those of the 2002 data used in Wennekers et al. (2005): there is a strong U-shaped relation between entrepreneurship

Table 7.1   Relating total entrepreneurial activity (2007) to the level of economic development, as measured by per capita income and innovative capacity

	Model 1: U-curved relationship with per capita income	Model 2: U-curved relationship with innovative capacity
Constant	21.4*** (7.2)	57.4*** (3.0)
Per capita income	–1.01*** (3.5)	–
Per capita income, squared	0.016*** (2.8)	–
GCR innovative capacity index		–21.2** (2.2)
GCR innovative capacity index, squared		2.15* (1.9)
Adjusted R^2	0.335	0.232
Observations	42	42

Note: Absolute t-values between parentheses. *** significant at 0.01 level; ** significant at 0.05 level; * significant at 0.10 level.

and level of economic development. The U-shape seems somewhat stronger in the case of per capita income (t-value is 2.8) than in the case of the innovation index (t-value is 1.9). The stability of the U-shape over the years (the relation is established both in 2002 and 2007) provides support for the idea that something fundamental happened in the economy and that this has to do with the role of entrepreneurship capital. I am aware that I attempt to draw conclusions with a time dimension using (cross-section) country data without one. This is allowed because the 42 countries have strongly diverging levels of economic development so that the temporal effect is implicit: countries tend to grow in terms of economic development.

The values of the adjusted R^2 (0.335 and 0.232) are certainly not low since this measure of 'explanation' on the right hand side of the equation is based upon just one phenomenon. However, obviously, there are many more phenomena influencing the relation between the level of entrepreneurship and that of economic development. These phenomena should capture all kinds of economic, technological, demographic and institutional differences. Wennekers et al. (2005) show that correction for several of these phenomena does not affect the U-shape relation. In Figure 7.1 a picture is drawn of the data and the estimated relation of model 1 where TEA (prevalence of early stage entrepreneurial activity) is related with per capita income (GDP per capita, in PPP).[8]

Above, I emphasize the (somewhat complicated) time serial interpretation of the correlation between entrepreneurship and economic

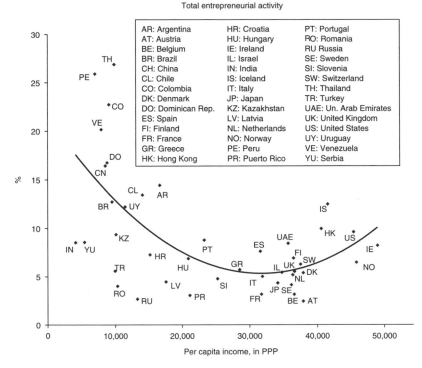

Figure 7.1 Total entrepreneurial activity (TEA) and GDP
Source: Bosma et al. (2008).

development. One can also look at it in a straightforward cross-sectional
fashion discriminating between emerging and developed economies.
Obviously, emerging economies (<US$25,000 per capita income) are on
the left hand side of Figure 7.1 while developed economies (>US$25,000
per capita income) are on the right hand side. We see that the level of
development has a different correlation with TEA for both groups of
economies. In the first group there seems to be a negative correlation
whereas in the second there seems to be a positive one. I am inclined to
carefully conclude that while developed economies should concentrate
on the switch from the managed towards the entrepreneurial economy,
emerging economies should also try and nurture the managed one. (See
also Naudé (2010) for a discussion of the relation between entrepreneurship and the level of economic development in the opposite poles of the
development spectrum.[9])

Contrasting the entrepreneurial and managed economy models

The occurrence of a regime switch suggests two contrasting models with a differing role of entrepreneurship. The model of the managed economy revolves around the links between stability, specialization, homogeneity, scale, certainty and predictability on the one hand and economic growth on the other. By contrast, the model of the entrepreneurial economy focuses on the links between flexibility, turbulence, diversity, novelty, innovation, linkages and clustering on the one hand and economic growth on the other. The models of the managed and the entrepreneurial economy can be compared by distinguishing between different groups of characteristics, including underlying forces, external environment characteristics, internal or firm characteristics and policy characteristics, as discussed later.[10]

Underlying forces

The first group of characteristics consists of three important underlying forces: localization versus globalization, change versus continuity and jobs *and* high wages versus jobs *or* high wages.

In the model of the managed economy, production labour and capital are the dominant production factors. The more mobile capital moves to where the cheapest labour (software) is or such labour moves towards capital once it is invested in plants (hardware). Knowledge is the dominant factor of production in the model of the entrepreneurial economy. It is more than just hard technical and scientific knowledge. It also comprises soft aspects like creativity, the ability to communicate and emotional intelligence. The competitive advantage in the entrepreneurial economy is driven by innovative activity, while knowledge spillovers are an important source of this innovative activity. Hence, in the model of the entrepreneurial economy, local proximity is important, with the region being the most important locus of economic activity, as knowledge tends to be developed in the context of localized production networks embedded in innovative clusters.

The model of the managed economy focuses more on continuity, while the model of the entrepreneurial economy thrives on change and even provokes it. Although innovation is present under the conditions of both change and continuity, the nature and the locus of innovative activity differ. The well-known distinction between incremental and radical innovations is helpful to elucidate this. Innovations are considered incremental when they are compatible with the core competence and technological trajectory of the firm or the industry. By contrast, a radical innovation can be defined as extending beyond the boundaries of the core competence and the technological trajectory of the firm or the industry. In the model of the managed economy change is absorbed within a given technological paradigm: the successful firm excels at incremental innovation. By contrast, in the model of the entrepreneurial economy, the capacity to break out of the technological lock-in imposed by existing paradigms is enhanced by the ability of economic agents to start new firms. Thus, incremental innovative activity along with diffusion plays a more important role in the model of the managed economy. While often requiring large investments in R&D, this type of innovative activity generates incremental changes in products along the existing technological trajectories.

One of the most conspicuous policy options in the model of the managed economy is that unemployment can be reduced only at the cost of lower wages. In the model of the entrepreneurial economy high employment can be combined with high wages and a low wage level does not necessarily imply high employment. An indication of the absence of a tradeoff between high wages and employment is the large variance in unemployment rates across OECD countries, although corporate downsizing has been ubiquitous. Small firms in general, and new ventures in particular, are the engine not only of employment creation,[11] but also of productivity (Erken et al. 2008). This is not due to the wage differential between small and large firms. On the contrary, the growth of new firms may not only generate greater employment, but also higher wages. New firm growth ensures that higher employment does not come at a cost of lower wages, but rather the opposite – higher wages. Under the model of the managed economy the job creation by small firms is associated with lower wages. Hence, while small firms generate employment at a cost of lower wages in the model of the managed economy, in the entrepreneurial economy model small firms may create both more jobs and higher wages (Acs and Fitzroy et al. 2002; Scarpetta et al. 2002).

The relevance for emerging countries lies in the idea that they have to create incentives for the knowledge embodied in their well-educated citizens to stay in the home country and exploit their knowledge in a (new) business instead of moving abroad. An example of a country which seems to be successful in doing so is India which houses numerous IT specialists doing work for clients across the globe, MBAs involved in number crunching for big investment banks in London and New York and so on. The opposite is true for a country like Poland which has seen a massive exodus of skilled workers which has actually forced local business to in-source labour from countries like Ukraine.

External environment

The second group of characteristics contrasts the external environment characteristics in the models of the managed and the entrepreneurial economies. Turbulence, diversity and heterogeneity are central to the model of the entrepreneurial economy. By contrast, stability, specialization and homogeneity are the cornerstones of the model of the managed economy.

Note, however, that a part of the entrepreneurial economy can also be 'exported' to another economy. Saxenian (2006) describes the concept of the 'new argonauts' by which she means highly skilled foreign employees who return to their home country to start up their own business exploiting knowledge and ideas that they have obtained in their previous employment. These 'exports' can influence this managed economy to become more sophisticated or more entrepreneurial or to create an entrepreneurial economy alongside the managed one.

Stability in the model of the managed economy results from a homogeneous product demand, resulting in a low turnover rate of jobs, workers and firms. The model of the entrepreneurial economy is characterized by a high degree of turbulence. Each year many new firms are started and only a subset of these firms survive. Nelson and Winter (1982) argue that the role of diversity and selection is at the heart of generating change. This holds for both the managed and the entrepreneurial economy models. However, what differs in these models is the management and organization of the process by which diversity is created as well as the selection mechanism. In the model of the managed economy research activities are organized and scheduled in departments devoted to developing novel products and services. The management of change fits into what Nelson and Winter (1982) refer to as the 'firm's routines'. The ability of incumbent businesses to manage the process of change pre-empts many opportunities for entrepreneurs to start new firms, resulting in a low start-up rate and a stable industrial structure. In the model of the entrepreneurial economy the process of generating new ideas, both within and outside of R&D laboratories, creates a turbulent environment with many opportunities for entrepreneurs to start new firms based upon different and changing opinions about different and changing ideas. In short, the innovation process in the managed economy is closed whereas that in the entrepreneurial economy is open.

Several theoretical arguments have suggested that the degree of diversity versus that of specialization accounts for differences in rates of growth and technological development (Acs and Fitzroy et al. 2002). Specialization of industry activities is associated with lower transaction costs and, therefore, greater (static) efficiency. Diversity of activities is said to facilitate the exchange of new ideas and, therefore, greater innovative activity and (dynamic) efficiency. Because knowledge spillovers are an important source of innovative activity, diversity is a prerequisite in the model of the entrepreneurial economy where lower transaction costs are preferably sacrificed for greater opportunities for knowledge spillover. In the model of the managed economy, there are fewer gains from knowledge spillovers. The higher transaction costs associated with diversity yield little room for opportunities in terms of increased innovative activity, making specialization preferable in the model of the managed economy.

The tradeoff between diversity and specialization focuses on firms while that between homogeneity and heterogeneity focuses on individuals. Modern communication and transport techniques destroyed many barriers. In a heterogeneous population of the entrepreneurial economy, communication across individuals tends to be more difficult and costly than in a homogeneous population: transaction costs are higher and efficiency is lower. At the same time, new ideas are more likely to emerge from communication in a heterogeneous than in a homogeneous world. Although the likelihood of communication is lower in a heterogeneous population, communication in this environment is more prone to produce novelty and innovation.[12] The lower transaction costs resulting from a homogeneous population in the model of the managed economy are not associated with high opportunity costs, because knowledge spillovers are relatively unimportant in generating innovative activity. However, knowledge spillovers are a driving force in the model of the entrepreneurial economy, offsetting the higher transaction costs associated with a heterogeneous population.

How firms function

The third group of characteristics contrasts firm behaviour in the models of the managed and the entrepreneurial economy: control versus motivation, firm transaction versus market exchange, competition and cooperation as substitutes versus complements and scale versus flexibility.

Under the model of the managed economy, labour is considered as indistinguishable from the other input factors. It is considered homogeneous and easily replaceable. Firms organize their labour according to the principles of command and control. Under the model of the entrepreneurial economy, the command and control approach to labour is less effective, as the competitive advantage of the advanced industrialized countries tends to be based on creating and validating new knowledge. This is accomplished by motivating workers to facilitate the discovery process and implementation of new ideas. Management styles emphasize the nurturing of interpersonal relationships, facilitating rather than supervising employees. In the entrepreneurial economy model, the focus of activities is on exploring new abilities, rather than exploiting existing ones.

Transaction costs economics distinguishes between exchange via the market and intra-firm transactions. Both Coase (1937) and Williamson (1975) emphasize that uncertainty and imperfect information increase the cost of intra-firm transactions. Knight (1921) argues that low uncertainty, combined with transparency and predictability of information, makes intra-firm transactions efficient relative to market exchange. In the managed economy model, where there is a high degree of certainty and predictability of information, transactions within firms tend to be more efficient than market exchange. By contrast, in the entrepreneurial economy, model market transactions are more efficient because of the high uncertainty. Since the mid-1970s the economic arena has become increasingly uncertain and unpredictable (Carlsson 1989), witnessed by a decrease in both mean firm size and the extent of vertical integration and conglomeration.

Models of competition generally assume that firms behave autonomously, whereas models of cooperation assume pervasive linkages among firms. These linkages take various forms, including joint ventures, strategic alliances and (in)formal networks etc. In the model of the managed economy, competition and cooperation are viewed as being substitutes. Firms are vertically integrated and primarily compete in product markets. Cooperation between firms in the product market reduces the number of competitors and reduces the degree of competition. In the model of the entrepreneurial economy, firms tend to be vertically independent and specialized in the product market. The higher degree of vertical disintegration under the model of the entrepreneurial economy implies a replacement of internal transactions within a large vertically integrated corporation with cooperation among independent firms. At the same time, there are more firms, resulting in an increase in both the competitive and cooperative interfaces. The likelihood of a firm competing or cooperating with other firms is higher in the entrepreneurial economy model.

Under the model of the managed economy, costs-per-unit are reduced through exploiting economies of scale. In product lines and industries where a large scale of production translates into a substantial reduction in average costs, large firms will have an economic advantage, leading to a concentrated industrial structure. Stable and predictable products, consumer tastes and lines of resource provision contributed to the success of the exploitation of economies of scale. The importance of scale economies has certainly contributed to the emergence and dominance of large corporations in heavy manufacturing industries, such as steel, automobiles and aluminium (Chandler 1977). The alternative source of reduced average costs is flexibility (Teece 1993), characterizing the entrepreneurial economy model. Industries where demand for particular products is shifting constantly require a flexible system of production that can meet such a whimsical demand.

Government policy

The final group of contrasting characteristics of the models of the entrepreneurial economy and the managed economy refers to government policy (Audretsch et al. 2007), including the goals of policy (enabling versus constraining), the target of policy (inputs versus outputs), the locus of policy (local versus national) and financing policy (entrepreneurial versus incumbent).

Under the model of the managed economy, public policy towards the firm is essentially constraining in nature. There are three general types of public policy towards business: antitrust policy (competition policy), regulation and public ownership. All three of these policy approaches restrict the firms' freedom to contract. Under the model of the managed economy, the relevant policy question is: how can the government prevent firms from abusing their market power? The entrepreneurial economy model is characterized by a different policy question: how can governments create an environment fostering the success and viability of firms? Whereas the major issues in the model of the managed economy are concerns about excess profits and abuses of market dominance, in the model of the entrepreneurial economy the issues of international competitiveness, growth and employment are important. In the managed economy model the emphasis is on constraining market power through regulation, whereas the focus in the entrepreneurial economy model is on stimulating firm – or rather industrial – development and performance through enabling policies.

Striking examples of how not to deal with this topic are abundant in almost every emerging country. The most obvious one is Venezuela which forced foreign investors to accept significantly less advantageous conditions for existing concessions in the oil sector. In addition, it has renationalized oil, cement and steel companies. Bolivia also nationalized its oil and gas industry. Other telling examples are regulation in Mexico pertaining to telecommunication, electricity and oil. Argentina has been trying to prescribe to companies what prices they should ask for their products as witnessed when the former president Kirchner urged Argentinians not to go to the Shell gas stations when the company was trying to pass on higher oil prices. Government intervention and efforts to minimize foreign influence do not only mean that the country foregoes opportunities for knowledge spillovers, but they will also have a negative effect on decisions regarding potential new foreign investments in the country which will adversely impact diversity and heterogeneity. Brazil created independent regulators in many sectors during the privatization boom of the 1990s. Since the current president took office in 2003, a different, more interventionist, approach has prevailed. An important example is the introduction of HD-television in Brazil where the ministry took an active role in the decision as to which standard the country should adopt. The government decided on the Japanese ISDB standard in return for Japanese investments in the Brazilian semiconductor industry, financing and technology transfers.

Governmental policy can involve targeting selected outputs in the production process versus targeting selected inputs. Because of the relative certainty regarding markets and products in the model of the managed economy, the appropriate policy response is to target outputs. Specific industries and firms can be promoted through government programmes. Whereas in the model of the managed economy production is based on the traditional inputs of land, labour and capital, in the entrepreneurial economy model it is mainly based on knowledge input. There is uncertainty about what products should be produced, how and by whom. This high degree of uncertainty makes it difficult to select appropriate outcomes and increases the likelihood of targeting the wrong firms and industries. Hence, the appropriate policy in the model of the entrepreneurial economy is to target inputs and in particular those inputs related to the creation and commercialization of knowledge. Government becomes the facilitator creating links and networks, creating forms of social innovation, proposing incentives to firms and knowledge institutes, stimulating special and functional flexibility of labour, etc.

The uncertainty associated with the outcomes of a process where knowledge is considered to be an important input means that policy-making is more difficult in this situation. Many emerging countries are lacking the necessary knowledge and experience for proper policy-making. Good examples of a natural way to overcome this problem can be found in Israel, Taiwan and India where highly skilled citizens have returned from abroad to set up new innovative businesses or invest venture capital in other start-ups. These individuals often take on the role of advisers to the government thus spreading the knowledge for input oriented policies (Saxenian 2006).

The locus of policy is a third characteristic where the models of the managed and entrepreneurial economy differ. Under the model of the managed economy the appropriate locus of policy-making is the national or federal level. The most important policy-making institutions tend to be located at the national level, although the targeted recipients of policy may be localized in one or a few regions. Under the model of the entrepreneurial economy, government policy towards business tends to be decentralized and regional or local in nature. This distinction in the locus of policy results from two factors (see also Chapter 13 by Nijkamp, this volume). First, because the competitive source of economic activity in the model of the entrepreneurial economy is knowledge, which tends to be localized in regional clusters, public policy requires an understanding of regional-specific characteristics and idiosyncrasies. Second, the motivation underlying government policy in the entrepreneurial economy is growth and the creation of jobs, to be achieved mainly through new venture creation. New firms are usually small and pose no oligopolistic threat on national or international markets. In the model of the entrepreneurial economy, no external costs – in the form of higher prices – are imposed on consumers in the national economy as is the case in the model of the managed economy. Fostering local economies imposes no cost on consumers in the national economy.

The question is whether local governments are actually equipped to design and implement local policy which stimulates businesses to capitalize on local advantages and mitigate local disadvantages. In addition, it is important to assess whether an appropriate system of checks and balances is in place to ensure that local policy-makers act in the most efficient manner.

Numerous illustrative examples can be found. I will mention three of them. Mexico is a country where decentralization has increased rapidly in the last decade although the necessary framework was lacking. As a result the effects of decentralization have not materialized as expected. However, for example, the Universidad Technológico de Monterrey in Mexico is cooperating with regional government and (potential) foreign investors to assess skills needed by business in the region and adapt its curriculum and its enrolment procedures in order to provide appropriate skilled labour. In addition, the university works together with the corporate world to create new products and new companies. The second example relates to the Baltic Sea region. After the fall of the Berlin wall, the countries in this area joined forces to study how cooperation between such diverse nations could lead to the development of a highly entrepreneurial region. Connecting economic actors through networking and information sharing makes it possible to enhance business and FDI opportunities, thus helping the poorer countries to catch up more quickly and the richer to penetrate a large market more easily (OECD 2007). However, the emerging countries in the region, such as Russia, Poland and the Baltic states, are still lacking the governance structures to reap the full benefits from this regional initiative despite extensive support from their neighbours which are more advanced in terms of governance.

An interesting example of localization is the phenomenon of the special economic zones in China. These are geographic entities allowed to pioneer the process of opening up to foreign investment since the 1980s. They integrate science with industry and trade. A different governance system and special rules were set up to ensure that local governments to adapt policy-making towards achieving the strategic goals that the central government set for these particular areas.

Finally, financing policies for business vary between the two models. Under the model of the managed economy, the systems of finance provide the existing companies with just liquidity for investment. Liquidity is seen as a homogeneous input factor. The model of the entrepreneurial economy requires a system of finance that is different from that in the model of the managed economy.[13] In the model of the managed economy, there is certainty in outputs as well as inputs. There is a strong connection between banks and firms in their joint efforts to foster growth. In the entrepreneurial economy model, certainty has given way to uncertainty requiring different financial institutions. In particular the venture and informal capital markets, providing finance for high risk and innovative new firms, play an important role in the model of the entrepreneurial economy. In this model liquidity loses its homogeneous image and is often coupled with forms of advice, knowledge and changing levels of involvement (business angels, incubators etc.).

Foreign financial institutions have acquired or set up businesses in many emerging countries. In many cases this has meant that local banks have lost most of their large corporate business to these foreign parties. Emerging countries could enhance the entrepreneurial part of their economy by stimulating local financial institutions to adopt modern ways of financing innovative new local business.

Concluding remarks

The model of the managed economy dominated most advanced economies until the late 1980s. It was based on relative certainty in inputs and outputs. Large plants and the ingenious interplay between man and machine were the cornerstones of this economy. Economies of scale increased dramatically. The model of the managed economy brought unprecedented growth. The joint effect of the computer and telecommunications revolutions and globalization has reduced the ability of the managed economies of Western Europe and North America to grow and create jobs. On the one hand, there is the advent of new competition from low cost, but relatively high educated and skill-intensive, countries in Central and Eastern Europe as well as in Asia. On the other hand, the telecommunications and computer revolutions have drastically reduced the cost of shifting, not just capital, but also information out of the high cost locations of Europe and into lower cost locations (Audretsch et al. 2010). Taken together, this joint effect implies that economic activity in high cost locations is no longer compatible with routinized tasks. Rather, the competitive advantage of high cost locations shifted to knowledge-based activities and in particular intellectual search activities. These activities cannot be costlessly transferred around the globe. Knowledge as an input into economic activity is inherently different from land, labour and capital. It is characterized by high uncertainty, high asymmetries across people and high transaction costs. An economy where knowledge is the main source of competitive advantage is more consistent with the model of the entrepreneurial economy. The essence of the model of the entrepreneurial economy is not just creating knowledge, but also exploiting it.

I do not want to argue that the managed economy is totally obsolete. There are large parts of modern advanced and emerging economies where routinized production is essential or where closed forms of innovation are successful. There are large parts where exploitation of what exists is important and where exploration of what does not exist is irrelevant. The modern economy is an economy of which the constellation differs drastically from that of 20 years ago. There is much to describe and to discover about the fundamental changes of the last twenty years.

Furthermore, there is a great deal to discover about what good policy practices are under the model of the entrepreneurial advanced economy (Audretsch et al. 2007). It seems obvious what the optimal use is of a machine, a running belt or an entire factory in the managed economy. But it is unclear what the value is of knowledge with its many soft and latent aspects such as creativity, communication and emotions. I hope that the above fourteen characteristics with their emphasis on the role of entrepreneurship capital may be helpful understanding the modern economy.

Emerging economies are in an inherently more complicated situation as can be summarized in the following points. First, we should acknowledge that while developed economies switch from the managed to the entrepreneurial economy, emerging economies face an even more challenging task. Just as emerging economies are a mix of an advanced and a developing one, they are also a mix of a managed and an entrepreneurial one. For instance, Indonesia has many traits of a managed economy considering that it has a history of promoting certain industries while constraining many others and policy-making is often centralistic. However, a good example of entrepreneurial policy is Indonesia's attitude towards fostering the development of small and medium enterprises (SMEs). Typically SMEs in Indonesia, and particularly Java, tend to cluster. According to Berry et al. (2002) a number of such firms have become successful exporters of rattan furniture, wood furniture and garments using the strength of subcontracting relationships with foreign investors and buyers as well as agglomeration economies achieved by clustering in selected locations. Berry et al. (2002) show that Indonesian SMEs participating in clusters are more likely to export and to adopt product and process innovations as compared to more dispersed and isolated firms. This is a direct result of the *Program Pembinaan dan Pengembangan Industri Kecil* which was started in the late 1970s to stimulate geographic concentration of small businesses. Such a concentration facilitates relatively cheap training in basic entrepreneurial skills for many SMEs at the same time.

Second, emerging economies usually have not fully finished the consolidation stage of the managed economy. Examples are inefficient and highly fragmented retail and hotel and catering sectors. Nevertheless, they have to try to develop or import parts of a yet newer economy.

Third, the managed part of an emerging economy goes well together with a concentrated power system where conformity and homogeneity play significant roles. This power system, combined with usually weaker democratic pressures in emerging economies, may frustrate the partial transition to an entrepreneurial economy where originality and diversity play important roles.

Fourth, a high degree of business informality means that while the state is confronted with missed revenues and information about the consequences of its regulatory initiatives, businesses underperform when it comes to access to formal credit sources and to legal protection.

Fifth, a drain of the brain, the creative and the entrepreneurial ones is no easy starting point for fostering a newer entrepreneurial economy.

Sixth, and hardly discussed above, there are diverse ways in which entrepreneurship can be detrimental to economic development, such as through its perverse allocation towards activities which are personally profitable but socially undesirable or through low quality entrepreneurship generating negative externalities (Naudé 2008). This effect can be prominent in emerging economies of many shapes as the Russian and the African examples show.

Obviously, many of these disadvantages are offset by advantages of emerging economies such as the opportunities of learning from the mistakes of the developed economies (catching-up mechanisms, returning highly skilled workers) and the informality of the culture (micro-credits). The variety among the emerging economies necessitates a more precise analysis than given above about what should be done to promote elements of the new entrepreneurial economy.

Acknowledgement

Madeleine Kemna and Matthijs van der Loos provided useful comments. This paper has been written in cooperation with the research programme SCALES, carried out by EIM and financed by the Dutch Ministry of Economic Affairs.

Notes

1. Being measured in terms of R&D, human capital and patented inventions.
2. Vernon (1970) predicts increased globalization to present an even more hostile environment to small business. Caves (1982) argues that the additional costs of knowledge activity constitute an important reason for expecting foreign investments to be mainly an activity of large firms. Chandler (1990) concludes that one has to be big in order to compete globally.
3. This process is known as 'breaking the knowledge filter': entrepreneurs are willing to spend costs to use existing but outside knowledge for their own production process. They provide a vital link between knowledge and productivity gains. See Acs et al. (2004) and Audretsch et al. (2009). Erken et al. (2008) show that entrepreneurship, next to R&D, plays a role explaining

'total factor productivity' for OECD countries in a recent period. See also Braunerhjelm et al. (2010).

4. These scholars have produced a large number of studies focusing mainly on three questions: (i) what are the gains to size and large-scale production? (ii) what are the economic and welfare implications of an oligopolistic market structure, that is, is economic performance promoted or reduced in an industry with just a handful of large-scale firms? and (iii) given the overwhelming evidence that large-scale production and economic concentration is associated with increased efficiency, what are the public policy implications?

5. Acs and Audretsch (1993); Birch (1987); Brock and Evans (1989); and Loveman and Sengenberger (1991).

6. Nascent entrepreneurs are busy setting up a business and have taken important steps. New entrepreneurs have businesses of less than three and a half years old.

7. The twelfth dimension of the so-called Global Competitive Index (WEF 2007: 20) is used.

8. By reporting the regression results of Table 7.1, I do not want to suggest that they describe the way entrepreneurship influences economic development. The relation between entrepreneurship and economic development is very complex. There are two causalities, lagged effects, measurement issues and several opposite effects (Thurik et al. 2008). I just want to emphasize that a regime switch occurred.

9. Naudé (2008) also discusses the threefold role of entrepreneurship in economic development: providing a long run effect breaking Malthusian stagnation, stimulating transformation from an agricultural to a post-industrial economy and generating innovation related productivity gains.

10. See Audretsch and Thurik (2001b, 2004) for more examples and references. Also see Audretsch (2007) for a brilliant and proficient but less organized account of the switch from the managed to the entrepreneurial economy.

11. See the 2008 special issue of *Small Business Economics*, 30(1) and in particular Fritsch (2008).

12. The concept of 'optimal cognitive distance' is connected to this phenomenon (Nooteboom et al. 2007).

13. The role of liquidity constraints should not be exaggerated in the entrepreneurial economy (Grilo and Thurik 2008).

8
The Impact of Institutions on Entrepreneurship in Developing Countries

José Ernesto Amorós

Introduction

There is a growing body of research investigating the relationship between entrepreneurship[1] and basic regional and national economic variables such as aggregate income and competitiveness (e.g. Acs and Armington 2004; Blanchflower 2000; Carree et al. 2002; Carree and Thurik 2003; van Stel et al. 2005; Wennekers et al. 2005). Empirical contributions based on the Global Entrepreneurship Monitor (GEM) research initiative show that variations in economic growth rates can be explained by differing rates of entrepreneurship (Reynolds et al. 1999; Zacharakis et al. 2000). As such the creation of new ventures[2] may contribute to the economic performance of countries and regions because entrepreneurial activities introduce innovation, create competition and enhance rivalry (Audretsch and Keilbach 2004; Wong et al. 2005). Nevertheless, the impact of these entrepreneurial efforts on economic growth differs not only between countries at similar levels of development (Carree et al. 2002, 2007) but also between countries at different stages of development (Acs and Amorós 2008; Wennekers et al. 2005), as well as among regions within a single country (Acs and Armington 2004; Belso-Martínez 2005; Hall and Sobel 2008).

In this context, entrepreneurship as the engine of economic growth is related to a combination of other determinants such as education levels, business climate and legal and political conditions (Bowen and De Clercq 2008; Grilo and Irigoyen 2006; Grilo and Thurik 2005; Hwang and Powell 2005; van Stel et al. 2005). Some of these 'macro-level' factors[3] can explain the *entrepreneurship rates* and also the *type* of entrepreneurial activities between countries and regions (Bowen and De Clercq 2008). Researchers have developed frameworks to explain some of the macro- (and micro-) determinants of entrepreneurship activities or entrepreneurial process (Reynolds et al. 1999, 2005; Sobel 2008; Verheul et al. 2002; Wennekers and Thurik 1999). These frameworks consider institutional factors to be the determinants of entrepreneurial dynamics.

This chapter focuses on a crucial determinant of entrepreneurship in developing (and advanced) countries: the *quality of institutions*.[4] Specifically, we explore the question: what kinds of institutions are related to the phenomenon of entrepreneurship in developing countries?

We focus on developing countries as there is a consensus that low and middle income countries have a relatively low degree of institutional quality compared to more advanced economies. This chapter therefore attempts, by contrasting developed and developing countries, to examine whether the quality of institutions affects the entrepreneurial dynamics.

Institutions, institutional quality and entrepreneurship

In economics, early contributions by Joseph Schumpeter (1911/1934, 1950), Frank Knight (1971) and Israel Kirzner (1973) represent not only examples of groundbreaking research but at the same time constitute the essential foundations for many theories of entrepreneurship. Developments in economics in the last few decades have also led to very interesting new formal models of entrepreneurship (Audretsch 2007; Audretsch and Thurik 2001b). Reynolds et al. (1999) introduce a general model, which argues that established business activity at the national level varies with the number of variables denominated as 'general national framework conditions', while entrepreneurial activity varies with the 'entrepreneurial framework conditions'. These conditions are related to the social, cultural and political context of a country, but the entrepreneurial framework conditions include the specific policy and governmental programmes that enhance the entrepreneurship dynamics of a country.[5] It is, however, remarkable that as Boettke and Coyne (2006: 124) note, 'only recently have economists begun to pay attention to the role of institutions and how they influence entrepreneurial behaviour'.

Government institutions can clearly influence the rate of entrepreneurship (see specifically also Chapters 11 and 12, this volume). Public policies can basically determine the entrepreneurial dynamics of a country or region by introducing specific entrepreneurship policies as well as by creating a general institutional structure conducive to entrepreneurship (Sobel et al. 2007). There is a flourishing body of literature examining the role of specific policies on entrepreneurship (Audretsch et al. 2007). This theoretical and empirical research reviews the characteristics of different entrepreneurship policies and evaluates their implementation (Hoffmann 2007; Stevenson and Lundström 2005, 2007). Other researchers also evaluate the impact of these policies but include extended criticisms about their effectiveness – or ineffectiveness (Li 2002; Parker 2007; Storey 2005). This body of literature is mainly based on developed country experiences. At this point it is important to note that the emphasis of this work on institutional quality is related to the preceding approaches regarding specific entrepreneurship policies. These policies 'emerge' from the general governmental environment and the interaction with this environment is a central determinant of entrepreneurship.[6]

As stated before, the second type of government influence related to institutional structures that determine the 'rules of the game' for entrepreneurship is less studied and is again focused mainly on the more developed economies (Sobel et al. 2007).

The efficient allocation of resources in an economy (in this case, the allocation of entrepreneurial talent) is expected to be quite different under different institutional structures. Institutions, as the basic set of constraints within which economic agents interact, will have a crucial effect on an economy. Different institutional environments, *ceteris paribus* (i.e. differences in the quality of institutions), have different effects on the level and/or type of entrepreneurship. An analogy may be useful here. Consider economic interaction as a game; it becomes quite evident that the rules of the game can shape, in a crucial sense, the outcome of the interaction (Buchanan 1991). Alternative structures of the rules can then be expected to lead to different outcomes.

But how does the quality of institutions in reality affect entrepreneurial activities and the decision of whether or not to become an entrepreneur? Following the basic tenets of neoclassical economic theory, entrepreneurship in this context must commence from an individualistic perspective. It is the economic agent who decides whether or not to undertake entrepreneurial activities or any other type of wage earning activities. It is the individual's rationale that determines the allocation of inputs across different activities when he or she is faced with a given budgetary constraint or a given environmental opportunity. Then, a model of labour choice can explain entrepreneurship.[7] Risk aversion also plays a role in the decision to be entrepreneur. For instance, Iyigun and Owen (1998) model a situation in which the accumulation of entrepreneurial and other professional skills cannot be undertaken simultaneously (although they both constitute elements of an aggregate production function). To the extent that entrepreneurship is a risky activity, agents are less likely to be entrepreneurs when good, safer alternatives are available. The model by Kihlstrom and Laffont (1979) differs from the above in terms of the attitudes of agents towards risk, where under conditions of general equilibrium with agents maximizing their expected utility, it is noted that agents who are less risk averse will tend to be entrepreneurs.

Note that the quality of institutions critically matters in this context. For instance, it is well known that if 'prices' do not convey accurate information as to the relative scarcities of different 'products' (Hayek 1945), then the allocation of resources will be misguided. It is evident that this analysis can be extended to the problem of the allocation of entrepreneurial effort (or, more generally, the allocation of labour). At the same time, risk perceptions and assessments can also be affected by institutional quality. An economy where the institutional framework does not safeguard an agent's economic freedom tends to be riskier in an objective sense,[8] affecting once again the manner in which the economy resolves its resource allocation problem. These cases represent particularly illustrative instances in which institutional variables dramatically influence the determinants of entrepreneurship.

To the extent that economic relations are carried out in a context where transactions costs are important, the significance of these latter variables are also relevant in the decision of whether to engage in entrepreneurial activities. As the costs of determining and enforcing contracts and of obtaining information on different market conditions are influenced by the quality of institutions (North 1990), this is another mechanism through which institutions matter for entrepreneurship.

The fact that institutional quality has important effects on the allocation of entrepreneurial talent in a given economy is highlighted by Baumol (1990). The work of Baumol is one of the first to argue that differences in entrepreneurship are the result of varying institutional elements across countries or regions. His contribution about the concept of productive, unproductive and destructive entrepreneurship not only links the rates (or level) of entrepreneurial activities to a specific context, but also relates the allocation of entrepreneurial efforts to institutional variables. Baumol's conjectures explain that countries (or regions) with better institutions have more productive entrepreneurship and less unproductive (or destructive) entrepreneurship. The

starting point of his work is the attractive egalitarian world where entrepreneurial talents are uniformly distributed across the population, but
where such talent is only conducive to economic growth, in terms of
it being harnessed productively under certain institutional conditions.
When the incentive structure of an economy leads agents to unproductive (rent-seeking) activities, we can expect that agents will follow suit.
For example, in a world where the largest 'prizes' are awarded to those
who undertake unproductive activities, the level of productive entrepreneurship will necessarily be smaller. Boettke and Coyne (2003) have
observed that entrepreneurship manifests itself differently across alternative institutional regimes and that only some of these expressions are
consistent with economic development.

In concluding this section, it is important to explain that some of the
arguments reviewed here have been the subject of empirical research,
which tends to corroborate that institutions (or, more accurately, institutional quality) have an important effect on economic outcomes.[9] But
only a few studies have inquired about the link between institutional
quality and entrepreneurship (Sobel 2008). Thus, it should be stated
again quite emphatically that institutional quality is an element that
should be present in any model and theory proposing to explain entrepreneurship. In this sense, the general research question is: if institutional variables are different depending on the country's degree of
development, does this situation affect the rates and types of entrepreneurship in a different manner? With an empirical approach, I explore
the relationship between some entrepreneurial rates utilizing the GEM
data and certain measures of the quality of institutions, using the World
Bank approach.

Empirical model

Data sources

The well-known GEM project represents a fundamental underpinning
to provide harmonized, internationally comparable data to evaluate
entrepreneurship activity across different countries. Also, GEM is useful
for studying the effects and the determinants of entrepreneurship. It is
generally recognized in the GEM reports that institutional quality plays
a key role as a determinant of entrepreneurship (Reynolds et al. 2005).
By the end of 2007, 60 different countries had participated in GEM, 32
of which are considered to be developing and emerging countries (see
the Table 8A.1 for a complete list and classification). GEM's database contains various entrepreneurial indicators that have been constructed on

the basis of a survey known as the 'adult population survey'. This survey helps GEM to estimate the percentage of the adult population (generally people between 18 and 64 years old) who are actively involved in starting a new venture. This indicator is called the *early stage entrepreneurial activity index* (also known as the total entrepreneurship activity index or TEA).[10] The GEM methodology disaggregates early-stage entrepreneurial activity according to two main entrepreneur motives. The first category is the opportunity-based entrepreneurs (OPP) who undertake action to create a new venture pursuing perceived business opportunities. There are the 'Schumpeterian entrepreneurs' who have a 'pull motive', such as the desire for independence or the purpose of increasing personal or family income, challenge, status and recognition. The second category is the necessity-based entrepreneurs (NEC), who are 'pushed' into entrepreneurship because 'being an entrepreneur' is the only option for subsistence. Although many studies recognize that the majority of entrepreneurial activity is the result of the search for business opportunities (Bolino 2000; Bosma et al. 2008; Carter et al. 2003; Feldman and Hessels et al. 2008; Kolvereid 1996), there is a relatively high prevalence of NEC entrepreneurs starting new endeavours in many low and middle income countries.

Data on the approximation of the countries' institutions and institutional quality were derived from the World Bank's 'Project on Governance'.[11] The motivation for this project lies – to use the same expression employed by the Bank's initiative – in the recognition that 'governance matters' (Kaufmann et al. 1999, 2008). The way in which governance is expected to make a difference to economic outcomes can be captured by the World Bank's definition of governance: 'We define governance as the traditions and institutions by which authority in a country is exercised for the common good.'[12] A product of this project is the Worldwide Governance Indicators (WGI). WGI has developed aggregate and individual governance indicators for 212 countries and territories covering the period 1996–2007. The WGI covers six dimensions of governance which are described in detail below (see 'Independent variables').

The relation between these variables and entrepreneurial decision-making is quite straightforward. Respect for the basic principles of a free market economy represents a basic condition for entrepreneurial activity.[13] To use a Schumpeterian term, entrepreneurship presupposes that an agent will be able to 'combine' different resources in different ways, which in turn implies that he or she has the right to do so without those resources being confiscated or facing other violations.

Detailed definitions of these variables and their measures are given below.

Dependent variables

Dependent variables are from the GEM databases covering the eight-year period, 2001–7 and 60 countries. The first dependent variable is the rate of OPP, defined as the percentage of the adult population who are involved in early stage entrepreneurial activity and who claim to be driven by the recognition of a business opportunity. These business opportunities could be a good proxy for Baumol's productive entrepreneurial activities.[14] By the year 2007, the GEM methodology had been improved and calculation of OPP rates revised. According to the new definition,

> ... those who chose recognition of an opportunity were asked whether the main driver behind pursuing this opportunity was (i) to increase their own income, (ii) to be independent or (iii) to maintain their income. The latter category was not considered as a genuine opportunity for the measures. (Bosma et al. 2008: 62)

The new OPP category includes an additional variable, 'improved opportunity' (IMPROPP), which is a measure of the proportion of opportunity-driven undertakings in early stage entrepreneurial activity, with theoretical values ranging from 0 to 100. This ratio can provide an indication 'of the anatomy' of opportunity entrepreneurship (Levie and Autio 2008), rather than population level rates (or volume). So, the OPP measure for 2007 is not totally comparable to previous years and will thus be used as control for 2007 in the panel models for testing for significant differences between periods. A specific model using IMPROPP only for the 2007 year and their correspondent independent variables is tested.

The third dependent variable is the rate of NEC. Again, it is the percentage of the country's adult population involved in entrepreneurship 'because they cannot find a suitable role in the world of work; creating a new business is their best available option' (Reynolds et al. 2005: 217). This measure is relevant for understanding entrepreneurship activities in developing countries. The GEM reports establish that low income countries have a high rate of entrepreneurial activity because a large part of the population has been unable to find other sources of employment. In some cases, this type of entrepreneurship could correspond to Baumol's unproductive entrepreneurial activities because in the developing countries, many of these activities are in the 'shadow' or informal economy. Furthermore, many of these entrepreneurs abandon their efforts once they have the opportunity to become employees. Based on the modified 2007 OPP, it is assumed that NEC for specific countries have increased during the year, so 2007 will again be used as a control.

Independent variables

I utilize the six WGI variables defined in exact terms according to Kaufmann et al. (2008: 7–8):

(a) Voice and accountability (VA), measuring perceptions of the extent to which a country's citizens are able to participate in selecting their government, as well as freedom of expression, freedom of association and a free media.

(b) Political stability and absence of violence (PS), measuring perceptions of the likelihood that the government will be destabilized or overthrown by unconstitutional or violent means, including politically motivated violence and terrorism.

(c) Government effectiveness (GE), measuring perceptions of the quality of public services, the quality of the civil service and the degree of its independence from political pressures, the quality of policy formulation and implementation and credibility of the government's commitment to such policies.

(d) Regulatory quality (RQ), measuring perceptions of the ability of the government to formulate and implement sound policies and regulations that permit and promote private sector development.

(e) Rule of law (RL), measuring perceptions of the extent to which agents have confidence in and abide by the rules of society and in particular the quality of contract enforcement, property rights, the police and the courts, as well as the likelihood of crime and violence.

(f) Control of corruption (CC), measuring perceptions of the extent to which public power is exercised for private gain, including both petty and grand forms of corruption, as well as 'capture' of the state by elites and private interests.

Clearly, some of these variables are related more directly with entrepreneurship activities (or total economy activities) but all variables are considered for the initial analysis. These indicators are measured following a normal distribution with a mean of zero and a standard deviation of one in each period. According to WGI, these variables virtually have scores between –2.5 and 2.5, with the higher scores corresponding to better outcomes. In order to test the different specifications including logarithmic, the scores are transformed to 0–5 scale. The WGI indicators are available biannually from 1996 and annually for the six-year period 2002–7. Thus, for this reason the 2001 measures are not available.[15]

Control variables

In addition to independent variables, the first control variable is the gross domestic product per capita (GDP pc) for the period 2002–7. The per capita income growth rate is a good proxy for measuring economic growth and is one of main sources for qualifying economic development (Wennekers et al. 2005). These variables are adjusted by the purchasing power parity per US dollars, GDP per capita (PPP). The data are taken from IMF's *World Economic Outlook Database* published in September 2007. To resolve the potential collinearity problem (some institutional variables are highly correlated with GDP), the models are retested, using a control variable for the country's degree of economic welfare: HINCOME with the value 1 for GEM's high income countries (see Table 8A.1). In order to control for the effect of the recalculated OPP, dummy variable Y2007 with value 1 is used for the countries participating in 2007. A correlation matrix for all variables is given in Table 8.1.

Methodology

The sections on the literature framework and variable descriptions note that the developing countries have relatively high rates of necessity-based entrepreneurial dynamics, while most developed nations have relatively high rates of productive entrepreneurs. Mindful of the general research proposition, in countries under *ceteris paribus* conditions,[16] the relationship between the institutional quality variables is positive for the opportunity entrepreneurial dynamics rates and negative for necessity entrepreneurship. In order to examine these relationships, we use a series of regressions following this general model:

$$E_{it} = f(WGI_{it}, X_{it})$$

where:
   E is entrepreneurial dynamics: OPP, IMPROPP or NEC;
   WGIs represent each of the World Bank's government variables;
   X is the control variables: GDP per capita (PPP) or HINCOME and Y2007;
   i is the country index and *t* is the time period.

Table 8.1 Correlations

	OPP	IMPROPP	NEC	VA	PS	GE	RQ	RL	CC	GDP	HINCOME
OPP	1	–	–	–	–	–	–	–	–	–	–
IMPROPP	-0.166	1	–	–	–	–	–	–	–	–	–
NEC	0.683**	-0.488**	1	–	–	–	–	–	–	–	–
VA	-0.322**	0.622**	-0.611**	1	–	–	–	–	–	–	–
PS	-0.408**	0.722**	-0.681**	0.719**	1	–	–	–	–	–	–
GE	-0.337**	0.782**	-0.670**	0.782**	0.816**	1	–	–	–	–	–
RQ	-0.328**	0.721**	-0.653**	0.787**	0.800**	0.950**	1	–	–	–	–
RL	-0.329**	0.773**	-0.683**	0.803**	0.837**	0.973**	0.947**	1	–	–	–
CC	-0.290**	0.817**	-0.638**	0.788**	0.815**	0.971**	0.936**	0.974**	1	–	–
GDP pc	-0.331**	0.766**	-0.687**	0.705**	0.724**	0.868**	0.833**	0.870**	0.863**	1	–
HINCOME	-0.316**	0.778**	-0.617**	0.655**	0.661**	0.811**	0.779**	0.821**	0.806**	0.880**	1

Note: ** significant at 0.01% level.

Models are estimated by pooling the cross-section of countries with the time series data on each country for the period 2002–7. Linear, logarithmic, inverse relations are verified, as is the quadratic specification, using a general-to-specific modelling procedure to test the better statistical fit.[17] In addition, a different intercept coefficient is specified for each country (fixed and random effects). The relationship between OPP and NEC entrepreneurial activities and the quality of institutions variables is tested. For 2007, only a simple ordinary least squares (OLS) linear model is used.

Results

The panel models on opportunity and necessity are performed using a generalized least squares (GLS) random effect specification but in order to use a less restrictive model a pooled OLS using time-clustered standard errors is also employed.[18] The first results confirm the potential problems of multicollinearity between some WGI variables that were advised in the correlation matrix. To solve this problem, VA, PS and CC are dropped from the panel models,[19] but for each variable a useful graphical analysis is considered. The first results from the regression models indicate that the R^2 values and the likelihood ratio tests are higher for the quadratic specification on opportunity-based entrepreneurial activities. Logarithmic specification is better on NEC, while linear specification is more suitable for improved opportunity.

Opportunity entrepreneurial activity

Linear, logarithmic, inverse and quadratic specifications using the OPP variable are tested. Quadratic specification (U-shape) has a better statistical fit (adjusted R^2 values) and superior statistical specification.

The results are shown in Table 8.2. In the GDP models, 'government effectiveness', GE and GE squared are significant (negative and positive, respectively); GDP and GDP squared are significant (negative and positive, respectively). The HINCOME models have the same results as the GE variables and HINCOME is significant and negative. This last result is consistent with the observation by Carree et al. (2007) who find that rich countries face a decreasing level of TEA. Compared with the whole period 2001–7, the control for the year 2007 is not significant, so significant variations of the 2007 OPP measures can be discarded. Even though the models are statistically significant and in accordance with previous research (Acs and Amorós 2008; Amorós and Cristi 2008; Wennekers et al. 2005), the observed relationships (U-shaped relationship) are not

Table 8.2   Opportunity-based entrepreneurship models

	OLS GDP model (Std. err. adjusted for 6 clusters in year)	GLS GDP model (Random effects)	OLS HINCOME model (Std. err. adjusted for 6 clusters in year)	GLS HINCOME model (Random effects)
GE	–10.104**	–12.709**	–12.009**	–14.107**
GE (squared)	2.665**	1.680**	3.478**	1.835**
RL	2.080	4.591	2.254	4.775
RL (squared)	0.895	0.659	0.645	0.709
RQ	3.751	6.755	3.562	6.768
RQ (squared)	–0.701	–0.878	–1.188	–0.889
GDP pc	–0.001***	–0.001**	–	–
GDP pc (squared)	$7.75^{E}{-}^{09}$***	$4.30E^{-09}$*	–	–
HINCOME	–	–	–1.853***	–1.633*
Y2007	–0.372*	–0.001	–0.777**	–0.142
Constant	13.091***	27.707***	9.234***	28.360***
R^2	0.445	0.329	0.376	0.3840
Wald chi^2	–	23.63***	–	21.43***
Observations	221	221	221	221
Groups	–	60	–	60

Note: * Significant at 0.10% level; ** significant at 0.05% level; *** significant at 0.01% level.

plausible explanations for the allocation of productive entrepreneurship with respect to the quality of institutions. The graphical analysis shows that countries with lower rates in their government variables (generally the low and medium income countries) exhibit a high degree of 'opportunity' entrepreneurial activities. Thus, even though GEM's opportunity rates for developing countries are high, they do not necessarily represent 'high quality' (productive) entrepreneurship activities (Bosma et al. 2008).

Improved opportunity

For this dependent variable two different series of WGI variables are tested. The results are shown in Table 8.3.

Even though high bivariate correlations and positive and significant one-to-one linear relationships for the six WGI variables can be observed for IMPROPP, some correlations disappear (or change to negative) in the OLS test with the introduction of GDP or HINCOME. For the GDP model using CC (control of corruption), PS (political stability)

Table 8.3   Improved opportunity-based entrepreneurship 2007 models

	GDP model 1	HINCOME model 1	GDP model 2	HINCOME model 2
CC	12.360**	11.480**	–	–
PS	3.849*	4.770**	–	–
RL	–8.962*	–9.420**	1.526	0.864
RQ	–	–	–1.186	–0.133
GE	–	–	6.610	6.020
GDP per capita	0.000	–	0.000	–
HINCOME	–	11.923***	–	11.639**
Constant	42.661***	45.030***	41.025***	43.739***
R^2	0.690	0.77	0.590	0.660
F	23.950***	34.55***	16.250***	21.160***
Observations	42	42	42	42

Note: * significant at 0.10% level; ** significant at 0.05% level; *** significant at 0.01% level.

and RL (rule of law), the first two are positive and significant, RL is negative and significant[20] and GDP is insignificant. In the HINCOME model, the results are similar but HINCOME is positive and significant. These last results are more plausible and confirm that those with high relative prevalence of improved opportunity-driven entrepreneurship are the high income countries[21] (Bosma et al. 2008). For the developing countries, the necessity motivated entrepreneurs constitute an important share of the TEA and, in many cases, the non-opportunity oriented (or necessity) entrepreneurial activities rates are above the OPP.

Necessity

In this model similar to OPP, random effects and the same WGI variables are used. Linear, logarithmic and inverse relations are verified, as is the quadratic specification. Logarithmic model being once best adjusted. The results are shown in Table 8.4.

Discussion

Overall findings

The findings presented in this chapter suggest that differences in institutional quality help to explain differences in entrepreneurship across developed and developing countries. A country's overall level of opportunistic entrepreneurial activities is not significantly affected by the

Table 8.4 Necessity-based entrepreneurship models

	OLS GDP model (Std. err. adjusted for 6 clusters in year)	GLS GDP model (Random effects)	OLS HINCOME model (Std. err. adjusted for 6 clusters in year)	GLS HINCOME model (Random effects)
ln(GE)	1.035	−0.924	−4.377	−2.969*
ln(RL)	−5.526*	−3.344**	−5.287	−5.305
ln(RQ)	0.940	2.817*	0.129	2.948
ln(GDP) per capita	−1.944***	−2.171***	–	–
HINCOME	–	–	−0.861**	−0.122
Y2007	0.028	0.147	−0.545*	−0.289*
constant	27.577***	25.182***	19.795***	8.672***
R^2	0.597	0.605	0.504	0.512
Wald chi^2	–	97.99***	–	60.36***
Observations	221	221	221	221
Groups	–	60	–	60

Note: * significant at 0.10 level, ** significant at 0.05 level, *** significant at 0.01 level.

WGI variables and exhibit a non-plausible U-shaped curve.[22] Acs and Amorós (2008: 127) note that the

U-shaped approach is useful in understanding the decline in self-employment in developing countries both across countries and over time, but not useful in explaining entrepreneurship (broadly defined). Second, the U-shaped approach is not very useful in explaining the role of developing countries in the efficiency-driven stage of development, either as they enter the efficiency-driven stage or leave the efficiency-driven stage.

Certainly the OPP measures for developing countries encompass many activities, which in comparison to those in the developed countries, do not constitute true opportunities or productive value added activities.

The positive relationships between improved opportunity-driven entrepreneurship activities utilized as a proxy for productive entrepreneurship and 'control of corruption', 'political stability' and high income countries indicate that real opportunity ventures can be allocated if the existing government institutions are of adequate quality. This has an important implication for entrepreneurs in the developing countries: the adoption of certain institutions has to precede productive entrepreneurial behaviour because these institutions, in this specific analysis, facilitate the right type of entrepreneurship (Boettke and Coyne 2006).

Finally, results of NEC entrepreneurship activities have important implications for the developing countries. The negative relationship between 'government effectiveness', 'rule of law' and GDP per capita confirm the influence of institutional quality on the allocation of entrepreneurship efforts. The results in general terms indicate that more economic development associated with better quality of institutions could reduce the prevalence rates of some unproductive entrepreneurial activities that are mainly motivated by necessity. For public policy, Leibenstein (1968: 83) suggests that attention be focused on:

> ... the gaps, obstructions, and impediments in the market network of the economy in question and on the gap filling and input completing capacities and responsiveness to different motivational states of the potential entrepreneurs in the population.

In this sense, government institutions should converge to enhance the efficiency of the market, as well as to provide a general environment that is open to motivated entrepreneurs (Levie and Autio 2008). For developing countries, this general environment is faced with the lack of regulations and rule of law (de Soto 2000), so many entrepreneurial efforts lead to large-scale, predominantly unproductive activities rather than the more desirable productive and real opportunity entrepreneurship. Thus institutional profiles in developing countries contrast with those of the high income developed economies that benefit from a well-established regulatory base and wide support for entrepreneurship (Manolova et al. 2008).

Limitations and future research

The exploratory nature of this research faces several limitations and the results are not conclusive. First, both GEM and WGI indicators are being improved continually. The IMPROPP variable is a good example of this. In this regard, it is difficult to state the pre-eminence of opportunity-based entrepreneurs over the necessity-based *per se*. Necessity entrepreneurs are not necessarily less successful (Block and Sandner 2009) and not all opportunity-based entrepreneurs create successful businesses with high impact on job creation and economic growth. Using GEM methodology some opportunity-driven entrepreneurs can be categorized following an overly simplistic approach because both push and pull factors are frequently involved in the reasons why people start new business ventures (Williams 2009). This is common in developing economies. On the other hand, some necessity entrepreneurs could be relevant for many economies because in many cases, despite the particularly small scale of the business, they can still be productive. For this reason further research needs to include additional analysis putting emphasis on the qualification of the entrepreneurship activities. For example, the GEM project has other variables that measure dimensions of high growth oriented entrepreneurship, innovation-driven or degree of internationalization (Hessels et al. 2008; Levie and Autio 2008).

The use of alternative entrepreneurial measures like self-employment indicators or new indexes could be useful in developing this line of research. Other measures of the quality of institutions like the *Index of Economic Freedom* (Heritage Foundation), *Economic Freedom of the World* (Fraser Institute), *Corruption Perception Index* (Transparency International) or other sources of government information like UNDP or the World Economic Forum could be complementary and help to define new models. These variables will possibly also help to resolve problems of collinearity by using different metrics. Using an approach based on a more specific regional focus or degree of development (for example, OECD countries, European Union countries, transition economies, Latin America, etc.) can help to improve the estimations.

Second, this chapter is restricted to national level data. An analysis at individual level might show different patterns. Another level is the region; a regional approach faces differences in institutional quality and this affects on entrepreneurship activities (Hall and Sobel 2008; Sobel 2008).

Finally, it is clear that any approach modelling entrepreneurship without explicitly considering institutional variables could be methodologically flawed. Moreover, the results of this chapter find that both entrepreneurship and other determinants (for example, GDP) can be influenced asymmetrically by the quality of institutions. Thus, in future research more robust and non-linear models need to be considered.

Concluding remarks

This chapter analysed the relationship between different types of entrepreneurial dynamics and the quality of government institutions during the period 2002–7. Even though these empirical results are not conclusive, as stated earlier, the study corroborates the significant and positive effects of the quality of institutions on opportunity entrepreneurial activities and significant and negative effects on necessity entrepreneurial rates.

These results have important implications for public policy. The results suggest that for developing countries in general, the quality of institutions alone does not enhance or improve entrepreneurship. These countries need to work in order to achieve stable regulatory and macroeconomic conditions (Amorós and Cristi 2008). This implies continuing efforts for the reduction of unemployment and necessity-based entrepreneurship. But this kind of public policy, although indispensable, is insufficient. If developing countries do not consider the promotion of productive entrepreneurship as a main concern in their policy agenda (Wennekers et al. 2005), they will only reduce necessity-based entrepreneurship without achieving higher growth through opportunity-based entrepreneurship. Such governmental decisions necessitate the creation of better national strategies to accelerate country growth and move more rapidly towards major innovation-based entrepreneurial activities (Acs and Amorós 2008). Developing countries must rationally organize their functions and seek to remove unnecessary barriers and controls that hamper entrepreneurial activity. They need to protect and stimulate property rights and introduce policies that support the creativity and efficiency of the private sector. With an adequate environment, including the quality of institutions, entrepreneurship can help to improve the economic and social conditions for developing economies.

Appendix

Table 8A.1 Participant countries in GEM 2002–7 and their income classification

Country	2002	2003	2004	2005	2006	2007		Country	2002	2003	2004	2005	2006	2007
High income countries								**Low and middle income countries**						
1 Australia	✦	✦	✦	✦	✦	–	32	Argentina	✦	✦	✦	✦	✦	✦
2 Austria	–	–	–	✦	–	✦	33	Brazil	✦	✦	✦	✦	✦	✦
3 Belgium	✦	✦	✦	✦	✦	✦	34	Chile	✦	✦	–	✦	✦	✦
4 Canada	✦	✦	✦	✦	✦	–	35	China	✦	✦	–	✦	✦	✦
5 Czech Republic	–	–	–	–	✦	–	36	Colombia	–	–	–	–	✦	✦
6 Denmark	✦	✦	✦	✦	✦	✦	37	Croatia	✦	✦	✦	✦	✦	✦
7 Finland	✦	✦	✦	✦	✦	✦	38	Dominican Rep.	–	–	–	–	–	✦
8 France	✦	✦	✦	✦	✦	✦	39	Ecuador	–	–	✦	–	–	–

Continued

Table 8A.1 Continued

Country	2002	2003	2004	2005	2006	2007		Country	2002	2003	2004	2005	2006	2007
High income countries								**Low and middle income countries**						
9 Germany	✦	✦	✦	✦	✦	–	40	Hungary	✦	–	✦	✦	✦	✦
10 Greece	–	✦	✦	✦	✦	✦	41	India	✦	–	–	–	✦	✦
11 Hong Kong SAR	✦	✦	✦	–	–	✦	42	Indonesia	–	–	–	–	✦	–
12 Iceland	✦	✦	✦	✦	✦	✦	43	Jamaica	–	–	–	✦	✦	–
13 Ireland	✦	✦	✦	✦	✦	✦	44	Jordan	–	–	✦	–	–	–
14 Israel	✦	–	✦	–	–	✦	45	Kazakhstan	–	–	–	–	–	✦
15 Italy	✦	✦	✦	✦	✦	✦	46	Latvia	–	–	–	✦	✦	✦
16 Japan	✦	✦	✦	✦	✦	✦	47	Malaysia	–	–	–	–	✦	–
17 Korea	✦	–	–	–	–	–	48	Mexico	✦	–	–	✦	✦	–
18 Netherlands	✦	✦	✦	✦	✦	✦	49	Peru	–	–	✦	–	✦	✦
19 New Zealand	✦	✦	✦	✦	–	–	50	Philippines	–	–	–	–	✦	–
20 Norway	✦	✦	✦	✦	✦	✦	51	Poland	✦	–	✦	–	–	–
21 Portugal	–	–	✦	–	–	✦	52	Romania	–	–	–	–	–	✦
22 Puerto Rico	–	–	–	–	–	✦	53	Russia	✦	–	–	–	✦	✦
23 Singapore	✦	✦	✦	✦	✦	–	54	Serbia	–	–	–	–	–	✦
24 Slovenia	✦	✦	✦	✦	✦	✦	55	South Africa	✦	✦	✦	✦	✦	–
25 Spain	✦	✦	✦	✦	✦	✦	56	Thailand	✦	–	–	✦	✦	✦
26 Sweden	✦	✦	✦	✦	✦	✦	57	Turkey	–	–	–	–	✦	✦
27 Switzerland	✦	✦	–	✦	–	✦	58	Uganda	–	✦	✦	–	–	–
28 Taiwan	✦	–	–	–	–	–	59	Uruguay	–	–	–	–	✦	✦
29 United Arab Emirates	–	–	–	–	✦	✦	60	Venezuela	–	✦	–	✦	–	✦
30 United Kingdom	✦	✦	✦	✦	✦	✦								
31 United States	✦	✦	✦	✦	✦	✦								

Note: ✦ = Country participating.
Source: Compiled by the author, based on GEM annual reports.

Acknowledgements

I am grateful to Juan Pablo Couyoumdjian who worked with me on previous related research and Oscar Cristi for helpful comments on an earlier draft. I thank Wim Naudé for the opportunity to participate in the UNU-WIDER project. Also acknowledged is the support of the Global Entrepreneurship Monitor Research Consortium. All errors are mine.

Notes

1. In the literature it is possible to find several definitions for entrepreneurship – see for instance the discussion in Chapter 1. Without a loss of generality, we refer to the definition of entrepreneurship used by the GEM project: 'adults

in the process of setting up a business [who] will (partly) and or currently be owning and managing an operating young business'.

2. As the previous chapter showed, the development of new technologies and the emergence of new business models have shifted from large corporations to small and new ventures over recent decades.

3. Micro-level research, in terms of formally modelling an agent's labour choice, has been undertaken by several economists, including Blanchflower and Oswald (1998), Iyigun and Owen (1998), Kihlstrom and Laffont (1979) and Lucas (1978). These studies suggest that a micro-foundational approach does indeed provide a useful theoretical framework in terms of examining the expected evolution of entrepreneurship. Consider, for example, the model presented by Lucas (1978). The central proposition of his model is that given the distribution of agents according to managerial talent, an increase in real wages tends to increase the opportunity cost of entrepreneurship. This, in turn, affects the allocation of labour across different activities. In terms of Lucas' analysis, the size distribution of firms tends to change in favour of larger firms as an economy grows wealthier.

4. I follow North's (1990) definition of institutions: 'Institutions are the humanly devised constraints that structure political, economic and social interaction.'

5. For complete measurements and methodology of the GEM model and entrepreneurial framework conditions, see Reynolds et al. (2005). For recent changes in GEM, see Bosma et al. (2008). Levie and Autio (2008) make an extensive empirical test of the GEM model using a review of Leibenstein's theories of entrepreneurship and economic development (1968, 1978, 1995) and link these theories with the entrepreneurial framework conditions.

6. On these issues, see the discussion in Storey (2005).

7. For different models along these lines, see Lucas (1978) and Lazear (2005).

8. This greater risk can be captured by examining the assessments of risk-rating agencies, as well as from the point of view of modern portfolio financial theory in terms of the higher returns demanded by the investors in these economies.

9. For seminal research on this question see, for example, the papers by Barro (1991), Keefer and Knack (1995) and Knack and Keefer (1997).

10. This index is based on the life-cycle of the entrepreneurial process which is divided into two periods: the first covers nascent entrepreneurs who have undertaken some action to create a new business in the past year but have not paid any salaries or wages in the last three months. The second category includes owners/managers of businesses that have paid wages and salaries for over three months, but less than 42 months.

11. For the complete World Bank Institute Initiative of Governance and Anti-Corruption Programme, see www.worldbank.org/wbi/governance.

12. It is interesting to note that this definition is quite similar to North's (1990) standard definition of institutions. See note 4.

13. On these issues, see also the analysis by Bjørnskov and Foss (2008), which suggests that many components of the economic freedom index that one would expect to be related to entrepreneurship do not seem to show any sort of relationship.

14. Even though the recognition of an opportunity is one of the 'central factors' of the entrepreneurship process (Timmons and Spinelli 2007), GEM's OPP measure can incorporate any type of entrepreneurial activity, including self-employment, and this can involve low growth or no-growth entrepreneurship. In the GEM data, nearly 50 per cent of all start-up attempts do not expect to create any jobs within five years (Autio 2007). Within Baumol's productive entrepreneurship activity approach, GEM's OPP measure probably does not 'fit' at all. This discussion will be taken up in the results section. The GEM methodology computes the high expectation TEA (HEA) index, which is the percentage of adult-aged population involved in TEA who expect to create 20 or more jobs within five years. GEM's 2007 *Executive Report* and 2007 *Global Report on High Growth Entrepreneurship* suggest that early-stage entrepreneurial activity in the middle and low income countries may be dominated more by low growth entrepreneurial initiatives. Unfortunately, this measure is not available for all the years and countries analysed here.

15. Different missing values procedures are inputted to calculate the 2001 rates, but the models with these values do not produce a better statistical fit (R^2). Therefore the model is calculated with only the available years.

16. Obviously other different economic, demographic, social and institutional factors exist, which influence entrepreneurial activity. See Wennekers et al. (2005: 298).

17. A series of Akaike tests and Schwarz tests, such as selection criteria for different models, are performed.

18. Hausman tests were used to prove the better specifications for each model. The null hypotheses for these tests are that there are no systematic differences between the fixed- and random-effects specifications. High p-values on OPP and NEC models would confirm this and support the use of random-effects specification. Nevertheless, these high p-values could be caused because the fixed effects estimates are very imprecise (i.e. featuring high standard errors). That is the reason to also use a pooled OLS estimator (with time-clustered standard errors) in addition to random-effects models, as the latter are more restrictive because they require strict exogeneity. See Wooldridge (2002: 257) for more information.

19. VA and PS, by definition, are 'less related' to economic activities. CC is highly correlated with RL. Nevertheless a model using all variables (not shown here) was performed with non-significant variations with respect to the restricted model. Also a variance inflation factor (VIF) test was performed, which corroborates the multicollinearity problem.

20. This result is probably a collinearity problem because CC is highly correlated with RL and this cross-section model has a relatively low number of observations.

21. Of the developing countries, only Chile and Uruguay have IMPROPP exceeding 50 per cent.

22. Acs and Szerb (2009) and Ahmad and Hoffmann (2008), among others, are developing new global entrepreneurship indices. The Global Entrepreneurship Index (GEI) has three subindexes that measure entrepreneurial activity, entrepreneurial strategy and entrepreneurial attitudes (Acs and Szerb 2009). The relationship between GDP growth and GEI index is

mildly S-shaped, rather than U-shaped. For example using 64 countries over the period 2006–8, with an emphasis on a developing region, Latin America, only one country was in the bottom half of the index: Chile ranked 26th, Colombia 35th, Uruguay 37th, Peru 41st, Argentina 42nd, Mexico 49th, Dominican Republic 53rd, Brazil 58th, Venezuela 49th, Bolivia 62nd and Ecuador 63rd.

9
Policy and Institutional Reform and Entrepreneurship in Developing Countries
Mina Baliamoune-Lutz

Introduction

Development economists acknowledge the role of institutional and policy reform on economic growth and development (see for example, Acemoglu et al. 2001, 2002, 2003; Baliamoune-Lutz 2009; Baliamoune-Lutz and Ndikumana 2007; Rodrik et al. 2004). Since these are expected to affect investment decisions and occupational choice, we could expect them to have an impact on entrepreneurship.

Institutional reform that affects taxes or liquidity constraints, for example, could have an impact on entrepreneurial activity (Djankov et al. 2008b; Gentry and Hubbard 2000; Guiso and Schivardi 2007). Thus, a channel through which institutional and policy reforms could affect growth could be through their interplay with entrepreneurial activities.

At the same time, however, entrepreneurship influences economic growth through its interaction with institutional and policy reforms. Intuitively, we may think that an improvement in trade and financial environments (policy reform) and/or enhanced institutional quality would lead to more entrepreneurial activities, *ceteris paribus*. It turns out that both theoretically and empirically this may not necessarily be the case.

The primary goal of this chapter is to explore how institutional and policy reforms affect the relationship between entrepreneurship and growth. Our analysis focuses in particular on the interplay between policy and institutional reforms and entrepreneurship (defined here as the ratio of self-employed to total non-agricultural employment, in per cent). Estimation results indicate that the interplay of entrepreneurship and trade and financial sector reforms is important. The empirical results indicate that the joint effect of trade reform and entrepreneurship on growth is negative, suggesting that trade reform reduces the positive effects of entrepreneurial ability, while the joint effect of financial sector reform and entrepreneurship has a non-linear effect on growth. Financial sector reform enhances the growth effects of entrepreneurship within a medium level range and reduces it at high levels of reform. Moreover, we find that the interplay of institutions and entrepreneurship does not seem to matter for the growth effects of entrepreneurship. The negative relationships between policy (trade and financial sector) reforms and entrepreneurship seem to validate the prediction of the Iyigun–Rodrik theoretical model that institutional reform works best in settings where entrepreneurial activity is weak while policy tinkering works best when entrepreneurial activity is vibrant[1] (Iyigun and Rodrik 2005) and are consistent with the findings reported in Baliamoune-Lutz (2007).

If we assume that a significant change in a country's openness to trade or in its ratio of credit to the private sector results from policy reform (viewed by Iyigun and Rodrik as institutional reform) instead of policy tinkering, then we may use indicators of trade openness and financial development as proxies for policy reform. In this chapter we consider changes in taxation or money supply or marginal changes in the structure of tariffs – that do not necessarily lead to significant changes in access to credit or trade openness – as policy tinkering. We do not test for the effect of policy tinkering, as the indicators we use are viewed as proxies for policy and institutional reform. However, while in their empirical estimation, Iyigun and Rodrik (2005) test for the effect of the interplay of entrepreneurship and trade reform only, we test for the interplay of entrepreneurship with institutional, trade and financial sector reforms. This allows us to try to identify which interactions matter for the growth effects of entrepreneurship.

Reforms, entrepreneurship and economic outcomes

Financial sector reforms are often implemented with the assumption that such reforms would lead to financial development, which in turn would promote growth and development. Recent empirical research on financial development and growth includes, among others, Beck et al. (2000), Benhabib and Spiegel (2000), Demetriades and Hussein (1996), Levine et al. (2000) and Shan (2005). Many empirical studies document that financial development causes growth. However, several others show that the evidence is either non-existent or weak or that there is reverse causality (see for example, Baliamoune-Lutz 2003; Demetriades and Hussein 1996; Shan 2005; Thornton 1996).

Similarly, the topic of the growth effects of trade liberalization and reform has been examined in a number of empirical studies (Baliamoune 2002; Baliamoune-Lutz and Ndikumana 2007; Dollar and Kraay 2004; Edwards 1993, 1998; Krueger 1998; Rodriguez and Rodrik 2000; Rodrik et al. 2004; Sachs et al. 1995). While some studies show that trade reforms have a positive impact on growth (see, for example, Dollar and Kraay 2004; Sachs et al. 1995; Sachs and Warner 1997), recent empirical studies (for example, Baliamoune-Lutz and Ndikumana 2007; Mukhopadhyay 1999; Rodriguez and Rodrik 2000) show that the growth effects of trade reforms may be non-existent, not systematic (Rodrik 2001) or negative. There is also empirical evidence that the effects may be contingent on pre-existing institutional settings (Addison and Baliamoune-Lutz 2006; Baliamoune-Lutz and Ndikumana 2007).

The role of institutions in development and growth has also been the subject of numerous studies (Acemoglu et al. 2003; Baliamoune-Lutz and Ndikumana 2007; Dollar and Kraay 2003; Easterly and Levine 2003; Knack and Keefer 1995; North 1990, 1991; Rodrik et al. 2004). For example, Acemoglu et al. (2003) argue that institutions have a significant effect on economic outcomes and on macroeconomic policies. Easterly and Levine (2003) show that institutions are the only channel through which tropics, germs and crops influence development. Similarly, Rodrik et al. (2004) conclude that there is empirical evidence of the primacy of institutions over trade and geography.

Baliamoune-Lutz (2007: 5) notes: 'entrepreneurship affects development through this process of innovation, investment, and market expansion'. Leff (1979: 47) writes, 'entrepreneurship clearly refers to the capacity for innovation, investment, and activist expansion in new markets, products, and techniques'. Baumol (1968) argues that it is the entrepreneur's job to find new ideas and put them to use. Indeed, the literature on entrepreneurship often stresses 'Schumpeterian entrepreneurship' and focuses on innovation as the main activity of the entrepreneur. Since innovation tends to require access to new technology and/or new ideas, such access can be greatly influenced by institutional and policy reforms.

Banerjee and Newman (1993) develop a theoretical model where capital markets are imperfect – so that wealthy individuals can become entrepreneurs while poor individuals are constrained to work for a wage – and show that the dynamics of occupational choice can influence the process of development through their effect on the distribution of income and wealth. Thus, institutional and financial sector reforms that would alter capital market imperfections could alter the growth effect of entrepreneurship. Moreover, Baliamoune-Lutz (2007) argues that the decision to allocate talent or entrepreneurial ability to productive rather than to unproductive activities[2] could depend on the relative rewards offered by society and:

> Since such rewards are usually governed by pre-existing policies and institutional settings we would expect a significant interaction between the allocation of entrepreneurship to productive (or unproductive) activities and policy and institutional reforms. (Baliamoune-Lutz 2007: 5)

Thus, here again the interplay of reforms and entrepreneurship may influence the growth effects of entrepreneurship.

The interplay of reforms and entrepreneurship is examined in the model developed in Iyigun and Rodrik (2005). The authors assume that investment decisions and policy outcomes are subject to uncertainty and use a theoretical model to study the interplay of institutional and policy reform and entrepreneurship and its impact on growth. Their findings indicate that the impact of institutional reform depends on the level of entrepreneurial activity. More specifically, Iyigun and Rodrik show that institutional reform has negative growth effects when entrepreneurial activity is strong and positive effects when entrepreneurial activity is weak. This is because reforms could impose a cost on the existing entrepreneurs while it may be neutral or even helpful to new ventures.[3]

Using a theoretical model where contractual problems between two entrepreneurs (partners) may arise, Acemoglu and Verdier (1998) show that less developed countries may find it optimal to maintain low property rights and a certain level of corruption. This is because enforcing property rights can be costly. The authors argue that since it is costly to reduce corruption and enforce property rights, the optimal allocation may also depend on the productivity of entrepreneurial activities. Thus, as Acemoglu and Verdier (1998: 1382) argue:

> ... it could be optimal for less developed economies, which may have less productive investment opportunities, to have a lower level of property right enforcement and more corruption.

Higher public wages can also be part of institutional reform, through their effects on the quality of bureaucracy and the level of corruption. The authors show that an increase in public wages can at the same time enhance the allocation of talent and cause entrepreneurial investment to increase. Acemoglu and Verdier (1998: 1383) conclude that:

> ... marginal improvement in the enforcement of property rights secured by higher bureaucratic wages may make it worthwhile for entrepreneurs to invest, increasing the expected return to entrepreneurship. Higher entrepreneurial returns, in turn, induce more agents to choose this occupation rather than public employment.

On the other hand, if a country maintains weak institutions, which would cause for example weak property rights, then this may induce individuals from the present generation to invest less in human capital and would not be able to benefit from improved institutional quality once it takes place and thus may vote against institutional reform (Acemoglu and Verdier 1998). In this case, some countries may persistently have low institutional quality and low investment. This, in turn, may suggest that in such countries, a large part of the self-employment will take place in the informal sector (remedial or subsistence entrepreneurial activity) where the level of human capital is generally low.

Data and methodology

The dependent variable is defined as the rate of growth in per capita income. We follow Iyigun and Rodrik (2005) and Baliamoune-Lutz (2007) and define the variable entrepreneurial intensity (ENT) as the ratio of self-employed to total non-agricultural employment[4] (data are from LABORSTA data set, ILO). The proxy for trade reforms (OPEN) is openness to international trade, measured by the ratio of the sum of imports and exports to GDP, in per cent. In this chapter, financial sector reform is proxied by domestic credit to the private sector (the variable CREDIT) as a percentage of GDP.[5] Our proxy for institutional reform (the variable ICRG) is the International Country Risk Guide (ICRG) composite index.[6] ICRG ratings are published by the Political Risk Services (PRS) Group and include economic, political and financial risk. These three categories of risk include scores for 22 risk components. The ICRG composite index is from World Development Indicators database. The index has values ranging from zero (highest risk) to 100 (lowest risk).

Data, except for data on the variable ENT, are from the World Bank's World Development Indicators database.

We initially include 44 developing and transition economies. We then try to test the robustness of our results by excluding countries that used to be in the group of developing countries but are currently included in the high income (developed countries) group, such as Singapore and South Korea for example, and excluding sub-Saharan African countries. The choice of the countries is dictated by data availability. The choice of the period (1990–2002) is dictated by the need to minimize cross-country disparity in the number of observations per country, since many developing countries do not have data on ENT prior to the 1990s, and to exclude the pre-transition period for Central and Eastern European countries.

We perform Arellano-bond GMM estimations on annual (unbalanced) panel data covering the period 1990–2002 and report the estimation results in Tables 9.2–9.5, along with the tests for the validity of the overidentifying restrictions (Sargan test) and second order autocorrelation. Based on the test results, we fail to reject the null in the case of both tests and all estimations. Thus, we conclude that there is not enough evidence to reject the hypothesis that the overidentifying restrictions are valid and the hypothesis that the average autocovariance in residuals of order 2 is zero.

Let us consider the following dynamic panel data model:

$$y_{i,t} = \delta + \alpha y_{i,t-1} + X_{i,t}\beta + \eta_i + \mu_{i,t} \tag{1}$$

where y is the rate of growth in income per capita, X is a row vector of the endogenous and exogenous factors determining income, η_i is the individual (country) fixed effect, and $\mu_{i,t}$ is a time varying error term. Then we apply the Arellano–Bond specification and obtain the following:

$$\Delta y_{i,t} = \Delta y_{i,t-1}\alpha + \Delta X_{i,t}\beta + \Delta \mu_{i,t} \tag{2}$$

The variables (on the right-hand side), INVEST (domestic investment as a ratio of GDP, in per cent), ENT, ICRG, OPEN and CREDIT, as well as their interactions, are considered to be endogenous. In addition to the endogenous variables, we control for the level of development by including per capita income, and we also include a regional dummy for Latin America (LAAM).[7] Lags dated t-2 are used as instruments for the endogenous variables.

Empirical results

Table 9.1 shows relevant correlation coefficients. We observe that the correlation between most variables and growth is rather weak. The highest correlation (0.35) that growth has is with the measure of institutional quality (ICRG). On the other hand, per capita income has strong positive linear correlation with ICRG, and weaker correlation with the investment ratio, openness to trade, and the indicators of financial reform (M2 and credit to the private sector). Interestingly, the association between ENT and the other variables is consistently negative and in some cases strong; –0.69 with income, and –0.45 with institutions and openness to trade.

The Arellano–Bond GMM estimation results are reported in Tables 9.2–5. First, we estimate the equations using the full sample (44 countries) and show the results in Table 9.2. Equation (1) portrays a simple model where we regress growth in per capita income on the investment ratio (INVEST), institutional reform (ICRG), trade reform (OPEN), financial reform (CREDIT) and entrepreneurial intensity (ENT). We also include a dummy variable for Latin America (LAAM). The results indicate that investment and institutional reform seem to have, as expected, a positive effect on growth. On the other hand, trade reforms and entrepreneurship do not seem to have a statistically significant positive impact (in fact, the variable ENT has a negative coefficient), while the proxy for financial reform shows up with a negative and highly significant coefficient.

In Equation (2), we account for the interplay of reforms (trade and financial reform) and entrepreneurial intensity. The results indicate that in both cases the interaction between these variables has a negative impact on growth, suggesting that reforms reduce the growth enhancing effects of entrepreneurial activity. Note that in Equation (2) the variables ENT and OPEN have a positive and highly significant coefficient, while the coefficient on the variable CREDIT is no longer significant (and is positive).[8]

In Equations (3)–(5) we test for the presence of non-linearity and also examine the growth effect of the interplay of institutional reform (ICRG) and ENT. There is support for a non-linear effect but only in the case of the interaction between financial reforms and entrepreneurship. Based on the results displayed in Table 9.2, we may conclude that the interplay of trade reforms and entrepreneurship has negative effects on growth if entrepreneurship is already vibrant and positive effects if entrepreneurial intensity is low.

Table 9.1 Correlation coefficients (p-value): pooled data

	ENT	GROWTH	INCOME	ICRG	OPEN	INVEST	CREDIT
GROWTH	−0.0085 (0.069)	–	–	–	–	–	–
INCOME	−0.691 (0.000)	0.062 (0.079)	–	–	–	–	–
ICRG	−0.453 (0.000)	0.347 (0.000)	0.605 (0.000)	–	–	–	–
OPEN	−0.448 (0.000)	0.038 (0.295)	0.213 (0.000)	0.413 (0.000)	–	–	–
INVEST	−0.294 (0.000)	0.286 (0.000)	0.316 (0.000)	0.420 (0.000)	0.418 (0.000)	–	–
CREDIT	−0.112 (0.017)	0.102 (0.007)	0.350 (0.000)	0.413 (0.000)	0.257 (0.000)	0.422 (0.000)	–
M2	−0.203 (0.000)	0.103 (0.005)	0.274 (0.000)	0.410 (0.000)	0.383 (0.000)	0.457 (0.000)	0.769 (0.000)

Notes: ENT: Entrepreneurial intensity, defined as the percentage of self-employment in total non-agricultural employment;

INCOME (pc): GDP per capita, PPP (constant 1995 international $). PPP value of income per capita in 1995 constant international dollars. PPP GDP is gross domestic product converted to international dollars using PPP rates;

GROWTH: The rate of annual growth in income per capita;

OPEN: Openness to trade, the sum of imports and exports as a percentage of GDP;

ICRG: International Country Risk Guide rating, published by the Political Risk Services (PRS) Group and includes three subcategories of risk; economic, political and financial risk. These categories include scores on 22 risk components. The World Bank publishes composite scores with values ranging from zero (highest risk) to 100 (lowest risk);

CREDIT: Domestic credit to private sector (percentage of GDP), refers to financial resources provided to the private sector, such as through loans, purchases of non-equity securities, and trade credits and other accounts receivable, that establish a claim for repayment. For some countries these claims include credit to public enterprises;

M2: Broad money (M1 plus M2) as a percentage of GDP; and

INVEST: Domestic investment as a percentage of GDP.

Source: Data on ENT are from LABORSTA data set produced by ILO. All other data are from World Bank World Development Indicators database (2005).

Table 9.2   Arellano–Bond GMM estimation, full sample (Dependent variable: growth of income per capita)

	(1)	(2)	(3)	(4)	(5)	(6)
Growth (lagged)	0.018 (0.048)	0.005 (0.046)	−0.029 (0.048)	0.018 (0.047)	0.021 (0.047)	
Endogenous variables						
INVEST	0.161** (0.065)	0.154** (0.066)	0.242*** (0.069)	0.245*** (0.068)	0.258*** (0.066)	
ICRG	0.280*** (0.044)	0.303*** (0.043)	0.317*** (0.046)	0.179 (0.117)	0.151 (0.119)	
OPEN	1.177 (1.624)	12.278*** (3.604)	14.028*** (4.149)	13.675*** (3.956)	12.353*** (3.791)	
ENT	−0.199* (0.106)	1.799*** (0.513)	3.107*** (1.192)	2.528** (1.174)	2.126 (0.162)	
CREDIT	−3.081*** (0.951)	0.536 (2.305)	2.247 (2.469)	1.635 (2.383)	0.966 (2.342)	
ENT X OPEN	–	−0.396*** (0.116)	−1.213*** (0.503)	−1.067*** (0.093)	−0.981** (0.469)	
ENT X CREDIT	–	−0.114* (0.062)	0.242** (0.096)	0.231** (0.096)	0.226** (0.095)	
ENT X OPEN_SQ	–	–	0.103* (0.056)	0.083 (0.054)	0.078 (0.052)	
ENT X CREDIT_SQ	–	–	−0.068*** (0.015)	−0.063*** (0.014)	−0.060*** (0.014)	
ENT X ICRG	–	–	–	0.0054 (0.003)	0.009 (0.014)	
ENT X ICRG_SQ	–	–	–	–	−0.00002 (0.00008)	
Exogenous variables						
LAAM	−0.074 (0.130)	−0.049 (0.131)	−0.012 (0.142)	−0.085 (0.139)	−0.148 (0.132)	
Number of obs.	345	345	345	345	345	
Sargan test[a], chi2	305.60	320.20	294.65	305.47	321.48	
M2[b], z; [pr > z]	−1.50 [0.13]	−1.67 [0.09]	−1.51 [0.13]	−1.36 [0.17]	−1.31 [0.19]	

Notes: [a]Sargan test of the validity of overidentifying restrictions; [b]Arellano–Bond test that average autocovariance in residuals of order 2 is 0; The constant is not reported; See Table 9.1 for variable definition; * significant at 0.10 level, ** significant at 0.05 level, *** significant at 0.01 level.

Source: Data on ENT are from LABORSTA data set produced by ILO. All other data are from World Bank World Development Indicators database (2005).

Table 9.3 Arellano–Bond GMM estimation (Dependent variable: growth of income per capita)

	Excluding high income countries			Excluding high income countries and SSA		
	(1)	(2)	(3)	(4)	(5)	(6)
Growth (lagged)	-0.045 (0.049)	-0.025 (0.050)	-0.026 (0.050)	-0.054 (0.049)	-0.019 (0.050)	-0.023 (0.049)
Endogenous variables						
INVEST	0.339*** (0.072)	0.335*** (0.075)	0.352*** (0.071)	0.364*** (0.074)	0.351*** (0.077)	0.355*** (0.073)
ICRG	0.297*** (0.046)	0.084 (0.123)	0.038 (0.125)	0.276*** (0.047)	0.062 (0.128)	0.101 (0.129)
OPEN	11.238*** (4.008)	12.593*** (4.145)	10.28*** (3.909)	7.871** (3.847)	8.236** (3.969)	7.528** (3.762)
ENT	2.426* (1.164)	1.091* (0.616)	1.004*** (0.654)	1.342 (0.115)	0.045 (0.675)	0.249 (0.703)
CREDIT	1.462 (2.475)	0.476 (2.464)	0.154 (2.428)	-0.985 (2.890)	-2.161 (2.890)	-1.216 (2.838)
ENT X OPEN	-0.914* (0.492)	-0.424*** (0.129)	-0.349*** (0.123)	-0.755 (0.481)	-0.316** (0.127)	-0.279** (0.121)
ENT X CREDIT	0.240** (0.095)	0.229** (0.095)	0.252*** (0.096)	0.496*** (0.158)	0.504** (0.160)	0.518*** (0.149)
ENT X OPEN_SQ	0.067 (0.055)	–	–	0.057 (0.054)	–	–
ENT X CREDIT_SQ	-0.066*** (0.015)	-0.058* (0.014)	-0.062*** (0.015)	-0.097*** (0.019)	-0.091*** (0.019)	-0.097*** (0.020)
ENT X ICRG	–	0.007* (0.003)	-0.0018 (0.011)	–	0.008* (0.004)	-0.0042 (0.011)
ENT X ICRG_SQ	–	–	0.0001 (0.0001)	–	–	0.0001 (0.0001)
Exogenous variables						
LAAM	-0.161 (0.155)	-0.299* (0.154)	-0.361** (0.148)	-0.225 (0.252)	-0.385** (0.161)	-0.366** (0.153)
TRANSITION						
Number of obs.	318	318	318	299	299	299
Sargan test[a], chi2	265.69	269.56	282.53	261.53	265.56	285.74
M2[b]; z; [pr > z]	-1.55 [0.12]	-1.32 [0.19]	-1.179 [0.23]	-1.57 [0.12]	-1.27 [0.21]	-1.21 [0.23]

Notes: [a] Sargan test of the validity of overidentifying restrictions; [b] Arellano–Bond test that average autocovariance in residuals of order 2 is 0; The constant is not reported; See Table 9.1 for variable definition; * significant at 0.10 level,** significant at 0.05 level, *** significant at 0.01 level.

Source: Data on ENT are from LABORSTA data set produced by ILO. All other data are from World Bank World Development Indicators database (2005).

Table 9.4 Arellano–Bond GMM estimation (Dependent variable: growth of income per capita) Including ENT squared and its interaction with other variables

	(1)	(2)	(3)	(4)
Growth (lagged)	−0.026 (0.048)	−0.026 (0.047)	−0.011 (0.049)	−0.013 (0.047)
Endogenous variables				
INVEST	0.237*** (0.070)	0.233*** (0.070)	0.147** (0.074)	0.251*** (0.069)
ICRG	0.243*** (0.046)	0.340*** (0.046)	0.364*** (0.049)	0.169 (0.123)
OPEN	12.217*** (4.087)	11.616*** (3.941)	11.925*** (4.355)	12.701*** (3.900)
ENT	0.945* (0.558)	0.991* (0.556)	1.479** (0.597)	0.727 (0.587)
CREDIT	1.662 (2.467)	1.323 (2.962)	1.607 (3.168)	1.495 (2.388)
ENT X OPEN	−0.333** (0.145)	−0.282** (0.126)	−0.307** (0.142)	−0.328*** (0.123)
ENT X CREDIT	0.248** (0.096)	0.294 (0.187)	−0.259* (0.150)	0.229** (0.096)
ENT X CREDIT_SQ	−0.066*** (0.015)	−0.068*** (0.016)	0.003 (0.016)	−0.062*** (0.014)
ENT X ICRG	–	–	–	0.003 (0.005)
ENT_SQ X OPEN	0.0011 (0.001)	–	–	–
ENT_SQ X CREDIT	–	−0.001 (0.001)	0.003 (0.016)	–
ENT_SQ X ICRG	–	–	–	0.0001 (0.0001)
Exogenous variables				
LAAM	−0.075 (0.139)	−0.033* (0.138)	−0.071 (0.144)	−0.155 (0.137)
Number of obs.	345	345	345	345
Sargan test[a], chi2	297.71	300.83	276.69	306.65
M2[b], z; [pr > z]	−1.51 [0.13]	−1.49 [0.14]	−1.50 [0.13]	−1.37 [0.17]

Notes: [a] Sargan test of the validity of overidentifying restrictions; [b] Arellano–Bond test that average autocovariance in residuals of order 2 is 0; The constant is not reported; See Table 9.1 for variable definition; * significant at 0.10 level, ** significant at 0.05 level, *** significant at 0.01 level.

Source: Data on ENT are from LABORSTA data set produced by ILO. All other data are from World Bank World Development Indicators database (2005).

Given that our full sample includes countries that have recently been added to the group of high income countries (for example, South Korea and Singapore) we adjust the sample by excluding all countries that are currently part of the high income group. We re-estimate the equations and report the results in columns (1)–(3) of Table 9.3. Next, we exclude sub-Saharan African countries and re-estimate the equations. We report the results in columns (4)–(6) of Table 9.3. The results are similar to those reported in Table 9.2 and, thus, we draw the same conclusions (except for the interplay of ENT and ICRG where we find weak evidence of a positive impact).

An alternative way to test this implication of the Iyigun–Rodrik theoretical model is to assess whether the interplay between the square of entrepreneurship and reforms is significant. We do this and report the results in Tables 9.4 and 9.5. The estimates in Table 9.4 where we use the full sample and Table 9.5 where we exclude high income countries[9]

Table 9.5 Arellano–Bond GMM estimation (Dependent variable: growth of income per capita) Including ENT squared and its interaction with other variables and excluding high income countries from the sample

	(1)	(2)	(3)
Growth (lagged)	−0.038 (0.049)	−0.024 (0.051)	−0.027 (0.049)
Endogenous variables			
INVEST	0.330*** (0.073)	0.269*** (0.078)	0.355*** (0.072)
ICRG	0.315*** (0.046)	0.323*** (0.048)	0.103 (0.125)
OPEN	9.320** (4.041)	9.708*** (4.199)	8.741** (3.844)
ENT	0.913* (0.544)	1.502*** (0.567)	0.513 (0.581)
CREDIT	0.231 (2.482)	−0.851 (3.231)	0.048 (2.409)
ENT X OPEN	−0.359** (0.141)	−0.358*** (0.132)	−0.303** (0.120)
ENT X CREDIT	0.260*** (0.095)	0.002 (0.001)	0.237** (0.095)
ENT X CREDIT_SQ	−0.063*** (0.014)	−0.174 (0.149)	−0.060*** (0.014)
ENT X ICRG	–	–	0.005 (0.005)
ENT_SQ X OPEN	−0.001 (0.001)	–	–
ENT_SQ X CREDIT	–	0.002 (0.001)	–
ENT_SQ X ICRG	–	–	−0.0001 (0.0001)
Exogenous variables			
LAAM	−0.289* (0.119)	−0.315** (0.159)	−0.361** (0.148)
Number of obs.	318	318	318
Sargan test[a], chi2	273.43	256.63	280.94
M2[b], z; [pr > z]	−1.51 [0.13]	−1.45 [0.15]	−1.28 [0.20]

Notes: [a] Sargan test of the validity of overidentifying restrictions; [b] Arellano–Bond test that average autocovariance in residuals of order 2 is 0; The constant is not reported; See Table 9.1 for variable definition. * significant at 0.10 level, ** significant at 0.05 level, *** significant at 0.01 level.

Source: Data on ENT are from LABORSTA data set produced by ILO. All other data are from World Bank World Development Indicators database (2005).

indicate that the interplay of the variable ENT squared and each of the reform proxies is statistically non-significant. It is important to note that the conclusions we outlined based on the previous results (Tables 9.2 and 9.3) remain strongly valid. In addition, we tried to control for human capital (the results are not reported in the chapter) by including total literacy rates and male and female literacy rates, as well as fertility rates, but the coefficients on all these variables are statistically insignificant, and the previous conclusions remain the same. Finally, we estimated the equations with a time dummy and the conclusions remain valid (see Table 9A.1). Thus, based on these results we may conclude that the growth effects of entrepreneurship seem, indeed, to depend on policy reform.[10]

Concluding remarks

This chapter examined the interplay of institutional and policy reforms and entrepreneurship and explored its effect on growth. More specifically, we tested an important implication of the Iyigun–Rodrik model (Iyigun and Rodrik 2005), that institutional reform would have negative (positive) effects if pre-existing entrepreneurial activity is vibrant (weak), while 'policy tinkering' will have a positive (negative) effects if pre-existing entrepreneurial activity is vibrant (weak). We did so by using panel data from developing and transition economies and estimating Arellano–Bond GMM growth equations where we include proxies for entrepreneurial intensity and institutional and policy reforms, as well as their interactions.

We found that the interplay of entrepreneurship and policy reforms has an influence on the growth effects of entrepreneurship. We showed that the joint effect of trade reform and entrepreneurship on growth is negative, suggesting that trade reform diminishes the positive effects of entrepreneurial ability on growth if entrepreneurial activity is vibrant. We found that the interplay of financial sector reform and entrepreneurship has a non-linear effect on growth. Financial reforms enhance the growth effects of entrepreneurship initially and diminish it at high levels of reform. Moreover, we show that the interplay of institutions and entrepreneurship does not seem to matter for the impact on growth.

The results related to the interplay of trade reform and entrepreneurial intensity are consistent with those derived in Baliamoune-Lutz (2007) and Iyigun and Rodrik's (2005) empirical estimation (although Iyigun and Rodrik view changes in openness to trade as institutional reform) using cross-sectional data from a group of developed and developing countries. With regard to the interplay of institutional reform and entrepreneurship the findings in the present study are different from those derived in

Baliamoune-Lutz (2007) where the author uses a sample of developed and developing countries and shows that this interplay has a positive effect on growth, implying that institutional reform could enhance the growth effects of entrepreneurship. It is possible that these differences stem from the fact that developed countries have much better institutions and thus the disparity in institutional reform would be more significant in a sample that includes developing and developed countries.

In summary, the empirical results suggest that trade and financial reforms can reduce the growth effects of entrepreneurship, although financial reforms seem to have a positive effect in early stages (low doses) of reform. On the other hand, institutional reform does not seem to influence the growth effects of entrepreneurship. Overall, these findings seem to be consistent with the predictions and arguments developed in Iyigun and Rodrik's (2005) theoretical model, if one assumes that a change in a country's openness to trade or in its ratio of credit to the private sector is a result of policy reform (also viewed by Iyigun and Rodrik as institutional reform), not policy tinkering. The growth effects of entrepreneurial activity seem to depend on pre-existing levels of entrepreneurship and on policy reforms. In settings where entrepreneurial activity is vibrant, reforms could have a negative outcome, while in settings with weak entrepreneurial activity reforms would enhance the growth effects of entrepreneurship. It is possible, for example, that in settings where entrepreneurial activity is strong, a trade or credit market reform would induce the incumbents to bribe or be part of other rent-seeking activities to access input or output markets or to eliminate possible competition (new entrants) which would have a negative effect on growth.

Appendix

Table 9A.1 Arellano–Bond GMM estimation (Dependent variable: growth of income per capita) Including time dummies

	(1) Full sample	(2) Excluding high-income countries	(3) Excluding high-income countries and SSA
Growth (lagged)	−0.037 (0.046)	−0.025 (0.049)	−0.021 (0.050)
Endogenous variables			
INVEST	0.303*** (0.066)	0.358*** (0.071)	0.355*** (0.073)
ICRG	0.384 (0.118)	0.062 (0.126)	0.117 (0.130)
OPEN	10.698*** (3.771)	9.734** (3.914)	7.272* (3.773)
ENT	1.792 (1.150)	0.752 (0.668)	0.176 (0.707)

Continued

Table 9A.1 Continued

	(1) Full sample	(2) Excluding high- income countries	(3) Excluding high- income countries and SSA
CREDIT	−0.143 (2.333)	−0.419 (2.445)	−1.244 (2.839)
ENT X OPEN	−0.931** (0.463)	−0.307** (0.125)	−0.252** (0.123)
ENT X CREDIT	0.186** (0.094)	0.227** (0.096)	0.473*** (0.164)
ENT X OPEN_SQ	0.081 (0.051)		
ENT X CREDIT_SQ	−0.048*** (0.015)	−0.055*** (0.015)	−0.089*** (0.021)
ENT X ICRG	0.011 (0.009)	0.0002 (0.011)	−0.003 (0.011)
ENTX ICRG_SQ	−0.00003 (0.00008)	−0.0001 (0.0001)	0.0001 (0.0001)
Exogenous variables			
LAAM	−0.130 (0.131)	−0.309** (0.150)	−0.327** (0.159)
Time	0.079*** (0.023)	0.046* (0.026)	0.027 (0.028)
Number of obs.	345	318	299
Sargan test[a], chi2	318.66	280.84	284.51
M2[b], z; [pr > z]	−1.19 [0.23]	−1.08 [0.28]	−1.14 [0.25]

Notes: [a] Sargan test of the validity of overidentifying restrictions; [b] Arellano–Bond test that average autocovariance in residuals of order 2 is 0; The constant is not reported; See Table 9.1 for variable definition. * significant at 0.10 level, ** significant at 0.05 level, *** significant at 0.01 level.

Source: Data on ENT are from LABORSTA dataset produced by ILO. All other data are from World Bank World Development Indicators database (2005).

Acknowledgement

The author is grateful to the International Center for Economic Research (ICER), Turin, Italy for a fellowship that supported this research. The usual disclaimer applies.

Notes

1. See Iyigun and Rodrik (2005) about the distinction between institutional reform and policy tinkering. Also, see the comments about the definition of policy and institutional reforms in Baliamoune-Lutz (2007).
2. Baumol (1990) and Colombatto and Melnik (2008) provide insightful discussions of the importance of the distinction between productive and unproductive entrepreneurship.
3. Iyigun and Rodrik (2005) take the view that only institutional reforms could have such an effect. In this chapter we assume that a significant policy change (for example, greater trade liberalization) could produce similar effects in developing and transition economies.
4. As noted in Baliamoune-Lutz (2007), some studies argue that an increase in self-employment in developing countries may indicate an increase in

informal activities, often as a result of the inability of less skilled workers to find jobs in the formal sector (Gong and Soest 2002). In this chapter, as in Baliamoune-Lutz (2007), we do not analyse the extent to which self-employment is part of the formal sector. Also, several recent studies have used data from the Global Entrepreneurship Monitor (GEM). However, GEM data do not include panel data for a sufficiently large sample of developing countries.

5. Several studies have stressed the role of capital market constraints in preventing entrepreneurship by low wealth agents (see for example, Blanchflower and Oswald 1998; Holtz-Eakin et al. 1994; Hurst and Lusardi 2004).

6. Studies that have used the ICRG composite index or specific ICRG index components – such as the rule of law, democratic accountability or the quality of bureaucracy – as proxies for the quality of institutions or institutional reform include Acemoglu et al. (2001); Brautigam and Knack (2004); La Porta et al. (1998).

7. All equations are also estimated using dummy variables for Asia, transition economies and sub-Saharan Africa (in separate estimations). Dummy variables for Asia and sub-Saharan Africa were statistically insignificant and the dummy for transition economies had a statistically significant positive coefficient. All conclusions on the relationships between the other RHS variables and growth remain unchanged.

8. All equations were also estimated using M2 instead of credit to the private sector (results are omitted from the chapter but may be obtained from the author) and the conclusions are the same.

9. Excluding SSA also yields similar results. Results are not reported here, but may be obtained from the author upon request.

10. An alternative interpretation could be that the growth effects of policy reform may depend on the level of pre-existing entrepreneurships.

10
Human and Social Capital in Entrepreneurship in Developing Countries

Gerrit Rooks, Adam Szirmai and Arthur Sserwanga

Introduction

Entrepreneurship scholars have recently started to pay attention to the interplay of human and social capital (Anderson and Miller 2003; Bosma et al. 2004; Brüderl and Preisendörfer 1998; Davidson and Honig 2003; Mosey and Wright 2007; Renzulli et al. 2000). Human capital refers to the knowledge and skills that economic actors have acquired, which can be employed for productive purposes, thereby generating income. Social capital can be understood as the immaterial and material resources that accrue to a group or individual by virtue of having a durable network of relationships.

Some entrepreneurship scholars argue that human and social capital are substitutes, while others see them as complements. Brüderl and Preisendörfer (1998) state that social capital compensates for shortcomings in human capital and Piazza-Georgi (2002) concludes that investment in human capital leads to a loss in social capital, since one is unable to invest simultaneously in both forms of capital. In the classical sociological literature, human and social capital are seen as complements, just as human and physical capital are increasingly seen as complements in the economic literature on growth and productivity (Abramovitz 1989; Szirmai 2008). Human capital is effective only in the 'right' social context (Burt 2001; Coleman 1988).

A shortcoming in the entrepreneurship literature is its focus on human and social capital in the advanced economies, while it has been argued that these aspects are critically important for developing countries (Woolcock 1998). This neglect of the developing countries is a weakness in the entrepreneurship literature in general (Bruton et al. 2008; Naudé 2008).

Human and social capital in entrepreneurship: Substitutes or complements?

Reflecting our increasing understanding of the processes of economic growth and development, the concept of capital has gradually been broadened over time. In the 1950s the emphasis was on physical capital accumulation and its contribution to economic growth, but capital accumulation left large portions of growth unexplained. In the 1960s and 1970s, Denison, Schultz and Becker introduced the notion of human capital, where investment in education and the quality of labour were seen as at least as important as investment in physical capital goods.

Contrary to the concept of human capital, which is by now widely accepted, social capital is still a somewhat contested concept, although some authors believe that the concept of social capital can serve as a bridge between theories and disciplines (Woolcock 1998).[1]

There are a number of definitions of social capital. One set can be summarized as resources that are potentially available from one's social ties. People can invest their scarce time and resources in strengthening their social ties and networks. Another set of definitions focuses on trust and norms as the solution to collective action problems. In this chapter we side with the former perspective. We adopt the view of Bourdieu, who gave the first systematic contemporary analysis of social capital. Bourdieu (1985: 248) defines the concept as:

> The aggregate of the actual or potential resources which are linked to the possession of a durable network of more or less institutionalized relationships of mutual acquaintance or recognition.

This also implies a choice for the micro-level. We focus on the social capital of entrepreneurial actors. Most existing studies in this regard have so far focused on entrepreneurship and social capital in the context of advanced economies. Until recently, there has been insufficient attention on the role of entrepreneurship in the very different context of developing economies. One exception is Honig (1998) who surveys 215 Jamaican informal micro-entrepreneurs. Honig finds that those entrepreneurs who had an education, also had a higher income. Also, if an entrepreneur was a church member who visited church semi-weekly, then the entrepreneur had a higher income as well. Honig's findings also suggest that the effects of human and social capital may vary between different business environments.

The human capital explanation of entrepreneurial success is that people who do better are more able individuals. They are the better educated, better skilled, healthier and more experienced people and these human resources help them to be more successful, effective and productive than those who possess less human capital. In this human capital view, it matters 'what you know'. Social capital explanations of success are based on the idea that people who do better are better connected to other people.

The notion that human and social capital are complementary forms of capital can be traced back to Coleman (1988). Coleman discusses the effect of social capital on the human capital of the next generation. He argues that social capital in the family as well as in the community promotes the formation of human capital. Without social capital there will be lower stocks of human capital. Burt (2001: 32) also considers human and social capital as complements: 'Social capital is the contextual complement to human capital.' In the perspective of Burt, human capital yields a higher profit, as it is complemented by social capital: it is 'what you know' and 'who you know'.

An opposite line of thinking is that human and social capital form substitutes. Piazza-Georgi (2002) argues that acquiring capital requires investments. People who invest much time in building up their human capital by getting an education will subsequently invest less time in social capital. Brüderl and Preisendörfer (1998) hypothesize that especially entrepreneurs who lack other sources of capital (human and financial) will be motivated to mobilize resources through their social network. According to Brüderl and Preisendörfer, this so-called 'network compensation hypothesis' might explain why many empirical studies do not find positive effects of social networks on business performance. Entrepreneurs who mobilize their networks are those who lack human and financial capital. Hence, effects of social capital are complemented with effects of human capital. The network compensation hypothesis was tested empirically using a sample of 1,849 business founders and the effects of different aspects of human capital on network support varied considerably. For instance, total years of schooling have a negative effect on the level of network support from strong ties such as family, while the same variable has a positive effect on the amount of network support from weak ties of the business founders. Based on their results, Brüderl and Preisendörfer (1998) call the evidence inconclusive.

In this chapter we formulate two working hypotheses. The first hypothesis is that the amount of social capital of a small entrepreneur is inversely related to his/her human capital (the network compensation hypothesis). Our second working hypothesis is that the effects of human and social capital on indicators of entrepreneurial performance are substitutable, rather than complementary.

Methodology

Study area

To study the interaction between human and social capital in a developing country, we use data from a recent survey conducted among Ugandan entrepreneurs in May 2008. Uganda is a developing country with a population of about 30 million people, some 40 per cent of whom are still living in poverty. Uganda is a very interesting country for studying entrepreneurship, since it is said to be one of the most entrepreneurial countries in the world. It has a total entrepreneurial average index (TEA) of 30 per cent of the working population (aged 16–64). About 3.1 million people are estimated to be entrepreneurs, the males accounting for about 65 per cent of the entrepreneurs (Walter et al. 2003, 2004). However, the business failure rate is reportedly high. On average, 30 per cent of the entrepreneurs shutdown their businesses within the first 12 months of operation. When business registration is used as an indicator of formalization, 66 per cent of Ugandan businesses are not registered in any way (informal enterprises) and 27 per cent do not pay any tax or any local market dues (Walter et al. 2003, 2004).

Survey design

The sampling procedure employed in the survey is based on the Global Entrepreneurship Survey approach for selecting respondents (see Walter 2003, 2004 for more details). The sample area is restricted to central Uganda. There are three other regions, but their inclusion would have been too costly. In central Uganda two different districts are covered, namely Kampala, the capital city and leading commercial town of Uganda, and one rural area, namely the Mpigi district, largely dependent on subsistence agriculture.

The Uganda Bureau of Statistics provided detailed maps of numbers, location and composition of households. A representative sample of populations aged 16–64 years was attained by taking a designated sample of households and selecting one adult per household at random.

Local government officials of the respective areas were helpful in providing and updating area registries of deaths and migrations and locating selected households. We use the Ugandan Bureau of Statistics' definition of a household 'as a group of people who normally eat together'. In case of ambiguity, only those who ate together the previous day are included in the composition of a given household. The local authorities were also helpful in making a distinction between residents who were entrepreneurs or non-entrepreneurs.

The sample was selected in a number of steps. First, parishes were selected. Next, local officials provided us with lists of households, indicating which households were entrepreneurs. From these lists some 750 entrepreneurial households and a control group of 250 non-entrepreneurial households were selected. The selection of households and subsequently of the respondents within the households was done randomly.

If there was more than one entrepreneur within the household, the adult entrepreneurial family members were numbered according to their age, assigning number one to the oldest and the highest number to the youngest household member The respondent was selected according to a random selection from a random numbers table: the second oldest person was selected if the chosen random number was a two, the fifth oldest if the random number was a five, etc. A similar procedure was chosen for the non-entrepreneurial households, with the difference that here every adult household member was assigned a number. In this chapter we analyse only the data for 733 entrepreneurs.

Since questionnaires could not be mailed, faxed or couriered to respondents in Uganda, the data had to be gathered via personal interviews. The interviews were carried out in May 2008. A team of ten interviewers were assembled and trained. The interviewers were all either graduate students or staff at Makerere University Business School (Kampala). All but one interviewer had extensive previous experience as an interviewer working for the Global Entrepreneurship Monitor (GEM) projects in 2003 and/or 2004. During the training, sampling procedures, translations of key terms in the questionnaires and handling of respondents were emphasized. Finally, the interviewers were field-tested to assess their ability to handle the data collection before they embarked on the exercise.

We devoted a substantial amount of time and effort to the construction and testing of the questionnaire. Three extensive pre-tests were carried out to fine tune the instrument to local circumstances and to ascertain the most appropriate way of asking the necessary questions.

The questionnaire consisted of mainly closed ended questions. Given the fact that many of the respondents had limited time for anything else apart from their own work, the questionnaires were inspired by simplicity and clarity, to exhaustively explore the variables.

Data collection

The data collection took place in the first two weeks of May 2008. In almost all cases we could trace the selected person and the selected person was willing to participate in the study. In Kampala there were five refusals; in Mpigi, two. Hence, we reached an unusually high response percentage of about 99.3 per cent. Each interview continued until the informant had completely described all the relevant issues. On average, an interview took 45–60 minutes.

The stratified sample consisted of 999 individuals aged 16–64 years. We oversampled entrepreneurs. Furthermore, we separated the urban and rural regions. The ratio of rural and urban areas in the sample (entrepreneurs and non-entrepreneurs) was in approximately equal proportions. Of the 504 rural and 495 urban respondents, 737 respondents were entrepreneurs and 262 non-entrepreneurs, allowing for comparisons between the two groups. Four of the 737 entrepreneurs were later discarded, because they belonged to the same enterprise.

Variables

Human capital

Human capital of entrepreneurs is determined according to three indicators. Respondents are asked to indicate their highest level of education. This variable 'years education', ranging from no schooling to a master's degree, is coded as the number of years. Two other variables measure the amount of experience an entrepreneur had gained working as an employee for a firm or as a manager before he or she decided to start his or her own business. The variable 'years experience manager' measures the years of experience that the entrepreneur had as a manager and the variable 'years experience employee' measures the years of experience as an employee.

Table 10.1   The sample

Number of respondents	Urban	Rural	Total
Non-entrepreneurs	123	139	262
Entrepreneurs	372	365	737
Total	495	504	999

Social capital

We measure the size of networks and available resources in the social network. To obtain network data we follow a standard ego-centred network approach (Burt 1984, 1997). We use three name generators to measure different aspects of the network of entrepreneurs. Multiple name generators are more reliable than single name generators for measuring the size and composition of the network (Marin and Hampton 2007). In the first name generator, we enquire about personal contacts with the following question: 'From time to time, most people discuss important personal matters with other people. Looking back over the last six months – who are the people with whom you discussed an important personal matter?' This provides indicators for the respondent's personal social capital. The second question was about contacts with whom business matters were discussed: 'From time to time, entrepreneurs seek advice on important business matters. Looking back over the last six months, who are the people with whom you discussed an important business matter?' This provides indicators for the informational social capital. The third question was about business contacts that could provide material support: 'If you were seeking material support for your business from other entrepreneurs, who, in the last six months, are those entrepreneurs?' This provides information on resource social capital. For every name generator question, the respondent was asked to list a maximum of five names. Limiting the number of alternatives is the standard way to cope with time constraints while maintaining measurement precision and decreasing measurement bias (Burt 1984: 315). There were a number of questions on each person cited in the name generator, referring to important issues such as the frequency of contacts with each person and a list of possible resources that might be obtained from the contact cite.

We construct two variables to measure social capital. The first variable, 'size', is the total number of unique contacts cited by entrepreneurs in the name generator. The second variable, 'network resources', is based on the question of possible resources a respondent could obtain via the contacts he/she cited. For every type of resource, the respondent would indicate whether he/she would be able to get the resource from the named contact. This variable is the aggregate of the resources he/she could obtain from the individuals in his/her network. We use four different types of material resources: financial, tools and machinery, premises or space and free labour.

Business success

We asked respondents whether their sales, number of customers and profits had changed compared to the previous year and by how much in percentage terms. We took the average percentage change of the three variables as our indicator of objective business success.

Innovativeness

To measure innovativeness, we use a set of five dichotomous items that measure whether the entrepreneur had introduced or invested in new or improved products or processes (see Table 10.2). These items are adapted from the first South African Innovation Survey (Oerlemans et al. 2004; Rooks et al. 2005). Innovativeness of small enterprises in the Ugandan context obviously refers to activities new to the firm, rather than to the market or to the world. We use a non-parametric items response model, the Mokken model (a probabilistic version of the Guttman scale), to measure the scalability of the items. This indicates

Table 10.2   Mean, range and scalability coefficient Mokken H for items measuring innovativeness and gestational activities

Item	Mean	Range	Mokken H
	Innovativeness		
In the last 3 years, have you invested resources:			
– to improve your (business) premises?	0.49	0–1	0.54
– to improve your (business) machineries or tools?	0.46	0–1	0.55
In the last 3 years, has your business introduced products or services that were new or improved to the market?	0.42	0–1	0.60
In the last 3 years, have you improved your products/services?	0.46	0–1	0.47
Do you plan to change your product-mix or service-mix within the next year?	0.59	0–1	0.58
	Gestational activities		
Have you prepared a business plan?	0.44	0–1	0.69
Is your plan written informally for internal use?	0.43	0–1	0.65
Is your plan written formally for external use?	0.06	0–1	0.71
Have you purchased any major items like equipment, facilities or property?	0.55	0–1	0.57
Have you developed projected financial statements (such as income and cash flow statements)?	0.37	0–1	0.54

that the items constitute a strong scale (Mokken H = 0.54). A Mokken H between 0.4 and 0.5 is considered to be a medium strong scale, above 0.5 is considered to be strong (Meijer and Baneke 2004; Mokken and Lewis 1982).

Gestational activities

The third dependent variable is an indicator of successful start-up. It assesses the progression of the exploitation process in terms of the number of gestation activities undertaken (Davidsson and Honig 2003). Davidsson and Honig identify 20 gestation behaviours. However, in the context of a developing country, many of these gestation behaviours, that is, applying for a patent, are not really applicable. We use a set of five dichotomous items that measures gestation behaviours (see bottom of Table 10.2). The Mokken model indicates that the items constitute a strong scale (Mokken H = 0.62).

Firm size and financial resources

In the absence of information on sales or turnover, as an indicator of firm size we use the number of workers employed in addition to the entrepreneur. In addition we collect data on changes in employment in the past four years, so as to get an idea of firm dynamics. Next, we also collect information on the financial resources invested in the firm.

Control variables

To control for possible conflicting effects, we include a number of control variables:

- Age is considered to be a factor in the probability of establishing a business. As individuals grow older, they are less likely to invest in the activities needed to start a new enterprise.
- Gender: In most countries gender is found to be a significant factor in the probability of establishing a business. To control for this, we include a dummy variable, 'gender' (female = 1).
- Marital status: The presence of a spouse is argued to be an aspect of social capital, thus having a positive influence on entrepreneurship (e.g. Davidsson and Honig 2003). However, empirical results are inconclusive (see e.g. Bosma et al. 2004; Donaldson and Honig 2003; Renzulli et al. 2000). To control for possible effects of having a spouse, we include a variable, 'married' (married = 1).

- Rural versus urban region: To control for possible conflicting effects of the sample regions, we include a dummy variable, 'rural' (rural region = 1; urban region = 0).
- Economic sector: We construct dummies for customer services, agriculture and manufacturing with trade and services as the baseline.
- Environmental context: We include a number of variables to control for the possible effects of entrepreneurial context. The first variable measures the dynamism of the entrepreneurial environment; the second gauges the competitive intensity that an entrepreneur experiences (competition).

Results

We use our new sample of 733 Uganda enterprises to provide a description of the country's entrepreneurs and to throw further light on this issue of Schumpeterian entrepreneurship.

Profile of entrepreneurship in the sample[2]

The first finding worth noting is the predominance of tiny enterprises: 64 per cent of the enterprises in our sample employed only one person and 85 per cent of the enterprises employed less than three people. There were only 25 enterprises (3.7 per cent) with ten or more employees. In most cases where the question about employment was not answered, we assume these to refer to enterprises without any employees, bringing the percentage of enterprises without employees to 11.7 per cent.

Most Ugandan enterprises were young; 55 per cent had started after 2004, 73 per cent after 2002 and 11.5 per cent or 81 firms had been established in 2008, the year that the survey was held.

Many of the larger firms were some kind of cooperative. For instance, a firm with 19 employees turned out to have 19 owners. Eight of the 22 firms with more than ten employees were cooperatives, with the same number of owners as the number of employed.

On average, 18 per cent of the persons employed in the enterprises were family members, a figure which, on the basis of the informal sector literature, was lower than expected. Surprisingly, the percentage of family labour was the lowest in firms with only one employee (a mere 9.6 per cent). It was quite substantial in firms with two to nine employees (27.5 per cent). In this category family employment was an important factor. In enterprises with more than ten employees, 17.1 per cent of the workforce consisted of family members.

Forty-two per cent of our entrepreneurs were female and only two of the 25 largest firms were run by women entrepreneurs. But apart from these exceptions, there was no clear relationship between size and gender. It is interesting to note that while female entrepreneurs were well represented in all sectors, they tended to be predominant in the service sector (consumer services plus business services, 52 per cent).

Of the 733 sample firms, 241 indicated that they were formally registered with the authorities. As might be expected, most of the larger firms were registered. Of the 25 firms with more than ten employees, 17 were registered. But the percentage of the smallest registered enterprises was not significantly different from the average (36.3 per cent).

Respondents were asked whether they had experienced the shutdown of a firm which they had been the owner in the past. They were also asked whether they expected to set up another enterprise in the future. This gave us four categories: (i) entrepreneurs who had experience only with their present firm, (ii) those with a history of entrepreneurship, (iii) entrepreneurs with no history but hoping to start up another firm in the future and (iv) entrepreneurs with both past history and future expectations. We consider the latter group to be the most dynamic one and refer to them as serial entrepreneurs (43.5 per cent of our sample fell in this category). When we cross-tabulate entrepreneurial history with firm size, we see that the larger firms tended to have significantly more serial entrepreneurs than the smaller ones (60 per cent of the firms with more than ten workers were serial entrepreneurs).

Most enterprises, including both tiny enterprises and some of the largest, were in consumer-oriented services (restaurants, lodging, recreation). The second most important activity was trade, where the very small enterprises dominated. Manufacturing accounted for around 11 per cent of the enterprises, with the larger firms dominant (around 20 firms had more than ten employees).

It is hard to measure the economic performance of micro-enterprises in a developing country. Respondents tended not to think in terms of economic concepts such as annual sales, turnover or profits. Even if they had an idea of their sales, they were very unwilling to provide such data to the interviewers, due to their fear of tax authorities. Therefore, one of the few measures we use for firm dynamism is employment growth. We find that not only were the firms usually minuscule, they also showed a marked lack of dynamism in terms of employment growth. Sixty-six per cent had no growth of employment whatsoever between 2005 and 2008, while 6.2 per cent indicated a decrease in employment: 10.9 per cent had been set up in 2008.

Only 15.6 per cent of the enterprises registered some growth of employment in the four-year period. In most cases, this referred to the hiring of one or two workers at the most (8.9 per cent and 2.5 per cent, respectively). There was a very small subset of dynamic enterprises exhibiting growth (less than 4 per cent of all enterprises).

Not surprisingly, there was a strong overlap between the set of larger firms and the more dynamic firms. Almost all of the larger firms experienced employment growth. In addition there were a small number of minuscule firms that had expanded their staff to five to eight persons. It is in this small subset that we should look for the dynamic Schumpeterian entrepreneurs.

Another indication of the nature of entrepreneurship is the amount of funds invested. The majority of the respondents had invested funds in their enterprise, but the sums were rather modest, varying from a low of UGX 1,000 (€0.40) to a high of UGX 100,000,000 (€44,000) for one exceptional enterprise. The average investment was UGX 786,082 (approximately €342). Average investments were highest in consumer-oriented services (UGX 1,182,229), followed by business services. Somewhat surprisingly, average investment was the lowest in manufacturing (UGX 335,865). Though modest, these sums were higher than the very small sums mentioned in the micro-entrepreneurship literature.

Broken down by firm size, we see that small enterprises predictably invested less than larger enterprises: entrepreneurs with 0–2 employees invested on average UGX 550,450 (€239), those with 3–9 employees invested UGX 1,238,060 (€538) and those with over 10 employees invested UGX 4,375,536 (€1,772). In sum, we can conclude that the majority of the enterprises were small, with limited access to investment and not dynamic in terms of employment growth.

Description of the networks of Ugandan entrepreneurs

In entrepreneurial research the size of the network is often equated with the amount of resources one can obtain from such a network. To measure the size of the entrepreneurial support, we use data from the three name generators that respectively measure personal network, business advice network and material support network. On average, the personal advice network consisted of 2.8 people; the business advice network 1.9 people and the material support network of 1.1 people. Hence, the average number of contacts mentioned totalled about six.

However, the same contact could be named more than once, since we asked about different aspects of the ego-centred network. Hence, it is likely that the networks show some overlap. This is related to the phenomenon of the so-called interlocking markets in developing countries. Markets are said to be interlocked if transactions in one market depend on transactions in other markets (Taslim 1988). We anticipate possible network overlap; for every contact named in two subsequent networks, the respondent was asked to indicate whether the contact had been mentioned before. If these double contacts are taken into account, the corrected average size of the total network was four. This implies that the network overlap was 33 per cent (6–4/6). Although no comparable data are available from other studies, the degree of overlap was lower than we had expected.

It is noteworthy that there was a big difference between male and female entrepreneurial networks. Networks of male entrepreneurs were substantially larger than those of their female counterparts (4.4 versus 3.3). Another noteworthy difference in network size was between rural and urban areas, with the networks of rural entrepreneurs substantially larger than those in the cities (five versus three).

It is often said that family plays a pivotal role in many African microenterprises. We find that the average entrepreneurial network consisted of 40 per cent family members. This figure was slightly higher in the personal network (42 per cent) and somewhat lower in the business advice (38 per cent) as well as in material support network (37 per cent). Again, there was a big difference between the networks of male and female entrepreneurs. The share of kin was notably higher for females than for males (50 per cent versus 33 per cent). Surprisingly, there was no difference in the proportion of kin between rural and urban entrepreneurs.

With regard to gender composition, most entrepreneur networks were rather homogeneous. Male entrepreneur networks consisted for 82 per cent of men, while female entrepreneur networks consisted for 60 per cent of men. Hence, females had the benefit of opposite gendered networks more often than males.

We asked respondents whether the ties were local (i.e. within their home village) or non-local (i.e. outside the village). It became apparent that on average 36 per cent of the ties were non-local. There was no significant difference between males and females in the locality of their ties, but the environment, whether rural or urban, did matter. Rural entrepreneurs had clearly more local networks than their urban counterparts (29 per cent versus 43 per cent).

Explaining social capital: The network compensation hypothesis

In this section, we examine the network compensation hypothesis which suggests that scarce time can either be devoted to accumulating human capital or to investing in social capital (social networks). The hypothesis suggests that there should be a significant negative correlation between indicators of human and social capital. If there is a shortage of human capital, it will be substituted for by social capital.

It is worth noting that this hypothesis should be distinguished from the question of substitutability of human and social capital, which refers to a framework in which the same 'outcome' can be realized with different combinations of 'inputs'. The network compensation hypothesis focuses on the actual empirical proportions of human and social capital.

As can be seen from Table 10.3, there are no significant negative correlations between human and social capital indicators. All correlations are positive, some of them significantly so. This is elaborated further in Table 10.4, which takes the social capital variables 'network size' and 'network resources' as the dependent variables and examines the relationships between human and social capital when control variables are added.

One of the most pronounced findings is the negative effect of gender. Females have significantly less social capital than males. On the other hand, being married is positively associated with social capital. Network size in rural areas is significantly higher than in urban areas. Finally, entrepreneurs in consumer services and agriculture have significantly more social capital than in other sectors.

The two regression tables confirm the initial conclusions from the bivariate correlations. There are no significant negative coefficients of the human capital variables, but there are various significant positive effects. Thus, both the years of education and the years of management experience have positive effects on network size. In sum, entrepreneurs

Table 10.3 Correlations between human and social capital

	Human capital indicators		
	Years of education	Years of management experience	Years of work experience
Network size	0.16	0.11**	0.03
Network resources	0.08*	0.09*	0.03

Note: * p<.05; ** p<.01 (two tailed tests).

Table 10.4 Determinants of social capital

	Network size	Network resources
Human capital		
Years of education	0.063 (0.025)*	0.042 (0.069)
Years of management experience	0.164 (0.061)**	0.407(0.176)*
Years of work experience	0.003 (0.023)	−0.034 (0.063)
Control variables: individual		
Marital status (married = 1)	0.374 (0.190)*	2.148 (0.626)
Age	0.003 (0.010)	−0.033 (0.026)
Gender (female = 1)	−0.936 (0.162)***	−1.886 (0.480)***
Control variables: enterprise		
Size enterprise	−0.004 (0.030)	0.029 (0.105)
Formally registered	0.120 (0.170)	1.485 (0.504)**
Age of enterprise	0.006 (0.015)	0.020 (0.043)
Number of co-owners	0.060 (0.050)	0.149 (0.172)
Control variables: environment		
Dynamism environment	0.046 (0.074)	0.201 (0.215)
Competitive pressure	−0.015 (0.085)	0.164 (0.249)
Region	1.778 (0.203)	0.449 (0.534)
Services	0.230 (0.168)	3.316 (0.523)***
Agriculture	−0.158 (0.273)	2.458 (0.695)***
Manufacturing	0.224 (0.354)	1.174 (0.741)
Constant	3.113 (0.421)	4.218 (0.236)
Number of observations	673	673
F	15.10*** (16, 656)	6.81*** (16, 656)
R^2	0.234	0.137

Note: Standard deviations in parentheses; *significant at 0.10%; **significant at 0.05%; *** significant at 0.001%.

with more human capital tended to have more developed social networks. This contradicts the network compensation hypothesis.

Determinants of entrepreneurial performance

We also analyse subjective business success, but have not included these results in this study. Subjective business success tells us more about the entrepreneurs' feelings of relative deprivation than about their performance. For instance, network resources are negatively associated with subjective business success. The more resources the network members have, the less successful the entrepreneur feels.

The analysis is performed at two levels. At the first level, we simply discuss and interpret the significant determinants of entrepreneurial performance. At the second level, we focus on the central question in this article, the complementarity or substitutability of human and social capital.

Substitutability versus complementarity, some methodological remarks

Applying the economic notion of substitutability of inputs to standard regression equations, we argue that a positive and significant coefficient for the two independent variables implies that they are substitutable. A significant regression coefficient implies a positive effect on the dependent variable, holding the other independent variable constant. Thus, by increasing one independent variable and reducing another or vice versa, the same outcome for the dependent variable can be found. Thus these two independent variables are substitutable.

With respect to the issue of substitutability, a positive and significant coefficient of the human capital variable and the social capital variable in the same equation means that they are substitutable. A positive coefficient for one variable and a non-significant coefficient for another means they are non-substitutable; similarly, a positive coefficient for one variable and a non-significant coefficient for the other also implies non-substitutability.

A positive and significant coefficient for the interaction term between human and social capital implies complementarity. A positive and significant coefficient for the interaction term and positive (and significant) coefficients for human and social capital imply complementarity, but with some substitutability at the margin. This reasoning is used to interpret the subsequent regression tables.

Endogeneity

As in our statistical model, we use the ordinary least square model in the equations explaining entrepreneurial performance. One objection to using this model in our case is that social capital may be conceived as an endogenous variable (see our explanation of social capital) because the amount of one's social capital depends, among others factors, on human capital. Our previous analyses show that although there are some significant relationships, we can explain only 10–20 per cent of the variance in social capital. Nevertheless, endogeneity may pose serious statistical problems.

To first investigate endogeneity we execute a so-called augmented regression test. We first perform a regression on social capital and include the residuals of this regression in a regression on our performance indicators. This test indicates endogeneity. To test whether this endogeneity has deleterious effects, we perform a Hausman-test using instrumental variables. As our instruments we use a number of variables that do not correlate with the error term of our dependent variables, but do correlate with social capital (the proportion of gender, kin and locality of ties within the network and marital status). The Hausman-test indicates that in most cases endogeneity is not a problem. The only problematic result is that the least squared coefficient of network resources in the regression of gestation activities is likely to be inconsistent. However, in our instrumental variables regression analysis of gestation activities, we see that the coefficient of network resources is higher than the least squares estimate. At this stage we decide to use our original social capital variables in the following analysis. The statistical problems due to endogeneity are only minor and using an instrumental variable approach to correct the problem is in itself often associated with major estimation problems (see, for instance, Bound et al. 1995).

Objective success

Table 10.5 presents four specifications with objective success as the dependent variable. The first specification includes all relevant background variables. In the second specification, we add interaction terms for the different human and social capital indicators. In the third column, we add other non-linear terms and find that the square of human capital and the square of network resources are significant. In column 4, we drop the non-significant control variables and all non-significant non-linear terms. This column is our preferred specification. A similar procedure is followed in the subsequent sections.

We find positive effects of years of education, firm size and the agricultural sector dummy, while being married has negative effects. The perceived dynamism of the environment also has a positive and significant coefficient.

In general, the degree of explained variation is very limited. Many of the coefficients are non-significant. With regard to substitutability, the results are somewhat mixed. The sign of education is positive, while the sign of network resources is negative and non-significant. This is an indication of non-substitutability. However, the sign of network resources squared is positive, indicating that there is some degree of substitutability of human capital and network resources at higher ranges of the variable network resources. None of the interaction terms is significant, which indicates an absence of complementarity effects.

Table 10.5 Determinants of objective success

	Model 1	Model 2	Model 3	Model 4
Human capital				
Years of education	0.011 (0.011)	0.009 (0.012)	0.023 (0.012)*	0.024 (0.011)*
Years of management experience	0.045 (0.042)	0.014 (0.056)	0.052 (0.035)	–
Years of work experience	-0.006 (.011)	-0.002 (0.013)	-0.006 (0.011)	–
Social capital				
Network size	-0.018 (0.024)	-0.024 (0.025)	-0.008 (0.023)	–
Network resources	0.010 (0.010)	0.012 (0.009)	-0.018 (0.013)	-0.011 (0.009)
Control variables: individual				
Marital status (married = 1)	0.014 (0.107)	0.005 (0.107)	–	–
Age	-0.012 (0.005)**	-0.011 (0.005)*	-0.014 (0.004)***	-0.013 (0.004)***
Gender (female = 1)	-0.058 (0.083)	-0.058 (0.083)	–	–
Control variables: enterprise				
Size enterprise	0.020 (0.006)**	0.020 (0.006)**	0.015 (0.005)**	0.014 (0.005)**
Formally registered	-0.076 (0.084)	-0.076 (0.084)	–	–
Age of enterprise	-0.003 (0.008)	-0.004 (0.008)	–	–
Number of co-owners	-0.014 (0.016)	-0.014 (0.016)	–	–
Control variables: environment				
Dynamism environment	0.119 (0.042)**	0.120 (0.042)**	0.127 (0.040)**	0.136 (0.038)***
Competitive pressure	-0.059 (0.039)	-0.061 (0.040)	–	–
Region	-0.097 (0.096)	-0.082 (0.097)	–	–
Customer oriented	-0.050 (0.092)	-0.040 (0.093)	–	–
Agricultural	0.221 (0.120)	0.191 (0.123)	0.300 (0.096)***	0.315 (0.095)***
Manufacturing	-0.012 (0.151)	-0.019 (0.151)	–	–

Social capital * human capital

Netw. res. * y. o. educ.	—	—	−0.002 (0.003)
Netw. size * y. o. educ.	—	—	−0.001 (0.010)
Netw. res. * y. man. exp.	—	—	0.000 (0.010)
Netw. size. * y. man. exp	—	—	0.025 (0.020)
Netw. res. * y. wo. exp.	—	—	0.006 (0.003)
Netw. size * y. wo. exp.	—	—	−0.005 (0.006)
Non-linear effects			
Years of education^2	0.004 (0.002)*	0.004 (0.002)*	—
Network size^2	—	−0.013 (0.006)*	—
Network resources^2	0.001 (0.001)*	0.002 (0.001)**	—
Network resources * region	—	0.022 (0.014)	—
Constant	0.257 (0.118)*	0.251 (0.122)*	0.704 (0.199)
Number of observations	698	695	672
F	7.39*** (6,691)	5.21*** (13, 681)	2.72*** (24, 647)
R^2	0.067	0.079	0.075

Note: Standard deviations in parentheses; * significant at 0.10%; ** significant at 0.05%; *** significant at 0.001%.

In interpreting these results, one should keep in mind the shortcomings of our performance indicator: perceived changes relative to the previous year. The time span is too short to accurately distinguish better or weaker performing enterprises.[3]

Gestation activities

Much more interesting results are noted for the dependent variable gestation activities (presented in Table 10.6). The dependent variable is the scale created by summing the answers to the five dichotomous questions on gestation activities, which are a good indication of entrepreneurial dynamism. Our preferred specification is specification 4.

The results for gestational activities are interesting. We have a high level of explained variance ($R^2 = 0.47$) and significant influences of human capital, network resources, interaction terms and squared variables. The first interesting finding is the difference between the effects of network size and network resources. Network resources have a positive effect on gestation activities, while network size has no significant effect. The second finding is that the square of network resources has a negative sign, indicating that the effects on gestation are non-linear, with positive effects dominating up to an optimum and negative effects setting in thereafter. The standardized beta of the non-quadratic term is much higher than that of the quadratic term. The direct positive influence of network resources is by far the most important effect.

There are positive effects of education. Formally registered enterprises are much more likely to engage in gestation activities than non-registered enterprises. It is somewhat surprising that rural entrepreneurs are more likely to consider gestation activities than urban entrepreneurs. Perceived competitive pressure also has a positive effect. Female entrepreneurs are significantly less prone to engage in gestation activities than males.

In terms of our analysis of substitution and complementarity, one needs to distinguish between network size and network resources. Education has a significant positive effect. Network size has no significant effect. In our methodological introduction, we interpret this as a lack of substitutability. In the case of network resources, the interaction term with education is positive and significant, indicating complementarity. But the positive coefficients of both the education and the network resources variables indicate that there is substitutability at the margin.

Table 10.6 Determinants of gestation activities

	Model 1	Model 2	Model 3	Model 4
Human capital				
Years of education	0.037 (0.013)**	0.037 (0.013)**	0.033 (0.014)*	0.034 (0.012)**
Years of management experience	0.052 (0.030)	0.113 (0.038)**	0.040 (0.029)	–
Years of work experience	-0.002 (0.015)	-0.005 (0.014)	-0.004 (0.014)	–
Social capital				
Network size	0.001 (0.033)	0.010 (0.032)	0.042 (0.033)	0.033 (0.031)
Network resources	0.080 (0.011)***	0.076 (0.011)***	0.123 (0.016)***	0.126 (0.014)***
Control variables: individual				
Marital status (married = 1)	0.362 (0.124)**	0.386 (0.124)**	0.267 (0.110)*	0.299 (0.109)*
Age	-0.002 (0.006)	-0.003 (0.006)	–	–
Gender (female = 1)	-0.314 (0.100)**	-0.306 (0.099)**	-0.213 (0.096)*	-0.215 (0.095)*
Control variables: enterprise				
Size enterprise	-0.010 (0.011)	-0.0009 (0.010)	–	–
Formally registered	0.411 (0.111)***	0.414 (0.112)***	0.394 (0.107)***	0.396 (0.107)***
Age of enterprise	-0.005 (0.008)	-0.003 (0.009)	–	–
Number of co-owners	-0.005 (0.020)	-0.007 (0.021)	–	–
Control variables: environment				
Dynamism environment	0.537 (0.052)***	0.536 (0.052)***	0.504 (0.051)***	0.507 (0.050)***
Competitive pressure	.064 (0.052)	0.058 (0.051)	–	–
Region (rural = 1)	1.633 (0.134)	1.623 (0.133)	1.489 (0.115)***	1.500 (0.115)***
Customer oriented	.384 (0.121)**	.358 (0.121)**	0.249 (0.111)*	0.239 (0.111)*
Agricultural	0.091 (0.178)	.143 (0.178)	–	–
Manufacturing	0.177 (0.187)	0.171 (0.185)	–	–

Continued

Table 10.6 Continued

	Model 1	Model 2	Model 3	Model 4
Social capital * human capital				
Netw. res. * y. o. educ.	–	0.008 (0.003)**	–	0.004 (0.002)**
Netw. size * y. o. educ.	–	–0.007 (0.007)	–	–
Netw. res. * y. man. exp.	–	–0.003 (0.009)	–	–
Netw. Size. * y. man. exp	–	–0.019 (0.019)	–	–
Netw. res. * y. wo. exp.	–	–0.004 (0.003)	–	–
Netw. size * y. wo. exp.	–	0.000 (0.008)	–	–
Non-linear effects				
Years of education^2	–	–	0.002 (0.002)	–
Network size^2	–	–	–0.010 (0.008)	–
Network resources^2	–	–	–0.002 (0.001)**	–0.002 (0.001)**
Network resources * region	–	–	–0.060 (0.019)**	–0.068 (0.015)***
Constant	0.625 (0.267)***	0.625 (0.267)***	1.026 (0.113)***	0.995 (0.109)***
Number of observations	673	673	703	703
F	40.54 (18, 654)	33.44 (24,648)	59.11 (15,687)	73.98 (12,690)
R^2	0.457	0.467	0.471	0.472

Note: Standard deviations in parentheses; * significant at 0.10%; ** significant at 0.05%; *** significant at 0.001%.

Innovative performance

In Table 10.7, the dependent variable is the scale of innovative performance, constructed by summing the positive responses to the five questions on innovative behaviour (see Table 10.2). Our preferred specification is model 4, which explains 36 per cent of the variation of the dependent variable.

Human capital has a positive effect on innovative performance. (Human capital is significant in all of our selected specifications.) Highly educated entrepreneurs are more innovative than those with more limited education.

The effects of social capital are very interesting. Network size has a significant negative effect on innovation. Being embedded in a large network can be an obstacle for innovative entrepreneurial behaviour. In contrast, network resources have an extremely significant positive effect. It is not the size of the network that matters, but the amount of resources that can be mobilized within the network.

Again, rural entrepreneurs are significantly more innovative than those in the cities. This is somewhat counterintuitive, as one would expect most innovation to take place in urban environments. Agricultural entrepreneurs are less innovative than entrepreneurs in other economic sectors.

There is an interesting negative interaction effect between network resources and regions. Network resources have a positive impact on innovative behaviour in general, but less so in rural areas than in urban areas. Finally the perceived dynamism of the environment has a positive effect on innovative behaviour.

With regard to the substitutability or complementarity of human and social capital, all interaction terms are non-significant in the preferred model. They are dropped from the equation. Thus, we find no complementarity effects. There are indications of substitutability between the years of education and network resources. Holding education constant, network resources increase innovative behaviour and vice versa. This implies that the same level of innovative performance can be achieved with different combinations of human and social (resource) capital.

No such substitutability is found for network size. Holding education constant, an increase in network size can even reduce innovative performance. Controlling for network resources, network size acts as negative social capital.

Table 10.7 Determinants of innovative performance

	Model 1	Model 2	Model 3	Model 4
Human capital				
Years of education	0.077 (0.017)***	0.076 (0.018)***	0.074 (0.017)***	0.068 (0.016)***
Years of management experience	0.003 (0.041)	0.130 (0.044)**	0.008 (0.051)	–
Years of work experience	−0.008 (0.018)	−0.004 (0.018)	0.011 (0.017)	–
Social capital				
Network size	−0.134 (0.041)**	−0.134 (0.041)*	−0.062 (0.038)	−0.080 (0.036)*
Network resources	0.137 (0.012)***	0.136 (0.012)***	0.170 (0.019)***	0.181 (0.010)***
Control variables: individual				
Marital status (married = 1)	0.231 (0.166)	0.240 (0.167)	–	–
Age	0.006 (0.007)	0.005 (0.007)	–	–
Gender (female = 1)	−0.266 (0.129)*	−0.296 (0.131)*	–	–
Control variables: enterprise				
Size enterprise	−0.002 (0.020)	−0.002 (0.018)	–	–
Formally registered	0.215 (0.142)	0.184 (0.142)	–	–
Age of enterprise	0.010 (0.012)	0.012 (0.012)	–	–
Number of co-owners	0.023 (0.023)	0.026 (0.021)	–	–
Control variables: environment				
Dynamism environment	0.453 (0.061)***	0.447 (0.061)***	0.445 (0.061)***	0.441 (0.057)***
Competitive pressure	−0.069 (0.070)	−0.070 (0.071)	–	–
Region (rural = 1)	1.402 (0.171)***	1.369 (0.168)***	1.269 (0.148)***	1.227 (0.147)***
Customer oriented	0.302 (0.157)	0.281 (0.156)	–	–
Agricultural	−0.400 (0.202)*	−0.362 (0.204)*	−0.431 (0.176)*	−0.415 (0.168)*
Manufacturing	0.222 (0.235)	0.229 (0.230)	–	–

Social capital * human capital

	(1)	(2)	(3)	(4)
Netw. res. * y. o. educ.	–	0.003 (0.003)	–	–
Netw. size * y. o. educ.	–	−0.015 (0.010)	–	–
Netw. res. * y. man. exp.	–	−0.017 (0.008)*	–	–
Netw. size. * y. man. exp	–	−0.014 (0.018)	–	–
Netw. res. * y. wo. Exp.	–	0.000 (0.000)	–	–
Netw. size * y. wo. exp.	–	−0.145 (0.009)	–	–
Non-linear effects				
Years of education^2	–	–	0.003 (0.003)	–
Network size^2	–	–	−0.014 (0.009)	–
Network resources^2	–	–	0.001 (0.001)	–
Network resources * region	–	–	−0.106 (0.022)***	−0.121 (0.018)***
Constant	1.587 (0.336)***	1.675 (0.337)***	1.821 (0.115)***	1.840 (0.087)***
Number of observations	671	671	708	708
F	30.45 (18, 652)	26.67 (24, 646)	33.26 (12, 698)	86.52 (7, 700)
R^2	0.356	0.357	0.365	0.361

Note: Standard deviations in parentheses; *significant at 0.10%; **significant at 0.05%; *** significant at 0.001%.

Concluding remarks

This chapter discussed the interplay of human and social capital in small firms in Uganda. It is based on a new representative survey amongst entrepreneurs, executed by the authors in May 2008.

The answer to the question of the substitutability or complementarity of human and social capital influencing entrepreneurial behaviour depends on the dependent variable. In the analysis of objective success, we find neither complementarity nor substitutability for the first order terms. The interaction terms are non-significant and there is no evidence of a direct significant influence of social capital on performance. The examination of the squared non-linear terms points to some degree of substitutability between years of education and network resources for higher levels of education.

In the case of gestation activities, there are no significant effects of network size, so that there can be no question of substitutability or complementarity with human capital. But the interaction term between years of education and network resources is positive and significant, pointing to complementarity between human and social capital. Also, the first order coefficients of years of education and network resources are positive, pointing to substitutability at the margin.

The most interesting results are found for innovative performance. Here there are significant positive effects of both years of education and network resources and a significant negative effect of network size. The negative effect of network size on innovativeness indicates that there can be no substitutability with human capital. But in the case of network resources, there is clear substitutability. A given degree of innovativeness can be achieved with either more human capital or more network resources.

Summarizing, we find hardly any effects for objective success, complementarity with substitution at the margin for gestation activities and substitution for innovative performance.

An important general insight emerging from our analysis is the need to distinguish between network size and access to network resources. Controlling for access to network resources, network size is either non-significant or significantly negative in influencing various dimensions of entrepreneurial performance. In the case of innovative behaviour, the size of a network is even an obstacle to entrepreneurial dynamism and can be perceived as a kind of negative social capital. This finding is consistent with the older literature on entrepreneurship in developing countries, where extended family networks in Africa and the Middle

East are seen as a major obstacle to entrepreneurial success. It is an important observation for modern quantitive network research.

Some other general findings are worth summarizing. Years of education have an important positive effect on all three dimensions of entrepreneurial behaviour. There are persistent negative effects of gender. Females have significantly smaller networks than males and have significantly less access to resources. Female entrepreneurs engage in less gestation activities and exhibit less innovative behaviour.

There are also systematic effects of the urban–rural divide. Rural entrepreneurs have significantly more access to network resources than their urban counterparts. They engage more in gestation activities and show more innovative behaviour than urban entrepreneurs. This contradicts common-sense expectation that more dynamism will be found in urban areas.

Appendix

Table 10A.1   Descriptive statistics

	Observations	Mean	Std deviation	Range
Dependent variables				
Objective success	728	0.011	0.998	–3.01, 3.02
Innovative performance	729	2.386	1.883	0, 5
Gestation activities	729	1.834	1.645	0, 5
Human capital				
Years of education	713	8.827	3.693	0, 20
Years of management experience	731	0.213	1.174	0, 15
Years of work experience	731	2.005	3.521	0, 32
Social capital				
Network size	731	3.944	2.290	0, 14
Network resources	731	6.187	6.281	0, 39
Control variables: individual				
Marital status (married = 1)	731	0.207	0.405	0, 1
Age	720	31.524	10.789	16, 64
Gender (female = 1)	732	0.421	0.494	0, 1
Control variables: enterprise				
Size enterprise	733	2.146	5.249	0, 100
Formally registered	727	0.366	0.482	0, 1
Age of enterprise	718	6.353	6.565	.5, 47
Number of co-owners	731	0.565	2.627	0, 40

Continued

Table 10A.1   Continued

	Observations	Mean	Std deviation	Range
Control variables: environment				
Dynamism environment	733	−0.003	1.006	−2.32, 2.12
Competitive pressure	730	3.830	0.949	1, 5
Region	730	0.493	9.500	0, 1
Customer oriented	733	0.363	9.481	0, 1
Agricultural	733	0.143	9.351	0, 1
Manufacturing	733	0.112	0.315	0, 1

Acknowledgements

We thank Bart Verspagen and Pierre Mohnen for valuable suggestions for and comments on the analysis of substitution and complementarity. We thank the participants of the 2007 UNU-WIDER Research Workshop on 'Entrepreneurship and Development' for their constructive comments and criticisms.

Notes

1. For an extended discussion of concepts, theories and approaches see Rooks et al. (2009).
2. For the detailed empirical tables underlying this section see Rooks et al. (2009).
3. Output indicators are notoriously difficult to collect in this type of research. Most studies use employment growth as a proxy indicator. We also experiment with employment growth as a dependent variable, but there is insufficient variation for any meaningful results.

Part IV
Entrepreneurship and the State

11
Is Pro-Active Government Support Needed for Entrepreneurship in Developing Countries?

Wim Naudé

Introduction

The dominant approach towards entrepreneurship promotion has in recent years been one of rolling back the state and reducing the perceived obstacles in the start-up and running of business firms so as to make it easier to 'do business'. Altenburg and von Drachenfels (2006) describe this as the 'new minimalist approach' to private sector development.

In this chapter I argue that this approach may at best be a necessary condition. It may not be sufficient. In fact, governance and doing business reforms are reactive measures. Instead, I argue that these measures need to be supplemented by more pro-active government and institutional support for entrepreneurship, in particular for *the type* of entrepreneurship which will stimulate economic growth and development. While regulatory reform which makes it easier to do business may increase the number of registered business firms, it may not result in the type of entrepreneurship which is most beneficial to growth.

Types of entrepreneurship

Private sector development depends on entrepreneurship, particularly the type of entrepreneurship that leads to new venture creation and growth. Such entrepreneurship is often lacking in many developing countries, where it is clear that large numbers of people are being pushed into informal and survivalist self-employment; that is, non-productive entrepreneurship.

These people are not entrepreneurs by choice and are, in the terminology of the Global Entrepreneurship Monitor (GEM) 'necessity entrepreneurs' – as studied in Chapter 8 by Amorós. The implication is that the ways in which entrepreneurship is most often measured, may not capture the differences between productive and non-productive (and even destructive – see Chapter 15) types of entrepreneurship. Often (see also Chapter 1) entrepreneurship is measured statically by the rate of business ownership or the rate of self-employment. This does not take into account the motivation of the entrepreneur. In poor countries, where less formal employment possibilities exist, self-employment rates are higher because of the need for survival (Gollin 2008). Using self-employment to judge the effectiveness of entrepreneurial policies or the impact of entrepreneurship on growth is therefore likely to be misleading.

To try and overcome the problems of measuring entrepreneurial motivations and thus of capturing the impact of different types of entrepreneurship, the GEM makes a distinction between 'opportunity'-motivated entrepreneurs and 'necessity'-motivated entrepreneurs.[1] The former can be seen as productive entrepreneurs, while the latter may be seen as informal/survivalist entrepreneurs. The GEM, and its measurement of these various types of entrepreneurship, are discussed by Amóros in Chapter 8 and hence are not repeated here. It can be noted that Sanders (2007: 339) argues that opportunity-motivated entrepreneurship is 'an important source of innovation'. In contrast, necessity-motivated entrepreneurs are the percentage of individuals who have started up their own firms 'because they cannot find a suitable role in the world of work creating a new business is their best available option' (Reynolds et al. 2005: 217). More detailed descriptions of GEM and comparisons with other cross-country datasets are summarized in Acs et al. (2008), Ardagna and Lusardi (2008) and Reynolds et al. (2005).

Literature review

Two strands of entrepreneurship literature are relevant for the purpose of this chapter. The first deals with the relationship between entrepreneurship and economic growth and suggests that the type of entrepreneurship may matter for growth. The second strand deals with the determinants of start-up rates, in particular regulatory barriers to entry such as start-up costs, minimum capital requirements and a lack of access to finance. This literature overlaps with the literature on the policy measures for promoting entrepreneurship. An exhaustive review of the literature falls outside the scope of this chapter; however, I will highlight some of the key findings and their salient features that are relevant for current purposes.

Entrepreneurship and economic growth

The theoretical literature has always seen entrepreneurship as essential for economic growth and development. Wennekers and Thurik (1999: 30) identify 13 distinct roles of an entrepreneur in economic growth. These include, amongst others, risk-taking, innovation, arbitrage and coordination of production factors. In various context and periods, different roles have been stressed as being more crucial for economic growth than others. Thus for instance in developing countries, where countries operate mostly within the technological production frontier, and where many markets may be missing, entrepreneurs move firms closer to the frontier through technological imitation[2] and more efficient allocation of labour and capital (Estrin et al. 2006; Leibenstein 1968). They provide competition and markets through arbitrage and a cost discovery function (see, for example, Hausmann and Rodrik 2003; Kirzner 1973). In more advanced economies, entrepreneurs push out the technological production function through radical and incremental innovation as described by Schumpeter (1911/1934). Nowadays the growth-enhancing role of entrepreneurs in advanced economies[3] is seen as transforming 'inventions into commercially viable products and processes' (Minniti 2008: 779). In all of these the crucial functions provided by the entrepreneur always go beyond mere business ownership or managerial functions ('routine' entrepreneurship) and often result in the creation of new firms offering new products and services.

As far as empirical tests of the relationship between entrepreneurship and economic growth are concerned, Nyström (2008) provides a summary of the literature. She lists 38 studies between 1996 and 2006 which quantify the relationship between entrepreneurship and economic performance. In these studies, entrepreneurship is measured either according to self-employment rates (most frequently), business ownership rates (e.g. Klapper et al. 2007), early stage entrepreneurial activity (start-up activity) (e.g. Wong et al. 2005) or even by the number of patents registered.[4] Economic performance is measured using either rates on employment, GDP growth or productivity growth. With the exception of three studies, the studies cited by Nyström (2008) focus exclusively on advanced economies, where governance is strong and doing business (DB) seemingly easier than in developing countries.

Nyström (2008) concludes that there is generally, at least over the long run, a positive relationship between entrepreneurship and economic performance. Her conclusion, however, could be too optimistic and too general. For instance in an earlier survey, Parker (2006) reports an ambiguous empirical relationship between the rates of self-employment and unemployment rates. Also, as I show next, a more nuanced relationship emerges when other definitions of entrepreneurship are used apart from self-employment rates.

Only a few studies to date utilize the GEM data to explore the macro-level relationship between growth and entrepreneurship (and between entrepreneurship and institutional features) and of those that do, all are currently plagued by methodological weaknesses. For instance, no study uses panel data methods (all use cross-section methods), none considers systematically the impact of governance and DB indicators on different motivations (opportunity or necessity) for entrepreneurship while others do not take endogeneity issues (reverse causality) and lags into account.[5] To examine the relationship between economic growth and entrepreneurship, one of the first studies to use GEM data, is Wong et al. (2005). As explanatory variable measuring entrepreneurship, Wong et al. use the GEM's measurement of 'high potential entrepreneurship' (HEA), spanning 37 countries for 2002. They find that only 'high potential' entrepreneurial activity is positively associated with economic growth.

Finally, small businesses in developing countries predominate and these are often seen to reflect entrepreneurship. However, Nyström's (2008) survey does not include studies which used small firms as a measure of entrepreneurship.[6] A survey of these would have indicated that the evidence that small businesses *per se* are good for growth, particularly in developing countries, is lacking. For instance Beck et al. (2003), using cross-country data, find no evidence that small business firm growth is associated with higher growth levels.

Start-up costs and regulations as barrier to entrepreneurship

Start-up costs and regulations refer to the efforts required to begin a firm. These differ in duration and content from country to country, but generally include aspects such as the cost, number of procedures and the time it takes to obtain a permit to operate a business, the costs of setting up a business, which often includes a fixed cost/sunk cost element and the regulations that needs to be adhered to in terms of labour and production and organization standards (Fonseca et al. 2001). As discussed by Guglielmetti in Chapter 5, the World Bank, in its DB indicators, measures start-up costs and regulations through four indicators: the number of procedures to be followed, the length of time it takes, the cost of start-up as a percentage of per capita income and the minimum capital required to start a business, also as a percentage of per capita income.

There are a number of good reasons why start-up costs and regulations may be needed and may even be beneficial for entrepreneurship. Three factors stand out. First, regulations are needed to protect the public and workers from potential fraud and exploitation by unscrupulous agents (Fonseca et al. 2007). Second, costs and regulations act as a mechanism to 'weed out' low quality entrepreneurs (Klapper et al. 2006) – see the discussion in Chapter 14. It is recognized that higher ability entrepreneurs can more easily overcome such regulatory barriers, a fact which results in generating a pool of entrepreneurs of higher average quality (Parker 2006). Third, start-up costs and regulations are very often a method for improving government revenue, especially where firms find it easier to avoid normal taxation (Klapper et al. 2006).

Despite these justifications for start-up costs and regulations for new firms, concerns have arisen from the accumulating evidence that start-up costs may be misused, and that this misuse may explain the wide variety in start-up rates and regulations across the world.[7] The main problems associated with start-up costs and regulations are corruption and rent-seeking, protection of incumbent firms and disincentives for firms to register. Thus, for instance, Djankov et al. (2002) find evidence that higher start-up costs and more regulation are associated with higher levels of corruption and a larger informal sector.[8] In their words 'regulation is pursued for the benefits of politicians and bureaucrats' (Djankov et al. 2002: 3). Where such corruption is tolerated or ineffectively controlled, start-up costs may not significantly deter entrepreneurs or act as 'filter' for good entrepreneurial talent (Klapper et al. 2006). Start-up costs may also rise as a reflection of incumbent entrepreneurs' influence. Parker (2006: 707) speculates that incumbent entrepreneurs may drive an increase in the regulation of business start-up that has been observed in many countries, to create barriers to entry for new firms. Thus start-up costs and regulations may be necessary, but may be misused and may exceed reasonble levels. The question is how will this affect entrepreneurial start-ups, particularly of the type of entrepreneurs most likely to drive economic growth?

The empirical evidence on the effect of start-up costs and regulations on entrepreneurship is mixed.[9] Data using self-employment as a measure of entrepreneurship often find a negative relationship and data using start-up rates (TEA) often find no statistically significant relationship.

For example, Klapper et al. (2006) – using cross-section data from a sample of EU countries and measuring 'entrepreneurship' as the number of new firms formally incorporated – find that entry costs and regulations result in fewer new firm incorporations, tend to keep out smaller firms, and reduce productivity through resulting in less competition. Likewise Fonseca et al. (2001) using self-employment data find evidence from OECD countries that start-up costs hinder entrepreneurial entry and result in lower employment.

In contrast, van Stel et al. (2007) using GEM data on entrepreneurial start-up rates from 39 countries find that capital costs and labour regulations do matter for start-ups, but that start-up costs are not significant. Ho and Wong (2007) also using GEM data, but only a cross-section of 37 countries for 2002, estimate the impact of financial constraints and entry regulations on entrepreneurship. They use as alternatively TEA, HEA a measure of entrepreneurship, opportunity-motivated entrepreneurship and necessity-motivated entrepreneurship. As controls Ho and Wong use GDP per capita and productivity growth. To measure start-up regulations, Ho and Wong compile a composite business cost index from the World Bank's DB indicators, and find that this only has a negative impact on opportunity-motivated entrepreneurship, and not on necessity-motivated or HEA.

Other recent studies that apply GEM data to study the determinants of entrepreneurship at the country level include Acs et al. (2008), Bowen and De Clerq (2008) and McMullen et al. (2008). Acs et al. (2008) use pooled, cross-sectional data across 40 countries to investigate the impact of regulatory barriers (taken from the DB indicators) and operational risk on the spread between formal and informal entrepreneurship. They compare in this regard the GEM data on start-up rates (TEA) with the World Bank Group Entrepreneurship Survey (WBGES) data on formal firm registrations, and make the assumption that the former measures 'entrepreneurship potential' and the latter 'actual entrepreneurship', so that the difference is 'lost entrepreneurship'. In their regression analysis they control for GDP per capita (although they do not use lags, thus do not take into account endogeneity problems), and control for the ratio of domestic credit to the private sector as a measure of financial development. They find that start-up costs significantly determine the amount of 'lost entrepreneurship', that is, the spread between the formal and informal sectors, and that start-up barriers appear to be more significant for formal entrepreneurs and less so for early stage entrepreneurship.

Bowen and De Clerq (2008) use GEM data on 40 countries over the period 2002–4 to determine that the proportion of a country's high growth entrepreneurs is a positive function of finance and education, and a negative function of corruption. They do not specifically test for start-up costs. Apart from corruption, they have no other governance related variables, although they include proxies for regulatory protection and regulatory complexity. They find that these measures are insignificant, however. McMullen et al. (2008) apply GEM data for 2002 on 37 countries to study the determinants of opportunity-motivated and necessity-motivated entrepreneurship. As independent variables they include ten measures of economic freedom and control for GDP per capita. They establish that opportunity-motivated entrepreneurship is higher in countries with more economic freedom, which can be taken to suggest indirectly that reforms to improve governance (such as to broaden voice and accountability) and lower restrictions on DB would stimulate opportunity-motivated entrepreneurship.

A shortcoming of the macro-level studies quoted above is that their methodologies contain a critical number of weaknesses. For instance in most case the authors restrict their estimators to ordinary least squares (OLS) in conjunction with using cross-section data – not exploiting possible panel data characteristics. In addition, they bias their estimates by including GDP per capita as a control variable on the right hand side of their estimating equations together with their independent variables (measures of economic freedom and operational risk), thus not taking into consideration the high level of correlation between these variables.

In contrast to the previously quoted studies quoted and the approach in this chapter, Ardagna and Lusardi (2008) use GEM data on the micro-level (they use individual data on more than 150,000 individuals surveyed across 37 countries in 2001 and 2002) to determine how a country's regulatory environment influences an individual's occupational decision to become an opportunity-motivated entrepreneur. As they use micro-level data they do not have the rate of opportunity-motivated entrepreneurship as dependent variable. Ardagna and Lusardi (2008) define a dummy variable to be equal to one if an individual has indicated that he or she started the firm to exploit an opportunity and equal to zero otherwise. They find that entry regulations (start-up costs, the time it takes and the number of procedures needed) reduce the positive effects that social networks and education have on the probability of someone becoming an opportunity entrepreneur. They also find that entry regulations make it less likely for unemployed individuals and young people to enter into entrepreneurship.

While Ardagna and Lusardi (2008) find that start-up costs and regulations can limit the benefits of social networks and education on entrepreneurship, Fonseca et al. (2007), using data from nine EU countries, find that start-up costs reduce the size of the positive effect that individual wealth (finance) has on the probability of an individual choosing to become self-employed. The relationship between start-up costs and education is further explored by Dulleck et al. (2006), with a theoretical model which departs from the assumption that higher education of the entrepreneur is a requirement for high growth firms to be successful. Then, a reduction in start-up costs leads to more people pursuing higher education, which in turn has positive spillover effects as it raises the available skills in the labour market overall. Using cross-country data they find evidence of a negative relationship between start-up costs and higher education enrolment rates.

Thus to conclude, although there is a growing number of studies that investigate the relationship between entrepreneurship and start-up costs, as far as can be determined, the direct impact of governance indicators on opportunity and necessity-motivated entrepreneurship has not been studied. The studies on the relationship between start-up costs and entrepreneurship tend to find mixed results, depending also on the definition for entrepreneurship. Furthermore, generalization of the results is difficult due to methodological weaknesses in these studies.

Methodology

Hypotheses and model

Based on previous sections, the following two hypotheses are formulated:

> *Hypothesis 1: The type of entrepreneurship matters for economic growth. In particular, economic growth is more likely to be driven by opportunity than necessity entrepreneurship.*

> *Hypothesis 2: The determinants of opportunity and necessity entrepreneurship are different. In particular, governance and DB indicators are unlikely to have a significant direct impact on opportunity entrepreneurship.*

Hypothesis 1 will be tested by estimating the following growth model:

$$Z_{it} = \alpha e_{it} + x_{it} \beta + c_i + u_{it} \tag{1}$$

For $i = 1, ... N$ (N=60) and $t = 2, ... T$ (T=5) and where z_{it} is the economic growth rate in country i at time I, e_{it} is alternatively opportunity and necessity entrepreneurship (as defined by the GEM), x_{it} is a $1 \times K$ vector of control variables as listed in Table 11.1. As indicated in the table some of these vary over time. Also in (1) c_i is unobserved country characteristics that is constant over the time period and influence z_{it} and u_{it} is a random error term with the usual properties.

Second, hypothesis 2 will be tested by estimating the determinants of opportunity and necessity entrepreneurship as follows:

$$e_{it} = \delta\, b_{it} + \gamma\, g_{it} + y_{it}\, \theta + d_i + \varepsilon_{it} \tag{2}$$

Table 11.1 Variables and data sources

Variable	Description	Source
Opp	Opportunity entrepreneurship. The percentage of adults in early stage entrepreneurial activity who are motivated to exploit a business opportunity. Covers approximately 60 countries over the period 2003–7.	Global Entrepreneurship Monitor
Nec	Necessity entrepreneurship. The percentage of adults in early stage entrepreneurial activity who are motivated to start a business due to a lack of employment opportunities. Covers approximately 60 countries over the period 2003–7.	Global Entrepreneurship Monitor
Startcost	The costs of starting up a business firm, measured as a percentage of per capita income. Covers 60 countries over the period 2003–7.	World Bank, DB Indicators
GDPPC	GDP per capita in constant values. Adjusted for PPP. Covers 60 countries over the period 2003–7.	World Bank, World Development Indicators Online
Growth	Percentage growth in real GDP per annum. Covers 60 countries over the period 2003–7.	World Bank, World Development Indicators Online
Credit	Amount of credit extended to the private sector as a percentage of GDP. Covers 60 countries over the period 2003–7.	World Bank, World Development Indicators Online
Patents	The number of patent applications filed by residents of a country. Covers 60 countries over the period 2003–7.	World Bank, World Development Indicators Online
Voice	Voice and accountability indicator. The indicator ranges between –2.5 and 2.5. Higher scores signify better outcomes.	World Bank, Worldwide Governance Indicators

Continued

Table 11.1   Continued

Variable	Description	Source
Political	Political stability indicator. The indicator ranges between –2.5 and 2.5. Higher scores signify better outcomes. Data for 60 countries for the period 2003–7 are used.	World Bank, Worldwide Governance Indicators
Gov	Government effectiveness indicator. The indicator ranges between –2.5 and 2.5. Higher scores signify better outcomes. Data for 60 countries for the period 2003–7 are used.	World Bank, Worldwide Governance Indicators
Reg	Regulatory quality indicator. The indicator ranges between –2.5 and 2.5. Higher scores signify better outcomes. Data for 60 countries for the period 2003–7 are used.	World Bank, Worldwide Governance Indicators
Law	Rule of law indicator. The indicator ranges between –2.5 and 2.5. Higher scores signify better outcomes. Data for 60 countries for the period 2003–7 are used.	World Bank, Worldwide Governance Indicators
Corrupt	Control of corruption indicator. The indicator ranges between –2.5 and 2.5. Higher scores signify better outcomes. Data for 60 countries for the period 2003–7 are used.	World Bank, Worldwide Governance Indicators
Capital	Gross fixed capital formation as percentage of GDP per annum. Covers 60 countries over the period 2003–7.	World Bank, World Development Indicators Online
Pop	Annual population growth. Covers 60 countries over the period 2003–7.	World Bank, World Development Indicators Online

Source: See text.

where e_{it} is alternatively opportunity and necessity entrepreneurship; b_{it} an indicator of the ease of DB in country i in period t; g_{it} an indicator of governance in country i in period t and y_{it} a 1×M vector of control variables (see Table 11.1). As in (1) d_i is unobserved country characteristics that are constant over the time period and influence e_{it} and ϵ_{it} is a random error term.

Estimator

Equations (1) and (2) will be estimated using both OLS as well as a random effects generalized least squares (GLS) estimator, given that panel data for 60 countries for the period 2003–7 are available. I use the random effects GLS estimator in order to exploit the properties of the panel data set. This is useful in the present case because there might be omitted factors which differ across time or across countries and which may influence GDP growth and entrepreneurial start-up rates. In the presence of such unobserved time invariant terms in the residual, the residual will be serially correlated and so OLS will not be efficient. The random effects estimator is a more efficient estimator. I use the Hausman test to determine whether the choice of a random effects estimator is statistically acceptable in the present case. For both equations (1) and (2) this test confirmed that the random effects estimator is appropriate.

Variables and data

The variables and data sources are listed and described in Table 11.1. As indicated, the data cover 60 countries[10] over the period 2003–7. A word about the choice of control variables is in order. For equation (1), x includes initial GDP per capita, population growth and gross fixed capital formation. This choice has been informed by economic growth theory, which considers countries with higher GDP per capita growing slower ('convergence') and considers greater inputs of labour (proxied by population growth) and capital as crucial drivers of growth. In case of equation (2) the control variables[11] include GDP per capita to control for the level of development (there is robust evidence that start-up rates vary across countries depending on GDP per capita), patents (as indicator of the creation of new opportunities/innovativeness in an economy), GDP growth (to test whether or not growth creates opportunities) and the amount of credit extended to the private sector (which proxies financial sector development/financial access, as for instance in Acs et al. 2008).

Empirical results

Descriptive overview

Table 11.2 summarizes the data. Mean values are shown for the entire sample, as well as separately for advanced and developing economies. For ease of reference start-up costs and governance indicators have been highlighted. This shows substantial differences between advanced and developing countries. While the sample mean for start-up costs is 16.9 per cent of per capita income, it is 9.63 per cent in the subsample of advanced economies, but three times higher on average in developing countries, at 29.4 per cent. Also, a comparison of the governance

Table 11.2 Summary of data

Variable	Number of observations	Mean for all countries	Mean for advanced economies	Mean for developing economies
Opp	184	6.49 %	5.03%	10.28%
Nec	187	2.52 %	1.30%	5.78%
Startcost	298	16.9 %	9.63%	29.4%
GDPPC	288	$20,002	$27,457	$7,008
Growth	288	4.81 %	3.94%	6.32%
Credit	281	57.9 %	105%	49.34%
Patents	157	21,898	25,307	10,020
Voice	300	0.628	1.018	−0.044
Political	300	0.263	0.678	−0.453
Gov	300	0.820	1.297	−0.004
Reg	300	0.741	1.181	−0.018
Law	300	0.609	1.132	−0.297
Corrupt	300	0.695	1.238	−0.244
Capital	256	22.09 %	21.95%	22.29%
Pop	295	0.89%	0.71%	1.18%

Source: Author's calculations based on World Bank and GEM data.

indicators shows that whereas these are all positive in advanced economies, they are all negative in developing countries. Indeed, the correlation coefficients between per capita GDP and the governance indicators are high, ranging between 0.70 in the case of voice and accountability to 0.87 in the case of rule of law. Table 11.2 also shows, however, that despite average start-up costs being three times as high on average in developing countries as in advanced economies, opportunity entrepreneurship rates are on average twice as high. Furthermore, GDP growth is on average almost twice as high in the sample of developing economies as in advanced economies.

The data in Table 11.2 therefore suggest that there might be a positive relationship between opportunity entrepreneurship and economic growth. It also shows that there does not seem to be a negative relationship between start-up costs and entrepreneurship – in the sample start-up costs are on average three times higher in developing economies than in advanced economies.

Regression results

Table 11.2 offers tentative support for the hypotheses put forward earlier. Thus, there is some indication that only opportunity entrepreneurship may matter for growth and that governance and DB indicators (start-up costs) are not strongly related to opportunity entrepreneurship (Table 11.2). Here I provide evidence on the statistical significance of these relationships using OLS and random effects GLS estimates.

Entrepreneurship and growth

Equation (1) was estimated using both OLS and random effects GLS, using as a measure of entrepreneurship alternatively opportunity and necessity entrepreneurship as defined by the GEM. Because the OLS and random effects GLS results are very similar, I report only the random effects GLS results in Tables 11.3 and 11.4.

Three remarks regarding the treatment of the right-hand side variables are in order. First, it will be seen that opportunity entrepreneurship enters as a lagged variable in (1). This is to avoid possible endogeneity problems, given that economic growth could be a determinant of opportunity entrepreneurship. Second, the governance indicators enter in first differences (indicated by 'd'), because the governance indicators in levels are significantly correlated with initial GDP capita. However, there is little correlation between changes in governance indicators and initial GDP per capita. The coefficients on the governance indicators would therefore capture the effects of improvements or deteriorations in the quality of governance on economic growth. Third, the governance indicators, being highly correlated with one another, are entered sequentially; the results contained in columns 2–7.

In Table 11.3 it can be seen that opportunity entrepreneurship is a significant determinant of economic growth, even when one controls for initial GDP per capita, population growth and fixed capital. It also remains significant when various governance indicators are included. It can also be seen that, with the exception of voice and accountability, all of the other governance indicators have a positive and significant impact on real GDP growth. Although opportunity entrepreneurship is significant, Table 11.3 suggests that the impact of governance indicators tends to be larger – the largest single impact on growth seems to come from improvements in the rule of law and the control of corruption. The results in Table 11.4 differ from those in Table 11.3, in that necessity entrepreneurship does not consistently appear as a significant determinant of real GDP growth. It is generally insignificant, with the only exceptions where government effectiveness and the rule of law enter into the equation. As in Table 11.3, all of the

Table 11.3 Random effects regression results for the impact of opportunity entrepreneurship on growth in GDP

Variable	(1) Without governance	(2) Voice and accountability	(3) Political stability	(4) Government effectiveness	(5) Regulatory quality	(6) Rule of law	(7) Control of corruption
Constant	4.6 (2.18)**	4.6 (2.2)**	4.4 (2.18)**	4.6 (2.09)**	4.50 (2.22)**	4.89 (2.14)**	5.07 (2.07)**
Opp (lagged)	0.14 (0.06)**	0.14 (0.06)**	0.14 (0.06)**	0.16 (0.06)**	0.17 (0.06)**	0.15 (0.06)**	0.13 (0.06)**
d.voice	–	0.14 (0.92)	–	–	–	–	–
d.political	–	–	2.41 (1.18)**	–	–	–	–
d.gov.	–	–	–	3.09 (1.00)**	–	–	–
d.reg.	–	–	–	–	3.78 (1.08)***	–	–
d.law	–	–	–	–	–	7.6 (2.08)***	–
d.corrupt	–	–	–	–	–	–	4.32 (1.23)***
Initial GDP	–0.00 (0.00)**	–0.00 (0.00)**	–0.00 (0.00)**	–0.00 (0.00)**	–0.00 (0.00)**	–0.00 (0.00)**	–0.00 (0.00)***
Pop.	–0.09 (0.44)	–0.08 (0.43)	–0.06 (0.45)	–0.15 (0.42)	–0.20 (0.44)	–0.10 (0.42)	–0.16 (0.42)
Capital	0.05 (0.09)	0.05 (0.09)	0.05 (0.09)	0.04 (0.08)	0.05 (0.09)	0.04 (0.09)	0.04 (0.08)
R^2	0.26	0.26	0.29	0.30	0.27	0.32	

Notes: Robust standard errors in parenthesis. * significant at the 1% level, ** significant at the 5% level, *** significant at the 10% level. Number of observations = 114, groups = 51.

Source: See text.

Table 11.4 Random effects regression results for the impact of necessity entrepreneurship on growth in GDP

Variable	(1) Without governance	(2) Voice and accountability	(3) Political stability	(4) Government effectiveness	(5) Regulatory quality	(6) Rule of law	(7) Control of corruption
Constant	4.31 (1.91)**	4.30 (1.91)**	4.27 (1.91)**	4.16 (1.83)**	4.34 (1.94)	4.19 (1.84)**	4.71 (1.84)**
Nec (lagged)	0.22 (0.15)	0.22 (0.15)	0.22 (0.14)	0.25 (0.15)*	0.24 (0.14)	0.29 (0.15)**	0.23 (0.144)
d.voice	–	0.11 (0.91)	–	–	–	–	–
d.political	–	–	2.13 (1.13)*	–	–	–	–
d.gov.	–	–	–	2.9 (0.97)**	–	–	–
d.reg.	–	–	–	–	3.45 (1.12)**	–	–
d.law	–	–	–	–	–	8.15 (2.30)***	–
d.corrupt	–	–	–	–	–	–	4.41 (1.25)***
Initial GDP	-0.00 (0.00)**	-0.00 (0.00)**	-0.00 (0.00)**	-0.00 (0.00)**	-0.00 (0.00)**	-0.00 (0.00)**	-0.00 (0.00)**
Pop.	-0.05 (0.42)	-0.04 (0.41)	-0.00 (0.42)	-0.09 (0.39)	-0.12 (0.41)	-0.08 (0.41)	-0.14 (0.41)
Capital	0.07 (0.08)	0.07 (0.08)	0.06 (0.08)	0.06 (0.08)	0.07 (0.08)	0.06 (0.08)	0.05 (0.08)
R² overall	0.27	0.26	0.31	0.31	0.27	0.34	0.30

Notes: Robust standard errors in parenthesis. Significance at the 1%, 5% and 10% levels respectively indicated by ***, ** and *. Number of observations = 115, groups = 51.

Source: See text.

governance indicators, with the exception of voice and accountability, have a positive and significant impact on real GDP growth. As for the control variables, initial GDP per capita enters significantly and with the right sign (negative) suggesting (slow) convergence. Capital also enters positively and significantly as was expected. Population growth turns out to be insignificant (although it is significant in the OLS results).

I can thus conclude that the results cannot reject Hypothesis 1.

Start-up costs, governance and entrepreneurship

The relationship between entrepreneurship and start-up costs (ease of DB) and governance indicators were estimated as per equation (2) using OLS and random effects GLS. As the OLS results are broadly similar, I report only the random effects panel data estimations and do so in Tables 11.5 and 11.6. Table 11.5 contains the results of the impact of start-up costs and governance indicators on opportunity entrepreneurship and Table 11.6 gives the results of their impact on necessity entrepreneurship. As far as the explanatory variables are concerned, GDP growth is entered with a lag (so as to avoid endogeneity problems) and because of multicollinearity the various indicators of good governance enter sequentially.

The results in Tables 11.5 and 11.6 are very similar, in that neither start-up costs nor governance have any statistically significant impact on either opportunity or necessity entrepreneurship. Amongst the control variables, GDP per capita is significantly (and negatively) related to both opportunity and necessity entrepreneurship – this confirms that at higher levels of development the opportunity costs (which include wage employment but also social benefits) of entrepreneurship increase. Thus countries with higher per capita GDP will be more likely to have lower opportunity and necessity entrepreneurship. GDP growth lagged has no statistically significant impact on entrepreneurship. However, in the case of opportunity entrepreneurship, credit extended to the private sector does turn out to be statistically significant. This finding is consistent with that of Bowen and De Clerq (2008) who find financial access to be a significant determinant of high growth entrepreneurship in the GEM data. Lack of access to finance/underdeveloped financial sector may therefore limit opportunity entrepreneurship.

Although much more needs to be done to identify the determinants of opportunity and necessity entrepreneurship, the results here cannot reject Hypothesis 2.

Table 11.5 Random effects regression results for the impact of start-up costs and governance on opportunity entrepreneurship

Variable	(1) Without governance	(2) Voice and accountability	(3) Political stability	(4) Government effectiveness	(5) Regulatory quality	(6) Rule of law	(7) Control of corruption
Constant	8.5 (1.95)***	8.36 (1.98)***	8.41 (2.00)***	8.52 (1.94)***	8.7 (1.97)***	8.37 (1.83)***	8.36 (1.94)***
Start-up costs	-0.02 (0.08)	-0.02 (0.09)	-0.04 (0.09)	-0.02 (0.09)	-0.03 (0.09)	-0.01 (0.09)	-0.01 (0.09)
d.Voice	–	0.43 (0.94)	–	–	–	–	–
d.Political	–	–	-1.95 (1.32)	–	–	–	–
d.Gov	–	–	–	0.20 (1.44)	–	–	–
d.Reg	–	–	–	–	-1.79 (1.55)	–	–
d.Law	–	–	–	–	–	3.89 (3.69)	–
d.Corrupt	–	–	–	–	–	–	0.93 (2.58)
GDP per capita	-0.00 (0.00)**	-0.00 (0.00)**	-0.00 (0.00)**	-0.00 (0.00)**	-0.00 (0.00)**	-0.00 (0.00)***	-0.00 (0.00)**
Patents	-0.00 (0.00)	-0.00 (0.00)	-0.00 (0.00)	-0.00 (0.00)	-0.00 (0.00)	-0.00 (0.00)	-0.00 (0.00)
Credit	0.02 (0.01)**	0.02 (0.007)**	0.02 (0.007)**	0.02 (0.00**)	0.02 (0.007)**	0.02 (0.01)*	0.02 (0.01)*
Growth (lag)	0.22 (0.15)	0.22 (0.16)	0.22 (0.15)	0.22 (0.16)	0.20 (0.15)	0.27 (0.18)	0.23 (0.17)
R^2	0.12	0.13	0.10	0.13	0.11	0.15	0.13

Notes: Robust standard errors in parenthesis. Significance at the 1%, 5% and 10% levels respectively indicated by ***, **, and *. Number of observations = 75, groups = 36.

Source: See text.

Table 11.6 Random effects regression results for the impact of start-up costs and governance on necessity entrepreneurship

Variable	(1) Without governance	(2) Voice and accountability	(3) Political stability	(4) Government effectiveness	(5) Regulatory quality	(6) Rule of law	(7) Control of corruption
Constant	4.69 (0.93)***	5.05 (0.95)***	4.78 (0.94)***	4.70 (0.93)***	4.72 (0.96)***	4.73 (0.94)***	4.78 (0.93)***
Start–up costs	0.05 (0.07)	0.04 (0.07)	0.05 (0.07)	0.05 (0.07)	0.05 (0.07)	0.05 (0.07)	0.04 (0.06)
d.Voice	–	–1.21 (0.62)	–	–	–	–	–
d.Political	–	–	1.07 (0.72)	–	–	–	–
d.Gov	–	–	–	–0.06 (0.53)	–	–	–
d.Reg	–	–	–	–	–0.13 (0.97)	–	–
d.Law	–	–	–	–	–	–0.99 (1.72)	–
d.Corrupt	–	–	–	–	–	–	–0.77 (1.15)
GDP per capita	–0.00 (0.00)***	–0.00 (0.00)***	–0.00 (0.00)***	–0.00 (0.00)***	–0.00 (0.00)***	–0.00 (0.00)***	–0.00 (00)***
Patents	–0.00 (0.00)	–0.00 (0.00)	–0.00 (0.00)	–0.00 (0.00)	–0.00 (0.00)	–0.00 (0.00)	–0.00 (0.00)
Credit	0.00 (0.00)	0.00 (0.00)	0.00 (0.00)	0.00 (0.00)	0.00 (0.00)	0.01 (0.04)	0.01 (0.04)
Growth (lag)	–0.03 (0.07)	–0.06 (0.08)	–0.04 (0.07)	–0.03 (0.07)	–0.03 (0.07)	–0.04 (0.08)	–0.04 (0.08)
R^2	0.45	0.45	0.47	0.45	0.45	0.44	0.44

Notes: Robust standard errors in parenthesis. Significance at the 1 %, 5% and 10% levels respectively indicated by ***, ** and *. Number of observations = 76, groups = 36.

Concluding remarks

The policy implication that emerges from this chapter is that the advocacy of better governance and an easier environment for DB may not be sufficient to encourage the type of entrepreneurship (opportunity-based) found to be a relevant for economic growth. Better governance and an easier environment even may not be necessary: despite poor governance and high start-up costs, the level of opportunity entrepreneurship is high in many countries, indicating that entrepreneurs may be able to overcome obstacles.

However, this does not mean that government support for entrepreneurship has no place. Indeed, I have pointed out that an approach to entrepreneurship based only on improving governance and lowering start-up costs is reactive. More pro-active measures, such as support for venture finance, education and training, particularly for technology entrepreneurship, may be needed in developing countries. The cases of China and India may be instructive in this regard. Both countries are ranked very low on the World Bank's (WB) index for the ease of DB – China is in 83rd and India in 120th position, among 178 countries in 2008. Despite this, productive entrepreneurship seems to be flourishing. Rates of opportunity-motivated entrepreneurship in China are high: between 2003 and 2007 the average annual rate was 8.2 per cent. Since 1978 a number of pro-active policy measures were introduced to support private sector development. A full discussion of these measures falls outside the scope of the present study, but it can be noted that these include the transformation and privatization of state owned enterprises (SOEs), learning from foreign firms through encouraging the inflow of FDI, the explicit encouragement of high-tech entrepreneurship (Rui and Yip 2008) and huge investments in infrastructure, particularly trade and transport-related infrastructure[12] (Dollar 2008). With respect to India, Athreye (2008) investigates the reason the country's software industry developed so rapidly despite its low ranking in the WB index. As she puts it:

> ... in theory, the Indian software industry should not have developed the way it did ... the software industry achieved its astonishing results despite the adverse conditions facing entrepreneurs. (ibid.: 2)

Mani (2008) documents the reasons for such success: pro-active government support policy including the extension of financial support schemes such as venture capital funds[13] to entrepreneurs. Apparently the Indian government did not assume that the supply of entrepreneurship would be automatically forthcoming to exploit the globally existing opportunities.

Finally, an interesting finding (particular given the results of Amóros in Chapter 8, this volume) is that there is a significant and positive impact of changes in governance on economic growth in the sample. One reason why this might happen is that better governance reduces destructive entrepreneurship (including rent-seeking) even though it does not raise opportunity entrepreneurship. The relationship between governance and destructive entrepreneurship is also discussed in Chapter 15.

The implication is that opportunity entrepreneurship and destructive entrepreneurship may be poor substitutes – the requirements for being a good opportunity-motivated entrepreneur may differ too substantially from the requirements from being good at rent-seeking). The lack of quantification of 'destructive' entrepreneurship prevents me from directly testing these conclusions and they must remain tentative until future research can provide more clarity. Private sector development through better governance and pro-active measures can be encouraged in ways which both support productive entrepreneurship and limit destructive entrepreneurship.

Notes

1. The GEM also measures what it terms 'high-potential' entrepreneurial activity (HEA), which measures the subjective expectation of the entrepreneur that his or her firm will employ more than 20 employees within five years (Wong et al. 2005: 345). Due to the difficulties inherent in using subjective expectations as proxy for productive, innovative entrepreneurship, and due to the fact that only about 5 per cent of respondents surveyed in GEM considered themselves to be high-potential, I will not use HEA in this chapter.
2. Schmitz (1989) highlights the importance of imitation by entrepreneurs and argues that it may be more important for the majority of developing countries than new knowledge generation.
3. According to Acs (2008: 2) 'for developed countries high impact entrepreneurship has become the main form of entrepreneurship driving their economies'.
4. Salgado-Banda (2007) uses patents as a measure for productive entrepreneurship and finds that it has a positive impact on economic growth in a sample of 22 OECD countries.
5. There is likely to be reverse causality between entrepreneurship and economic growth, and entrepreneurship may affect growth only after a certain lag (see e.g. Carree and Thurik 2008).
6. Although small firms are sometimes used as a measure of entrepreneurship, they are not necessarily synonymous with entrepreneurship or entrepreneurial ventures (Wennekers and Thurik 1999). Most small firms

are run by managerial business owners rather than entrepreneurs (Carree et al. 2002).

7. Theoretical models have also been provided to show that start-up costs can lower the relative number of individuals who choose to self-employment as an occupational choice (e.g. Fonseca et al. 2001) and that start-up costs reduce the positive effect of wealth holdings on the decision of individuals to enter self-employment (Fonseca et al. 2007).

8. If this also holds in the present sample, then we should expect in section five to find a positive relationship between necessity entrepreneurship and start-up costs across countries – which we do not, however, find in the present sample.

9. In the review here, I focus on studies concerned with the relationship between start-up or entry regulations and costs and entrepreneurship. I do not review studies which investigate other constraints such those posed by, for example, taxes (see Gentry and Hubbard 2000), finance (e.g. Blanchflower and Oswald 1998; Ho and Wong 2007) and closure procedures (e.g. Acs et al. 2008).

10. The countries and territories included are: Argentina, Australia, Austria, Belgium, Brazil, Canada, Chile, China, Colombia, Croatia, Czech Republic, Denmark, Dominican Republic, Ecuador, Finland, France, Germany, Greece, Hong Kong, Hungary, Iceland, India, Indonesia, Ireland, Israel, Italy, Jamaica, Japan, Jordan, Kazakhstan, Korea, Latvia, Malaysia, Mexico, Netherlands, New Zealand, Norway, Peru, Philippines, Poland, Portugal, Puerto Rico, Romania, Russia, Serbia, Singapore, Slovenia, South Africa, Spain, Sweden, Switzerland, Taiwan, Thailand, Turkey, Uganda, United Arab Emirates, United Kingdom, United States, Uruguay and Venezuela.

11. I will indicate below that where appropriate I have used lagged values of GDP per capita and GDP growth in the regressions so as to avoid endogeneity (reverse causality) problems.

12. According to Dollar (2008: 10) 'The combination of low tariffs, efficient customs, and efficient ports means that large numbers of firms in China are very well connected to the international market.'

13. According to Mani (2008: 2) 'Although the absolute level of venture capital investments in India is low, it has been growing at a rate of 90 per cent over the last few years and at this rate of growth, the industry is set to match Europe by 2009 or 2010.'

12
Entrepreneurship and the Developmental State
William Lazonick

Introduction

In Chapter 2 I provided the basic outlines of the theory of innovative enterprise, with a particular focus on why and how it provides the essential analytical link between entrepreneurship and development. With Part II and III of this book having detailed the measurement of entrepreneurship, the role of institutions, and the previous chapter by Naudé having identified the need for a pro-active (instead of only a reactive) role for the state *vis-à-vis* entrepreneurship, I will in this chapter focus on the relationship between the 'developmental state' and the innovative enterprise.

Social conditions of innovative enterprise

My starting point is the observation that an analysis of the functions of entrepreneurship in the innovation process as done in Chapter 2 shows that the success or failure of the entrepreneur is highly dependent on the set of social relationships in which she is embedded. The need for organizational integration and financial commitment generally means that the entrepreneur must share strategic control with professional managers and financiers. Large numbers of participants in the firm's hierarchical and functional division of labour need to be motivated to work together for a sustained period of time towards the achievement of collective goals.

At the level of the business enterprise, the collective character of the innovation process reflects the reliance of the entrepreneur on the skills and efforts of other enterprise participants in the exercise of strategic control, the management of organizational integration and the mobilization of financial commitment.

Comparative historical research on innovative enterprises across advanced nations and over time has revealed distinctive patterns in social structures that support the transformation of strategic control organizational integration and financial commitment into innovative outcomes (Lazonick 2007c). I call these distinctive social structures 'social conditions of innovative enterprise'. Historically, as particular forms of these social conditions have provided the foundations for the growth of innovative enterprises in a national economy, and as enterprises characterized by these social conditions have grown to dominate resource allocation in the national economy as a whole, these social conditions of innovative enterprise themselves have become national norms for business behaviour that have shaped the form and content of national governance, employment and investment institutions. It is now widely recognized among scholars of comparative political economy that there exists a wide array of 'varieties of capitalism' that can provide the institutional bases for economic development (see e.g. Lazonick 2007b). I will use examples from Britain, Japan, Italy and the United States to illustrate.

Britain as workshop of the world

A century ago, Britain still had the highest level of GDP per capita in the world, and one could identify the industrial districts around Manchester, Sheffield and Birmingham as the reasons why Britain could be known as the 'workshop of the world'. The thousands of relatively small companies that populated these districts produced commodities such as cotton textiles and metal housewares for export to markets around the world. Enterprise governance was based on either proprietorships or, as in the case of cotton spinning, highly localized, single plant limited liability firms. In the leading export sectors, of which cotton textiles was by far the most important, new ventures used local stock markets to raise funds for rapid investments in new factories to respond to cyclical booms in demand. The foundation for British global supremacy in these industries was the availability of large local supplies of unionized labour with specialized craft skills (Farnie 1979; Farnie and Abe 2000; Lazonick 1983).

In periods of strong product market demand, the ready availability of specialized craft labour induced new specialized manufacturing firms, often started by entrepreneurial craft workers, to set up in these districts. The growth of a district induced other firms to invest in regionally specific communication and distribution facilities for the supply of materials, the transfer of work in progress across vertically specialized firms and the marketing of output. Regional concentration encouraged vertical specialization, which in turn eased firm entry into a particular specialty, thus resulting in high levels of horizontal competition. Firms could be owned and managed by the same people or in the case of the limited liability spinning companies a single manager would direct the one-factory firms. There was no need to invest in the types of managerial organization that by the late nineteenth century were becoming central to the growth of firms and the development of the economies of the United States and Germany. In the industrial districts, economies of scale were, as Alfred Marshall (1890) argued, external, rather than internal, to the firm.

The Third Italy

By the 1920s, the British industrial districts entered a decline from which they would never recover (Elbaum and Lazonick 1986). A half century later, however, the remarkable growth of the 'Third Italy', based on industrial districts of small-scale enterprises clustered in Emilia-Romagna around Bologna, in Veneto outside of Venice, and in Tuscany in the vicinity of Florence, led some Italian economists, most notably Becattini (1992) and Brusco (1982), to look to the work of Marshall for an analytical framework for understanding the developmental dynamics that these districts possessed. Given the expansion of these industrial districts on the basis of relatively small-scale enterprises, one could rightly point to the role of entrepreneurship as a significant force in the development of the Third Italy. At the same time, a more fundamental analysis of the development of these industrial districts revealed how individual entrepreneurship was embedded in and supported by a highly collective social structure. For example, in an influential essay entitled 'The Emilian Model: Productive Decentralization and Social Integration' originally published in Italian in 1980 and translated into English two years later, Brusco (1982: 167) presented 'a dynamic analysis of the interaction of the between the productive structure, the labour market and the principal political institutions in Emilia-Romagna'.

There were a number of good reasons to refer to the Third Italy as 'Marshallian' industrial districts, as Becattini in particular was wont to do. The industrial activities of these districts focused on, among other things, textiles, footwear and light machinery just as the British districts had done. Each industrial activity was populated by large numbers of vertically specialized proprietary firms in which craft labour was a prime source of competitive advantage and of which many entrepreneurs had previously been craft workers. Yet there were a number of major differences between the nineteenth-century industrial districts that Marshall observed and those that could be found in the Third Italy a generation after the end of the Second World War. The identification of these differences is of central importance for the analysis of how entrepreneurial activity flourishes and reaches its limits, in different social contexts.

The first major difference was the sheer diversity of specialized production by small firms in the Third Italy. Large numbers of the relatively small Italian firms were truly entrepreneurial as, within their specialized industrial activity, firms competed by differentiating their products for higher income and more sophisticated markets. While one could certainly find such entrepreneurial firms in the British industrial districts of the late nineteenth century, those districts and their constituent firms contributed to the growth of the British economy primarily through a system of mass production of standardized goods, even if it was one based on the proliferation of relatively small firms and craft labour.

The second characteristic of the Italian industrial districts that distinguished them from the British was the extent to which in Italy collective institutions supported the innovative activities of small firms. In the Italian districts, regional universities were important suppliers of both new knowledge and educated labour, quite in contrast to the craft-based provision of these inputs in the British districts. Brusco emphasized the importance of the 'red' local governments in Emilia-Romagna in promoting policies to support the activities of small enterprises and in particular in facilitating cooperatives that provided these firms with 'real services' related to financing, business administration, marketing and training that they could not provide for themselves and which profit-seeking specialized firms did not find it worthwhile to supply (Brusco 1992; Brusco and Pezzini 1990). While consumer cooperatives sprung up in the British industrial districts of the late nineteenth century – with the Lancashire town of Rochdale acquiring fame as the pioneer of the consumer cooperative movement – producer cooperatives were rare.

The third distinguishing characteristic of the Italian industrial districts that became more evident in the 1990s was the extent to which, in some districts and in some industries, 'leading' firms could emerge, drawing on the resources of the industrial districts while, through their own internal growth, transforming the innovative capability of the districts. A problem with the British industrial districts when they were confronted by competitive challenges in the first half of the twentieth century was that dominant firms failed to emerge to lead the restructuring of the districts. Indeed, over the past decade a major concern among many observers of Italian industrial districts has been whether the competitive advantage of regions based on a multitude of small entrepreneurial firms can be maintained when they are confronted by the rise of dominant global enterprises.

In Italy, a well-known early case of the emergence of a dominant firm is Benetton, a family firm in the Veneto area, known along with Emilia-Romagna and Tuscany for its industrial districts. Benetton grew from the last half of the 1960s by maintaining control over marketing, design and logistics (including the rapid replenishment of fast-selling shop inventories) while outsourcing production to small producers in its home region (and then increasingly abroad) and establishing a global brand name by franchising retail shops around the world (and subsequently investing in its own 'megashops') (Harrison 1994). A similar dynamic of enterprise growth can be found in the rise of Natuzzi, since the early 1990s a leading global brand in upholstered furniture. Based in a newer industrial district in the south of Italy, Natuzzi has combined a tightly integrated vertical supply chain with its own global marketing capabilities to outcompete the more specialized but once dominant furniture manufacturers in Emilia Romagna (Belussi 1999). In 2006 Natuzzi had record sales so far of €735 million and at the end of the year employed 8,133 people (3,590 in Italy and 4,543 abroad). As demonstrated in the cases of Benetton and Natuzzi, even in industries that are not high-tech, the overwhelming tendency is for entrepreneurial firms to grow large and dominate their industries; one can offer as a particularly well-known example Wal-Mart, the US retailing giant, launched as an entrepreneurial firm in the small town of Bentonville, Arkansas in 1950, that as of January 2010 employed 2.1 million people worldwide, generating US$405 billion in revenues and over US$14 billion in profits.

Japan's transformation

If one wants to understand the vulnerability of the 'Marshallian industrial district' in long run historical perspective, one should go back to the 1920s and 1930s when the Japanese cotton textile industry outcompeted the once powerful British cotton textile industry in global competition. While the Japanese had the advantage of much lower wages and much longer working hours than the British, Japan's main source of long run competitive advantage in global competition was the higher productivity that its industry generated. The Japanese industry's high productivity was in turn based on the investment strategies and organizational structures of ten dominant 'spinning' companies (which from the beginning of the twentieth century also integrated weaving), all of which had been entrepreneurial start-ups in the 1870s and 1880s. These spinning companies relied on the global trading companies of the Japanese *zaibatsu*, most notably Mitsui and Mitsubishi, to supply them with cotton and sell their yarn and cloth, as well as, increasingly, on indigenous Japanese textile machine manufacturers to supply them with the latest equipment (Mass and Lazonick 1990).

In the 1920s, one entrepreneurial Japanese textile machinery company in particular took advantage of the opportunity presented by the rapid growth of the nation's cotton textile industry, and by the 1930s its weaving innovations had enabled Japan to become the world leader not only in the export of cotton cloth, but also in the export of machinery for the weaving of cotton cloth. That firm was the Toyoda Automatic Loom Company. During the 1930s Toyoda strategically transferred its considerable capabilities in mechanical engineering and manufacturing to the development of automobiles under the name of Toyota Motor Company (changing the 'd' to a 't' in the family name so that its motor vehicles would not be mistaken for its now famous weaving machines) (Mass and Robertson 1996; Wada 2006).

Of much greater importance for present purposes, however, is the fact that the growth of Toyota was both central to and emblematic of the transformation of Japan from a poor nation in the 1940s to a rich nation in the 1980s. When in the 1980s and 1990s many 'non-neoclassical' scholars followed Johnson (1982) in focusing on the role of the 'developmental state' in the Japanese 'economic miracle', they generally failed to analyse the role of 'innovative enterprise' in this transformation (see Woo-Cumings 1999). As a direct result, they ignored two fundamental phenomena in the link between entrepreneurship and economic development.

First, they have missed the importance of enterprise strategy organization and finance in the transformation of entrepreneurial firms into innovative firms. The contribution of the developmental state in Japan to the wealth of the nation cannot be understood in abstraction from the growth of companies such as Toshiba, Hitachi, Toyota, Matsushita, Sony and Canon. While the Japanese state provided various forms of support for these companies, especially in the realm of bank-based finance, it was a combination of strategy organization and finance internal to these companies that made them successful and gave the state's industrial policy a chance of reinforcing that success. One needs a theory of innovative enterprise to understand not only the role of entrepreneurship in economic development but also the role of the state.

The United States as developmental state

One can make the same argument for the importance of the growth of dominant firms in the process of economic development for the world's richest economy, the United States. Except, and here is the second phenomenon that Western scholars of the developmental state have entirely missed, in terms of technological innovation over the past century and to the present, *the US state has been far more developmental than the Japanese state.* Scholarly works have been written on particular industries – for example, agriculture (Ferleger and Lazonick 1993), airliners (Van der Linden 2002), aircraft engines (Constant 1980), computers (National Research Council 1999), the Internet (Abbate 2000), biotechnology (Lazonick and Tulum 2009) – that support this proposition.

As for Silicon Valley, the world's leading high-tech industrial district, the developmental state has been of central importance throughout its history. In agreement with this statement, judging from a 1984 article entitled 'Venture Capital & the Growth of Silicon Valley', is William R. Hambrecht, founder and principal of Hambrecht & Quist, a preeminent Silicon Valley investment banking and venture capital firm. 'There were three major catalytic events that occurred [from 1935 to 1950] that propelled our country into a position of technological leadership', Hambrecht (1984: 74) wrote. First, in the mid-1930s, the United States received a wave of European refugees, including some of the world's most prominent scientists and engineers. Second, during the Second World War the US government made massive investments in research and development. And third, in the aftermath of the Second World War, under the 'GI Bill', the US government paid for the university tuition and subsistence costs of millions of people who might not otherwise have been able to afford a higher education. As Hambrecht (1984: 75) summed up the impact: 'A group of European scientists and engineers and the newly trained American engineers, fresh from their experiences in the R&D labs, went back to the universities and trained a whole new generation of engineers who in the 1950s and 1960s created the micro-electronics revolution.'

In the biotechnology industry, which has been booming in the 2000s, the flow of resources has been much more one way from the government to firms (Goozner 2004; Lazonick and Tulum 2009). Through the National Institutes of Health (NIH), the US government has long been the nation's (and the world's) most important investor in knowledge creation in the medical fields. Since its inception in 1938 through 2009, US taxpayers invested US$706.4 billion in 2009 in the work of the NIH. In 2009 US Congress appropriated US$30.4 billion to fund the work of the NIH. In its 27 centres and institutes in Bethesda, Maryland, the NIH supports the medical research of 6,000 scientists and technicians. But in-house research absorbs less than 10 per cent of the NIH budget and administration another 9 per cent. In 2009 NIH awarded more than 80 per cent of its total funds for research, training, fellowships and R&D contracts in the form of '50,000 competitive grants to more than 325,000 researchers at over 3,000 universities, medical schools and other research institutions in every state and around the world'.[1]

The business sector has direct access to, and can appropriate high returns from, this state-funded research. In 1978 intense lobbying by the National Venture Capital Association and the American Electronics Association, both with their centres of gravity as cohesive trade associations in Silicon Valley, convinced the US Congress to lower the capital gains tax rate from almost 50 per cent to 28 per cent, thus reversing a 36-year trend towards higher capital gains taxes (Lazonick 2009: ch. 2). The Bayh-Dole Act of 1980 gave universities and hospitals clear property rights to new knowledge that resulted from US government-funded research so that they could license the results of their research to new technology firms. The main motivation for Bayh-Dole was the growing number of biotech inventions emanating from NIH research that, it was argued, would be left unexploited but for the Act's less restrictive conditions for the transfer of intellectual property. In 1980 as well, a Supreme Court decision that genetically engineered life forms are patentable facilitated the opportunity for the types of knowledge transfers that Bayh-Dole envisioned. The magnitude of the gains that could be reaped from biotech start-ups became apparent when Genentech, founded in 1976, raised US$36 million in its initial public offering (IPO) in 1980, to be followed by, at the time, the largest IPO in US history, the US$107 million raised by Cetus, another San Francisco Bay area company that dated from 1971.

In 1983 another important inducement to biotech investment followed in the form of the Orphan Drug Act, which gave generous tax credits for research and experimentation as well as the possibility of seven-year market exclusivity for companies that developed drugs for 'rare' diseases. It was argued that without these financial incentives many potential medicinal drugs that could be developed for relatively small markets would remain 'orphans': pharmaceutical or biotech companies would not have been willing the make financial commitments of the size and duration required to nurture these drugs from infancy to adulthood. By December 2006 the Food and Drug Administration had designated 1,674 orphan drug submissions that made these companies eligible for the tax credits and had granted market exclusivity on 301 drugs that had reached the approval stage. A number of these orphan drugs are now 'blockbusters' with US$1 billion or more in annual sales. The US government, through its Medicare and Medicaid programmes, moreover, remains the leading source of effective demand for these high priced biotech products (Lazonick and Tulum 2009).

In sum, the United States has had, and still possesses, a formidable developmental state. As for Japan, it was able to grow rich without its state being as developmental as that of the United States precisely because its firms could take advantage, through licensing and joint ventures, of knowledge created in the United States and other advanced Western nations. Nevertheless, the further development and utilization of this knowledge to engage in indigenous innovation required that the Japanese firms have sufficient 'absorptive capacity'. The cases of the Toyoda automatic loom and the Toyota automobile, already mentioned, are examples of such indigenous innovation.

To have this absorptive capacity and engage in indigenous innovation, a nation has to have already made the most strategic and most expensive investment of them all: investment in a public system of primary, secondary and tertiary education. The economic institutions that support entrepreneurship and innovation in the United States and Japan may differ radically, but what these as well as other advanced economies have in common are long histories of massive investments in their educational systems.

US government investment began with the Morrill Land Grant Act of 1862, out of which emerged a nationwide system of higher education oriented towards industrial development, including universities such as MIT, Cornell, Michigan, Purdue, Iowa and University of California Berkeley (Ferleger and Lazonick 1994). In the development of Silicon Valley, the key player was Stanford University, a private university founded in 1885 on the basis of railroad wealth. From the 1930s Stanford oriented itself to support industrial development. The key 'public entrepreneur' was Frederick Terman. With an electrical engineering doctorate from MIT, Terman was a professor of engineering at Stanford in the 1930s, spent the Second World War directing the Harvard University Radio Research Lab, returned to Stanford after the war as its dean of engineering and became the University's provost in the 1950s. Two of Terman's students in the 1930s were William Hewlett and David Packard, who in 1939, on the urging of Terman, founded the eponymous firm adjacent to Stanford.

The founding of Hewlett Packard (HP) reflected Terman's vision of Stanford as a high-tech industrial district that would spawn start-ups (Leslie and Kargon 1996). In the Boston area, Georges Doriot, a professor at Harvard Business School had a similar vision. After the Second World War, Doriot and a number of academic and business leaders in the Boston area, through the pioneering venture capital firm, American Research & Development, made a conscious and successful attempt to commercialize the military technologies that had accumulated at the MIT, by far the most important university in the nation for military research (Hsu and Kenney 2005). The result by the 1950s was the emergence of 'Route 128' in the Greater Boston area as the world's leading high-tech industrial district.

Highly aware of these efforts on the East Coast, in his 1946–7 Dean's Report of the Stanford School of Engineering, Terman issued a call for the western United States to make use of its institutions of higher education to foster indigenous innovation (quoted in Leslie 1993: 55):

> The west has long dreamed of an indigenous industry of sufficient magnitude to balance its agricultural resources. The war advanced these hopes and brought to the west the beginning of a great new era of industrialization. A strong and independent industry must, however, develop its own intellectual resources of science and technology, for industrial activity that depends upon imported brains and second hand ideas cannot hope to be more than a vassal that pays tribute to its overlords, and is permanently condemned to an inferior competitive position.

Towards strong and independent industry in emerging and developing countries

In the post-Second World War decades, economies such as Japan, South Korea and Taiwan would adopt precisely the above perspective on industrial development, with the education of the population as the foundation.[2] In the case of Japan, laws dating back to 1886 made primary education universally free and compulsory, and by 1909 98 per cent of all school-age children went to primary school (Koike and Inoki 1990). Japan also developed a system of higher education from the late nineteenth century that sent its graduates into industry (Yonekawa 1984). Additionally, also from the late nineteenth century, Japanese companies engaged in the practice of sending university-educated employees abroad for extended periods of time to learn about Western technology (see, for example, Fukasaku 1992). Of utmost importance to Japan's post-Second World War development was the fact that for decades Japanese industrial enterprises had made university-educated engineers integral to their managerial organizations (Morikawa 2001).

These investments in education meant that in 1960 only 2.4 per cent of Japan's population aged 15 and over had no schooling while on average its population had 7.78 years of schooling (the US figures were 2.0 per cent and 8.49 years). By contrast, in 1960 the no-schooling proportions were in South Korea 42.8 per cent, Taiwan 37.3 per cent, Singapore 46.2 per cent and Hong Kong 29.7 per cent, while the average years of schooling of these populations were in South Korea 4.25, Taiwan 3.87, Singapore 4.30 and Hong Kong 5.17 (Barro and Lee 2000). A major challenge that faced the would-be 'Asian Tigers' was to transform their national educational systems into a foundation for industrial development. In South Korea, as the most dramatic example, average years of schooling of the 15-plus population rose from 7.91 years in 1980 to 10.84 in 2000, surpassing Japan's 2000 figure of 9.47 and not far behind the US figure of 12.05 (Barro and Lee 2000). By the last half of the 1990s South Korea had the highest number of PhDs per capita of any country in the world (Kim and Leslie 1998: 154).

India, a nation with 680 million people aged 15 or over in 2000 compared with South Korea's 37 million, has not invested in such a dramatic transformation of its mass education system. In 1960 the Indian 15-plus population included 72.2 per cent with no schooling and had on average 1.68 years of schooling. In 2000 India's no-schooling figure remained high at 43.9 per cent, while the average years figure was only 5.06. India, with one-sixth of the world's population, has one-third of the world's illiterates. Nevertheless in the post-Second World War decades, given the size of its population and the legacy of British colonial rule, India did have large numbers of university graduates – so many in fact that as late as the first half of the 1990s India's problem was less brain drain and more the nation's millions of educated unemployed. In British fashion, Indian university students favoured the study of science over engineering. In the 1950s and 1960s, however, the Indian government, with the assistance of US universities and foundations, invested in the system of Indian Institutes of Technology that are currently of critical importance to high-tech development in that nation. Over the past decade educated Indians have also been far and away the most numerous of all nationalities in following global career paths to the United States, on temporary work visas and as permanent residents, for graduate education and work experience (see Lazonick 2009: ch. 5).

For those nations that made these investments in education, since the 1960s the development strategies of East Asian nations have interacted with the investment strategies of US-based high-tech companies to generate a global labour supply.[3] This process has entailed flows of US capital to East Asian labour as well as flows of East Asian labour to US capital. As a result new possibilities to pursue high-tech careers, and thereby develop productive capabilities, have opened up to vast numbers of individuals in East Asian nations. Many found the relevant educational programmes and work experience in their home countries. But many gained access to education and experience by following global career paths that included study and work abroad, especially in the United States.

For East Asian nations, these global career paths have posed a danger of 'brain drain': the career path could come to an end in the United States (or another advanced economy) rather than in the country where the individual had been born and bred. Education and experience in the United States created, however, valuable 'human capital' that could potentially be lured back home. A major challenge for the East Asian nations has been the creation of domestic employment opportunities, through a combination of FDI, strategic government initiatives and the growth of indigenous businesses, to enable the career paths of global nationals to be followed back home, thus transforming a potential 'brain drain' into an actual 'brain gain'.

Historically, FDI by multinational enterprises (MNEs) has been an important source of high-tech employment creation in these nations, mainly because even when they have gone to these countries in search of low wage labour, the multinational corporations (MNCs) have also employed indigenous scientists, engineers and managers. US MNCs such as Motorola in South Korea from 1967, Intel in Malaysia from 1972 and Texas Instruments (TI) in India from 1985 created some of the first attractive opportunities for nationals to pursue high-tech careers at home.

The greatest impact on innovation and development comes, however, from the creation and growth of indigenous firms. When high-tech employment is dependent on MNEs, there are limits to the transfer of high quality employment to the host nation, whereas indigenous companies maintain strategic control over the location of job creation. Many of the founders of these indigenous companies

have been part of the 'reverse brain drain' from the advanced economies (Saxenian 2006). Some founders and many key employees have
followed career paths entirely at home, going from MNCs to indigenous companies.

In the case of South Korea, indigenous investments by government
and business rather than FDI have since the late 1980s driven the
development of domestic high-tech capabilities. In the 2000s these
indigenous investments are creating new opportunities for high end
investment by MNCs in South Korea, including new investments by
a company such as Motorola that has been doing business there for
almost 40 years. In contrast, in the absence of leading indigenous high-
tech companies, Malaysia's growth still remains highly dependent on
the upgrading strategies of MNEs such as Intel. Like Motorola in South
Korea, Intel originally went to Malaysia in search of low wage assembly labour in a politically stable country that had made a commitment
to mass education. And like Motorola Korea, Intel Malaysia upgraded
its capabilities over time, employing a higher proportion of high skill
labour in higher value added activities at rising wages.

Like Motorola in South Korea and Intel in Malaysia, TI originally
went to India in the mid-1980s in search of low wage labour. TI, however, was not searching for low skill labour. What first attracted TI to
India was the availability of highly educated engineers and program-
mers, albeit at much lower wages than would have had to be paid in the
United States. Over time TI expanded and upgraded its Indian operations, employing larger numbers of educated labour to design increasingly complex products. Two decades after TI came to India, the nation
is experiencing a growth dynamic in which, with both skill levels and
wages rising, indigenous companies such as Tata Consultancy Services,
Infosys and Wipro are taking the lead, and in which MNEs are being
attracted to India more for the high quality of its high-tech labour supply than for its low cost.

A similar process of indigenous innovation has been taking place in
China, but with the difference that indigenous Chinese companies such
as Lenovo, Founder and Huawei Technologies have emerged to serve
the growing Chinese consumer and business markets, and have drawn
upon the capital goods expertise of MNEs such as Intel, TI, Motorola
and HP to develop higher quality, lower cost products. Some of these
companies – Lenovo, Founder and Huawei are prime examples – have
become leading competitors not only in China but also internationally
(Feng and Zhang 2007; Lu 2000; Lu and Lazonick 2001; Xie and White
2004; Zhang 2009). While there are large numbers of Chinese high-tech

employees who have acquired higher education and work experience in the United States, the vast majority have been receiving education and experience in China.

Given the growth dynamic that has taken hold in these nations, sheer size ensures that Indians and Chinese will dominate the expansion of the global high-tech labour supply. Combined, the population of India and China is 33 times that of South Korea and Taiwan. India and China have rapidly growing domestic markets that both provide demand for the products of indigenous companies and give their governments leverage with MNEs in gaining access to advanced technology as a condition for FDI. While India and China offer indigenous scientists and engineers rapidly expanding employment opportunities at home, vast numbers of their educated populations are studying and working abroad. Aided by the ongoing liberalization of US immigration policy (impeded just temporarily by the reaction to 9/11), the global career path is much more of a 'mass' phenomenon for Indian and Chinese scientists and engineers than it has been for the Koreans and Taiwanese. History tell us that, following global career paths, more and more Indian and Chinese high-tech labour will migrate back to their countries of origin, where as Saxenian (2006) has shown, they have been an important source of high-tech entrepreneurship.

The cases of South Korea and Taiwan should give pause to arguments that investments in knowledge-intensive sectors are not of much relevance to the very poor nations such as those in Africa. While most African nations are certainly not well-positioned to compete in high-tech industry, it must be remembered that South Korea's GDP per capita was only 10 per cent of that of the United States in 1960 and 13 per cent in 1970, while that of Taiwan was just 13 per cent in 1960 and 20 per cent in 1970 (Maddison 2007). In 2003 South Korea's GDP per capita was 54 per cent of that of the United States and Taiwan's 60 per cent. In the 1980s and 1990s through 'indigenous innovation' – improvements on technologies that are transferred from abroad – these nations, like Japan about a quarter century before, transformed themselves from poor nations into rich nations. Now China and India, with one-third of the world's population, are also developing rapidly on the basis of indigenous innovation.

It would be very misleading to attribute the development of China and India to a sudden emergence of entrepreneurship. There is no doubt that entrepreneurship has been unleashed in these nations. It is a phenomenon, however, that is only explicable through an analysis of the changing social conditions of innovative enterprise.

Concluding remarks

National investment in educating the labour force is the foundation of economic development. This investment must be done ahead of demand, thus creating the problems of brain drain and the educated unemployed. The solution to these problems is domestic employment provided by government agencies, MNCs and indigenous businesses that can make use of an educated labour force, absorbing those who have not gone abroad and eventually attracting back a portion of those who have.

In need of study are the conditions under which these employment opportunities are created. Entrepreneurship or the formation of new indigenous firms is one way in which this employment can be created. But, in higher value added industries, entrepreneurship assumes a supply of entrepreneurs who have already secured not only the relevant education but also the substantial work experience needed to give them an intimate knowledge of the technological, market and competitive conditions of the particular industries in which they will launch new ventures.

National investments in a primary, secondary and tertiary educational system provide a foundation for a portion of the indigenous population to secure advanced education and high-tech work experience. The sources of a supply of indigenous entrepreneurs include: (i) government employment in research institutes and educational institutions, (ii) employment at MNEs operating within the nation and (iii) employment abroad that culminates in 'reverse brain drain'. The histories of South Korea and Taiwan show that these three sources of entrepreneurship all played roles in the process of creating the entrepreneurs who were involved in creating the indigenous enterprises that led the remarkable transformation of their economies from the late 1960s to the early 1990s. Eventually these indigenous enterprises themselves became sources of entrepreneurs who could start new 'spinoffs'. The same dynamic is now working itself out in India and China. Further research is needed to document in detail this process of creating a supply of effective entrepreneurs in developing economies.

A critical dimension of the development process is the sharing of the gains from innovative enterprise. Policies to promote development must take into account the need for the government to share in the gains so that it can reinvest in the education of the labour force as well as in physical infrastructures. The labour force also needs to share in the gains of innovative enterprise so that it can enjoy a higher standard of living and augment the level of domestic consumer demand. In a developing economy such as China, the challenge at this point is not economic growth but rather the great increase in income inequality that accompanies it. We need to understand better how incentives can be created to promote entrepreneurial ventures in developing economics while ensuring an equitable distribution of the gains from innovation.

The areas for further research identified here entail challenges to economic orthodoxy concerning both the efficacy of market forces and the inefficacy of state intervention. I have argued that, contrary to prevailing ideology, even in the advanced economies, governments contribute to development by protecting and subsidizing indigenous industry. The standard argument against government subsidy and protection of industry is based on the theory of the market economy with its optimizing firms that simply respond to market forces. It is a theory that is fundamentally flawed when it seeks to show the superiority of perfect competition over an industrial structure in which some firms have gained a dominant share. The theory of the market economy fails to ask how, within an industry, some firms can through innovation gain a competitive advantage over other firms and drive the development of the economy.

In contrast, the theory of innovative enterprise that I have laid out in Chapter 2 explains why governments can support the process of development by subsidizing and protecting infant firms in infant industries. In particular, it provides a critical response to the neoclassical contention that state intervention and subsidies to industry can only undermine the economic progress of a nation. Chang (2002) has shown that neoclassical ideology has been instrumental in 'kicking away the ladder' of industrial policy that the developed nations have themselves climbed to become rich, thus seeking to deny developing nations from scaling the same heights. The theory of innovative enterprise provides the micro-foundations for understanding the conditions under which such industrial policy might succeed.

In effect, the dynamics of the innovating firm explain why in the face of established international competition, tariff protection or some other type of subsidy may be necessary to transform the high fixed costs of an innovative strategy into low unit costs. It also explains why the success or failure of state support for industry will depend on the social conditions of innovative enterprise. Within this framework, state subsidy provides the firms that constitute a national industry with a source of financial commitment while they are engaging in indigenous innovation and have yet to transform the high fixed costs of that innovation strategy into low unit costs. But financial commitment in and of itself does not, and cannot, ensure the success of an innovative investment strategy. Given the financial commitment provided by tariff protection or other types of subsidies, it matters who exercises strategic control and what types of investments in organizational learning they make.

Arguments for the efficacy of state subsidy for developing economies need to specify the 'business model' that will combine strategic control organizational integration and financial commitment to generate innovation as a foundation for economic development. The theory of innovative enterprise does not 'explain' economic development. That explanation must be sought in the social conditions of innovative enterprise that prevail in a particular time and place. The theory of innovative enterprise provides a coherent analytical framework for researching the characteristics of those conditions and for devising policies that, for the sake of economic development, can help to ensure that relevant conditions of innovative enterprise are in place. Innovative enterprise, I have argued, is the essential, and logical, link between entrepreneurial ventures and the development state.

Acknowledgements

I have benefited greatly from comments on an earlier draft of this chapter (and Chapter 2) by Wim Naudé and Tony Shorrocks of UNU-WIDER, as well as by participants at the conference on 'Rethinking Development in the Age of Globalization', Southern New Hampshire University, 6–8 April 2007.

Notes

1. http://www.nih.gov/about/budget.htm
2. Indeed, in the late 1960s and early 1970s Terman and his disciples were key advisers to the Koreans in the setting up of what became the Korea Advanced Institute of Science and Technology – KAIST (see Kim and Leslie 1998).
3. The following draws on Lazonick (2009: ch. 5).

13
Entrepreneurship, Development and the Spatial Context: Retrospect and Prospects

Peter Nijkamp

Introduction

This chapter offers an overview of the rich literature on entrepreneurship in relation to geographic-locational conditions and regional development policy. Regional development has been a permanent source of interest among scientists and policy-makers. Regional growth theory has over the years become an important branch of modern economic growth analysis. In the past, locational and resource conditions (e.g. accessibility) used to play a significant role (witness the traditional interest in infrastructural conditions including information and communication technology, ICT), but in more recent years, the attention has shifted towards issues like sustainable development and competitive advantages of regions. This trend is also reflected in endogenous economic growth theory and the new economic geography. In this context, we also observe greater interest in entrepreneurship, leadership and regional innovative/creative culture in which the knowledge society also plays a critical role (see also Helpman 2004). This has had far-reaching implications for development economics, for instance, by placing more emphasis on market efficiency, tradition/trust and the self-organizing capacity of regions.

In general, we observe not only more interest in efficiency and innovative modes of business activities (witness the emphasis on strategic performance management in corporate organizations), but also a thorough interest in the innovativeness of public sector operations (see Windrum and Koch 2008). Against this background, the strategic driving forces of regional development (such as education, training, R&D,

incubator initiatives, creative city actions) are increasingly receiving attention. This merger of public and private sector initiatives as a joint focus on the knowledge and innovation sector is sometimes called the 'triple helix' concept (cf. Shane 2003). This is a promising policy support concept, as it is possible to engage local entrepreneurship through joint ventures.

The drivers of growth in a regional system may be classified according to six factors:

- *Human capital*: productive contribution by labour and cognitive talent of people;
- *Entrepreneurial capital*: productive contributions from smart business activities and innovative attitudes;
- *Financial capital*: financial resources available to support commercial production;
- *Social capital*: interactive resources among economic agents, e.g. in the form of network access and use, that support economic synergy;
- *Knowledge capital*: productive contributions by R&D and education, reflected in patents, concessions, and local spin-offs; and
- *Creative capital*: original and unplanned contributions that support the economic sustainability of local business initiatives.

Clearly, regional competitiveness and effective entrepreneurship are two sides of the same coin. Already since the early history of economics (Adam Smith, Ricardo), good entrepreneurship has been regarded as the critical success factor for economic performance. The notion of entrepreneurial competition was developed more fully a century ago by Marshall. A really groundbreaking contribution to the analysis of entrepreneurship from a broad historical perspective was offered by Joseph Schumpeter in his book *The Theory of Economic Development* (1911/1934). Starting from a circular flow of goods and money of a given size in a static context, he argues that without growth or economic progress there is no scope for entrepreneurship: history will then repeat itself. However, if the exogenous circumstances are changing, the circular equilibrium will also change. This disturbance of an equilibrium towards a new position is called 'creative destruction'. One of the driving forces for a change towards a new equilibrium is formed by innovation which means a breakthrough of existing patterns of production and productivity. Innovation is thus a creative *modus operandi* of an entrepreneur and induces a process of economic growth. Clearly, flexibility and vitality of the economic system is a *sine qua non* for an adjustment ('resilience') after a disturbance in the original equilibrium position.

Innovation and entrepreneurship are regarded as key factors for high economic performance in a competitive economy (Acs 2002; Suarez-Villa 1996). The unprecedented and accelerated economic growth in the past decades has to a large extent taken place in and was spurred on by the information and telecommunications sector (Roller and Waverman 2001), through which the advanced knowledge economy could be materialized. However, the fruits of the modern knowledge economy are not equally spread over all regions, but exhibit a clear regional and local differentiation (Acs and de Groot et al. 2002; Nijkamp and Poot 1997; Porter 2003; Roper 2001). The spatial dimensions of innovation, production and knowledge dissemination have become an important field of study (Fischer and Varga 2003). The innovation literature shows that different analytical frameworks appear to offer different explanatory findings, such as the new economic geography, the new growth theory and the new economics of innovation (Acs 2002). Such differences in empirical findings emerge, *inter alia*, from the role and seedbed conditions of knowledge production, the appropriability of knowledge in a broader spatial network, as well as the filters and barriers in knowledge spillovers. Knowledge creation and acquisition have nowadays also become part of modern industry and of advanced entrepreneurship (Capello 2002; Shane and Venkataraman 2000). Not surprisingly, the impact of policy on innovation and entrepreneurship in a regional setting has recently received broad attention in the scientific literature.

Since the 1980s, economic research has witnessed an avalanche of interest in innovative behaviour of firms, in particular in the context of regional competitive conditions (for a review, see Bertuglia et al. 1997; Fischer and Fröhlich 2001). Regions (including cities) are increasingly regarded as important nodes of production, consumption, trade and decision-making and play a critical role in global modes of production and transportation. Locality and globality are two sides of the same coin in an open network. The conventional comparative advantage perspective on regions is no longer sufficient to explain the relative economic performance of regions in a global economy, as participation in ICT networks, educational systems and business culture are also important economic success factors. This awareness has had important implications for regional growth theory culminating in the popularity of the 'new' growth theory (for an overview see Nijkamp and Poot 1998).

The focus on knowledge as a factor *par excellence* for business performance ties in with the present emphasis on endogenous growth theory, which takes for granted that economic growth does not automatically emerge from technological innovation as 'manna from heaven', but is the result of deliberate actions and choices of various stakeholders, including the government. Government policy in a modern society, however, is no longer a controlling strategy, but a facilitating strategy through which, by means of investments in R&D, education, training and knowledge centres etc., the seedbed conditions may be created for successful entrepreneurial performance.

The birth, growth, contraction and death process of enterprises has become an important field of research in so-called firm demographics (van Wissen 2000). This new field of research is concerned with the analysis of the spatio-temporal change pattern of firms from a behavioural analytical perspective (cf. Nelson and Winter 1982). Recent interesting studies in this field can be found, *inter alia*, in Brüderl and Schussler (1990), Carroll and Hannan (2000) and Siegfried and Evans (1994). Many studies on growth processes of firms originate from industrial economics or organization and management disciplines, often complemented with notions from geography, demography or psychology (e.g. Caves 1998; Evans 1987; Gertler 1988; Hayter 1997; Stintchcombe et al. 1968).

Empirical research has shown that in most cases enterprises change their strategies (products, markets etc.) in an incremental way. From historical research it appears that radical adjustments do take place, but occur infrequently (Mintzberg 1978). In evolutionary economics it is emphasized that organizations develop, stabilize and follow routines. These routines may change over time, but in the short run they function as stable carriers for knowledge and experience. This causes a certain degree of 'inertia'. Related to the latter point is the core concept of search behaviour. Organizations are not invariant, but change as a result of search for new solutions when older ones fail to work. Search behaviour follows routines, for example, based upon perceptions 'coloured' by the previous situation and biases in information processing (see van Geenhuizen and Nijkamp 1995). The study of the development trajectories of individual firms from a spatio-temporal perspective is sometimes called 'company life history analysis' (van Geenhuizen 1993). It uses mainly a case study approach and aims to trace and explain the evolution of firms over a longer period. Particular attention is then given to entrepreneurial motives for corporate change at the microlevel. Factors to be considered are, *inter alia*, the business environment, leadership, links between strategic and operational change, human resource management and coherence in management (see Pettigrew and Whipp 1991). Information acquisition – e.g. through participation in networks of industries – is of course also an important element to be considered. In this context, the local 'milieu' (e.g. through *filières*) may also play an important role.

The regional nexus

Structural change and economic development are usually seen as the outgrowth of new and creative combinations of economic activity. The dynamics in this development process can largely be ascribed to innovative behaviour of risk-taking entrepreneurs. It is noteworthy that studies on entrepreneurship have shown in the course of economic history a fluctuating pattern of interest among economists. Illuminating examples can be found in the works of Schumpeter (1911/1934) and Galbraith (1967). An interesting overview can be found in Hébert and Link (1989), who address the motives and economic background of entrepreneurship; in their rather comprehensive study they distinguish the German, Chicago and Austrian schools of thought. In general, there appears to be a broad consensus that the entrepreneurial act is pursued by a risk-taking rational businessman in a small-scale setting, who dares to choose new, potentially beneficial directions and to explore less travelled pathways. Innovative acts are not generated by formal policies, but by challenging stress situations in a competitive environment that may bring about high revenues but also unexpected losses. From an evolutionary perspective, the 'animal spirit' is the driving force in a real entrepreneurial climate.

The globalization trend in the past decades has prompted the emergence of an open space economy, with a high degree of imports/exports of capital, labour, information and knowledge across the border. International migration and spatial mobility of firms exhibit a similar pattern. The last part of the twentieth century has witnessed a massive downsizing and drastic restructuring of many corporate firms. This new economic area, based less on the traditional inputs of natural resources, labour and capital, and more on the inputs of knowledge and ideas, is often labelled as the 'entrepreneurial economy'. This new age takes for granted the Schumpeterian ideas on risk-taking entrepreneurship as the basis for innovation and economic progress. Paradoxically, the increased degree of uncertainty creates also many opportunities for small and young firms, and hence leads to higher rates of entrepreneurship. Entrepreneurship affects the economy both directly and indirectly, and at various levels, through innovation, competition and restructuring (Wennekers and Thurik 1999). Empirical investigations have shown that both a higher rate of new business start-ups and a higher rate of turbulence (the sum of start-ups and closures) enhance, after a certain time lag, economic growth and job creation (Carree and Thurik 2003). Clearly, entrepreneurship is not only a driver for economic growth, competitiveness and job creation, but also a vehicle for personal development and the resolution of social issues.

It is widely recognized that the region has become a fundamental basis of economic and social life. The national level of observation, though still important, is no longer the uniquely privileged point of entry to our understanding of economic development and all the more so given the fact that the barriers between national economies are, in certain respects, breaking down, at least in Europe (Scott and Storper 2003).

Innovation and entrepreneurship are not equally distributed among sectors and regions. In the past two decades we have witnessed a renewed interest in the seedbed conditions for small and medium sized enterprises (SMEs), as it was recognized that the innovative potential of the SME sector was very high (Acs 2002; Acs and Audretsch 1990). Many start-ups appear to be small-scale in nature and hence it is no surprise that new entrepreneurship is often found in the SME sector. The current economic conditions reflect also new types of industrial organization among commercial firms (e.g. network constellations) in which entrepreneurship plays a key role. It is therefore conceivable that in recent years the action-oriented concept of entrepreneurship is back on the stage with a particular view to the regional and network conditions for the emergence of innovative and competitive entrepreneurship (Danson 1995; Davidsson 1995; Deakins 1999; Foss and Klein 2002; Nijkamp 2003; Pineder 2001; Preissl and Solimene 2003; Stam 2003). Entrepreneurship means a sailing under very uncertain and changeable weather conditions, driven by survival strategies in a competitive and sometimes antagonistic world (Mehlum et al. 2003; Stough et al. 2002). In such evolutionary economic developments, due attention is to be given to incubation conditions and technogenesis processes which drive regional growth.

Regional economics in the past decades has made a successful attempt to uncover the complexities of the modern space economy. It has led to important integrations of scientific perspectives, such as an integration of agglomeration theory and location theory, trade theory and welfare theory or growth theory and entrepreneurship (including industrial organization). The blend of rigorous economic analysis and geographical thinking has furthermore induced a bridge between two traditionally disjointed disciplines, while this synergy has laid the foundations for innovative scientific cross-fertilization of both theoretical and applied nature in the important domain of regional development. The region has become a natural fruitful anchor point for an integrated perspective on the dynamics in the space economy, such as regional development in the context of changing labour conditions or spatial innovation in the context of metropolitan incubator conditions (Florida 2002).

There is clearly a wealth of literature on regional convergence/divergence and on the factors determining structural disparity. In the past decades we have also witnessed the rise of many applied studies (e.g. Abreu 2005; Barro 1991; Kormendi and Meguire 1985), in which extensive databases were analysed in a comparative perspective.

In light of the previous observations, regions face two imperatives in a market-driven world. First, they have to be concerned with socio-economic welfare, notably employment. Job creation, an important indicator of economic growth, is central to the wealth creating process of a regional economy. The second imperative is the ability to develop the economy. Development includes two interrelated processes: structural change and productivity improvement (Malecki 1997a). These processes take place in a multifaceted force field.

Regional development manifests itself as a spatially uneven change in a system of regions. Regional divergence, rather than regional convergence, is a common phenomenon that has attracted thorough attention from both the research community and policy agencies. The standard neoclassical view of regional growth would predict that low wage regions would acquire productive investments from high wage regions and/or export cheap labour to these areas. Then, the market system in the longer run would lead to an equalization of factor payments, so that in the final equilibrium, a convergence among regions would occur. In reality, this simplified model is subjected to many restrictive assumptions (full mobility, absolute cost differences, no institutional inertia, complete foresight on profitable investments, constant returns to scale), so that an equilibrium may be very hard to achieve. Regional change at the end is the result of entrepreneurial activity in which innovations (new or improved products and processes, new management styles, locations) are key factors.

Entrepreneurship has acquired central importance among the processes that affect regional economic change. Entrepreneurs are essential actors of change, and they can act to accelerate the creation, diffusion and application of new ideas. In doing so, they not only ensure the efficient use of resources but also take initiatives to exploit business opportunities (OECD 1998). A central reason for the interest by policy-makers in entrepreneurship is its apparent capacity – based on US experience (OECD 1989) – to create, directly and indirectly, employment and wealth. An important indication of the significance now attached to entrepreneurship is the OECD study on *Fostering Entrepreneurship* to increase economic dynamism by improving the environment for entrepreneurial activity (see OECD 1998).

This chapter makes a modest attempt to review the current literature on entrepreneurship. It is not a literature on a phenomenon that has reached a mature equilibrium, but one that is still vigorously developing. Clearly, to review such an expanding field constitutes an almost impossible task, at least with regard to completeness of coverage.

The entrepreneurial hero

Modern economic and technological systems are indeed in a state of flux. Consequently, recent years have witnessed an avalanche of interest in entrepreneurship, in particular the critical success factors of the modern 'entrepreneurial hero' and the wider urban and regional development implications of emerging entrepreneurship in favourable seedbed areas. It goes without saying that in the recent past also the conditions that facilitate proper entrepreneurship policy or the opportunities of public–private partnership constellations have received increasing attention. Research in this field has focused in particular on fact finding, on theory development and on modelling contributions and has aimed to get a better understanding of this complex multi-actor force field. Contributions have been made by representatives from different disciplines, in particular economics, regional science, industrial organization and behavioural psychology. And in this context, the critical importance of knowledge and information in our ICT-driven world is increasingly recognized and it has become an important field of study.

Entrepreneurship is a phenomenon that takes several forms and appears in small and large firms, in new firms and established firms, in the formal and informal economy, in legal and illegal activities, in innovative and traditional concerns, in high risk and low risk undertakings, and in all economic sectors (OECD 1998). Apparently, entrepreneurship is a multifaceted phenomenon that can be viewed from different angles. Entrepreneurship has been a topic of long-standing concern in economics, but there remains little consensus on the concept of entrepreneurship (Hébert and Link 1989). An extensive review is found in Fischer and Nijkamp (2008).

Different authors stress different facets of entrepreneurship. Schumpeter (1911/1934), for example, emphasizes the creative component. For Schumpeter the creativity of entrepreneurship lies in the ability to perceive new economic opportunities better than others do, not only in the short-term as arbitrageurs, but also in the long-term as fillers of innovative niches (Suarez-Villa 1989). While in Schumpeter's concept risk-taking is not a definitional component, Knight (1921) emphasizes the entrepreneur's role as dealing with risk in a context in which entrepreneurship is separable from the control of the firm. More recently, Schultz (1980) has chosen to define entrepreneurship as the ability to deal with disequilibria rather than the ability to deal with uncertainty. Risk does not enter prominently into this concept of entrepreneurship. In his view, definitions of entrepreneurship which are uncertainty-based cannot logically relegate risk to a position of little or no importance. Finally, several other economists including Piore and Sabel (1984) stress the network character of entrepreneurship, a new form of entrepreneurship based on innovative activities carried out in clusters of firms. A review of the conceptual and operational definitions of entrepreneurship can be found in Bögenhold (2004).

Innovation has become a fashionable topic in modern economics, but the foundations of this concept date back to Marshall (1890), who introduced the notion of industrial districts, in which a strong spatial concentration of (usually smaller) firms may be found and where each of these firms is specialized in one (or a few) elements of the production process of the main economic activity in the area concerned. This concentration is not only the consequence of market-driven economic and technological efficiency requirements, but is also anchored in the region's cultural, institutional and socio-economic value systems (such as trust, cooperation and social support systems). Industrial districts have in general major advantages, in particular, lower production costs, reduced transaction costs, rise in efficiency of production factors deployed and enhancement of dynamic efficiency (cf. Gordon and McCann 2000; Lever 2002; Porter 2000). Such economic technological clusters form the seedbed conditions for modern entrepreneurship (Rabellotti 1997). An extensive description and typology or regional clusters in Europe can be found in the 'Observatory of European SMEs' (European Commission 2002) in which a distinction is made between regional clusters, regional innovation network and regional innovation systems. A review of the literature on regional clusters is given in Asheim et al. (2006).

The OECD (1998) identifies three important characteristics of entrepreneurship that have emerged in the light of the above views. First, entrepreneurship involves a dynamic process in which new firms are starting up, existing firms are growing and unsuccessful ones are restructuring or closing down. A second characteristic of entrepreneurship is that – to the extent that it implies control of the process by the entrepreneur-owner – it tends to be identified with small business where the owner(s) and manager(s) are the same.

Finally, entrepreneurship entails innovation. This view stems from Schumpeter's (1911/1934) suggestion that entrepreneurial innovation is the essence of capitalism and its process of creative destruction embodied in new products, new production processes and new forms of organization.

In both science and policy circles, it is nowadays widely accepted that knowledge is the key to success, and that explains why with the advent of the ICT revolution so much emphasis is placed on the promises offered by our modern knowledge society (cf. Audretsch and Thurik 1999; Nijkamp and Stough 2002). The ICT sector in combination with drastic changes in the industrial organization will exert profound influences on modern spatial economic systems. These dynamic developments will undoubtedly create a new urban and regional scene dominated by the digital economy (Cairncross 1997). The ICT sector may in principle create the conditions for a dispersal of economic activity, but the network constellations of a modern industrial system will at the same time call for close interactions favouring agglomeration forces. What we actually observe in recent years is a reinforced position of urban nodes in global networks (Castells 1996; Preissl and Solimene 2003; Scott and Storper 2003). Furthermore, the ICT orientation of urban areas induces also a clear emphasis on knowledge infrastructure and knowledge transfer in urban agglomerations, a process which itself induces both centripetal and centrifugal urban development (Kolko 2002; Smith 2001). Learning and training mechanisms in a modern urban and entrepreneurial setting are apparently the key conditions for economic performance. In a recent book, Drennan (2002) demonstrates clearly that the ICT sector flourishes best in large urban concentration, as this favours scale advantages and human interaction. In conclusion, our world is showing unprecedented techno-economic dynamics, with far-reaching implications for the space economy.

A frequently used measure of innovative activities is the output of the knowledge production process measured in terms of patent applications. But innovation is a phenomenon that is difficult to capture empirically. Patent-related measures have two important limitations (Fischer et al. 2006). First, the range of patentable inventions constitutes only a subset of all R&D outcomes, and second, patenting is a strategic decision and, thus, not all patentable inventions are actually patented. As to the first limitation, purely scientific advances devoid of immediate applicability as well as incremental technological improvements, which are too small to pass for discrete, codifiable inventions, are not patentable. The second limitation is rooted in the fact that it may be optimal for firms not to apply for patents even though their inventions would satisfy the criteria for patentability. Therefore, patentability requirements and incentives to refrain from patenting limit the measurement based on patent data. R&D-related data, while important, relate to the input of the knowledge production process, as opposed to innovations achieved.

In the traditional regional economics literature we already find that space offers discriminating economic conditions. And also nowadays we realize that, despite the ICT sector, knowledge and entrepreneurship are not ubiquitous goods that are freely available everywhere, but have clearly geographical and institutional backgrounds. There is an avalanche of recent studies on the geography of innovation and economic progress (see e.g. Boekema et al. 2000; Brons and Pellenbarg 2003; Gallup et al. 1999; van Oort 2004). Notwithstanding the 'death of distance', physical geography is nowadays still a major determinant of competitive economic conditions, such as access to main transport and communication arteries.

Driving forces of entrepreneurship

Clearly, geographical space is not able to create sufficient conditions for innovative developments or novel institutional arrangements, but it is important in that it may embody necessary or desirable conditions for new forms of behaviour in both the private and the public domain. The urban incubation theory is a nice illustration of this argument. The recent interest in the new economic geography has clearly pointed out the critical importance of spatial accessibility in regard to the emergence of innovative attitudes and of institutional support mechanisms (Acemoglu et al. 2001; Hall and Jones 1999). Such institutional ramifications are not only related to regulatory systems such as property rights or stable political regimes, but also to self-organized modes of cooperation and competition in the private sector. The main challenge from a research perspective is the identification of promising human capital conditions from a regional-institutional perspective, while taking account of the self-organizing potential of business life in a given area (Lundvall 1992; Norton 2001; Oakey 1996). The concept of a 'learning economy' has to be mentioned in this context as well, as this notion indicates that evolution is not a rectilinear development, but is dependent on deliberate choices and cognitive feedback decisions of humans in an uncertain environment, who respond endogenously to new challenges and to creative opportunities offered by social and economic interaction. This new mode of producing and interacting is a major departure from Fordist mass production methods in the past.

Regional development is a dynamic phenomenon with a permanent change in business activities. This change may be caused by innovation, by decline and by the birth and death of firms. The development of the SME sector plays a critical role in spatial dynamics, as many forms of creative entrepreneurship are found in this sector. Clearly, the regional system (education, social support system, culture, accessibility etc.) plays an important role in the changing conditions for entrepreneurship. Entrepreneurial adjustment patterns are thus of decisive importance for convergence or divergence patterns in regional systems. But the fundamental question remains: which are the drivers of new business investments and new entrepreneurial modes of operation?

Mass production in large-scale concentrations has been a prominent success factor in the age of industrialization. Labour specialization and – later on – capital specialization was a *sine qua non* for a productivity rise that was needed to survive in a competitive economy or to become a winner in a growing market. Mass production, however, creates also a high degree of path dependency, lock-in behaviour and hence inertia in large-scale enterprises, with the consequence of a low degree of flexibility and adaptability to new circumstances. In the course of history we have learned that mass production is not the only mode of industrial organization, but is also accompanied and sometimes even facilitated by SMEs, which have often demonstrated a surprising ability to adopt new production possibilities (including distribution and logistics) (cf. Marsili 2001; Suarez-Villa 1989). The fact that 'big size' is not always the optimal level of a firm has been thoroughly analysed by You (1995), who offers four explanatory frameworks:

- *Technological*: the optimal scale of a firm is determined by economies of scale and scope as well as by the span of control, so that the optimal firm size is the result of scale economies and diseconomies;

- *Institutional*: according to the transaction cost theory (see Coase 1937; Williamson 1985), the governance of a complex undertaking with many activities may cause high internal transaction costs, so that it may be more beneficial to resort to the market for specific activities (e.g. non-core activities);
- *Organizational*: the type of industrial organization (e.g. monopoly, oligopoly or monopolistic competition) is reflected in the market share of a firm, which is in turn determined by the price, the product uniformity (or specialty) and the managerial structure; and
- *Dynamics*: due to path dependency, lock-in behaviour, cultural environment, age of the firm and other determinants, the past situation of the firm may impact on its future size.

Although the industrial revolution has created the seedbed conditions for large-scale industries, the importance of small-scale activities has to be mentioned here. The existence – and sometimes resurrection – of a strong SME sector in various regions or urban districts was already noted by Marshall (1890) and later on by many industrial economists, who observed that innovative behaviour of existing or new firms does not necessarily increase their firm size. Examples may be found in many industrial districts (e.g. Lyon, Solingen, Sheffield, Rhode Island), where differentiated market orientation, flexible modes of production, and regional governing institutions controlling a balance between competition and cooperation were the most prominent features. This model was called *flexible specialization* (for details, see Piore and Sabel 1984; Sabel and Zeitlin 1985) and was based on networks of partly competing, partly cooperating firms involved in production and/or distribution of goods in a given region. Innovation was the driving force of these networks, which were subject to permanent change, depending on market conditions and competition. The strong feature of flexible specialization was the high degree of craftsmanship and skills of all actors involved in a clearly visible regional profile. When market conditions were changing, new networks could spontaneously emerge, so that the market positions could be kept. This industrial constellation could only be maintained under conditions of flexibility and mutual support of all actors involved.

The entrepreneurial event takes shape through the interaction of two sets of factors: personal (micro-) factors and environmental (macro-) factors. Much of the literature on entrepreneurship has focused on the micro-factors, the characteristics of an individual to become an entrepreneur and to start a new firm. These studies focus on the role of factors such as personality, educational attainment and/or ethnic origin (Lee et al. 2004). Personality studies find that entrepreneurship is associated with characteristics such as alertness to business opportunities, entrepreneurial vision and pro-activity (Chell et al. 1991). Research on personality, moreover, finds that entrepreneurs exhibit greater individualism than non-entrepreneurs do (McGrath et al. 1992).

Roberts (1991) emphasizes aspects of local culture and attributes as critical to building a local environment that fosters entrepreneurship. Even though cultural attitudes are formed through complex processes that are not well understood, it is a generally accepted view that cultural factors affect the way in which business is done. Such factors, for example, influence the willingness to cooperate with others and may reinforce trust and personal reputation that can reduce transaction costs in doing business. Conversely, an environment characterized by mistrust may oblige entrepreneurs to spend time and money to protect against the potentially opportunistic behaviour of those with whom they work. This may deter some of the entrepreneurial activity (OECD 1998). But there has been little research analysing systematically the impact of trust/mistrust on entrepreneurship.

High levels of entrepreneurial activity are often ascribed to cultural attributes. Culture, indeed, seems to play a critical role in determining the level of entrepreneurship within a region. Other things being equal, an environment in which entrepreneurship is esteemed and in which stigma does not attach to legitimate business failure will almost certainly be conducive to entrepreneurship. In the US the strong pro-entrepreneurial culture has assisted in shaping institutional characteristics of the economy that facilitate business start-ups, rewards firms based on their economic efficiency, and allows low cost exit for entrepreneurs who succeed, fail or simply want to move on to a new venture. A further striking aspect of the US entrepreneurial environment is the ample availability of risk capital and generally well-functioning market mechanisms for allocating this efficiently across a wide range of size, risk and return configurations (OECD 1998).

The key aspect of favourable entrepreneurial environments, however, is – as emphasized by Malecki (1997a) – thriving networks of entrepreneurs, other firms and institutions, providing capital, information and other forms of support. The theoretical notion of the *milieu* introduced by the GREMI group (Groupement de Recherce Européen sur les Milieux Innovateurs) epitomizes these characteristics (Maillat 1995). Entrepreneurial development is most likely to be successful in larger urban regions, especially in metropolitan regions, where innovativeness, an entrepreneurial climate and business opportunities are relatively abundant (Malecki 1997a).

Nowadays, with the advent of the ICT sector favouring network formation, such constellations based on flexible specialization are usually called *virtual organizations* or *virtual enterprises* (cf. Cooke and Morgan 1993). They refer to organization networks that have a flexible structure, that are governed by trust and innovative spirit, and that resemble for the outer world one unambiguously identifiable and complete organization. The control and command structure is not always very clear and may be flexible as well. According to Hale and Whitlam (1997: 3): 'The virtual organization is the name given to any organization which is continually evolving, redefining and reinventing itself for practical business purposes.' Virtual enterprises may vary in appearance. Examples of this organizational model are (Noorman 2002):

- *Internal virtual organization*: an organization comprising relatively autonomous teams which can be flexibly employed (Campbell 1997); illustrations can be found in virtual offices and lean offices;
- *Stable virtual organization*: an industrial model based on an outsourcing of non-core activities to a relatively small and fixed number of intermediaries;
- *Dynamic virtual organization*: large-scale but flexible cooperation between industrial organizations based on ad hoc opportunistic market motives (cf. Upton and McAfee 1996); and
- *Web-enterprise*: an organization centred around a (temporary) network of experts in a given field, sharing knowledge management and information for dedicated purposes.

The advances in the ICT sector have, of course, induced the transition to virtual network activity. It is clear that a wide variety of virtual enterprises is emerging nowadays. Their common feature is the trend to shorten product life cycles, to be subject to permanent innovation pressure, to be information-oriented, to be driven by high quality targets (zero defect), to operate in non-hierarchical modes, to be market-oriented through learning-by-using interactions and to take care of the entire value chain (cf. Morgan 1991).

The regional action space

A region is a spatially organized entity that offers the geographic seedbed conditions for entrepreneurship and their spatial network constellations, both physically and virtually. The governance of such a complex network organization is fraught with many problems, as innovative behaviour cannot so much be steered by policy. But policy can create support mechanisms through which self-reliance, self-esteem and confidence may be shaped. This requires in particular proper administrative support systems that favour business trust via non-bureaucratic, flexible and tailor-made governance initiatives.

Despite much variety, we observe in almost all cases a decentralized mechanism for governing cooperative relationships. Cooperation becomes volatile, but needs rules and trust. Consequently, the principle of trust has become a popular concept; it is less based on emotion than on economic rationality which may be more transaction-specific (Dasgupta 1988; Granovetter 1985; Linders et al. 2005). Consequently, there may be a need for more institutional support systems or various forms of institutional embeddedness in order to prevent destruction of human capital for ad hoc purposes (cf. Hagen and Choe 1998). This brings us to a major issue for public policy: is a non-formal public–private governance mechanism feasible that ensures the public interest (e.g. a stable regional development) and enhances private performance (e.g. innovative behaviour)? Availability of resources, smart infrastructure and proper education and training systems, accompanied by close interactions between the business world and the public sector, are critical success factors in this context (Stough 2003). It goes without saying that the spatial context of innovation and entrepreneurship needs an intensive research effort in order to understand the complex mechanism of regional and urban economic development.

In the literature on technological innovation and regional growth – following the rise of the new growth theory – three major drivers of growth were outlined: the knowledge base, innovative culture and action and public infrastructure.

Entrepreneurship does not take place in a wonderland of no spatial dimensions, but is deeply rooted in supporting geographic-locational support conditions (such as favourable urban incubation systems, venture capital support conditions, accessibility and openness of urban systems, diversity and stress conditions in the urban environment, heterogeneous and highly skilled labour force, communication and information infrastructures, collective learning mechanisms etc.). With the advent of the modern sophisticated communication and network structures, the action radius of entrepreneurs has significantly increased (see e.g. Reggiani and Nijkamp 2006). Consequently, the geography of entrepreneurship and innovation has become an important field of research in modern regional economics, in which the dynamics of firms are receiving major attention.

There are various reasons why of all types of firm dynamics new firm formations have attracted most attention (van Geenhuizen and Nijkamp 1995). Perhaps most significant is the fact that new firms provide new jobs. A second reason is that new firms are often involved in the introduction of new products and processes in the market. Accordingly, they may provide a major challenge to established firms and encourage them to improve their product quality and service or to reduce prices. On the other hand, it should be recognized that newly established firms face relatively large risks, due to lack of organizational experience and cohesion. As a consequence, the death rate among start-ups is relatively high and tends to decrease over time. Many entrepreneurs appear to die at a young age. It is clear that successful new enterprises contribute significantly to the economy and employment in the region concerned. There is, however, usually a large sectoral and geographical variation among the success or survival rates of new entrepreneurs (Acs 1994).

The study of the development trajectories of individual firms from a spatio-temporal perspective is sometimes called 'company life history analysis' (van Geenhuizen 1993). It mainly uses a case study approach and aims to trace and explain the evolution of firms over a longer period. Particular attention is then given to entrepreneurial motives for corporate change at the micro-level. Factors to be considered are, *inter alia*, the business environment, leadership, links between strategic and operational change, human resource management and coherence in management (see also Pettigrew and Whipp 1991). Information acquisition, for example through participation in networks of industries, is of course also an important element to be considered. In this context, the local 'milieu' may also play an important role.

It is a widely held belief that metropolitan environments offer favourable incubator conditions for creative entrepreneurship, as in this setting the conditions for proper human resource management (e.g. by means of specialized training and educational institutes) and labour recruitment are most favourable (see, for example, Davelaar 1991; Lagendijk and Oinas 2005; Leone and Struyck 1976; Pred 1977; Thompson 1968). But it should be recognized that various non-metropolitan areas also offer favourable seedbed conditions to the management of corporate change. The reason is that in many non-metropolitan areas the information needs are met in localized learning mechanisms, based on a dynamic territorial interplay between actors in a coherent production system, local culture, tradition and experiences (Camagni 1991; Storper 1993).

This view comes close to the one which puts a strong emphasis on the trend for localization in less central areas where doing business is a final resort or a survival strategy. Advocates of the latter idea adhere to a vertically disintegrated and locationally fixed production, based on a shift to flexible specialization. Some empirical evidence on non-urban seedbeds is found in high technology regions such as Silicon Valley, Boston, the M4 Corridor, and in semi-rural areas such as the Third Italy. Although the success of economic restructuring in these regions – as a result of many high-tech start-up firms – is, without doubt, due to the pervasiveness of the trend for flexible specialization, concomitant localization is not sufficiently proven (Gertler 1988; van Geenhuizen and van der Knaap 1994). Aside from a trend towards localization there is a trend towards globalization, associated with the growing influence of multinational corporations and their global networking with smaller firms (Amin 1993).

In the light of the previous observations it may be argued that modern entrepreneurship is based on associated skills of a varied nature. An entrepreneur is certainly an opportunity seeker, but in so doing he or she needs to have an eye on the rapidly changing external environment. As a consequence, firm demography is a multidimensional field of research in which psychology, sociology, marketing, political science, economics, finance and management come together. A demographic approach to entrepreneurship may unravel various components of the spatio-temporal dynamics of both existing and new firms. In-depth case study research as advocated in company life history analysis is certainly necessary to identify motives and barriers concerning successful entrepreneurship, but there is also a clear need for more analytical comparative research leading to research synthesis and transferable lessons.

An interesting example of the latter type of research approach can be found in a study by Breschi (2000), who conducts a cross-sector analysis of the geography of innovative activities. Using the evolutionary concept of a technological regime he is able to identify the background factors of variations in spatial patterns of innovations, viz. knowledge base, technological opportunities, appropriability conditions and cumulativeness of technical advances. Undertaking more of such studies might advance the idea that geography counts in a modern entrepreneurial age. Cities offer important seedbed conditions for modern entrepreneurship in an open network economy, but this role is by no means exclusive. We observe at the same time local niches or shells in isolated areas which offer due protection or incubation for creative entrepreneurial abilities. Important stimulating factors may be the presence of training and educational facilities, an open business culture, venture capital, public support, local suppliers and subcontractors and so forth. Consequently, the geographic landscape of modern entrepreneurship is varied and calls for intensified research efforts aimed at more synthesis.

Entrepreneurial interactions

A new phenomenon in modern economies is the emergence of inter-woven global networks (Castells 1996) which allow for global interaction and communications, a process through which market areas may obtain worldwide coverage (e.g. through the Internet). Consequently, interaction costs, transaction costs and transportation costs form an interconnected portfolio of new market opportunities (and impediments) for modern business firms. Against this background, it is plausible that communication potential and knowledge are nowadays seen as critical success factors for the 'global entrepreneur'. The pathway towards global business is not easy to find; there is no single recipe, so that learning strategies are of great importance here. To reduce the risk of misinvestments, there is much scope for collective learning strategies which manifest themselves in two configurations, viz. network participation and geographical agglomeration. At present, both forces are at work simultaneously and have created the new geographic landscape at the beginning of the new millennium (see also van Geenhuizen and Ratti 2001).

Entrepreneurship means also the management of business network constellations. An interesting and fairly comprehensive review of the relationship between entrepreneurship and network involvement is given by Malecki (1997b). The local environment (including its culture, knowledge base and business attitude) appears to act as a critical success factor for new forms of entrepreneurship, a finding also obtained by Camagni (1991). Apparently, the local 'milieu' offers various types of networks which tend to encourage the 'entrepreneurial act' (Shapero 1984).

It should be emphasized that the chain entrepreneurship – competition, innovation, growth – is not a rectilinear one. Innovation is a critical factor that functions in an open multi-actor system with concurrent phases of decisions and plan implementations, where the demand side (i.e. the customer) is the driving force (Prahalad and Ramaswamy 2004). Innovation policy at the firm level with various risks bears increasingly a resemblance to smart portfolio management. But in the particular case of innovation, a balance has to be found between uncertain exploration and risky exploitation (March 1991). Entrepreneurs are the foundation stones of the innovation process, as they have to create new combinations of people and products, through the creation of idea generators, product champions, proper support systems and mentors, venture mechanisms and effective gatekeepers (see also Katz 2003).

The modern ICT is a centrepiece in the rise of both local and global networks. ICT not only induces faster and more reliable communications, but prompts also a change in firm interaction, management practice, labour acquisition and spatial structure of entrepreneurship (Beuthe et al. 2004). In addition, ICT favours both business-to-business commerce and business-to-consumer commerce. The use of Internet and e-commerce means a significant and historically unprecedented rise in productivity, a phenomenon that can be ascribed to network externality theory, which explains increasing returns, first mover advantages and coordination advantages (see e.g. Economides 1996; van Geenhuizen and Nijkamp 2004; Wigand 1997). It is clear that creative entrepreneurship finds its roots nowadays in the modern ICT sector which induces a clear knowledge orientation.

Malecki and Poehling (1999) have given a very valuable review of the literature on this issue; learning by doing, supported by inter-firm network collaboration, enhances the competitive potential of new firm initiatives. They observe a variety of network configurations, such as suppliers or customer networks, local networks of neighbouring firms, professional networks and knowledge networks, which all may contribute to a better entrepreneurial performance. Empirical research in this area, however, is still scarce and there would be scope for more systematic comparative investigations into the knowledge drivers of modern entrepreneurship. It is certainly true that information and knowledge are important assets in an enterprise, but the economic evaluation of such knowledge (e.g. as a private good or a public good with a non-rivalry character) needs to be studied more thoroughly (Shane and Venkataraman 2000).

An interesting illustration of the importance of local networks for new firm formation can be found in the literature on ethnic entrepreneurship (Waldinger 1996). Many cities in a modern industrialized world are confronted with a large influx of foreign migrants (see, for example, Baycan-Levent et al. 2009; Borjas 1992, 1995; Brezis and Temin 1997; Gorter et al. 1998; McManus 1990). The socio-economic problems involved have created enormous tension and have prompted many policy initiatives on housing, job creation, education etc. But the successes of such policies have not yet been impressive. The seedbed conditions for active economic participation are often weak, as a result of low levels of skill, language deficiencies, cultural gaps and stigmatization. One of the more recent promising efforts has been to favour ethnic entrepreneurship, so that socio-cultural minorities, through a system of self-employment, might be able to improve their less favoured position. Ethnic entrepreneurship has different appearances, e.g. production for the indigenous ethnic market or low skilled activities, but increasingly we see also an upgrading of the ethnic production sector (e.g. shops, software firms and consultancy).

In a survey study, van Delft et al. (2000) demonstrate that the access to and use of local support networks is a critical success factor for various urban policy programmes addressing the new immigrants. Such networks may relate to socio-economic support, provision of venture capital or access to the urban community at large. The importance of social bonds and kinship relationships is also emphasized by several other authors (for instance, Borooah and Hart 1999; Boyd 1989; Chiswick and Miller 1996). In general, such networks appear to create various externalities in terms of entrepreneurial spirit, search for opportunities, self-organization and self-education and business information and access to local markets.

But it is noteworthy that such network connections are geared towards the geographical space in which ethnic entrepreneurs operate. It should be added that in most cities ethnic networks are not uniform, but reflect local cultures from the country of origin. Many ethnic entrepreneurs operate in volatile markets and, although network participation is needed to cope with many market uncertainties, business or social networks are usually not sufficient to survive in a competitive environment (Barrett et al. 1996). There is a need for more thorough empirical research on the motives and performance of ethnic entrepreneurs (see also Masurel et al. 2002).

Concluding remarks

This chapter on entrepreneurship and regional development has looked at two strands of literature in regional economics, viz. regional growth theory and entrepreneurship/innovation theory. In the past these two mainstream theories have developed in a rather disjointed way, but more recently we have witnessed a clear tendency towards cohesion and integration (Capello and Nijkamp 2009). This new direction emerged mainly from two origins, namely more emphasis on the micro-foundations for regional economic growth and the introduction of network theory as an integrating paradigm for spatial economic dynamics.

Regional growth theory already has a long history in both regional economic and welfare theory. Neoclassical growth theory has provided an important cornerstone for our understanding of the drivers of regional development; it has acted as an analytical framework in which learning principles – and other productivity enhancing measures – played a crucial role. In the past decades these contributions have been complemented with endogenous growth theory in which the determinants of economic growth (e.g. infrastructure, knowledge systems, technology) were no longer seen as external forces, but as important vehicles for growth that could be influenced by explicit and deliberate policy choices of both public and private actors. Furthermore, the new economic geography provided another complement, namely the importance of agglomeration economies in the space economy, in particular in the context of monopolistic competition. These new directions have prompted more applied work on spatial convergence in a multiregional system. They have also stimulated a badly needed research shift towards more realism in applied regional economic research, in particular in areas such as: accessibility, economies of scale, sustainability, proximity, monopolistic competition, knowledge systems and innovation. In the new research trend a much more prominent place has been given to the importance of entrepreneurship.

In this modern research framework the entrepreneur is increasingly conceived of as the critical change agent who has to reach the highest performance in a competitive system. He or she has to face externalities of various kinds (e.g. in industrial districts), but is also the creator of new initiatives, as witnessed in the current innovation literature. From a spatial perspective the entrepreneur has to excel in terms of local embeddedness, global orientation, exploitation of proximity advantages, use of clustering and network principles and access to advanced knowledge circuits.

New research would have to address in particular the following issues:

• The question of how locational choices of entrepreneurs (including the decision to stay at the same location) are linked to innovation theory;
• The multifaceted influence of entrepreneurial motivations in relation to the firm's social capital on the strategic performance of a firm (Kourtit et al. 2009);

- The seedbed conditions for the creation of new entrepreneurs (in particular, the development of a multidisciplinary-oriented production function for entrepreneurs); and
- The impact assessment of contextual factors (such as local leadership, institutional support systems, entrepreneurial culture, trust principles etc.) on the emergence of successively local and regional entrepreneurship.

It goes without saying that the next years will require the full attention of entrepreneurship research to regional development analysis. Entrepreneurship and regional development prompt indeed a rich variety of research questions to regional scientists. It is a domain where industrial organization, cultural geography, location theory, business economies and technology form an intertwined nexus. From a macro- or global perspective, the region is a strategic niche in a global development. But from a micro-perspective, the region is shaped by innovative actions of risk-seeking entrepreneurs. Competition, trust, network organization and public policy are ingredients for win-win situations at local level.

Our review of this complex field has clearly demonstrated the linkages of the theme of 'entrepreneurship and regional development' to other research domains, such as network theory, spatial externalities, cultural behavioural theory, innovation theory and endogenous growth theory. For a dynamic entrepreneurial and regional growth theory, the interwoven connection of entrepreneurial life cycles, industrial life cycles and (multi)regional life cycles is a fascinating research issue, not only from a theoretical viewpoint, but also from an applied modelling perspective (Bruinsma et al. 2009). A particularly fascinating and policy-relevant question is how knowledge investments and spillovers are related to dynamic spatial processes. It goes without saying that in this field a wealth of research questions and answers are still waiting to be tackled. There is a great need for creative combined micro-meso-macro growth analyses at a regional level. Quantitative modelling has so far not kept pace with the research challenges in the past decade.

14
Non-State Sovereign Entrepreneurs and Non-Territorial Sovereign Organizations

Jurgen Brauer and Robert Haywood

Introduction

Diagnostically, this chapter revolves around the concept of non-state sovereign entrepreneurs. We first focus on the concept of the sovereign, particularly the sovereign state, inasmuch as it relates to local and global governance and, in turn, pertains to violent social conflict. Finding that state sovereignty lies at the crux of the inability to deal with violent social conflict in a timely manner, we then shift our attention to consider a different solution approach, namely that of non-state sovereign actors and the entrepreneurship required to form non-territorial sovereign organizations that might address violent social conflict effectively, efficiently and reliably. The link to economic development – the theme of the other contributions to this book – is given by the connection between peace and security and economic development. Rather than addressing the direct link between entrepreneurship and development, this chapter speaks to an indirect link: from entrepreneurship for peace to peace as a precondition for development.

Varieties of entrepreneurship

Commercial entrepreneurship and political entrepreneurship

Entrepreneurs are more easily named than defined – for the United States, one twentieth-century list includes Bill Gates (Microsoft), Sam Walton (Wal-Mart), Ted Turner (CNN), Henry Ford (Ford Motor Company), Ray Kroc (McDonald's and franchising) and Fred Smith

(FedEx) – but one way or another character attributes such as envisioning and pursuit of commercial market opportunities, provision of leadership and risk assumption are mentioned. Entrepreneurs do not need to start from scratch (Ray Kroc took over someone else's business and then built it up), be singular (Bill Gates' quieter co-founder of Microsoft was Paul Allen) or become multibillion dollar businesses.

Risk-taking as a character trait of entrepreneurs has been traced to Richard Cantillon (c.1730) but the precise term appears to originate with Jean-Baptiste Say (1803: Book I, Chapter V) who applies it to a person who sees market opportunity by combining capital and labour that are not necessarily his own. Joseph Schumpeter (1942) extended this to one who sees opportunity in a particular kind of innovation, namely one that competitively destroys fellow businessmen's markets by offering superior products or services for sale. Hence the celebrated phrase 'creative destruction'. Even better, instead of merely creating an improved water mill, gas lamp or card catalogue, the invention of 'disruptive technologies', such as steam power, electric lights or modern-day information technology, created entirely new industries from scratch (a process *The Economist* calls 'creative creation').[1]

Whereas the entrepreneur is an agent of change, entrepreneurship refers to a process, and, at least since Schumpeter, much thought has been given to governmental policies that would condition the economic environment so as to enable this process to function with minimal friction and call forth the agents on demand.[2] If economy-wide growth and subsequent prosperity are driven by entrepreneurship, then the proper role of government lies in providing a nurturing institutional environment such as minimalist, and unbiased, regulation, a stable legal framework and sound money. In economic theory this has led to the formulation of new theories of economic growth (e.g. Romer 1990). But the empirical literature that aims to causally and precisely relate Schumpeterian entrepreneurship to economic growth – to link micro-activity to macro-outcomes – remains unsettled, certainly for developing economies.

Usually confined to commercial society, it is recognized that the attributes of entrepreneurship carry over to other fields such as political, social, religious and academic entrepreneurs.[3] In addition to goods and services, certain agents in society produce 'bads' and 'disservices'. Entrepreneurs and entrepreneurship can be productive or unproductive or even destructive (e.g. Baumol 1990).

Paraphrasing *The Economist*, one also might speak of 'destructive destruction'. Specifically with respect to war and other violent social conflict, social scientists such as Kenneth Boulding, Jack Hirshleifer and Gordon Tullock developed concepts such as contest success functions and appropriation and coercion-based economics (as compared to production- and exchange-based economics), and the toolkit of neoclassical economics is applied to phenomena such as rent-seeking, organized crime, rebellion and revolution, civil war and terrorism. More recently it has been broadened further and is labelled security economics. The now voluminous literature of economics and quantitative political science provides evidence of both micro- and macroeconomic causes and consequences of destructive political entrepreneurship.[4]

Social entrepreneurship and sovereign entrepreneurship

A third type of entrepreneurship is seen in the profit and not-for-profit (non-taxed) social entrepreneurs who necessarily combine commercial with socio-cultural or socio-political aspirations. Prominent examples include Amnesty International, Greenpeace, International Alert, Global Witness and Doctors without Borders, each of which, in one way or another, deal with violent social conflict and whose presence in or absence from conflict zones can make a drastic difference to the affected populations. All need to raise revenue, and all need to control cost so as to maximize resource flow towards their respective missions. At the same time, all were started by one or more persons with an entrepreneurial vision. All innovated and created a market, yet we are not aware of much scholarly attention having been given to them in the conflict literature.

The Skoll Centre for Social Entrepreneurship at Oxford University's Saïd Business School defines social entrepreneurship as

> ... the product of individuals organisations, and networks that challenge conventional structures by addressing failures – and identifying new opportunities – in the institutional arrangements that currently cause the inadequate provision or unequal distribution of social and environmental goods.

Another way of putting this – if only for emphasis – is to say that instead of a commercial entrepreneur also delivering, in an Adam Smithian world, unintended public benefits, social entrepreneurs aim to deliver public benefits that also yield non-incidental private benefits to them.[5] In contrast to foundations (e.g. Rockefeller, Ford or Gates) which are funded by endowment, today's social entrepreneurs stake their own economic livelihood on their ability to raise money and sell a 'social' product or service. And under the motto of 'doing well by doing good', a number of today's efforts are even organized along profit lines.[6]

In addition to commercial, political and social entrepreneurship, a fourth type is sovereign entrepreneurship. It is well-known that states offer different baskets of services at different prices (tax rates). So long as freedom of movement (migration) is guaranteed, people and corporations sort themselves into jurisdictions – sovereignties – of their choice based, in part, on the particular mix of services and costs a sovereign provides.[7] For example, some Caribbean states are favourite offshore locations for financial firms, and due to more flexible operating conditions and tax structures, shipping companies are flagged in Liberia or Panama. Likewise, states compete for skilled workers generally (e.g. Canada, Australia, New Zealand) or for particular skills specifically (e.g. in health services). Within and between states, jurisdictions advertise communal amenities, natural beauty, cultural offerings, educational opportunities or restful quietude. Others offer effective, efficient and reliable commercial regulation. Entities such as Hong Kong and Dubai have been entrepreneurial in carving out specific roles for themselves in the international marketplace.

Some see this type of sovereign competition as a threat to sovereignty, while others believe that this type of competition can motivate sovereigns to provide better governance (van Veen 2007). There is no doubt that a sovereign who wishes to attract foreign resources will need to forgo more policy options than one that is unconcerned about attracting foreign resources. As closed North Korea and open Singapore show, sovereigns are free to make that choice. However, there is nothing in the international system that shields them or their citizens from the consequences of their choices. Sovereigns should not expect to have absolute autonomy and still enjoy international insurance against making poor choices. Rather, the question is whether a sovereign's subjects may have that expectation or even the right of insurance against sovereign failure, a complex set of issues to which we now turn.

Failed governance and the sovereign prize

The sovereign state: Attributes and purposes

Today, sovereignty refers to self-rule of a people in a given territory, however that rule might be culturally sanctioned and operationally exercised. The present international system consists of an assemblage of self-ruling sovereignties that has its origin in the 1648 Peace of

Westphalia. A modern sovereign state takes on (at least) three fundamental attributes:

1. *The sovereign has legitimate authority*: authority is acknowledged
   power and not just the potential use of coercive force. The sovereign derives authority from some legitimizing source, which can be
   either/both internal (often ideological) and external (recognition by
   other sovereigns).
2. *The sovereign has supremacy*: there is no authority above a sovereign
   and all authority within the sovereign's realm is inferior to it.
3. *The sovereign has territory*: a state is defined as supreme within its
   territory.

Sovereigns, being supreme within their territory, operate as *de jure*
equals to each other. Interactions between territories remain the exclusive domain of sovereigns. They can encourage, discourage or prohibit
such interactions. No institutions above them exercise legitimate, bind-
ing authority.[8]

The central purpose of such sovereignty is to facilitate governance
within the realm, that is, to establish rules, laws, regulations and
enforcement mechanisms. State-based governance is called government
and comprises legislative, executive and judicial aspects. Non-state
forms of governance exist alongside the state. Every family and firm
has its own procedural and behavioural norms and rules and formal or
informal enforcement mechanisms.[9] Families and firms are governed
societies without the accoutrement of statehood. For example, nomadic
tribes used family relationships to establish the first governed societies without a fixed relationship to territory. Some of these societies
still exist today, and sometimes in conflict with Westphalian states.[10]
Similarly, religions exercise authority over the faithful based on their
beliefs, not their geographic home. Empires extended some degree of
authority over territories where they had large commercial interests.
Thus empire-wide laws applied to individuals recognized by the centre
of the empire, but vassal lords often held legal sway over local populations. In all these non-state cases, attributes one and two of modern-day
sovereignty tend to hold – that is, authority and supremacy (certainly
for firms, less so for modern families) – but attribute three in particular
(defined territory) does not.

Externally, sovereigns can voluntarily form or join institutions by
mutual agreement with other sovereigns and put limitations on their
behaviour. The United Nations is one such treaty organization. Being

voluntary, withdrawal from membership is possible and thus sovereignty is maintained. The Charter of the United Nations and a series of declarations, resolutions and concrete acts associated with post-Second World War decolonization simplified and strengthened the concept of sovereignty, particularly with regard to a sovereign's absolute control over a defined territory.

The United Nations General Assembly's Friendly Relations Declaration of 24 October 1970 states that 'no State or group of States has the right to intervene, directly or indirectly, for any reason whatsoever, in the internal or external affairs of any other State'.[11] The non-interference model of state sovereignty is a foundational part of today's international legal framework. Indeed, Article 1(1) of the International Covenant on Civil and Political Rights states as the first human right that 'all peoples have the right of self-determination. By virtue of that right they freely determine their political status and freely pursue their economic, social and cultural development.'[12] The sovereign state has been the principal means by which global society has implemented the principle of self-determination.

Non-interference of one sovereign in another's affairs is a prerequisite for self-determination and thus for the realization of all the other rights and values a community seeks. As seen in the Charter of the United Nations, the Westphalian system demonstrates a belief that armed interventions are almost always predatory in nature. Therefore, the principle of state sovereignty now largely operates to protect weak states from predation by the strong, hence the vociferous resistance by some states to the United States' war against Iraq, started in 2003, and the equally determined resistance by states to grapple effectively and decisively with cases such as Sudan and Zimbabwe. Thus the purpose of external state-to-state voluntary, mutual agreements also is governance, in this case the governance of state-to-state relations within the international system of sovereign states.

Incentive problems of state-based governance

Although the legal framework for sovereignty is contemporary, that does not mean that sovereigns operate today unambiguously within that framework. Nor does it mean that such a framework, focused on the state as the sole legitimate actor in international relations, provides a sufficient foundation for effective, efficient and reliable global governance.

For example, the lack of concern for sovereign responsibility once sovereign rights have been captured has become a contentious issue. Today it is widely accepted by global civil society that a sovereign should be the agent of its people, individually or communally. When people confer rule-making power on an agent, they confer rights to speak and act on behalf of the collective, and that right is conferred with an understanding that the sovereign will act in their collective interest and for their benefit. But these rights can and often are usurped, not only but especially in multi-tribe or multi-nation states when one group wishes to assert rights over one or more of the others by dint of grasping the reins of, and therefore the international protection granted to, statehood. In the absence of countervailing political, cultural and commercial institutions within or outside the state, the absolute power granted to a sovereign encourages the abuse of sovereignty. Usurpation of power is facilitated and enhanced when other sovereigns in the Westphalian system accept their obligation not to intervene. Consequently, successful political entrepreneurs are generally welcomed into the fold so long as they do not directly threaten the interests of other sovereigns.

Former Australian foreign minister Gareth Evans characterizes the acceptance of internal state violence by other states under the Westphalian system as the 'institutionalization of indifference', and cites former US American Secretary of State Robert Lansing as remarking, in conjunction with his role as a member of the Paris Peace Treaty negotiation team in 1919, that 'the essence of sovereignty is the absence of responsibility' (Evans 2008: 18). Sovereignty is synonymous with immunity from outside discipline. No matter how horrific the process of usurping state power or of putting opposition movements down, a sovereign state can rightfully expect the inaction of other sovereigns. Although vigorously keeping an external balance of power between and among each other, sovereigns under the Westphalian system grant each other an internal monopoly on violence, even to the extent of granting an effective right to rule through violence, oppression or rigged elections.

This grant amounts to *a priori* immunity from prosecution for even the most blatant immoral and inhumane treatment of a state's subjects. It also amounts to an incentive for internal opponents to organize *coup d'états*, assassinations or insurrections to seize the reins of sovereignty. Sovereignty is contestable and offers a lucrative winner-take-all prize, namely the sovereign right of absolute control over territory, its entire people and all other resources within. The (bloody) contest for the prize of sovereignty stems from such grand power.

Driving this contest is the fact that once won, other sovereigns tend to accept the winner as a legitimate sovereign into the international community of states with little concern about the legitimacy of the contest or of the regime itself. Rather than encouraging self-determination, sovereignty in some places has allowed the victor to harass and even destroy peoples within its territory. The state's monopoly on violence, combined with the principle of non-interference, give the sovereign an incomparable edge in any domestic dispute. In essence, any sovereign is acceptable to other sovereigns, no matter how that sovereignty has been come by or how it is being sustained.

The Westphalian obstacle

Even when limited to the realm of human security, an increasing number of issues are challenging the basis of the Westphalian system and demand behaviours that are contrary to Westphalian doctrines. A sampling of them includes the following:

- Global civil society now widely agrees that some state behaviours are so outrageous as to constitute intolerable crimes against humanity and require that limits be placed on Westphalian sovereign immunity. The Responsibility to Protect (R2P) movement asserts that if a sovereign cannot or will not protect its own subjects from mass atrocities then it is the responsibility of other sovereigns to protect them, even if that requires armed intervention. This violates a number of sovereign rights, among them the right to monopoly on the use of force, the inviolability of territory, control of borders and suzerainty over citizens.[13]
- The recently established International Criminal Court (ICC) in The Hague is meant to begin to overcome some of the inadequacies of the Westphalian system. It required a great deal of effort to establish, largely due to the fear of state sovereigns of the development of a supra-state authority. Consequently, only citizens of sovereigns who agree to be bound by ICC jurisdiction may be tried under its authority (or any person committing a crime in a state that has acceded to the ICC Statutes). This limits the ability of the court to prosecute specific cases. The ICC is further restrained in that by a majority vote of the United Nations Security Council sovereign states may prevent the prosecution of a specific case and any veto in the Security Council can stop an intended ICC prosecution.[14]
- Non-state military and criminal organizations are increasingly challenging the system of international relations. Sovereign states that do not or cannot wholly control their territory, such as tribal areas in Pakistan, nevertheless are held responsible for the activities that go on there. Other sovereigns, feeling threatened by those activities, may seek retribution against the incapable sovereign and/or may

violate international norms through direct intervention, risking war in the process.[15]

- Even in the presence of international treaty obligations, prohibitions in regard to weapons of mass destruction (WMD) are difficult to monitor and enforce due to policy independence and sovereign control over territory. Thus only limited enforcement mechanisms are incorporated into WMD treaties due to these concerns. Technology has made WMD much more destructive and deliverable, than the weapons of 400 or even 50 years ago. The Westphalian system has not developed a structure to deal effectively with imminent, anticipated or potential threats. Such systems are needed or individual states will assert their sovereign rights to self-defence, as the United States has done, in potentially premature, chaotic and dangerous ways.

- Inter-state wars are the ultimate dispute settlement method under the Westphalian system. Because states are the highest form of political authority, only inter-state armed violence can solve disputes where at least one state is unwilling to accept negotiation or moral persuasion, as is a sovereign's right. The reliance of the Westphalian system on military power and war as the ultimate arbiter is inherently at odds with the strong desire of most people to make law and proper governance the ultimate arbiter.

These are but a sample of issues pertaining to violent social conflict, the resolution of which is impeded by the Westphalian system and the current norms of state-based governance. Westphalia is the obstacle. It is imperative that we recognize that dependence on sovereign states is no longer meeting the needs of diverse societies on Earth.[16] It is not meeting people's needs within the state, nor is it maintaining appropriate relations between and among them, nor does it facilitate effective governance of crucial global issues.

Along these lines Stephen Krasner of Stanford University refers to sovereignty as 'organized hypocrisy' (Krasner 1999). Similarly, Andreas Osiander calls it the 'Westphalian Myth' (Osiander 2001). More than 20 years ago, Daniel Bell, a Harvard sociologist, noted that the 'nation-state is becoming too small for the big problems of life, and too big for the small problems of life' (Bell 1987: 14). Professor Louis Henkin, a Columbia University specialist in international law, was even more critical. He wrote that:

[Sovereignty's] birth is illegitimate, and it has not aged well. The meaning of sovereignty is confused and its uses are various, some of

them unworthy, some even destructive of human values ... The pervasiveness of that term is unfortunate, rooted in mistake ... Sovereignty
is a bad word, not only because it has served terrible national mythol-
ogies; in international relations, and even in international law, it is
often a catchword, a substitute for thinking and precision ... for legal
purposes, at least, we might do well to relegate the term to the shelf
of history as a relic from an earlier era ... As applied to a state, elements long identified with 'sovereignty' are inevitably only meta-
phors, fictions, fictions upon fictions.[17]

These are but a sample of the extensive number of writers and practitioners gravely concerned about the consequences of continuing to meet
the need for effective, efficient and reliable global governance of serious global issues utilizing a sovereign state-based model of international
relations. As global governance exceptions proliferate and as more issues
are at odds with the system of state actors, it appears that these occur-
rences are linked to an underlying cause: the inherent inability of the
Westphalian system to guide humankind in creating effective, peaceful
and just global institutions of governance. Another approach or at least
an alternative, parallel or complementary approach is needed.

Non-state sovereign entrepreneurship

In our view, the problems of local or global governance, including violent conflict within and between states, can be ascribed not merely
to the faulty exercise of state sovereignty but to its very existence.
Whatever proximate solutions are proposed, such as R2P civil society
engagement which defers to the United Nations Security Council or
the UN Global Compact which seeks to harness commercial society
under a United Nations umbrella, ultimate solutions must address the
restoration of effective, efficient and reliable governance and legitimate
sovereignty beyond the state.

Ultimate solutions must address the creation of what we term Inclusive
Governance Networks, or effective, efficient and reliable governance
and legitimate sovereignty beyond the nation-state, characterized by
the inclusion of commercial and civil society, alongside government,
as legitimate sovereign actors. Yet, virtually the entire academic and
public discussion regarding global governance carries the terms of reference of the Westphalian-type, United Nations, state-based system.
But unlike global civil and commercial society, the members of that
system are, ironically, the least global players. They cannot but act with

parochial interests in mind. Thus, due to its design, state-based global governance is unlikely to succeed.

What is needed is an enforceable, rules-based global structure that elevates the legitimate role of civil and commercial society. Sovereigns must exist in the pre-1648 sense: universal assertion of authority and supremacy, but non-territorial – or encompassing territorial, that is, global. Like what the Roman Church once thought it was – universal, free from parochial interests, with governance exercised through increasingly local nodes – effective global governance will only come through the expansion of legitimate roles for civil and commercial societies within appropriate issue domains.

The question arises of how this can possibly be achieved today. Our suggestion looks to non-state sovereign entrepreneurs (NSEs) and increased legitimate space for non-territorial sovereign organizations (NSOs). NSE deals with the rise of transboundary non-state actors as they impinge on and aim to supplement and supersede certain powers of sovereign states. Global civil and commercial society must engage in the innovative search for and operation of sovereign, that is, rule-making and rule-enforcing, yet non-state (non-territorial) powers.

Non-state sovereign governance already exists

Even though the state predominates in international relations, an important observation is that there exist, and have always existed, a number of non-state governance structures, including global ones, that derive their coherence, effectiveness and cultural legitimacy from identities based on non-national, non-state attributes. Religious beliefs offer one example. The Roman Catholic Church or the communities of Jews or Muslims or other faith traditions, precede – and all territorially transcend – the sovereign state. Each asserts and exercises sovereignty over its respective spiritual domain. They formulate, promulgate and enforce religious law upon their believers. They once claimed and severely enforced monopoly rights over their subjects' fealty, loyalty and lives. Many adherents still fervently believe in, and identify with, the exercise of canonical rights even as competing forms of non-religious sovereignty have evolved. While the Vatican has diplomatic standing (since 1929), the leader of Tibetan Buddhism, the Dalai Lama, does not. In times past, the situation was reversed: to be viewed as legitimate, that is, sanctioned (blessed), leaders of secular entities needed formal recognition by heads of spiritual entities.

For many of today's world citizens, universal social movements and global corporations, identification with nation or state has become nominal, even notional. To them, nationalism and statism are passé: the relevant scope (and sometimes identity) is their issue or their industry. Geographical territory, the very basis of the sovereign state, is decidedly less important to them than it once was. Many of these have achieved legitimacy through their expertise or operant values.

A striking commercial example of non-state sovereign global governance is provided by ICANN, the Internet Corporation for Assigned Names and Numbers. Its mission 'is to coordinate, at the overall level, the global Internet's systems of unique identifiers and in particular to ensure the stable and secure operation of the Internet's unique identifier systems'.[18]

Clearly, the scope of ICANN's activity is global, and it is the ultimate rule-making body in designing and assigning Internet domain names, a task that is vital to the stability of the Internet. ICANN assigns domain name suffixes for states and territories such as Palestine, Hong Kong, Taiwan and the Vatican (ps, hk, tw and va, respectively), without consideration for their sovereign status. After the Assembly of Kosovo declared the Republic of Kosovo an independent sovereign state in February 2008, Kosovo used the World Economic Forum in June that year to appeal to be granted its own domain name suffix. ICANN deferred that decision to another non-state global governance organization, the International Organization for Standardization (ISO) which, according to its ISO3166–1 standard, makes the call as to what entities qualify for mail routing, currency and other codes. As of 23 September 2008, Abkhazia, Transnistria, Somaliland and South Ossetia also were on the list of would-be recipients of their own domain name system (DNS) codes. Like Kosovo, all are or recently were, embroiled in war.[19] The DNS has become a symbol of statehood, yet it is granted by two non-state actors.

ICANN is a private, non-profit, California-registered, public-benefit corporation, operating under Californian law, not United States federal law. Governments have no direct decision-making powers in the operations of ICANN. All powers are vested in ICANN's Board of 15 voting members. The majority of the board members are selected by a nominating committee which seeks 'to ensure that the ICANN board is composed of members who in the aggregate display diversity in geography, culture, skills, experience and perspective'. Nationality and statehood are deliberately excluded. Moreover, 'notwithstanding anything herein to the contrary, no official of a national government or a multinational entity established by treaty or other agreement between national governments may serve as a director'.

In the event of instability of the DNS, ICANN can form a crisis management team to determine what intervention it should take to ensure or restore stability to the system. It could credibly be argued that this is at least as critical to the world as is the stability of the telephone system. But the stability of the telephone system is controlled by the International Telecommunications Union (ITU), which is an intergovernmental treaty organization of the United Nations. While non-state actors may become associates, only state members have voting rights in the controlling organs of the ITU. The ITU is a prototypical Westphalian structure for inter-state coordination and has a function for the telephone network that closely parallels ICANN's function for the Internet.

Instead of civil and commercial society being accredited observers to an intergovernmental organization such as the ITU, ICANN literally inverts this familiar governance structure. Member governments each appoint one 'accredited' representative to ICANN's Governmental Advisory Committee (Art. XI, Section 2(1)e). The Governmental Advisory Committee then may select from its members a single non-voting board liaison officer (one of six such non-voting officers). In ICANN the private corporation takes on the voting role of the sovereigns in the ITU and the sovereigns take on the non-voting observer status of 'sector member'. Yet the rules of ICANN are just as enforceable on the states as are the rules of the ITU. Because the state is no longer supreme, this governance organization cannot be reconciled with the Westphalian concept of the sovereign state.

There is no inherent reason why the ITU should not have been able to exercise sovereign control over the Internet. That it did not suggests that its governing structure was too slow to adapt to the emergence of a new globe-spanning technology. Yet that technology still needed a way to organize itself or be organized and ICANN emerged to provide reliable Internet governance. It is legitimized by expertise, effectiveness and shared values, not by a democratic process.[20]

Once one starts looking, examples of existing non-state global governance with some degree of sovereign power can be multiplied. There is no question for instance that Microsoft Corporation's Windows operating system is, in effect, a non-state, sovereign, global governance standard. And Microsoft recently enforced the standard when it blocked pirated Windows software from operating properly in China.[21] The company also has worked to have the various versions of Windows declared a global standard by global standard setting bodies, and this is important because these bodies are not states, nor associations of states (as shown later on). It is a common, but largely unrecognized, practice for non-state actors to engage in global norm formulation, standard setting and rule-making with self-regulation and self-enforcement: in other words to engage in non-state sovereign global governance.

Non-territorial sovereign organizations are not non-governmental organizations

At this juncture, it is useful to highlight why organizations such as ICANN are *not* non-governmental organizations but are non-territorial sovereign organizations. The key insight – the one that drives the entire chapter – is that NGOs are subsumed under and subject to the state (or to their multistate organizations). Unlike NSOs, NGOs possess neither rule-making authority nor supremacy. Amnesty International and Greenpeace are influential global civil society actors, but unlike NSOs they have no legitimate source from which they could derive rule-making and rule-enforcing authority, as they lack supremacy within their issue domain. Crucially, however, both NGOs and NSOs are non-territorial, transboundary organizations.

As a matter of logic, the taxonomy of organizations should be rewritten as follows:

- State organizations (territorial or boundary organizations)
  - single state organization (e.g. any and all states)
  - multistate organization (e.g. EU, AU, ICAO, ITU, WTO)*
- Non-territorial organizations (non-state or transboundary organizations)
  - non-territorial non-sovereign organizations (the former NGOs)
    - civil society organizations (e.g. Greenpeace)
    - commercial society organizations (e.g. IATA, WTTC)*
- Non-territorial sovereign organizations (NSOs)
  - civil society sovereign organizations (e.g. the International Committee of the Red Cross, the International Olympic Committee, FIFA and other examples to be discussed)
  - commercial society sovereign organizations (e.g. ICANN, ISO and other examples provided later on)

Non-state sovereign global entrepreneurship

The seemingly anomalous non-state global governance example of ICANN is not unique.[22] Other examples of non-state groups involved in global sovereign governance include the following. All were driven by entrepreneurs, some specifically with the objective of stopping or mitigating violent social conflict.

- Undoubtedly, due to its role in the peace and security field, a non-state actor of great interest is what now is called the International Committees of the Red Cross and Red Crescent, founded in 1863. This movement consists of several components, the most pertinent of which is the International Committee of the Red Cross (ICRC). The key entrepreneur behind the ICRC was Henry Durant, a businessman. ICRC spawned the initial and subsequent formulation of international laws of war and international human rights. Originally concerned with the treatment of battlefield wounded soldiers, the ICRC played a central and essential role in the First Geneva Convention, the International Convention for the Amelioration of the Condition of the Wounded and Sick in Armed Forces in the Field. This treaty got sovereigns to recognize the principle that helping the wounded, on or off the battlefield, was to be regarded as a neutral act. Since that initial Convention in 1864, the ICRC has effectively pressured states to extend ICRC protections under the rules of war to include naval warfare, prisoners of war and civilians.[23]
- The position of organized religions and their manifest, secular organizations, such as the Roman Catholic Church has already been alluded to. Clearly they exercise global, sovereign governance functions, yet with the exception of Vatican State, they are non-state organizations. The Vatican showed its entrepreneurial spirit by becoming a state in 1929,[24] but there is of course no question about the Church's social mission of ministering to the poor, sick, wounded and abandoned.
- Within commercial society, an important governing role is played by the ISO. The ISO is a private, non-profit organization composed of standards institutes nominally arrayed by states, but none are recognized, nor may they act, as representatives of states in any formal, official or sovereign way. Moreover, while some state standards institutes are indeed official government entities, many are either wholly private or are public–private joint ventures. The ISO sets standards and the world follows them, quite outside formal Westphalian channels. Currently, the ISO is working on a 'societal security' series of standards (ISO22300) and is conducting preparatory work on 'social responsibility' standards (ISO26000) that may directly address peace and security concerns. It is not inconceivable that, in future, it might formulate and promulgate a state sovereignty standard and that states can elect to be 'ISO certified', just as companies do now.[25]

- Arguably one of the stronger non-state actors in the world is the Fédération Internationale de Football Association (FIFA), the world body that regulates the sport of football (soccer). Its position as the ultimate governing body over the world's most popular sport allows it to assert itself in the political affairs of sovereign states. One recent example comes from Europe, when the state of Poland sacked the entire board of Poland's national football association for what FIFA determined to be non-football related (political) reasons. FIFA was able to use the credible threat of barring the Polish national football team from upcoming World Cup qualifying matches to compel the Polish government to reinstate the board and its president. An examination of FIFA's website shows that this is no isolated instance.[26]

Examples of non-state sovereign global governance entrepreneurship are numerous. In addition to ICANN, ICRC, ISO and FIFA, one may consider:

- The International Union for the Conservation of Nature (IUCN) is an environmental organization and, like the ISO and ICRC, a private institution with huge influence on environmental and related state laws and regulations. To appreciate the example, compare it to certain EU laws that need state ratification. The EU is a state-based association; the IUCN is a non-state association. But in either case, top level rule-making is filtered 'down' for local adoption. Thus the IUCN may very much be considered as fulfilling sovereign, rule-making functions, with execution and enforcement delegated to states.
- Like FIFA, the Olympic Movement also is a private sports body with global rule-making and enforcement powers. Interestingly, because of governance failures among Westphalian-type states it was a deliberate attempt at non-state peace-making between and among states. The driving entrepreneur behind the Olympic Movement was Pierre de Coubertin and its prominent symbol of the five interlocking, multicoloured rings that represent the (then) five continents is important inasmuch as the symbol rejects statism. It refers to people on land, not to subjects in states.[27]
- The Kimberley Process Certification Scheme and VISA Inc. are other examples of global governance that are driven by non-state sovereign entrepreneurs, one coming off a global civil society movement that includes state and commercial participation, the other, like the Microsoft Corporation example, coming off a purely global commercial undertaking.[28]

- The International Accounting Standards Board is a non-state academic and practitioner-driven body that sets global norms to which even the United States government (through the Securities and Exchange Commission) recently acceded.[29]
- The International Chamber of Commerce was founded in 1919 by an entrepreneurial Frenchman, Etienne Clémentel and established its own International Court of Arbitration whose rulings are accepted by states.[30]
- Medieval guilds set standards and enforced them, quite in the absence of states acting as governance bodies.
- Grounded in Islamic law, the informal money transfer network known as *hawala* is wholly based on trust and honour with presumably canonical but certainly not secular legal recourse in case of non-performance.[31]

Although state consent may be involved in some cases of non-state sovereignty, states may not posses *de jure* or *de facto* veto over these entrepreneurial activities. If the membership of a World Consumers' Union for instance decided henceforth not to purchase product or service X from state Z, there is nothing states could do about this. States, after all, are just one form of social organization and if global civil society arranges itself in alternative, if simultaneous, ways then alternative modes of sovereign governance can evolve.

Concluding remarks

Stable and prosperous societies share three fundamental aspects. Their people are fully represented by their cultural, economic and political institutions, in short, by civil society, commercial society and political society (government). Civil society receives and allocates resources based on moral suasion. Commercial society receives and allocates resources through markets. Governments receive and allocate resources through power. Inclusive governance networks rely upon all three social realms and provide stability as each social realm resolves problems differently, supports and restrains the others and is distinct but dependent on the others for long-term legitimacy and continued functioning.[32]

Civil and commercial societies have transcended state boundaries and now operate with global presence. There is nothing that intrinsically binds them to a single state. Only the state and its sovereign are intrinsically territorially bound and without global scope. That the Earth is divided into entities that mutually recognize each other as sovereign states does not make any particular state global but instead emphasizes the division of the globe into insular states. Global governance, as currently practised, is run by distinctly non-global players.

In this context, it is crucial to understand that our argument does not advocate the replacement of the sovereign state by civil and/or commercial non-state sovereign organizations. Instead, we propose that (i) presently, civil and commercial society are subsumed under, and subject to, the powers of a state-based system, (ii) this social arrangement is at times dysfunctional and the root cause of the inability to address adequately local and global problems that are increasing in number and severity and (iii) to rectify these problems, the balance between and among civil, commercial and political society needs to be realigned such that rule-making and enforcement is no longer vested solely in the state.

Despite their powers of coercion, states do not have a monopoly on resources. Most of the accessible wealth in the world is held by the civil and commercial sectors of society. These resources could become available to support alternative local and global governance systems through a variety of fee-for-service arrangements. For example, if global airlines, tourism and shipping industries did not have to carry the cost of numerous security provisions (e.g. defensive measures, higher insurance costs, forgone revenues), part of the cost saving could be charged as fees for the governance structures that reduced the risks. Unlike the British and Dutch East India companies, modern world corporations have no desire to raise and maintain their own armed forces. The new commercial empires like Accor, Allianz, Aramco, BHP Billiton, DeBeers, Embraer, Google, Herstal, Lenovo, Maersk, Mittal, Samsung, Tata, Toyota or Vodafone, to name a few, easily possess the scope and reach of their colonial predecessors but without imperial sovereign ambitions. Today's corporate private security forces, whether in-house or contracted, are a necessary but otherwise unwelcome cost that corporations would rather not carry. Modern corporations do not wish to behave like state sovereigns; nor do they wish to maintain private military forces to ensure the security of their assets. Most are willing, even eager, to conform to local rules and regulations, and to have local sovereigns ensure the security of their assets and staff. Most just want to get on with business. To get their wish, more forward-looking, entrepreneurially driven action is required by business than is current practice or expectation and civil society should assist commerce rather than looking askance at it. Because peace reduces the cost of business and increases revenue, commercial society (i.e. business and business associations) can be encouraged to become constructive players in shaping an agenda for peace as part of their broader non-state global governance agenda. As demonstrated, there already exist many examples of commerce being engaged in state-transcending global governance structures, institutions and organizations. This should also be applicable to the arena of peace and security worldwide. This, in turn, would assist economic development as well.

Acknowledgements

This chapter was conceived while Brauer was the One Earth Future Foundation's research director. The views expressed here are ours and should not necessarily be ascribed to the Foundation. We thank Jeffrey French and Matthew Bunch for research and drafting assistance. By invitation, a version of this paper was delivered as a keynote address for UNU-WIDERs Project Workshop on 'Entrepreneurship and Conflict' held at the International Conflict Research Institute (INCORE), University of Ulster, Londonderry, Northern Ireland, 20–21 March 2009. We thank our hosts and workshop participants for their interest and comments.

Notes

1. On the term entrepreneur, see for example, Sobel (2007) or the Wikipedia entry. On entrepreneurship, also see the extensive survey in *The Economist* magazine (12 March 2009) and the sources cited there.
2. By analogy, if the entrepreneur is the spark, then workers and managers serve as engine and oil, respectively, in the machinery of economics.
3. We use the phrase commercial society as an alternative to the more common term business. Commercial society consists of private sector commercial operations of all types and their collective organizations such as Chambers of Commerce and labour unions which do not fit well within the rubrics of civil society or government. However, when chambers of industry or labour unions are staffed by government appointment and funded through mandated taxes we would classify them as part of government. This would also apply to state-owned enterprises that operate at fiat prices rather than market prices.
4. Destructive political entrepreneurs may just be failed constructive entrepreneurs. Had the English king's forces won, would we not today regard George Washington as a failed entrepreneur? On security economics, see for example, Brück (2005); Brück et al. (2008); Brauer and van Tuyll (2008: especially chs. 3 and 8).
5. Indeed, in addition to intended public benefits they may also deliver unintended public benefits, for example, when better health care provision directly benefits not only the affected population but also their employers.

6. There are several foundations whose mission it is to bring social entrepreneurs into being. Among them are the Ashoka, Schwab and Skoll Foundations (see for example: Skoll: www.sbs.ox.ac.uk/skoll). None as yet appears to have set up a social entrepreneurship incubator.
7. See Tiebout (1956).
8. Even inter-state organizations like the UN are not above this authority due to the voluntary nature of such institutions. That sovereign states exist outside of and even withdraw from these organizations demonstrates that sovereignty continues to reside within the sovereign state in inter-state organizations. Sovereigns only relinquish *de jure* sovereignty when they choose to do so.
9. State and non-state governance interact. For example, labour law circumscribes what a firm may or may not do in regard to its workforce and family law sets strictures on how parents deal with their children. Similarly, civil and commercial activity can filter through and influence state-wide lawmaking, especially in democracies.
10. The Roma in Europe and the Bedouin in Kuwait/Saudi Arabia are examples of nomadic peoples who have been discriminated against by states. As recently at 1993 between 10,000 and 25,000 Roma lost their Czech citizenship because, being nomadic, they could not meet the residency requirements set by the Czech Republic when it separated from Slovakia.
11. See UN General Assembly, Declaration of Principles of International Law Concerning Friendly Relations and Co-operation Among States in Accordance with the Charter of the United Nations, 24 October 1970. Available at: www.unhcr.org/refworld/docid/3dda1f104.html. Adopted by General Assembly resolution 2625 (XXV) of 24 October 1970.
12. International Covenant on Civil and Political Rights, G.A. res. 2200A (XXI), 21 UN GAOR Supp. (No. 16) at 52, UN Doc. A/6316 (1966), 999 U.N.T.S. 171, entered into force 23 March 1976. See www1.umn.edu/humanrts/instree/b3ccpr.htm
13. On the history of R2P see www.responsibilitytoprotect.org. Although initiated with the support of some states, the R2P project is civil society-based. Notwithstanding claims on the R2P web site that all governments have 'endorsed' R2P, the text of the relevant United Nations General Assembly resolution (UNGA A/60/L.1*, 20 September 2005, §§138–40) is put in the usual careful, diplomacy language. In the end, §139 is quite clear that, as before, any non-peaceful intervention is left up to a resolution of the United Nations Security Council on a case-by-case basis.
14. See http://untreaty.un.org/cod/icc/statute/romefra.htm, Article 16: 'Deferral of investigation or prosecution. No investigation or prosecution may be commenced or proceeded with under this Statute for a period of 12 months after the Security Council, in a resolution adopted under Chapter VII of the Charter of the United Nations, has requested the Court to that effect; that request may be renewed by the Council under the same conditions.'
15. Relatedly, the high seas fall under no one's sovereignty. And yet there are increasing problems. Near-shore piracy is covered as near-shore areas fall within sovereign jurisdictions, but high seas areas do not.
16. Most of the extant forms of global governance are based on arrangements by and for states. Treaty organizations such as the United Nations system,

WTO, NATO, ASEAN and the AU only admit states to membership and are held hostage to sovereign interests rather than to the common interests of the global community, the peoples and their environment as a whole. On the AU, see Kioko (2003).

17. Krasner (1999); Osiander (2001); Bell (1987: 14); Henkin (1999, as cited by Linde 2006: fn. 235); and Henkin 1995: 8–10.
18. See www.icann.org/en/general/bylaws.htm
19. See http://blog.icann.org/?p=357
20. Another example of existing non-state global governance occurs when global markets adopt a state's currency as if it were their own. From criminal networks to the global petroleum trade to independent countries such as Panama (since 1904), Ecuador (2000), East Timor (2000) and El Salvador (2001), the United States dollar has become *de jure* legal tender, yet the government of the United States has no direct power over these adoptions (hence we consider them non-state). The dollar is legal tender even in two British dependencies: the British Virgin Islands (1959) and the Turks and Caicos Islands (1973). In addition, the dollar is *de facto* tender in many war-torn societies and tourist destinations around the world (e.g. Afghanistan, Cambodia and Uruguay). Small non-EU European states (Vatican State, Monaco and San Marino) have adopted the euro in consequence of currency unions with EU member states, and Andorra, Montenegro and Kosovo adopted the euro unilaterally, even though they are not EU members.
21. When pirated software is loaded, it activates an update function, and Microsoft then can, and has, interfered with the proper operation of the computers on which the pirated software was loaded.
    - ICAO = International Civil Aviation Organization, ITU = International Telecommunications Union, WTO = World Trade Organization, IATA = International Air Transport Association, WTTC = World Travel and Tourism Council. The first three are public sector, state-based organizations, the latter two are commercial sector, non-state, non-sovereign organizations.
22. Nor is it without problems. As is well-known, the state of the People's Republic of China is overtly blocking selected Internet signals. This is akin to non-state cell phone operators blocking transmission signals in states or (see note 21) to Microsoft blocking software from functioning in China.
23. Durant's four co-founders were Gustave Moynier, Dr Louis Appia, Dr Théodore Maunoir and Henri Dufour. Durant and the ICRC received the Nobel Peace Prize on four occasions, in 1901, 1917, 1944 and 1963. The seven principles of the Movement are humanity, impartiality, neutrality, independence, voluntary service, unity and universality. The full name of the International Red Cross is The International Red Cross and Red Crescent Movement (www.redcross.int). It comprises National Red Cross and Red Crescent Societies (the National Societies), the International Committee of the Red Cross and the International Federation of Red Cross and Red Crescent Societies. See www.icrc.org
24. In 1648, Pope Innocent X issued the Bull *Zelo Domu Dei*, in which the Vatican rejected the sovereign rights nascent states arrogated unto themselves in the Peace of Westphalia. The Bull says that 'all such provisions have been, and are of right, and shall perpetually be, null and void, invalid,

iniquitous, unjust, condemned, rejected, frivolous, without force or effect, and no one is to observe them, even when they be ratified by oath' (www. shsu.edu/~his_ncp/Thirty.html). Defeated, the Vatican made common cause and, today, enjoys the rights of sovereignty it once condemned, the only religion with a recognized head of state. It acquired statehood in 1929 under Pope Pius XI. Pope John Paul II revised the Vatican's constitution on 26 November 2000. Politically, it is a dictatorship. Translated from German, Article 1(1) of its constitution reads: 'As head of Vatican State, the Pope owns full legislative, executive and judicial powers.' ['Der Papst besitzt als Oberhaupt des Vatikanstaates die Fülle der gesetzgebenden, ausführenden und richterlichen Gewalt.'] (See www.vatican.va/vatican_city_state/legislation/documents/scv_doc_20001126_legge-fondamentale-scv_ge.html). The Vatican is not a member of the United Nations but, by UN General Assembly resolution A/RES/58/314 of 1 July 2004, the Holy See 'shall be accorded the rights and privileges of participation in the sessions and work of the General Assembly and the international conferences convened under the auspices of the Assembly or its other organs of the United Nations, as well as in United Nations conferences as set out in the annex to the present resolution' (http://daccess-dds-ny.un.org/doc/UNDOC/GEN/N03/514/70/PDF/N0351470.pdf?OpenElement).

25. State sovereigns might be held accountable through civil society recognition of an alienability of sovereignty from its territory or by withdrawal of external recognition if a sovereign fails to meet recognized social responsibilities. Many academic and non-profit organizations have created indices that measure aspects of sovereign performance. In this regard, an ISO Sovereign Rights and Responsibilities Standard may be achievable. Some arrangement for a civil sector-driven imposition of trusteeship or receivership upon a sovereign could be developed when sovereign performance standards are not met. In the past, sovereigns have attempted to operate state trusteeships or receivership programmes with limited success (Krasner 2004). Perhaps a non-state driven effort might be worth a try.

26. Recently FIFA has also begun to use its power to try to fight racism in Europe and elsewhere and has banned fans from home games as penalties for racist chants. Given the 'national' identification and passion the game can arouse, it is extraordinary to note how (nation) states are compelled to submit to FIFA rulings. In addition, although the current discussion of limiting the number of 'foreign' nationals playing in 'national' club teams may, if implemented, violate EU labour laws, the very fact that such a discussion can be conducted in all seriousness demonstrates the considerable non-state sovereign global governance powers that FIFA holds.

27. Australia, in 1894, was not yet a separate state – at the time it consisted of six self-governing Crown Colonies – and Antarctica although known as an ice mass was not yet recognized as a separate landmass. On the Olympic Movement, its history, Charter, constituent bodies and organization see multimedia.olympic.org/pdf/en_report_122.pdf

28. 'The Kimberley Process is a joint governments, industry and civil society initiative to stem the flow of conflict diamonds.' See www.kimberleyprocess.com. For a history of VISA Inc. see corporate.visa.com/about-visa/our-business/history-of-visa

29. See www.iasb.org/Home.htm
30. See www.iccwbo.org and www.iccwbo.org/court
31. As it was suspected of serving as a conduit for terror-related financing, hawala gained prominence in the wake of the 11 September 2001 attacks on the United States. The Western-style banking and finance sector of course also has served illicit purposes. Even when it is wholly legal, it still can run into global governance-related performance problems as the world economic crisis of 2008 and onward demonstrates. Meanwhile, hawala continues, as it must, because much of the world's population lives outside the formal, Western-style private and state banking sectors.
32. These are practical divisions of a unitary whole in which each person is involved in all three aspects: civic work, commerce and governing.

Part V
Conclusion

15
Entrepreneurship and Economic Development: Policy Design

Wim Naudé

The aim of this volume was to take stock of the new insights that are emerging on the role of entrepreneurship in economic development, and to identify the challenges that will continue to drive research in the future. An important challenge, raised in particular in Chapters 8, 9 and 11, is the design of policies that will encourage productive entrepreneurship. Governments and development agencies across the world are devoting substantial resources to encourage entrepreneurship. This is especially evident in the small business and private sector development support programmes promoted by departments of trade and industry, and development agencies within the UN and the World Bank, to name but a few.

It should be noted that appropriate policies for entrepreneurship, particularly in developing countries where institutional checks and balances are often not robust, should take into account that entrepreneurship may not always promote economic development. Although the chapters in this book generally take the view that entrepreneurship is good for economic development (or rather, for economic growth) an important recognition made right from the start was that entrepreneurship, and entrepreneurship policies, may not always contribute to growth. Hence in Chapter 2 Lazonick, with reference to the differences faced in starting up a new firm and in managing and getting a firm to grow, warned that 'policies that place too much stress on entrepreneurship as the key to economic development can undermine the collective and cumulative process of organizational learning required for innovation'. Other chapters point to the need for supportive institutions to be in place in order for entrepreneurship and entrepreneurship policies to be effective – see for instance the chapters by Amorós (Chapter 8), Baliamoune-Lutz (Chapter 9), Naudé (Chapter 11) and

319

Lazonick (Chapter 12). As Baliamoune-Lutz points out, 'Intuitively, we may think that...policy reform...would lead to more entrepreneurial activities, *ceteris paribus*. It turns out that both theoretically and empirically this may not necessarily be the case.'

As far as concrete advice for policy design is concerned in light of the above, three questions need to be asked by a government or development agency when considering support to entrepreneurs: first, *should* entrepreneurship be supported? Second, *could* entrepreneurship be supported? And third, if the answers to the first two questions are positive, what are the most effective means of support?

In addition to these three questions, policy design should also be concerned with two evolving perspectives regarding the role of entrepreneurship policy: first, whether the stage of a country's (and a government's) development matters for its policy emphasis, and second, what the implications are for the growing importance of global public goods and the need, as described by Brauer and Haywood in Chapter 14, for non-state sovereign entrepreneurs.

Should entrepreneurship be supported?

The answer to that question depends on the definition of entrepreneurship that the policy-maker or development agency has in mind. Many so-called entrepreneurship support programmes are more specifically programmes that support small and micro-firms and the self-employed. However, small and micro-firms are not necessarily synonymous with entrepreneurship: many of these firms do not contribute significantly to economic growth and development (Wennekers and Thurik 1999). Also, as was pointed out in the introductory chapter and reiterated in the chapters of Desai (Chapter 4), Guglielmetti (Chapter 6) Amorós (Chapter 8) and Naudé (Chapter 11), many people turn to self-employment out of necessity or out of the desire to evade regulations, taxes and other agents' predatory activities.

It can be understood, based on the discussions of Desai (Chapter 4), Klapper et al. (Chapter 5), Amorós (Chapter 8), Baliamoune-Lutz (Chapter 9) and Naudé (Chapter 11) that as development proceeds, proportionately fewer people will choose to be self-employed. Self-employment may thus be indicative of productive, unproductive, evasive and destructive forms of entrepreneurship, and may therefore be an unreliable guide as to the effectiveness of policies to stimulate productive entrepreneurship, and of measuring the impact of entrepreneurship on economic growth.

Moreover, many small business support programmes may not be supportive of entrepreneurship *per se*. Schramm (2004: 105) describes most small business support programmes as poverty and livelihood oriented, tending to 'involve cottage industries that add little to the economy in terms of productivity or growth'. Empirical evidence that small business development *per se* will be good for growth is lacking. Beck et al. (2003) find no evidence that small business firm growth is associated with higher growth levels, and Parker (2006) reports that there is an ambiguous empirical relationship between the rate of self-employment (often taken as a measure of entrepreneurship) and unemployment rates. Audretsch and Thurik (2004) point out that many small business support programmes are in fact undertaken for social and political reasons rather than for economic motivations.

Not only may such small business support programmes be ineffective in supporting entrepreneurship, they may even be disadvantageous to entrepreneurship. This possibly counter-intuitive conclusion was implicit in the previous section on destructive entrepreneurship where it is argued that increasing the rate of self-employment through, for example, small business policies (such as micro-finance) could lower the quality of the entrepreneurship pool in a country or region, and this could have negative external effects on high ability entrepreneurs.

Thus, the discussion so far would suggest that the type of entrepreneurship to be supported should rather be 'high potential' entrepreneurship, that is individuals with high ability to be entrepreneurs, where the likelihood of firm growth is higher (as was argued in the previous section, firm size depends, among other things, on entrepreneurial ability). The fundamental policy implication is that *not all persons should allocate their talent towards becoming entrepreneurs, but those with high entrepreneurial ability should be assisted to become entrepreneurs*. And moreover, based on Chapter 5 by Leora Klapper and co-authors, one can add that such high entrepreneurial ability should be channelled from the informal to the formal sector of the economy. As they state in their chapter:

> [The] previous literature highlights the potential advantages of formal sector participation, including police and judicial protection (and less vulnerability to corruption and the demand for bribes), access to formal credit institutions, the ability to use formal labour contracts, and greater access to foreign markets. We argue that firms that choose to stay informal might be unable to realize their full growth potential and that 'high growth' entrepreneurship is most likely to happen through formally registered firms.

One implication, a central message of Chapter 5, is that the formalization of firms should be encouraged through cheaper and more efficient business registration procedures.

The finding that governments *should* support high ability, high potential entrepreneurs, even via taxes, can be based on the fact that there may be significant externalities: the private costs and benefits of entrepreneurship are likely to diverge in many instances from social costs and benefits. Thus, it has been suggested that the private benefits from the innovation of entrepreneurs is smaller than the social benefits, which reduces the incentives for entrepreneurs to provide these 'services'. Furthermore, the positive relationship between the stock of entrepreneurs and the levels and rates of human capital formation in an economy, as posited and tested for by Dias and McDermott (2006) implies that policies which can increase productive entrepreneurship can also speed up the structural transformation of an economy. These positive externalities imply that entrepreneurship should be supported through some form of subsidy.

However, there may be cases where the social costs of 'unproductive' or 'evasive' entrepreneurship may be higher than its private benefits, and where low ability entrepreneurs may crowd out higher ability entrepreneurs, as mentioned earlier. In such cases, some form of taxation and/ or regulation of entrepreneurial entry may be called for. Strong policy implications have emanated from the work of De Meza and Webb (1987, 1999), Coelho et al. (2004) and Ghatak et al. (2007) on the effects of low ability entrepreneurs on economic development. More radical proposals have included entrepreneurial entry to be more heavily regulated and entrepreneurs to be taxed higher (for instance through a tax on interest), so as to weed out low ability entrepreneurs. Such taxes have been argued to improve both social and the private welfare of entrepreneurs (Kanniainen and Poutvaara 2007).[1] It also implies that provision of subsidized credit/finance to start-ups may have perverse or neutral effects on economic growth, since this will lower the quality of the pool of entrepreneurs, and create an adverse selection problem which banks might try to overcome by raising required collateral (Ghatak et al. 2007). Other policy proposals have included raising wage rates. This would be good for both workers as well as entrepreneurs, because the average quality of entrepreneurship will increase with higher opportunity costs, which will result in lower borrowing costs and encourage high ability entrepreneurs to start up. Wage rates could for instance be raised through an intervention that increases average productivity (Ghatak et al. 2007).

Could entrepreneurship be supported?

There is a strand of literature, associated with the Austrian School, which is of the opinion that government is unable to raise the supply or quantity of entrepreneurship, but can merely influence the allocation of entrepreneurial ability. In the words of Coyne and Leeson (2004: 247) 'government policy cannot create entrepreneurship'. All that the government should do in this view, is to 'get the institutions right', that is, ensure protection of property rights and a well-functioning legal system and to maintain macroeconomic and political stability and competitive tax rates. This will at least minimize opportunities for 'destructive' entrepreneurship as discussed. In Chapter 11 this 'mini-malist view' of entrepreneurship support was critically discussed.

Not all will agree that government is unable to influence the sup-ply of entrepreneurship. Arguments in favour of governments' ability to raise the supply of entrepreneurship centre around a government's ability to lower entry costs and regulations (see for instance Chapter 5 in this book), support innovative activities (e.g. R&D), and whether or not – and how – government can improve entrepreneurial ability in a country. The wide range of entrepreneurship rates across countries, even when controlled for variations in institutional quality, would sug-gest that specific policies and regulations – such as start-up costs – may have an influence on the supply of entrepreneurs.

While not indicative of causality between start-up rates and start-up costs, the fact that high start-up costs are associated with low start-up rates in developed countries such as Japan, the Netherlands, Switzerland and Sweden could suggest that the supply of high quality entrepre-neurship could be influenced. In fact, a key policy of the European Commission to increase the supply of entrepreneurship in the EU is through education and programmes to make people aware of the poten-tial of entrepreneurship as an occupation.

What are the best ways of supporting entrepreneurship for economic development?

The book collectively makes the case for the support of high ability, high potential entrepreneurship, both in terms of support for raising the quantity (supply) as well as the allocation of entrepreneurial talent. A number of further questions arise.

First, what type of policies could stimulate the supply of entrepre-neurship? From the chapters in this book three types of policies may be identified: those aimed at raising the entrepreneurial ability; policies aimed at raising the non-pecuniary benefits of entrepreneurship; and policies to address the levels of start-up costs and business regulation.

How can entrepreneurial ability – *ex ante* not observable – be improved? Holmes and Schmitz (1990: 266–7) argue that entrepreneurial ability can be improved through 'experience, training, schooling and improvements in health'. In Chapter 10 Rooks et al. also discussed the possibility that social networks could improve (or support) entrepreneurial ability, finding a complementarity between human and social capital in their sample. Of course, education, better health and social capital (or networks) can influence returns from entrepreneurship (as it improves entrepreneurial ability), as well as from wages (it makes for more productive workers). Therefore, *a priori*, the effects of education and health investments and social capital on entrepreneurship may be ambiguous. Certainly, some evidence suggests that the type of knowledge imparted (e.g. more practical, general education) is important, and also suggests that in building entrepreneurial capacity tacit knowledge and learning by doing may be vital. Thus, if existing successful entrepreneurs of high ability can share their knowledge and act as trainers or mentors for younger or nascent entrepreneurs, more effective strengthening of entrepreneurial ability may occur. In this regard, Kanniainen and Poutvaara (2007) have suggested that more successful firms may be sold if the incumbent entrepreneur (having demonstrated high entrepreneurial ability) can be supported – perhaps even subsidized – to impart some of his/her tacit knowledge of the firm and its environment to the new incoming entrepreneur.

Entrepreneurial ability can also be improved through complementary support for R&D. Imitation may be a better policy in developing countries, but only after macroeconomic stability and uncertainty have been addressed in many countries. However, in developed countries R&D policies, to stimulate innovation and competitiveness, are seen as key policies to support entrepreneurship. It was shown elsewhere that the existence of vertical complementarity between intermediate inputs and final goods production, as described in the model of Ciccone and Matsuyama (1996), suggests the case for government support of R&D activities and general start-up costs, as these are shown in their model to have both pecuniary and technological externalities.

Entrepreneurs may be also be enticed the improvement of the non-pecuniary benefits of entrepreneurship, considered mainly to be accomplished by improving the 'culture' of entrepreneurship in a society. It may also be important to create a climate in which greater investments in entrepreneurial ability may be forthcoming. Chapters 4, 5 and 6 of this book are particularly concerned about the climate for entrepreneurship in development countries. Thus, a climate that is less critical of inequality, business failure and personal independence may be more conducive to entrepreneurship. This has raised the possibility that governments can foster an 'entrepreneurial culture' in society as a way to raise productive entrepreneurship. One way, for example, would be to encourage role models of entrepreneurs (Giannetti and Simonov 2004: 272).

There is little evidence, however, that governments can decisively change cultural or social norms. Various authors argue that culture tends to be resistant to change and is stable over long periods (Licht 2007). It has also been argued that because many entrepreneurs are motivated by non-pecuniary gains, policy efforts to stimulate entrepreneurial entry by reducing the costs of exit (e.g. through making bankruptcy procedures less onerous) may not be effective (Licht 2007).

However, to the extent that these may reduce the stigma attached to failing and to encourage re-entry into business for habitual entrepreneurs, a positive impact on entrepreneurship may result. There may be two justifications for wanting to encourage such habitual entrepreneurship. One is that many firms fail due to the poor ability of entrepreneurs, but that some entrepreneurs actively learn during this process and improve their ability, so that they may be more successful the second time. Second, many firms fail due to bad luck, and too stringent bankruptcy laws might prevent entrepreneurs of high ability from being able to achieve their potential (Cressy 2006).

The quantity of entrepreneurship may also be influenced by start-up costs and regulations. As is discussed in the chapters by Leora Klapper and co-authors (Chapter 5) and Naudé (Chapter 11) there is growing empirical evidence that entry costs and regulation may discourage productive entrepreneurs from starting up a firm. The policy implication that follows is that entry costs and regulations should be reduced.

From the discussion in this book, particularly Chapter 11, such a policy implication should take into consideration a country's level of development and the extent of pro-active government support. For instance, in underdeveloped countries with high levels of corruption, the entry barriers may be a source of rents to corrupt officials, so that these barriers may not keep out dishonest entrepreneurs and will make reform or abolition of these barriers difficult. Thus in such a situation the removal of barriers, if it can be achieved, may have relatively more positive effects in that more entrepreneurs of ability could now enter the market, sources of rent-seeking/ unproductive activities could be eliminated, and competition levels improve. Once these gains have been made – and governance has been improved – some limited form of regulation may be reimposed so as to protect the public from dishonest entrepreneurs.

The second broad strand of policy measures aims to shift high ability entrepreneurs away from unproductive, destructive or evasive forms of entrepreneurship towards productive entrepreneurship. In this regard much of the current literature is in line with Amorós (Chapter 8) and Baliamoune-Lutz (Chapter 9) whose chapters suggest that the most important 'policy' for improving productive entrepreneurship is to get the institutional framework in a country right.[2] An appropriate institutional framework is one that ensures entrepreneurs can capture the profits or rewards of their activities. This requires secure property rights (Wiggens 1995), the rule of law (Parker 2007), reasonable levels of taxes on profits, currency convertibility, contract enforcement and financial stability, as well as the 'fostering of opportunities' for new entrepreneurs through competition policy (Dutz et al. 2000).

Building appropriate institutions in underdeveloped countries is notoriously difficult. A number of factors complicate institutional design, suggesting that although there may be certain core universal requirements, a one-size-fits-all approach to institutional design may be inappropriate.

For one, institutions are endogenous (Acemoglu et al. 2005) and relatively little is known about the co-evolution of institutions, entrepreneurial behaviour and a country's stages of development (Fogel et al. 2006).

Second, institutional reform itself is an ongoing, dynamic process that needs to be managed with care with regard to its speed and consistency (Estrin et al. 2006). It can cause uncertainties to emerge that can have unwanted outcomes for productive entrepreneurship, such as the entrenchment of former elites and a rise in rent-seeking behaviour (Naudé 2009).

Third, initial conditions may matter for the dynamics and success of institutional strengthening. These include the distribution of income and wealth before the commencement of institutional reforms and institutional building. High wealth inequalities may be associated with lower start-up rates.

The uncertainties associated with institutional design and strengthening and its relationship with entrepreneurship has led Naudé (2009a) and Naudé and Gries et al. (2008) to recommend the decentralization of entrepreneurial support programmes, as far as it is possible. Such calls are also based on the agglomeration of economic activity which implies that space (location) matters for entrepreneurial success. That the spatial elements and hence the decentralization of entrepreneurship support is important is dealt with in some detail in Chapter 7 by Thurik, and in Chapter 13 by Nijkamp. The latter chapter specifically deals with the need for regional innovation systems and the role of the entrepreneur as a driver in such systems.

Two perspectives framing policy design

Finally, the design of policies to support productive entrepreneurship needs to be complemented or framed by two perspectives: first, whether the stage of a country's (and a government's) development matters for its policy choices or policy emphasis, and second, what the implications are of the growing importance of global public goods and the need, as described by Brauer and Haywood in Chapter 14, for non-state sovereign entrepreneurs.

Stage of development and entrepreneurship policy design

A robust, if sometimes controversial idea, in development studies is that a country goes through various stages in the development process (e.g. Porter 2004; Rostow 1960). Within development economics, it is well-recognized that countries undergo structural transformation from being predominantly agricultural based and rural to being largely service and manufacturing based and urban (Gries and Naudé 2010). This recognizes that different types of industries develop or evolve over the course of the development path (Lin, in Lin and Chang 2009) and that different types of industries entail different types of entrepreneurship. This in turn requires different types of support from the government. In Chapter 11 Naudé discusses the case for pro-active government support for entrepreneurship. Now it is time to confront this with the fact that a government's ability to take such pro-active measures may very well depend on the level of its development. The nature and capability of the state *vis-à-vis* a country's level of economic development therefore needs to be considered in the design of appropriate entrepreneurship policies.

Hart (2001) makes a distinction between a 'developmental state' and a 'regulatory state', arguing that a developmental state, which is more hands-on and leading in the development process, is more appropriate when a country's industry will benefit from centralization and intervention – that is, where the firm and the entrepreneur are still operating well within the technological frontier. A similar argument is made by Phan et al. (2008) in a study of entrepreneurship in emerging countries. They conclude:

> ... studies of entrepreneurial regions across the world... have under-scored the critical role of governments at different levels in the emer-gence of these regions... the magnitude of government influence, which is significant in the early stages of development, seems to decline in later stages relative to other factors... The explanations for this vary from the traditional factor substitution wherein government kick-starts the development of a sector, which then becomes attractive for private capital to accumulate, to the post-modern institutionaliza-tion, in which the development of such institutions as intellectual property regimes engender capital accumulation. (ibid.: 325)

Phan et al. (2003) suggest that in the early stages of development, government intervention will be needed to address market failures and to kick-start growth. The relationship between the private sector and government through various phases of development is summarized in Table 15.1.

In the table the left hand column refers to three stages of develop-ment: the factor-driven, the efficiency-driven and the innovation-driven stage, as described by Porter (1990, 2004). In the middle column this is set against the dominant private sector mode and on the right hand side column against the type of state orientation most conducive for the development of the private sector mode. This indicates that at an early stage of development the entrepreneurial base is still small, and that private sector activity is mainly in dispersed, low productivity tra-ditional activities. At such a stage of development, states are very often fragile, as discussed by Guglielmetti in Chapter 6. The major develop-ment challenge here is to transfer the state from being fragile to being facilitating. In other words, the state establishes legitimacy, authority and capacity, and starts to put in place basic framework conditions for investment and productivity growth. This will enable a core of entre-preneurship to emerge, most often in accordance with the country's comparative advantage[3] and will prepare the economy towards the effi-ciency-driven path.

To fully embark on this path of efficiency-driven growth, however, the state needs to expand its intervention in the economy to 'defy' the comparative advantage through a range of selective policies – see for instance Amsden (1989) on industrial policies in East Asia's success.

Table 15.1   The entrepreneurship–policy nexus through the stages of a country's development

Stage of development	Private sector mode	Type of state orientation
Factor-driven: Production most intensive in unskilled labour and natural resources.	*Traditional economy:* Dominance of primary sectors. Specialization in cash crops, mineral extraction. Spatially dispersed production. Small entrepreneurial base.	*Fragile or facilitating:* Establishing authority, capacity and/or legitimacy important to move from fragile to facilitating. No industrialization under fragile state conditions. Facilitating state aims at establishing conducive business environment (property rights, stability, rule of law, accessibility). Functional and broad-based industrial and business development policies gradually implemented.
Efficiency-driven: Production more efficient, and movement towards technology frontier starts.	*Managerial economy:* Manufacturing sector grows. Greater product diversification. Larger firms, SOE and MNEs dominate. 'Fordist' production by obtaining productivity growth through economies of scale. Growing clustering.	*Developmental or facilitating:* Developmental state to use active and selective (industrial) policies to encourage domestic technological capability formation. As the economy develops, this role may change towards the facilitating role focusing on industrial policies aimed at high technological innovation.
Innovation-driven: Production of high tech goods and innovative to expand the technological frontier.	*Entrepreneurial economy:* Rise in services sector. High value added manufacturing activities dominate with greater specialization. High tech clusters stabilizes. Reemergence of small businesses on both national and international markets.	*Facilitating:* The state promotes basic framework conditions. Substantial focus on innovation, technology. Market competition, market development through entry of new entrepreneurial firms important.

Source: Author's compilation based on the discussions in Acs and Szerb (2009), Altenburg (2009) and Porter (2004).

This will allow, for instance, economies of scale to be reaped, which will encourage self-reinforcing agglomerations, facilitate growth in firm size,[4] and will see a greater role for instance for state-owned enterprises (SOEs) and multinational enterprises (MNEs). At this stage it is important for policy support to take into account the nature and profile of indigenous entrepreneurs. For example in the 1950s and 1960s in Singapore and Korea, where a strong local entrepreneurial base was judged to be lacking, policies (particularly under the rubric of industrial policies) were first aimed at complementing and strengthening the domestic entrepreneurial base, through the entry of more foreign entrepreneurship and the provision of much financial support to allow entrepreneurs to take on greater risks with regard to imitation and foreign technology adoption (Nelson and Pack 1999). And in Taiwan and Japan, where the entrepreneurial base was already fairly strong, limitations were placed on foreign entrepreneurs during the early stages of development.

At some point, the country's development will be such that it needs a flexible approach towards entrepreneurial support policies in order to shift from being interventionist and selective, towards being less interventionist and more functional. Many countries embark on trade liberalization during this phase of their development. Examples include the EU, the USA and India. China's two-track approach since 1978 can be seen as a variant of this shift, whereby the shift is gradually introduced by allowing a more liberalized private sector economy to develop without disbanding state-owned enterprises. For instance Siebert (2007: 899) remarks that 'the Chinese now show a larger acceptance of the market economy than the three large continental countries of Europe'. He describes how the Chinese reforms fostered the emergence of more productive enterprises not by dismantling or privatizing state-owned enterprises upfront (as in Eastern Europe or some African countries) but by maintaining these and 'simply by letting new economic activities develop outside the government controlled sector' (ibid.: 900). China also allowed the growing class of private sector entrepreneurs to influence the evolution of the institutional framework shaping its industrial policy – described as 'institutional entrepreneurship' (Li et al. 2006).

Thurik's Chapter 7 considers the transition from managerial economy to entrepreneurial economy (or from the efficiency- to the innovation-driven stage) to be due to the simultaneous rise in the importance of knowledge and the entrepreneur in production. As he puts it, the 'entrepreneurial economy is the political, social and economic response to an economy increasingly dominated by knowledge as the production factor, but also by a different, yet complementary factor that had been overlooked: entrepreneurship'. In such a context or stage of development, support for entrepreneurship has tended to focus on the formation and function of regional clusters (see also Nijkamp's chapter) and their linkages with the rest of the economy, on technological innovation, and on venture capital support (see Lazonick's chapters). In such a context, the need for flexibility has also led to a reevaluation of entrepreneurial support to SMEs. As Nijkamp eloquently comments in Chapter 13:

> Mass production in large-scale concentrations has been a prominent success factor in the age of industrialization. Labour specialization and – later on – capital specialization was a *sine qua non* for a productivity rise that was needed to survive in a competitive economy or to become a winner in a growing market. Mass production, however, creates also a high degree of path dependency, lock-in behaviour and hence inertia in large-scale enterprises, with the consequence of a low degree of flexibility and adaptability to new circumstances. In the course of history we have learned that mass production is not the only mode of industrial organization, but is also accompanied and sometimes even facilitated by SMEs, which have often demonstrated a surprising ability to adopt new production possibilities.

While the above discussion has raised some pertinent issues on the design of entrepreneurship policies in relation to the stage of a country's economic development, this is still a relatively uncharted area. There is as yet no substantial literature on the relationship between the stages of development, the evolving nature of entrepreneurship and the orientation of the state. It is likely to be confounded by difficulties for governments and international development organizations to identify their stage of development, due to the fact that stages overlap (as the third column in Table 15.1 suggests), that some countries may leapfrog stages and that the instruments and measurements to guide appropriate policies at each stage are not well understood. In the latter regard Avanzini's entrepreneurship indicators presented in Chapter 3 as well as Acs and Szerb's (2009) Global Entrepreneurship Index (GEI) may assist in linking entrepreneurship policy design across different stages. However, the entrepreneurship indicators presented in Chapter 3 and the GEI are still untested. Clearly, substantial scope for further research remains in this area.

Entrepreneurship beyond the nation-state

A second perspective for framing the design of entrepreneurship support policies is that consideration of the need for entrepreneurship
beyond the nation-state. In this regard Brauer and Haywood (Chapter
14) have made a novel contribution by emphasizing the essential limitations of the nation-state to deal with the growing number of global
challenges (including global public goods). The challenges include global climate change, insecurity, violent conflict and terrorism, migration
and the vulnerability to financial and economic shocks magnified by
globalization. As Brauer and Haywood emphasize in their chapter: 'It is
imperative that we recognize that dependence on sovereign states is no
longer meeting the needs of diverse societies on Earth. It is not meeting
people's needs within the state, nor is it maintaining appropriate relations between and among them, nor does it facilitate effective governance of crucial global issues.'

Hence Brauer and Haywood discuss the increasing prominence of
social entrepreneurs, and include in the list of 'social entrepreneurs'
organizations working across sovereign states, such as Amnesty
International and Greenpeace. However, as these 'have no legitimate
source from which they could derive rule-making and rule enforcing
authority ... they lack supremacy within their issue domain'. Accordingly,
the call is made for non-state 'sovereign' entrepreneurs (NSEs) who do
have the ability to make and enforce rules. Would such NSEs be able to
make progress in terms of providing more effective governance of global
challenges? The examples given by Brauer and Haywood of ICANN and
FIFA are intriguing and raise further questions of how and under what
conditions NSEs can arise, how these can be promoted and by whom,
and what the relationship between NSEs and sovereign states would
involve once NSEs start to pose more serious threats to the perceived
'internal matters' of the latter. Clearly, a large research agenda remains,
but one that is important in light of the growing global public good
nature of many of the world's current economic development challenges. Consider in conclusion just one area related to global climate
change, namely energy production. Energy production contributes significantly to carbon dioxide emissions. However, most energy production is sovereign state- owned or controlled. Agreements on reducing
the carbon footprint of energy production could be better regulated
and enforced through a non-territorial sovereign organization (NSO)
in energy. Such an NSO could set guidelines and monitor for example, the taxation of carbon-intensive energies, R&D on new forms of

energy, subsidization of clean energy etc. This could be consistent with a greater entry of private entrepreneurs into the energy market, which would require global competition policy, regulation and market entry/exit policies for energy provision, food production, industrial production and transport. Future global economic development may critically hinge on the success of NSEs and NSOs.

Concluding remarks

Promoting the type of entrepreneurship that will contribute to economic development will need to raise both the quantity as well as the quality of entrepreneurial ability. The message from this book is that the *quantity* of entrepreneurship can be raised through, for instance, education (the type may be important), culture, increased awareness of entrepreneurship as an occupational choice, learning by doing and in particular through a developmental state that provides these. The role of the latter may differ, depending to the stage of a country's development.

The *quality* of entrepreneurship can be improved through incentives that will entice those individuals with the highest entrepreneurial ability to become entrepreneurs and entice other self-employed back into wage employment. Herein selection mechanisms (e.g. entry regulations), allowing entrepreneurs to 'specialize' in entrepreneurship (i.e. stimulating habitual entrepreneurship) and providing state-led support to overcome market imperfections may be important.

The content of these policies may in many instances run counter to received wisdom and practices. For instance, not all education may benefit entrepreneurship since the opportunity costs for the highly educated in entrepreneurship may be higher. Entry regulations may fulfil a positive function. Credit subsidies for start-ups may dilute the quality of the entrepreneurial pool with adverse spillover effects on talented entrepreneurs.

In addition to policy measures aimed at raising the quantity and quality of entrepreneurship, institutional building was emphasized in this book as being at the core of productive entrepreneurship. In particular, institutions provide the appropriate incentives for the productive *allocation* of entrepreneurial ability. Thus measures to increase the quantity and quality of entrepreneurs when they are uncertain about their rewards from productive entrepreneurship may result in increased rent-seeking, or evasion of regulations and tax measures. Here, macroeconomic stability, positive economic growth and ensuring a reduction in uncertainty in the economic environment are important. Furthermore, strengthening institutions such as property rights, contract enforcement, the rule of law and reasonable taxation are necessary (although not sufficient) requirements to limit perverse forms of entrepreneurship.

If these measures are successful in raising the quantity and quality of entrepreneurship and in providing incentives for the guiding of entrepreneurial ability towards activities that support economic growth, the result in many poor and underdeveloped countries would be to see an initial *reduction* in the rate of entrepreneurship as measured by the self-employed or business ownership rate. High ability entrepreneurs will create jobs, increase the average size of firms, raise incentives for education and migration to urban agglomerations and the modern economy, diversify an economy by uncovering its production possibilities, and demonstrate and facilitate the adoption of new technology. Ultimately this would result in an economy whose structure is dominated by the service sector, populated by high technology firms and highly (appropriately) educated workers. Opportunities for self-employment in high growth potential service/innovation oriented small firms would multiply, and would raise the rate of self-employment. Sustained growth will then depend on how entrepreneurial ability interacts with available opportunities, and how opportunities for global development can be utilized (or global threats minimized) by new manifestations of entrepreneurship operating beyond the sphere of the nation-state.

However, not enough is known about the dynamics of institutions in developing countries, or of the nature and requirements for NSEs and NSOs, and of their impact on the quantity, quality and allocation of entrepreneurial ability. This should form an important part of the research agenda on entrepreneurship in development. In conclusion, given the important research agenda it is hoped that this book will stimulate further research at the intersection of the fields of entrepreneurship and development economics.

Notes

1. Criticism of the taxation of entrepreneurs, especially in developing countries where self-employment is often a response against excessive regulation and an absence of strong property rights (evasive entrepreneurship) is summarized by Kanniainen and Poutvaara (2007) who also point to the positive externalities generated by entrepreneurs in developing contexts. Extensions and refinements of the models of De Meza and Webb (1987, 1999) by Parker (2003) suggest a less strong possibility for 'over-investment' to occur.

2. It has been argued that entrepreneurs may themselves bring force to bear for appropriate institutional change. Li et al. (2006: 5) call such entrepreneurs 'institutional entrepreneurs' defined as 'innovative person[s] who start or expand his [/her] business venture and in the process help destroy the prevailing non-market institutions in order for his [/her] business venture to be successful'.

3. Indeed, Justin Lin defines a 'facilitating state', as a 'state that facilitates the private sector's ability to exploit the country's areas of comparative advantage' (Lin and Chang 2009: 484).

4. Market failures often prevent firms from growing. An empirical regularity associated with the failure of economic development in much of SSA is the failure of small firms, especially indigenous firms, to grow. In contrast, the growth in firm size is a 'stylized fact' of economic development. It depends, however, crucially on entrepreneurship – specifically entrepreneurial talent or ability as illustrated by Murphy et al. (1991). Market failures result in the misallocation of entrepreneurial talent.

References

Abbate, J. (2000) *Inventing the Internet* (Cambridge, MA: MIT Press).

Abramovitz, M. (1989) 'Thinking about Growth' in M. Abramovitz (ed.) *Thinking about Growth and Other Essays on Economic Growth and Welfare* (Cambridge: Cambridge University Press).

Abreu, M. (2005) *Spatial Determinants of Economic Growth and Technology Diffusion* (Amsterdam: Tinbergen Institute).

Acemoglu, D., Johnson, S. and Robinson, J. (2001) 'The Colonial Origins of Comparative Development', *American Economic Review*, 91(5): 1369–401.

Acemoglu, D., Johnson, S. and Robinson, J. (2002) 'Reversal of Fortune: Geography and Institutions in the Making of the Modern World Income Distribution', *Quarterly Journal of Economics*, 117(4): 1231–94.

Acemoglu, D., Johnson, S. and Robinson, J. (2005) 'Institutions as the Fundamental Cause of Long-Run Growth', Working Paper 10481 (Cambridge, MA: NBER).

Acemoglu, D., Johnson, S. Robinson, J. and Thaicharoen, Y. (2003) 'Institutional Causes, Macroeconomic Symptoms: Volatility, Crises and Growth', *Journal of Monetary Economics*, 50: 49–123.

Acemoglu, D. and Verdier, T. (1998) 'Property Rights, Corruption and the Allocation of Talent: A General Equilibrium Approach', *The Economic Journal*, 108(450): 1381–403.

Acs, Z. J. (ed.) (1994) *Regional Innovation, Knowledge and Global Change* (London: Frances Pinter).

Acs, Z. J. (2002) *Innovation and the Growth of Cities* (Cheltenham: Edward Elgar).

Acs, Z. J. and Amorós, J. E. (2008) 'Entrepreneurship and Competitiveness Dynamics in Latin America', *Small Business Economics*, 31(3): 305–22.

Acs, Z. J. and Armington, C. (2004) 'Employment Growth and Entrepreneurial Activity in Cities', *Regional Studies*, 38(8): 911–28.

Acs, Z. J. and Audretsch, D. B. (1990) *Innovation and Small Firms* (Cambridge, MA: MIT Press).

Acs, Z. J. and Audretsch, D. B. (1993) 'Conclusion' in Z. J. Acs and D. B. Audretsch (eds) *Small Firms and Entrepreneurship: An East–West Perspective* (Cambridge: Cambridge University Press).

Acs, Z. J., Audretsch, D. B., Braunerhjelm, P. and Carlsson, B. (2004) 'The Missing Link: The Knowledge Filter and Entrepreneurship in Endogenous Growth', Discussion Paper 4783 (London: CEPR).

Acs, Z. J., de Groot, H. L. F. and Nijkamp, P. (eds) (2002) *The Emergence of the Knowledge Economy* (Berlin/New York: Springer).

Acs, Z. J., Desai, S. and Hessels, J. (2008a) 'Entrepreneurship, Economic Development and Institutions', *Small Business Economics*, 31(3): 219–34.

Acs, Z. J., Desai, S. and Klapper, L. (2008b) 'What Does Entrepreneurship Data Really Show?, *Small Business Economics*, 31(3): 265–81.

Acs, Z. J., Fitzroy, F. R. and Smith, I. (2002) 'High-Technology Employment and R&D in Cities: Heterogeneity vs Specialization', *Annals of Regional Science*, 36(3): 373–86.

Acs, Z. J. and Szerb, L. (2009) 'The Global Entrepreneurship Index (GEINDEX)', *Foundations and Trends in Entrepreneurship*, 5(5): 341–435.

Addison, A. and Baliamoune-Lutz, M. (2006) 'Economic Reform when Institutional Quality is Weak: The Case of the Maghreb', *Journal of Policy Modeling*, 28: 1029–43.

Addison, T. and Brück, T. (2009) 'The Multi-Dimensional Challenge of Mass Violent Conflict' in T. Addison and T. Brück (eds) *Making Peace Work: The Challenge of Social and Economic Reconstruction* (Basingstoke: Palgrave Macmillan for UNU-WIDER).

Ahmad, N. and Hoffmann, A. N. (2008) 'A Framework for Addressing and Measuring Entrepreneurship', OECD Statistics Working Paper 2 (Paris: OECD).

Ahmad, N. and Seymour, R. G. (2008) 'Defining Entrepreneurial Activity: Definitions Supporting Frameworks for Data Collection', Working Paper STD/DOC(2008)1 (Paris: OECD Statistics Directorate).

Aidis, R. and van Praag, M. (2004) 'Illegal Entrepreneurship Experience', *Journal of Business Venturing*, 22(2): 283–310.

Alesina, A., Ozler, S., Roubini, N. and Swagel, P. (1992) 'Political Instability and Economic Growth', Working Paper 4173 (Cambridge MA: NBER).

Alesina, A. and Perotti, R. (1993) 'Income Distribution, Political Instability and Investment', mimeo (Cambridge, MA: Harvard University).

Altenburg, T. (2009) 'Industrial Policy for Low and Lower-Middle Income Countries', paper presented at the UNU-WIDER, UNU-MERIT and UNIDO Workshop on 'Pathways to Industrialization in the 21st Century: New Challenges and Emerging Paradigms', Maastricht, the Netherlands, 22–23 October.

Altenburg, T. and von Drachenfels, C. (2006) 'The New Minimalist Approach to Private Sector Development: A Critical Assessment', *Development Policy Review*, 24(4): 387–411.

Amin, A. (1993) 'The Globalization of the Economy: An Erosion of Regional Networks?' in G. Grabher (ed.) *The Embedded Firm: On the Socioeconomics of Industrial Networks* (London: Routledge).

Amorós, J. E. and Cristi, O. (2008) 'Longitudinal Analysis of Entrepreneurship and Competitiveness Dynamics in Latin America', *International Entrepreneurship and Management Journal*, 4(4): 381–99.

Amsden, A. (1989) *Asia's Next Giant: South Korea's Late Industrialisation* (Oxford: Oxford University Press).

Anand, P. B. (2009) 'Infrastructure Development in Post-Conflict Reconstruction' in T. Addison and T. Brück (eds) *Making Peace Work: The Challenge of Social and Economic Reconstruction* (Basingstoke: Palgrave Macmillan for UNU-WIDER).

Anderson, A. R. and Miller, C. J. (2003) ' "Class Matters": Human and Social Capital in the Entrepreneurial Process', *Journal of Socio-Economics*, 32(1): 17–36.

Antonelli, G. (2009) 'Emerging Powers: The New Socio-Economic Scenario', keynote speech at the MIUR–PRIN 2007 and Openlock Project Workshop on 'Globalization, Local Development and Emerging Powers. The Role of Innovation Policies', University of Bologna, Italy, 6–7 February.

Ardagna, S. and Lusardi, A. (2008) 'Explaining International Differences in Entrepreneurship: The Role of Individual Characteristics and Regulatory Constraints', Working Paper 14012 (Cambridge, MA: NBER).

Arndt, C. and Oman, C. (2006) *Uses and Abuses of Governance Indicators* (Paris: OECD).

Arruñada, B. (2007) 'Pitfalls to Avoid when Measuring Institutions: Is Doing Business Damaging Business?', *Journal of Comparative Economics*, 35: 729–47.

Asheim, B., Cooke, P. and Martin, R. (eds) (2006) *Clusters and Regional Development* (London: Routledge).

Athreye, S. (2008) 'Economic Adversity and Entrepreneurship-Led Growth: Lessons from the Indian Software Sector', paper presented at the UNU-WIDER and UNU-MERIT workshop on 'Entrepreneurship, Technological Innovation and Development', Maastricht, the Netherlands, 30–31 October.

Audretsch, D. B. (2007) *The Entrepreneurial Society* (Oxford: Oxford University Press).

Audretsch, D. B., Aldridge, T. and Oettl, A. (2009) 'Scientist Commercialization and Knowledge Transfer' in Z. J. Acs, D. B. Audretsch and R. J. Strom (eds) *Entrepreneurship, Growth and Public Policy* (Cambridge: Cambridge University Press).

Audretsch, D. B., Grilo, I. and Thurik, R. (2007) *The Handbook of Research on Entrepreneurship Policy* (Cheltenham: Edward Elgar).

Audretsch, D. B., Grilo, I. and Thurik, R. (2010) 'Globalization, Entrepreneurship and the Region' in M. Fritsch (ed.) *Handbook of Research on Entrepreneurship and Regional Development* (Cheltenham: Edward Elgar, forthcoming).

Audretsch, D. B. and Keilbach, M. (2003) 'Entrepreneurship Capital and Economic Growth', available at: http://www.dur.ac.uk/resources/dbs/businessschool/research%20paper%20005.pdf

Audretsch, D. B. and Keilbach, M. (2004) 'Entrepreneurship and Regional Growth: An Evolutionary Interpretation', *Journal of Evolutionary Economics*, 14(5): 605–16.

Audretsch, D. B., Keilbach, M. and Lehmann, E. (2006) *Entrepreneurship and Economic Growth* (Oxford: Oxford University Press).

Audretsch, D. B. and Thurik, R. (eds) (1999) *Innovation, Industry Evolution and Employment* (Cambridge: Cambridge University Press).

Audretsch, D. B. and Thurik, R. (2001a) 'Linking Entrepreneurship to Growth', STI Working Paper 2001/2 (Paris: OECD).

Audretsch, D. B. and Thurik, R. (2001b) 'What is New about the New Economy: From the Managed to the Entrepreneurial Economy', *Industrial and Corporate Change*, 10(1): 267–315.

Audretsch, D. B. and Thurik, R. (2004) 'A Model of the Entrepreneurial Economy', Discussion Paper 2004–12 on Entrepreneurship, Growth and Public Policy (Jena: Max Planck Institute).

Audretsch, D. B., Thurik, R., Verheul, I. and Wennekers, S. (eds) (2002) *Entrepreneurship: Determinants and Policy in a European-US Comparison* (Boston, MA and Dordrecht: Kluwer Academic Publishers).

Auer, P. (2007) *From Job Security to Labour Market Security: Flexi-Curity for Reducing Labour Market Segmentation?* (Geneva: ILO).

Autio, E. (2007) 'GEM's Report 2007: Global Report on High-growth Entrepreneurship' (Babson Park, MA: Babson College and London: London Business School).

Avanzini, D. B. (2008) 'Composite Entrepreneurship Indicators: Theoretical Derivation and General Methodology', unpublished manuscript (Santiago: Catholic University of Chile).

Avanzini, D. B. (2009) 'Designing Composite Entrepreneurship Indicators: An Application using Consensus PCA', Research Paper 2009/41 (Helsinki: UNU-WIDER).

Bakvis, P. (2006) 'How the World Bank & IMF Use the Doing Business Report to Promote Labour Market Deregulation in Developing Countries', ICFTU/Global Union publications, available at: http://www.icftu.org/www/PDF/doingbusinessicftuanalysis0606.pdf

Balcerowicz, E., Balcerowicz, J. and Hashi, I. (1999) 'Barriers to Entry and Growth of Private Companies in Poland, the Czech Republic, Hungary, Albania and Lithuania', CASE Report 14 (Warsaw: Center for Social and Economic Research).

Baliamoune-Lutz, M. (2002) 'Assessing the Impact of One Aspect of Globalization on Economic Growth in Africa', Discussion Paper 2002/91 (Helsinki: UNU-WIDER).

Baliamoune-Lutz, M. (2003) 'Financial Liberalization and Economic Growth in Morocco: A Test of the Supply-Leading Hypothesis', *Journal of Business in Developing Nations*, 7: 31–50.

Baliamoune-Lutz, M. (2007) 'Entrepreneurship, Reforms and Development: Empirical Evidence', Working Paper 38/2007 (Turin: ICER).

Baliamoune-Lutz, M. (2009) 'Human Well-Being Effects of Institutions and Social Capital', *Contemporary Economic Policy*, 27(1): 54–66.

Baliamoune-Lutz, M. and Ndikumana, L. (2007) 'The Growth Effects of Openness to Trade and the Role of Institutions: New Evidence from African Countries', Policy Paper 6 (Boston, MA: Boston University, Institute for Economic Development).

Banerjee, A. V. and Newman, A. F. (1993) 'Occupational Choice and the Process of Development', *Journal of Political Economy*, 101(2): 274–98.

Barrett, G., Jones, T. and McEvoy, D. (1996) 'Ethnic Minority Business: Theoretical Discourse in Britain and North America', *Urban Studies*, 33(4/5): 783–809.

Barro, R. J. (1991) 'Economic Growth in a Cross Section of Countries', *Quarterly Journal of Economics*, 106(2), 407–43.

Barro, R. J. and Lee, J.-W. (2000) 'International Data on Educational Attainment: Updates and Implications', Working Paper 42 (Cambridge, MA: Harvard Center for International Development).

Baumol, W. J. (1968) 'Entrepreneurship in Economic Theory', *American Economic Review*, 58: 64–71.

Baumol, W. J. (1990) 'Entrepreneurship: Productive, Unproductive and Destructive', *Journal of Political Economy*, 98(5): 893–921.

Baumol, W. J. (2009) 'Entrepreneurship, Competition and World Trade' in D. B. Audretsch, R. Litan and R. Strom (eds) *Entrepreneurship and Openness: Theory and Evidence* (Cheltenham: Edward Elgar for the Kauffman Foundation).

Baycan-Levent, T., Nijkamp, P. and Sahin, M. (2009) 'New Orientations in Ethnic Entrepreneurship: Motivation, Goals and Strategies of New Generation Ethnic Entrepreneurs', *International Journal of Foresight and Innovation Policy*, 5(1–3): 83–112.

Becattini, G. (1992) 'The Marshallian Industrial District as a Socio-Economic Notion' in F. Pyke, G. Becattini and W. Sengenberger (eds) *Industrial Districts and Inter-firm Cooperation in Italy* (Geneva: International Institute for Labour Studies).

Beck, T., Demirguc-Kunt, A. and Levine, R. (2003) 'Small and Medium Enterprises, Growth and Poverty: Cross-Country Evidence', Policy Research Working Paper 3178 (Washington, DC: World Bank).

Beck, T., Demirguc-Kunt, A. and Levine, R. (2005) 'SMEs, Growth and Poverty: Cross-Country Evidence', *Journal of Economic Growth*, 10(3): 199–229.

Beck, T., Levine, R. and Loayza, N. (2000) 'Finance and the Sources of Growth', *Journal of Financial Economics*, 58 (1/2): 261–300.

Behrens, A. (2007) 'Entrepreneurship Indicators: Performance, Determinants and Impact', presented at a OECD/Eurostat meeting.

Bell, D. (1987) 'The World and the United States in 2013', *Daedalus*, 116(3): 1–31.

Belso-Martínez, J. A. (2005) 'Equilibrium Entrepreneurship Rate, Economic Development and Growth: Evidence from Spanish Regions', *Entrepreneurship and Regional Development*, 17(2): 145–61.

Belussi, F. (1999) 'Path-Dependency versus Industrial Dynamics: An Analysis of Two Heterogeneous Districts', *Human Systems Management*, 18: 161–74.

Benhabib, J. and Spiegel, M. (2000) 'The Role of Financial Development in Growth and Investment', *Journal of Economic Growth*, 5(4): 341–60.

Berg, J. and Cazes, S. (2007) 'The Doing Business Indicators: Measurement Issues and Political Implications', Economic and Labour Market Paper 2007/6 (Geneva: ILO).

Berry, A., Rodriguez, E. and Sandee, H. (2002) 'Firm and Group Dynamics in the Small and Medium Enterprise Sector in Indonesia', *Small Business Economics*, 18(1–3): 141–61.

Bertuglia, C. S., Lombardo, S. and Nijkamp, P. (eds) (1997) *Innovative Behaviour in Space and Time* (Berlin, Heidelberg and New York: Springer).

Beuthe, M., Himanen, V., Reggiani, A. and Zamparini, L. (eds) (2004) *Transport, Development and Innovation in an Evolving World* (Berlin, Heidelberg and New York: Springer).

Binzel, C. and Brück, T. (2007) 'Analyzing Conflict and Fragility at the Micro-Level', paper presented at the UNU-WIDER Conference on 'Fragile States–Fragile Groups' (Helsinki, Finland), 15–16 June.

Birch, D. (1987) *Job Creation in America* (New York: Free Press).

Bjørnskov, C. and Foss, N. (2008) 'Economic Freedom and Entrepreneurial Activity: Some Cross-Country Evidence', *Public Choice*, 134(3–4): 307–28.

Blanchflower, D. G. (2000) 'Self-Employment in OECD Countries', *Labor Economics*, 7: 471–505.

Blanchflower, D. G. and Oswald, A. J. (1998) 'What Makes an Entrepreneur?', *Journal of Labor Economics*, 16(1): 26–60.

Block, J. and Sandner, P. (2009) 'Necessity and Opportunity Entrepreneurs and Their Duration in Self-employment: Evidence from German Micro Data', *Journal of Industry, Competition and Trade*, 9(2): 117–37.

Boekema, F., Morgan, K., Bakkers, S. and Rutten, R. (eds) (2000) *Knowledge, Innovation and Economic Growth* (Cheltenham: Edward Elgar).

Boettke, P. J. and Coyne, C. J. (2003) 'Entrepreneurship and Development: Cause or Consequence', *Advances in Austrian Economics*, 6: 67–88.

Boettke, P. J. and Coyne, C. J. (2006) 'Entrepreneurial Behaviour and Institutions' in M. Minniti (ed.) *Entrepreneurship: The Engine of Growth*, Volume 1 (Westport, CT: Praeger Press).

Bögenhold, D. (2004) 'Entrepreneurship: Multiple Meaning and Consequences', *International Journal of Entrepreneurship and Innovation Management*, 4(1): 3–10.

Borjas, G. (1992) 'Ethnic Capital and Intergenerational Mobility', *Quarterly Journal of Economics*, 107(1): 123–50.

Borjas, G. (1995) 'Ethnicity, Neighbourhoods and Human Capital Externalities', *American Economic Review*, 85(3): 365–90.

Borooah, V. K. and Hart, M. (1999) 'Factors Affecting Self-Employment among Indian and Caribbean Men in Britain', *Small Business Economics*, 13: 111–29.

Bosma, N., Jones, K., Autio, E. and Levie, J. (2008) *Global Entrepreneurship Monitor 2007 Executive Report* (Babson Park, MA: Babson College, London: London Business School).

Bosma, N., van Praag, M., Thurik, R. and de Wit, G. (2004) 'The Value of Human and Social Capital Investments for the Business Performance of Start-ups', *Small Business Economics*, 23 (3): 227–36.

Botero, J., Djankov, S., La Porta, R., Lopez-de-Silanes, F. and Shleifer, A. (2004) 'The Regulation of Labour', available at: http://www.doingbusiness.org/documents/labor_June04.pdf

Bound, J., Jaeger, D. A. and Baker, R. M. (1995) 'Problems with Instrumental Variables Estimation when the Correlation between the Instruments and the Endogenous Explanatory is Weak', *Journal of the American Statistical Association*, 90: 443–50.

Bourdieu P. (1985) 'The forms of capital' in J. G. Richardson (ed.) *Handbook of Theory and Research for the Sociology of Education* (New York: Greenwood), pp. 241–58.

Bowen, H. P. and De Clercq, D. (2008) 'Institutional Context and the Allocation of Entrepreneurial Effort', *Journal of International Business Studies*, 39: 747–67.

Boyd, M. (1989) 'Family and Personal Networks in International Migration: Recent Developments and New Agendas', *International Migration Review*, 23(3): 638–70.

Brauer, J. and van Tuyll, H. (2008) *Castles, Battles and Bombs* (Chicago, IL: University of Chicago Press).

Braunerhjelm, P., Acs, Z. J., Audretsch, D. B. and Carlsson, B. (2010) 'The Missing Link: The Knowledge Filter and Entrepreneurship in Endogenous Growth', *Small Business Economics*, 34(2): 105–25.

Brautigam, D. and Knack, S. (2004) 'Foreign Aid, Institutions and Governance in Sub-Saharan Africa', *Economic Development and Cultural Change*, 52(2): 255–85.

Breschi, S. (2000) 'The Geography of Innovation: A Cross-Sector Analysis', *Regional Studies*, 34(3): 111–34.

Brezis, E. S. and Temin, P. (eds) (1997) *Elites, Minorities and Economic Growth* (Amsterdam: North-Holland).

Brock, W. A. and Evans, D. S. (1989) 'Small Business Economics', *Small Business Economics*, 1(1): 7–20.

Brons, M. and Pellenbarg, P. H. (2003) 'Economy, Culture and Entrepreneurship in a Spatial Context' in T. Marszal (ed.) *Spatial Aspects of Entrepreneurship* (Warsaw: Polish Academy of Sciences).

Brück, T. (2005) 'An Economic Analysis of Security Policies', *Defence and Peace Economics*, 16(5): 375–89.

Brück, T., Karaisl, M. and Schneider, F. (2008) 'A Survey on the Economics of Security', final report for the European Commission, Directorate-General for Justice, Freedom and Security (Berlin: Deutsches Institut für Wirtschaftsforschung).

Brüderl, J. and Preisendörfer, P. (1998) 'Network Support and the Success of Newly Founded Businesses', *Small Business Economics*, 10(3): 213–25.

Brüderl, J. and Schussler, R. (1990) 'Organizational Mortality', *Administrative Science Quarterly*, 35: 530–7.

Bruinsma, F., Kourtit, K. and Nijkamp, P. (2009) 'Tourism, Culture and e-Services: Evaluation of e-Service Packages', *Innovative Marketing*, 4: 32–50.

Brusco, S. (1982) 'The Emilian Model: Productive Decentralisation and Social Integration', *Cambridge Journal of Economics*, 6(2): 167–84.

Brusco, S. (1992) 'Small Firms and the Provision of Real Services' in F. Pyke and W. Sengenberger (eds) *Industrial Districts and Local Economic Regeneration* (Geneva: International Institute for Labour Studies).

Brusco, S. and Pezzini, M. (1990) 'Small-Scale Enterprise in the Ideology of the Italian Left' in F. Pyke, G. Becattini and W. Sengenberger (eds) *Industrial Districts and Inter-Firm Cooperation in Italy* (Geneva: International Institute for Labour Studies).

Bruton, G. D., Ahlstrom, D. and Obloj, K. (2008) 'Entrepreneurship in Emerging Economies: Where are we Today and Where Should the Research Go in the Future?', *Entrepreneurship Theory and Practice*, 32(1): 1–14.

Buchanan, J. M. (1991) 'The Economy as a Constitutional Order' in J. M. Buchanan (ed.) *The Economics and the Ethics of Constitutional Order* (Ann Arbor, MI: University of Michigan Press).

Burt, R. S. (1984) 'Network Items and the General Social Survey', *Social Networks*, 6: 293–339.

Burt, R. S. (1997) 'A Note on Social Capital and Network Content', *Social Networks*, 19(4): 355–73.

Burt, R. S. (2001) 'Structural Holes Versus Network Closure as Social Capital' in N. Lin, K. Cook and R. S. Burt (eds) *Networks and Organizations* (New York: Walter de Gruyter).

Bygrave, W. D. and Hofer, C. W. (1991) 'Theorizing about Entrepreneurship', *Entrepreneurship Theory and Practice*, 16(2): 13–22.

Cairncross, F. (1997) *The Death of Distance* (Boston, MA: Harvard Business School Press).

Camagni, R. (1991) *Innovation Networks: Spatial Perspectives* (London: Belhaven Press).

Campbell, J. (1997) 'Knowledge Management in the Virtual Enterprise' in J. Jackson and J. V. D. van der Wielen (eds) *Proceedings of the Second International Workshop on Telework* (Tilburg: Work and Organization Research Center).

Canadian Press (2008) 'Declaration Issued after the Group of 20 Summit in Washington', 15 November: 15.

Cantillon, R. (c. 1730) *Essay on the Nature of Trade in General* (translated from French) (London: Fletcher Gyles).

Capello, R. (2002) 'Entrepreneurship and Spatial Externalities: Theory and Measurement', *Annals of Regional Science*, 36(3): 387–402.

Capello, R. and Nijkamp, P. (eds) (2009) *Handbook of Regional Growth and Development Theories* (Cheltenham: Edward Elgar).

Carlsson, B. (1989) 'The Evolution of Manufacturing Technology and Its Impact on Industrial Structure: An International Study', *Small Business Economics*, 1(1): 21–38.

Carree, M. and Thurik, R. (2003) 'The Impact of Entrepreneurship on Economic Growth' in D. B. Audretsch and Z. J. Acs (eds) *Handbook of Entrepreneurship Research* (Dordrecht: Kluwer Academic Publishers).

Carree, M. and Thurik, R. (2008) 'The Lag Structure of the Impact of Business Ownership on Economic Performance', *Small Business Economics*, 30(1): 101–11.

Carree, M., van Stel, A., Thurik, R. and Wennekers, S. (2002) 'Economic Development and Business Ownership: An Analysis Using Data of 23 OECD Countries in the Period 1976–1996', *Small Business Economics*, 19(3): 271–90.

Carree, M., van Stel, A., Thurik, R. and Wennekers, S. (2007) 'The Relationship between Economic Development and Business Ownership Revisited', *Entrepreneurship and Regional Development*, 19(3): 281–91.

Carroll, G. R. and Hannan, M. T. (2000) *The Demography of Corporations and Industries* (Princeton, NJ: Princeton University Press).

Carter, N. M., Gartner, W. B., Shaver, K. G. and Gatewood, E. J. (2003) 'The Career Reasons of Nascent Entrepreneurs', *Journal of Business Venturing*, 18(1): 13–39.

Castells, M. (1996) *The Rise of the Network Society* (London: Blackwell).

Caves, R. E. (1982) *Multinational Enterprise and Economic Analysis* (Cambridge: Cambridge University Press).

Caves, R. E. (1998) 'Industrial Organization and New Findings on the Turnover and Mobility of Firms', *Journal of Economic Literature*, 36(4): 1947–82.

Chandler, A. D. (1962) *Strategy and Structure: Chapters in the History of the American Industrial Enterprise* (Cambridge, MA: MIT Press).

Chandler, A. D. (1977) *The Visible Hand: The Managerial Revolution in American Business* (Cambridge, MA: Harvard University Press).

Chandler, A. D. (1990) *Scale and Scope: The Dynamics of Industrial Capitalism* (Cambridge, MA: Harvard University Press).

Chang, H.-J. (2002) *Kicking Away the Ladder: Development Strategy in Historical Perspective* (London: Anthem Press).

Channel, W. (2008) 'Uses and Abuses of Doing Business Indicators', available at: http://www.businessenvironment.org/dyn/be/docs/149/Channell.pdf

Chaudhuri, K., Schneider, F. and Chattopadhyay, S. (2006) 'The Size and Development of the Shadow Economy: An Empirical Investigation from States of India', *Journal of Development Economics*, 80(2): 428–43.

Chell, E., Hawarth, J. M. and Brearley, S. (1991) *The Entrepreneurial Personality: Concepts, Cases and Categories* (London: Routledge).

Chenery, H. B. and Srinivasan, T. N. (1988) 'Preface to the Handbook' in H. B. Chenery and T. N. Srinivasan (eds) *Handbook of Development Economics*, Volume 1 (Amsterdam: North-Holland).

Chiswick, B. R. and Miller, P. W. (1996) 'Ethnic Networks and Language Proficiency among Immigrants', *Journal of Population Economics*, 9(1): 19–35.

Ciccone, A. and Matsuyama, K. (1996) 'Start-up Costs and Pecuniary Externalities as Barriers to Economic Development', *Journal of Development Economics*, 4: 33–59.

Coase, R. H. (1937) 'The Nature of the Firm', *Economica*, 4(16): 386–405.

Coelho, M. P., de Meza, D. and Reyniers, D. J. (2004) 'Irrational Exuberance, Entrepreneurial Finance and Public Policy', *International Tax and Public Finance*, 11: 391–417.

Coleman, J. S. (1988) 'Social Capital in the Creation of Human Capital', *American Journal of Sociology*, 94: 95–120.

Collier, P. (1994) 'Demobilization and Insecurity: A Study in the Economics of the Transition from War to Peace', in J.-P. Azam, D. Bevan, P. Collier, S. Dercon, J. Gunning and S. Pradhan 'Some Economic Consequences of the Transition from Civil War to Peace', Policy Research Working Paper 1392 (Washington, DC: World Bank).

Collier, P. (2006) 'Economic Causes of Civil Conflict and their Implications for Policy', mimeo (Oxford: Oxford University).

Collier, P. and Gunning, J. (1995) 'War and Peace and Private Portfolios', *World Development*, 23(2): 233–41.

Collier, P. and Hoeffler, A. (2002) 'Aid, Policy and Growth in Post-Conflict Societies', Policy Research Working Paper 2902 (Washington, DC: World Bank).

Colombatto, E. and Melnik, A. (2008) 'Founders and Funders: An Introduction to Entrepreneurship and Venture Capital', New Perspectives of Political Economy, Vol. 4.

Constant II, Edward W. (1980) *The Origins of the Turbojet Revolution* (Baltimore, MD: Johns Hopkins University Press).

Cooke, S. and Morgan, M. (1993) 'The Network Paradigm: New Departures in Corporate and Regional Development', *Environment and Planning D: Society and Space*, 11: 543–64.

Cooper, N. (2006) 'Peaceful Warriors and Warring Peacemakers', *The Economics of Peace and Security Journal*, 1: 19–23.

Cortinovis, I., Vela, V. and Ndiku, J. (1993) 'Construction of a Socioeconomic Index to Facilitate Analysis of Health in Data in Developing Countries', *Social Science and Medicine*, (36): 1087–97.

Cowling, M. and Bygrave, W. (2002) 'Entrepreneurship and Unemployment: Relationships between Unemployment and Entrepreneurship in 37 Nations Participating in the Global Entrepreneurship Monitor', available at: www.babson.edu/entrep/fer/babson2003/xxii/xxii-p1/xxii-p1.html

Coyne, C. J. and Leeson, D. T. (2004) 'The Plight of Underdeveloped Countries', *Cato Journal*, 24(3): 235–49.

Cressy, R. (2006) 'Why do Most Firms Die Young?', *Small Business Economics*, 26: 103–16.

Cusmano, L., Morrison, A. and Rabellotti, R. (2008) 'Catching up and Sectoral Systems of Innovation: A Comparative Study on the Wine Sector in Chile, Italy and South Africa', Working Paper 48299 (Walla Walla, WA: American Association of Wine Economists).

Dallago, B. (1990) *The Irregular Economy: The Underground Economy and the Black Labour Market* (Dartmouth: Aldershot).

Danson, M. W. (1995) 'New Firm Formation and Regional Economic Development', *Small Business Economics*, 7: 81–7.

Dasgupta, P. (1988) 'Trust as a Commodity' in D. Gambetta (ed.) *Trust: Making and Breaking Cooperative Relations* (Oxford: Basil Blackwell).

Davelaar, E. J. (1991) *Incubation and Innovation: A Spatial Perspective* (Aldershot: Ashgate).

Davidsson, P. (1995) 'Culture Structure and Regional Levels of Entrepreneurship', *Entrepreneurship and Regional Development*, 7(1): 41–62.

Davidsson, P. (2004) *Researching Entrepreneurship* (New York, NY: Springer).

Davidsson, P. and Honig, B. (2003) 'The Role of Social and Human Capital among Nascent Entrepreneurs', *Journal of Business Venturing*, 18(3): 301–31.

Davis, T. (2006) 'Understanding Entrepreneurship: Developing Indicators for International Comparisons and Assessments', Report on the OECD's Entrepreneurship Indicators Project and Action Plan (Paris: OECD).

Davis, T. (2007) 'Entrepreneurship Indicators Project: Developing Comparable Measures of Entrepreneurship and the Factors that Enhance or Impede it', paper presented at the 'World Forum on Statistics Knowledge and Policy Workshop on Entrepreneurship Indicators', OECD Statistics Directorate, 27 June (Istanbul, Turkey).

De Meza, D. and Webb, D. (1987) 'Too Much Investment: A Problem of Assymetric Information', *Quarterly Journal of Economics*, 102(2): 281–92.

De Meza, D. and Webb, D. (1999) 'Wealth, Enterprise and Credit Policy', *Economic Journal*, 109(455): 153–63.

De Soto, H. (1989) *The Other Path: The Invisible Revolution in the Third World* (New York: Harper and Row).

De Soto, H. (2000) *The Mystery of Capital: Why Capitalism Triumphs in the West and Fails Everywhere Else* (New York: Basic Books).

Deakins, D. (1999) *Entrepreneurship and Small Firms* (London: McGraw Hill).

Demetriades, P. O. and Hussein, K. A. (1996) 'Does Financial Development Cause Economic Growth? Time-Series Evidence from 16 Countries', *Journal of Development Economics*, 51(2): 387–411.

Diamantaras, K. I. and Kung, S.-Y. (1996) *Principal Component Neural Networks: Theory and Applications* (New York: Wiley).

Dias, J. and McDermott, J. (2006) 'Institutions, Education and Development: The Role of Entrepreneurs', *Journal of Development Economics*, 80: 299–328.

Djankov, S., Freund, C. and Pham, C. S. (2008) 'Trading on Time', available at: http://www.doingbusiness.org/Documents/TradingOnTime_APR08.pdf

Djankov, S., Ganser, T., McLiesh, C., Ramalho, R. and Shleifer, A. (2008a) 'The Effect of Corporate Taxes on Investment and Entrepreneurship', draft paper, date accessed 15 March 2009.

Djankov, S., Ganser, T., McLiesh, C., Ramalho, R. and Shleifer, A. (2008b) 'The Effect of Corporate Taxes on Investment and Entrepreneurship', Working Paper 13756 (Cambridge, MA: NBER).

Djankov, S., Hart, O., McLiesh, C. and Shleifer, A. (2008) 'Debt Enforcement Around the World', *Journal of Political Economy*, 116(6): 1105–49.

Djankov, S., La Porta, R., Lopez-de-Silanes, F. and Shleifer, A. (2002) 'The Regulation of Entry', *Quarterly Journal of Economics*, 117(1): 1–37.

Djankov, S., La Porta, R., Lopez-de-Silanes, F. and Shleifer, A. (2003) 'Courts', available at: http://www.doingbusiness.org/documents/LexPaperAug211.pdf

Djankov, S., La Porta, R., Lopez-de-Silanes, F. and Shleifer, A. (2008) 'The Law and Economics of Self-Dealing', *Journal of Financial Economics*, 88: 430–65.

Djankov, S., McLiesh, C. and Shleifer, A. (2007) 'Private Credit in 129 Countries', *Journal of Financial Economics*, 84: 299–329.

Dollar, D. (2008) 'Lessons from China for Africa', Policy Research Working Paper 4531 (Washington, DC: World Bank).

Dollar, D. and Kraay, A. (2003) 'Institutions, Trade and Growth', *Journal of Monetary Economics*, 50(1): 133–62.

Dollar, D. and Kraay, A. (2004) 'Trade, Growth and Poverty', *The Economic Journal*, 114(493): F22–F49.

Drennan, M. P. (2002) *The Information Economy and American Cities* (Baltimore, MD: Johns Hopkins University Press).

Dulleck, U., Frijters, P. and Winter-Ebmer, P. (2006) 'Reducing Start-Up Costs for New Firms: The Double Dividend on the Labour Market', *Scandinavian Journal of Economics*, 108(2): 317–37.

Dutz, M. A., Ordover, J. A. and Willig, R. D. (2000) 'Entrepreneurship Access Policy and Economic Development: Lessons from Industrial Organisation', *European Economic Review*, 44: 739–47.

Earle, J. S. and Sakova, Z. (1999) 'Entrepreneurship from Scratch: Lessons on the Entry Decision into Self-Employment from Transition Economies', Discussion Paper 79 (Bonn: Institute for the Study of Labour).

Earle, J. S. and Sakova, Z. (2000) 'Business Start-ups or Disguised Unemployment? Evidence on the Character of Self-Employment from Transition Economies', *Labour Economics*, 7: 575–601.

Easterly, W. (2001) 'The Lost Decade: Developing Countries' Stagnation in Spite of Policy Reform 1980–1998', *Journal of Economic Growth*, 6: 135–57.

Easterly, W. and Levine, R. (2003) 'Tropics, Germs and Crops: How Endowments Influence Economic Development', *Journal of Monetary Economics*, 50(1): 3–39.

Economides, N. (1996) 'Network Externalities, Complementarities and Innovation', *European Journal of Political Economy*, 12(2): 211–33.

Edwards, S. (1993) 'Openness, Trade Liberalization and Growth in Developing Countries', *Journal of Economic Literature*, 31(3): 1358–93.

Edwards, S. (1998) 'Trade, Productivity and Growth: What do We Really Know?', *The Economic Journal*, 108: 383–98.

Elbaum, B. and Lazonick, W. (eds) (1986) *The Decline of the British Economy* (Oxford: Oxford University Press).

Erken, H., Donselaar, P. and Thurik, R. (2008) 'Total Factor Productivity and the Role of Entrepreneurship', Jena Economic Research Papers 2008–019 (Jena: Friedrich Schiller University and Max Planck Institute of Economics).

Estrin, S., Meyer, K. E. and Bytchkova, M. (2006) 'Entrepreneurship in Transition Economies', in M. Casson, B. Yeung, A. Basu and N. Wadeson (eds) *The Oxford Handbook of Entrepreneurship* (Oxford: Oxford University Press).

European Commission (2002) 'Observatory of Regional SMEs 2002/3. Regional Clusters in Europe', Brussels: European Commission, available at: http://ec.europa.eu/regional_policy/innovation/pdf/library/regional_clusters.pdf

Evans, D. (1987) 'The Relationship Between Firm Growth, Size and Age', *Journal of Industrial Economics*, 35(4): 567–81.

Evans, G. (2008) *The Responsibility to Protect: Ending Mass Atrocity Crimes Once and For All* (Washington, DC: Brookings Institution Press).

Eyraud, F. and Saget, C. (2005) *The Fundamentals of Minimum Wage Fixing* (Geneva: ILO).

Fagerberg, J. and Godinho, M. (2005) 'Innovation and Catching up' in J. Fagerberg, D. Mowery and R. Nelson (eds) *The Oxford Handbook of Innovation* (Oxford: Oxford University Press).

Farnie, D. A. (1979) *The English Cotton Industry and the World Market, 1815–1896* (Oxford: Oxford University Press).

Farnie, D. A. and Abe, T. (2000) 'Japan, Lancashire and the Asian Market of Cotton Manufacturers, 1980–1990' in D. A. Farnie, T. Nakaoka, D. J. Jeremy, J. F. Wilson and T. Abe (eds) *Region and Strategy in Britain and Japan* (London: Routledge).

Feldman, D. C. and Bolino, M. C. (2000) 'Career Patterns of the Self-employed: Career Motivations and Career Outcomes', *Journal of Small Business Management*, 38(3): 53–67.

Feng, K. and Zhang, M. (2007) 'Governance and Learning Under Transition Economy: The Case of the Chinese Telecom Equipment Sector' paper prepared for the conference on 'Innovation and Competition in the Global Communications Technology Industry', INSEAD, Fontainebleau, France, 23–24 August.

Ferleger, L. and Lazonick, W. (1993) 'The Managerial Revolution and the Developmental State: The Case of U.S. Agriculture', *Business and Economic History*, 22(2): 67–98.

Ferleger, L. and Lazonick, W. (1994) 'Higher Education for an Innovative Economy: Land-Grant Colleges and the Managerial Revolution in America', *Business and Economic History*, 23(1):116–28.

Fischer, M. M. and Fröhlich, J. (eds) (2001) *Knowledge, Complexity and Innovation System* (Berlin: Springer).

Fischer, M. M. and Nijkamp, P. (2008) 'Entrepreneurship and Regional Development' in R. Capello and P. Nijkamp (eds) *Handbook of Regional Growth and Development* (Cheltenham: Edward Elgar).

Fischer, M. M., Scherngell, T. and Jansenberger, E. (2006) 'The Geography of Knowledge Spillovers between High-Technology Firms in Europe. Evidence from a Spatial Interaction Modelling Perspective', *Geographical Analysis*, 38(3): 288–309.

Fischer, M. M. and Varga, A. (2003) 'Spatial Knowledge Spillovers and University Research', *Annals of Regional Science*, 37(2): 303–22.

Florida, R. (2002) *The Rise of the Creative Class* (New York: Basic Books).

Fogel, K., Hawk, A., Morck, R. and Yeung, B. (2006) 'Institutional Obstacles to Entrepreneurship' in M. Casson, B. Yeung, A. Basu and N. Wadeson (eds) *The Oxford Handbook of Entrepreneurship* (Oxford: Oxford University Press).

Fonseca, R., Lopez-Garcia, P. and Pissarides, C. A. (2001) 'Entrepreneurship, Start-Up Costs and Employment', *European Economic Review*, 45: 692–705.

Fonseca, R., Michaud, P.-C. and Sopraseuth, T. (2007) 'Entrepreneurship, Wealth, Liquidity Constraints and Start-Up Costs', *Comparative Labor Law and Policy Journal*, 28: 637–74.

Foss, N. J. and Klein, P. G. (eds) (2002) *Entrepreneurship and the Firm* (Cheltenham: Edward Elgar).

Fox, L. (2006) 'Minimum Wage Trends: Understanding Past and Contemporary Research', Briefing Paper 178 (Washington, DC: Economic Policy Institute).

Freudenberg, M. (2003) 'Composite Indicators of Country Performance: A Critical Assessment', STI Working Paper 2003/16, Industry Issues (Paris: OECD).

Fritsch, M. (2008) 'How Does New Business Formation Affect Regional Development? Introduction to the Special Issue', *Small Business Economics*, 30(1): 1–14.

Fukasaku, T. (1992) *Technology and Industrial Development in Pre-War Japan: Mitsubishi Nagasaki Shipyard, 1884–1934* (Milton Park: Routledge).

Galbraith, J. K. (1956) *American Capitalism: The Concept of Countervailing Power* (Boston, MA: Houghton Mifflin Co).

Galbraith, J. K. (1967) *The New Industrial State* (London: Routledge).

Gallup, J. L., Sachs, J. D. and Mellinger, A. D. (1999) 'Geography and Economic Development', Working Paper 6849 (Cambridge, MA: NBER).

Garrett, T. A. and Wall, H. J. (2006) 'Creating a Policy Environment for Entrepreneurs', Working Paper 2005–064B (St. Louis, MO: Federal Reserve Bank of St. Louis, Research Division).

Gentry, W. and Hubbard, R. G. (2000) 'Entrepreneurship and Household Savings', *American Economic Review*, 90(2): 283–87.

Gertler, M. (1988) 'The Limits of Flexibility: Comments on the Post-Fordist Vision of Production and its Geography', *Transactions of the Institute of British Geographers*, 17: 410–32.

Ghatak, M., Morelli, M. and Sjöström, T. (2007) 'Entrepreneurial Talent, Occupational Choice and Trickle Up Policies', *Journal of Economic Theory*, 137(1): 27–48.

Giannetti, M. and Simonov, A. (2004) 'On the Determinants of Entrepreneurial Activity: Social Norms, Economic Environment and Individual Characteristics', *Swedish Economic Policy Review*, 11: 269–313.

Glimstedt, H., Lazonick, W. and Xie, H. (2006) 'The Evolution and Allocation of Stock Options: Adapting US-Style Compensation to the Swedish Business Model', *European Management Review*, 3(3): 156–76.

Gollin, D. (2008) 'Nobody's Business but My Own: Self-Employment and Small Enterprise in Economic Development', *Journal of Monetary Economics*, 55(2): 219–33.

Gompers, P., Lerner, J. and Scharfstein, D. (2005) 'Entrepreneurial Spawning: Public Corporations and the Genesis of New Ventures, 1986 to 1999', *Journal of Finance*, 60(2): 577–614.

Gong, X. and Soest, A. (2002) 'Wage Differentials and Mobility in the Urban Labour Market: A Panel Data Analysis for Mexico', *Labour Economics*, 9(4): 513–29.

Goozner, M. (2004) *The $800 Million Pill: The Truth Behind the Cost of New Drugs* (Berkeley, CA: University of California Press).

Gordon, I. R. and McCann, P. (2000) 'Industrial Clusters: Complexes Agglomeration and/or Social Networks', *Urban Studies*, 37(3): 513–32.

Gorter, C., Nijkamp, P. and Poot, J. (eds) (1998) *Crossing Borders* (Aldershot: Ashgate).

Granovetter, M. S. (1985) 'Economic Action and Social Structure: The Problem of Embeddedness', *American Journal of Sociology*, 91(3): 481–510.

Gries, T. and Naudé, W. A. (2009) 'When to Start a New Firm? Modelling the Timing of Novice and Serial Entrepreneurs', Research Paper 2009/39 (Helsinki: UNU-WIDER).

Gries, T. and Naudé, W. A. (2010) 'Entrepreneurship and Structural Economic Transformation', *Small Business Economics*, 34(1): 13–29.

Grilo, I. and Irigoyen, J. M. (2006) 'Entrepreneurship in the EU: To Wish and not to Be', *Small Business Economics*, 26(4): 305–18.

Grilo, I. and Thurik, R. (2005) 'Entrepreneurial Engagement Levels in the European Union', *International Journal of Entrepreneurship Education*, 3(2): 143–68.

Grilo, I. and Thurik, R. (2008) 'Determinants of Entrepreneurial Engagement Levels in Europe and the US', *Industrial and Corporate Change*, 17(6): 1113–45.

Guiso, L. and Schivardi, F. (2007) 'What Determines Entrepreneurial Clusters?', Working Paper 200616 (Cagliari: University of Cagliari and Sassari, Centre for North South Economic Research).

Gwatkin, D. R., Rustein, S., Johnson, K., Pande, R. P. and Wagstaff, A. (2000) 'Socio-Economic Differences in Health, Nutrition and Population in Brazil, Ethiopia, Nigeria and Vietnam' (Washington, DC: HNP/Poverty Thematic Group of the World Bank).

Hagen, J. M. and Choe, S. (1998) 'Trust in Japanese Interfirm Relations: Institutional Sanctions Matter', *Academy of Management Review*, 23: 589–600.

Hale, R. and Whitlam, P. (1997) *Towards the Virtual Organization* (London: McGraw-Hill).

Hall, J. C. (2008) 'Randall G. Holcombe, Entrepreneurship and Economic Progress', *Review of Austrian Economics*, 21(2–3): 219–22.

Hall, J. C. and Sobel, R. S. (2008) 'Institutions, Entrepreneurship and Regional Differences in Economic Growth', *Southern Journal of Entrepreneurship*, 1(1): 69–96.

Hall, R. E. and Jones, C. (1999) 'Why Do Some Countries Produce so Much More Output per Head than Others', *Quarterly Journal of Economics*, 10: 463–83.

Hambrecht, William R. (1984) 'Venture Capital & the Growth of Silicon Valley', *California Management Review*, 26(2): 74–82.

Hampel-Milagrosa, A. (2008) 'A Combined Qualitative and Quantitative Approach to Address Gender Issues in the Doing Business Project', paper presented at the World Bank's Independent Evaluation Group (IEG) and the Doing Business Team in Washington, DC, USA, 24–26 September.

Harrison, B. (1994) 'The Small Firms Myth', *California Management Review*, 36(3): 142–58.

Hart, D. M. (2003) 'Entrepreneurship Policy: What It Is and Where It Came From' in D. M. Hart (ed.) *The Emergence of Entrepreneurship Policy* (Cambridge: Cambridge University Press).

Hart, J. A. (2001) 'Can Industrial Policy be Good Policy?', paper presented at the conference on 'The Political Economy of Policy Reform' (Tulane University, New Orleans, USA), 9–10 November.

Hausmann, R. and Rodrik, D. (2003) 'Economic Development as Self-Discovery', *Journal of Development Economics*, 72(2): 603–33.

Hayek, F. A. (1945) 'The Use of Knowledge in Society', *American Economic Review*, 35(4): 519–30.

Hayter, R. (1997) *The Dynamics of Industrial Location* (Chichester: John Wiley).

Hébert, R. M. and Link, A. N. (1989) 'In Search of the Meaning of Entrepreneurship', *Small Business Economics*, 1(1): 39–49.

Helpman, E. (2004) *The Mystery of Economic Growth* (Cambridge: Belknap Press).

Henkin, L. (1995) *International Law: Politics and Values* (Amsterdam: Martinus Nijhoff Publishers).

Henrekson, M. (2007) 'Entrepreneurship and Institutions', *Comparative Labor Law and Policy Journal*, 28: 717–42.

Hessels, J., van Gelderen, M. and Thurik, R. (2008) 'Entrepreneurial Aspirations, Motivations and their Drivers', *Small Business Economics*, 31(3): 323–39.

Ho, Y.-P. and Wong, P.-K. (2007) 'Financing, Regulatory Costs and Entrepreneurial Propensity', *Small Business Economics*, 28: 187–204.

Hoffmann, A. N. (2007) 'A Rough Guide to Entrepreneurship Policy' in D. B. Audretsch, I. Grilo and R. Thurik (eds) *The Handbook of Entrepreneurship Policy* (Cheltenham: Edward Elgar).

Hoffmann, A. N., Larsen, M. and Oxholin, A. S. (2006) 'Quality Manual of Entrepreneurship Indicators', Version 2 (Copenhagen: FORA).

Holmes, T. J. and Schmitz, J. A. (1990) 'A Theory of Entrepreneurship and Its Application to the Study of Business Transfers', *Journal of Political Economy*, 98(2): 265–94.

Holtz-Eakin, D., Joulfarian, D. and Rosen, H. S. (1994) 'Entrepreneurial Decisions and Liquidity Constraints', *Rand Journal of Economics*, 25(2): 334–47.

Honig, B. (1998) 'What Determines Success? Examining the Human, Financial and Social Capital of Jamaican Microentrepreneurs', *Journal of Business Venturing*, 13(3): 371–94.

Hotelling, H. (1933) 'Analysis of a Complex of Statistical Variables into Principal Components', *Journal of Educational Psychology*, 24: 417–41.

Hsu, D. and Kenney, M. (2005) 'Organizing Venture Capital: The Rise and Demise of American Research & Development, 1946–1973', *Industrial and Corporate Change*, 14(4): 579–616.

Hurst, E. and Lusardi, A. (2004) 'Liquidity Constraints, Household Wealth and Entrepreneurship', *Journal of Political Economy*, 112(2): 319–47.

Hwang, H. and Powell, W. W. (2005) 'Institutions and Entrepreneurship' in S. Alvarez, R. Agarwal and O. Sorenson (eds) *Handbook of Entrepreneurship Research: Disciplinary Perspectives* (New York: Springer).

Independent Evaluation Group (IEG) (2008) *Doing Business: An Independent Evaluation. Taking the Measure of the World Bank – IFC Doing Business Indicators* (Washington, DC: World Bank).

International Bank for Reconstruction and Development and World Bank (2004) *Doing Business in 2004: Understanding Regulation* (Washington, DC: World Bank and Oxford University Press).

International Bank for Reconstruction and Development and World Bank (2005) *Doing Business in 2005: Removing Obstacles to Growth* (Washington, DC: World Bank and Oxford University Press).

International Bank for Reconstruction and Development and World Bank (2006) *Doing Business in 2006: Creating Jobs* (Washington, DC: World Bank and Oxford University Press).

International Bank for Reconstruction and Development and World Bank (2007) *Doing Business 2007: How to Reform* (Washington, DC: World Bank and Oxford University Press).

International Bank for Reconstruction and Development and World Bank (2008a) *Doing Business 2008* (Washington, DC: World Bank and Oxford University Press).

International Bank for Reconstruction and Development and World Bank (2008b) *Doing Business: Change to the Methodology, 2004–2007*, available at: http://www.doingbusiness.org/MethodologySurveys/methodologyNoteArchive.aspx

International Bank for Reconstruction and Development and World Bank (2008c) *Doing Business 2009: Comparing Regulation in 181 Economies* (Washington, DC: World Bank and Oxford University Press).

International Bank for Reconstruction and Development and World Bank (2009) *Doing Business 2010: Reforming through Difficult Times* (Washington, DC: World Bank and IFC and Palgrave Macmillan).

International Development Association (IDA) (2007) *Country Policy and Institutional Assessments. Questionnaire 2007*, available at: http://siteresources. worldbank.org/IDA/Resources/CPIA2007Questionnaire.pdf

International Labour Organization (ILO) (2007) 'In Asia, Informal Work Shifts but Remains Massive', available at: www.ilo.org.

Iyigun, M. and Owen, A. L. (1998) 'Risk, Entrepreneurship and Human-Capital Accumulation', *American Economic Review*, 88(2): 454–7.

Iyigun, M. and Rodrik, D. (2005) 'On the Efficacy of Reforms: Policy Tinkering, Institutional Change and Entrepreneurship' in T. Eicher and C. G. Penalosa (eds) *Institutions and Growth* (Cambridge, MA: MIT Press).

Johnson, C. (1982) *MITI and the Japanese Miracle: The Growth of Industrial Policy, 1925–1975* (Stanford, CA: Stanford University Press).

Johnson, S., Kaufman, D., Shleifer, A., Goldman, M. I. and Weitzman, M. L. (1997) 'The Unofficial Economy in Transition', *Brookings Papers on Economic Activity*, 2: 159–239.

Jolliffe, I. T. (2002) *Principal Component Analysis*, Second Edition (New York: Springer).

Kanniainen, V. and Keuschnigg, C. (eds) (2005) *Venture Capital, Entrepreneurship and Public Policy* (Cambridge, MA and London: MIT Press).

Kanniainen, V. and Poutvaara, P. (2007) 'Imperfect Transmission of Tacit Knowledge and Other Barriers to Entrepreneurship', *Comparative Labor Law and Policy Journal*, 28: 675–93.

Kaplan, R. S. and Norton, D. P. (1992) 'The Balanced Scorecard: Measures That Drive Performance', *Harvard Business Review*, January–February: 71–80.

Kaplan, R. S. and Norton, D. P. (1993) 'Putting the Balanced Scorecard to Work', *Harvard Business Review*, September–October: 2–16.

Karhunen, K. (1946) 'Zur Spektraltheorie Stochastischer Prozesse', *Annales Academiae Scientiarum Fennicae*, Series A1, Mathematica-Physica, 34: 1–7.

Katz, R. (2003) *The Human Side of Managing Technological Innovation* (Oxford: Oxford University Press).

Kaufmann, D., Kraay, A. and Mastruzzi, M. (2008) 'Governance Matters VII: Aggregate and Individual Governance Indicators, 1996–2007', Policy Research Working Paper 4654 (Washington, DC: World Bank).

Kaufmann, D., Kraay, A. and Zoido-Lobatón, P. (1999) 'Governance Matters', Policy Research Working Paper 2196 (Washington, DC: World Bank).

Kauffman Foundation (2007) 'On the Road to an Entrepreneurial Economy: A Research and Policy Guide, Version 2.0', available at: www.kauffman.org

Keefer, P. and Knack, S. (1995) 'Institutions and Economic Performance: Cross-Country Tests Using Alternative Institutional Measures', *Economics and Politics*, 7(3): 207–27.

Keen, D. (1994) *The Benefits of Famine: A Political Economy of Famine and Relief in Southwestern Sudan. 1983–89* (Princeton, NJ: Princeton University Press).

Kihlstrom, R. and Laffont, J. J. (1979) 'A General Equilibrium Entrepreneurial Theory of Firm Formation Based on Risk Aversion', *Journal of Political Economy*, 87(4): 719–48.

Kim, D.-W. and Leslie, S. W. (1998) 'Winning Markets or Winning Noble Prizes? KAIST and the Challenges of Late Industrialization', *Osiris*, 2nd Series, 13: 154–85.

Kioko, B. (2003) 'The Right of Intervention under the African Union's Constitutive Act: From Non-interference to Non-intervention', *International Review of the Red Cross*, 85(852): 807–25.

Kirzner, I. M. (1973) *Competition and Entrepreneurship* (Chicago, IL: University of Chicago Press).

Kirzner, I. M. (1997) 'Entrepreneurial Discovery and the Competitive Market Process: An Austrian Approach', *Journal of Economic Literature*, 35: 60–85.

Klapper, L., Amit, R. and Guillén, M. F. (2008) 'Entrepreneurship and Firm Formation Across Countries' in J. Lerner and A. Schoar (eds) *International Differences in Entrepreneurship* (Cambridge, MA: NBER).

Klapper, L., Amit, R., Guillen, M. F. and Quesada, J. M. (2007) 'Entrepreneurship and Firm Formation across Countries', Policy Research Working Paper 4313 (Washington, DC: World Bank).

Klapper, L., Laeven, L. and Rajan, R. (2006) 'Entry Regulation as a Barrier to Entrepreneurship', *Journal of Financial Economics*, 82 (3): 591–629.

Knack, S. and Keefer, P. (1995) 'Institutions and Economic Performance: Cross Country Tests Using Alternative Institutional Measures', *Economics and Politics*, 7(3): 207–27.

Knack, S. and Keefer, P. (1997) 'Why Don't Poor Countries Catch-up? A Cross-National Test of an Institutional Explanation', *Economic Inquiry*, 35(3): 590–602.

Knight, F. H. (1921) *Risk, Uncertainty and Profit* (New York: Houghton Mifflin).

Koike, K. and Takenori, I. (eds) (1990) *Skill Formation in Japan and Southeast Asia* (Tokyo: University of Tokyo Press).

Kolko, J. (2002) 'Silicon Mountains, Silicon Molehills: Geographic Concentration and Convergence of Internet Industries in the US', *Information Economics and Policy*, 14: 211–32.

Kolvereid, L. (1996) 'Organizational Employment versus Self-Employment: Reasons for Career Choice Intentions', *Entrepreneurship Theory and Practice*, 20(3): 23–31.

Kormendi, R. and Meguire, P. (1985) 'Macroeconomic Determinants of Growth', *Journal of Monetary Economics*, 16(4): 141–63.

Kourtit, K., Nijkamp, P. and de Waal, A. (2009) 'Strategic Performance Management and Creative Industry', *International Journal of Foresight and Innovation*, 5: 65–82.

Krasner, S. D. (1999) *Sovereignty: Organized Hypocrisy* (Princeton, NJ: Princeton University Press).

Krasner, S. D. (2004) 'Sharing Sovereignty: New Institutions for Collapsed and Failing States', *International Organization*, 29(2): 85–120.

Krueger, A. O. (1998) 'Why Trade Liberalisation is Good for Growth', *The Economic Journal*, 108(450): 1513–22.

Kuesel, C., Maenner, U. and Meissner, R. (eds) (2008) *The Social and Ecological Market Economy: A Model for Asian Development?* (Eschborn: GTZ).

La Porta, R., Lopez-de-Silanes, F., Shleifer, A. and Vishny, R. W. (1998) 'Law and Finance', *Journal of Political Economy*, 106(6): 1113–55.

Lagendijk, A. and Oinas, P. (2005) *Proximity, Distance and Diversity* (Aldershot: Ashgate).

Lazear, E. P. (2005) 'Entrepreneurship', *Journal of Labor Economics*, 23(4): 649–80.

Lazonick, W. (1983) 'Industrial Organization and Technological Change: The Decline of the British Cotton Industry', *Business History Review*, 57(2): 195–236.

Lazonick, W. (2007a) 'Innovative Enterprise and Economic Development' in Y. Cassis and A. Colli (eds) *Business Performance in the Twentieth Century: A Comparative Perspective* (Cambridge: Cambridge University Press).

Lazonick, W. (2007b) 'The US Stock Market and the Governance of Innovative Enterprise', *Industrial and Corporate Change*, 16(6): 983–1035.

Lazonick, W. (2007c) 'Varieties of Capitalism and Innovative Enterprise', *Comparative Social Research*, 24: 21–69.

Lazonick, W. (2009) *Sustainable Prosperity in the New Economy? Business Organization and High-Tech Employment in the United States* (Kalamazoo, MI: W. E. Upjohn Institute for Employment Research).

Lazonick, W. (2010a) 'The Chandlerian Corporation and the Theory of Innovative Enterprise', *Industrial and Corporate Change*, 19(1): 317–49.

Lazonick, W. (2010b) 'The Explosion of Executive Pay and the Erosion of American Prosperity', *Entreprises et Histoire*, 57 (forthcoming)

Lazonick, W. and Tulum, Ö. (2009) 'US Biopharmaceutical Finance and the Sustainability of the Biotech Boom', paper presented at the Sloan Industry Studies Conference (Chicago, IL), 29 May (revised July).

Lee, S. and McCann, D. (2007) 'Measuring Labour Market Institutions: Conceptual and Methodological Questions on "Working Hours Rigidity"' in J. Berg and D. Kucera (eds) *In Defence of Labour Market Institutions: Cultivating Justice in the Developing World* (Basingstoke: Palgrave Macmillan and Geneva: ILO).

Lee, S. Y., Florida, R. and Acs, Z. J. (2004) 'Creativity and Entrepreneurship: A Regional Analysis of New Firm Formation', *Regional Studies*, 38(8): 879–89.

Leff, N. (1979) 'Entrepreneurship and Economic Development: The Problem Revisited', *Journal of Economic Literature*, 17: 46–64.

Leibenstein, H. (1968) 'Entrepreneurship and Development', *American Economic Review*, 58(2): 72–83.

Leibenstein, H. (1978) *General X-Efficiency Theory and Economic Development* (Oxford: Oxford University Press).

Leibenstein, H. (1995) 'The Supply of Entrepreneurship' in G. M. Meier (ed.) *Leading Issues in Economic Development* (New York: Oxford University Press).

Leitão da Silva Martins, S. P. (2007) 'Indicators for Measuring Entrepreneurship: A Proposal For A Scoreboard', *Industry & Higher Education*, 21(1): 85–97.

Leone, R. A. and Struyck, R. (1976) 'The Incubator Hypothesis: Evidence from Five SMSAs', *Urban Studies*, 13(3): 325–31.

Leslie, S. W. (1993) *The Cold War and American Science: The Military-Industrial Complex at MIT and Stanford* (New York: Columbia University Press).

Leslie, S. W. and Kargon, R. H. (1996) 'Selling Silicon Valley: Frederick Terman's Model for Regional Advantage', *Business History Review*, 70(4): 435–72.

Lever, W. F. (2002) 'Correlating the Knowledge-Base of Cities with Economic Growth', *Urban Studies*, 39(5–6): 859–70.

Levie, J. and Autio, E. (2008) 'A Theoretical Grounding and Test of the GEM Model', *Small Business Economics*, 31(3): 235–63.

Levine, R., Loayza, N. and Beck, T. (2000) 'Financial Intermediation and Growth: Causality and *Causes*', *Journal of Monetary Economics*, 46: 31–77.

Li, D. D., Feng, J. and Jiang, H. (2006) 'Institutional Entrepreneurs', *American Economic Review*, 96(2) 358–62.

Li, W. (2002) 'Entrepreneurship and Government Subsidies: A General Equilibrium Analysis', *Journal of Economic Dynamics and Control*, 26(11): 1815–44.

Licht, A. N. (2007) 'The Entrepreneurial Spirit and What the Law Can Do About It', *Comparative Labor Law and Policy Journal*, 28: 817–62.

Lin, A. (2006) 'Shanghai Bar Association Goes After Foreign Firms', *New York Law Journal*, 18 May, available at: www.law.com/jsp/llf/PubArticleLLF.jsp? =1147856732635.

Lin, J. and Chang, H.-J. (2009) 'Should Industrial Policy in Developing Countries Conform to Comparative Advantage or Defy it? A Debate between Justin Lin and Ha-Joon Chang', *Development Policy Review*, 27(5): 483–502.

Linde, C. (2006) 'The U.S. Constitution and International Law: Finding the Balance', *Journal of Transnational Law and Policy*, 15(2): 305–39.

Linders, G. J., de Groot, H. L. F. and Nijkamp, P. (2005) 'Economic Development, Institutions and Trust' in R. Boschma and R. Kloosterman (eds) *Learning from Clusters* (Dordrecht: Springer).

Loveman, G. and Sengenberger, W. (1991) 'The Re-emergence of Small-scale Production: An International Comparison', *Small Business Economics*, 3(1): 1–37.

Lu, Q. (2000) *China's Leap into the Information Age: Innovation and Organization in the Computer Industry* (Oxford: Oxford University Press).

Lu, Q. and Lazonick, W. (2001) 'The Organization of Innovation in a Transitional Economy: Business and Government in Chinese Electronic Publishing', *Research Policy*, 30(1): 35–54.

Lucas, R. E. (1978) 'On the Size Distribution of Firms', *Bell Journal of Economics*, 9(2): 508–23.

Lucas, R. E. (1988) 'On the Mechanics of Economic Development', *Journal of Monetary Economics*, 22(1): 3–39.

Lundvall, B. (ed.) (1992) *National Systems of Innovation* (London: Pinter).

Maddison, A. (2007) 'Historical Statistics for the World Economy, 1–2003AD', available at: http://www.ggdc.net/maddison/

Maillat, D. (1995) 'Territorial Dynamics, Innovative Milieus and Regional Policy', *Entrepreneurship and Regional Development*, 7(2): 157–65.

Malecki, E. J. (1994) 'Entrepreneurship in Regional and Local Development', *International Regional Science Review*, 16: 119–53.

Malecki, E. J. (1997a) *Technology and Economic Development* (Harlow: Addison Wesley Longman).

Malecki, E. J. (1997b) 'Entrepreneurs, Networks and Economic Development' in J. A. Katz (ed.) *Advances in Entrepreneurship, Firm Emergence and Growth*, Volume 3 (Greenwich, CT: Jai Press).

Malecki, E. J. and. Poehling, R. M (1999) 'Extroverts and Introverts: Small Manufactures and their Information Sources', *Entrepreneurship and Regional Development*, 11: 247–68.

Mani, S. (2008) 'The Growth of Knowledge-Based Entrepreneurship in India, 1991–2007: Analysis of Its Evidence and Constraints', paper presented at the

UNU-WIDER and UNU-MERIT workshop on 'Entrepreneurship, Technological Innovation and Development', Maastricht, the Netherlands, 30–31 October.

Manolova, T. S., Eunni, R. V. and Gyoshev, B. S. (2008) 'Institutional Environments for Entrepreneurship: Evidence from Emerging Economies in Eastern Europe', *Entrepreneurship Theory and Practice*, 32(1): 203–18.

Marin, A. and Hampton, N. K. (2007) 'Simplifying the Personal Network Name-Generator: Alternatives to Traditional Multiple and Single Name-Generators', *Field Methods*, 19(2): 163–93.

Marshall, A. (1890) *Principles of Economics*, reprinted in 1997 (London: Prometheus).

Marsili, O. (2001) *The Anatomy and Evolution of Industries: Technological Change and Industrial Dynamics* (Cheltenham: Edward Elgar).

Mass, W. and Lazonick, W. (1990) 'The British Cotton Industry and International Competitive Advantage: The State of the Debates', *Business History*, 32(4): 9–65.

Mass, W. and Robertson, A. (1996) 'From Textiles to Automobiles: Mechanical and Organizational Innovation in the Toyoda Enterprises, 1895–1933', *Business and Economic History*, 25(2): 1–37.

Masurel, E., Nijkamp, P., Tastan, M. and Vindigni, G. (2002) 'Motivations and Performance Conditions for Ethnic Entrepreneurship', *Growth and Change*, 33(2): 238–60.

Mazzoleni, R. and Nelson, R. R. (2007) 'Public Research Institution and Economic Catch-Up', *Research Policy*, 36: 1512–28.

McChesney, F. S. (1987) 'Rent Extraction and Rent Creation in the Economic Theory of Regulation', *Journal of Legal Studies*, 16: 101–18.

McCormick, B. and Wahba, J. (2000) 'Overseas Employment and Remittances to a Dual Economy', *The Economic Journal*, 110(463): 506–34.

McGrath, R. G., MacMillan, I. C. and Scheinberg, S. (1992) 'Elitists, Risk-Takers and Rugged Individualists? An Exploratory Analysis of Cultural Differences between Entrepreneurs and Non-Entrepreneurs', *Journal of Business Venturing*, 7: 115–35.

McManus, W. S. (1990) 'Labour Market Effects of Language Enclaves', *Journal of Human Resources*, 25(2): 228–52.

McMillan, J. and Woodruff, C. (1999a) 'Dispute Prevention without Courts in Vietnam', *Journal of Law, Economics and Organization*, 15: 637–58.

McMillan, J. and Woodruff, C. (1999b) 'Interfirm Relationship and Informal Credit in Vietnam', *Quarterly Journal of Economics*, 114: 1285–320.

McMillan, J. and Woodruff, C. (2002) 'The Central Role of the Entrepreneurs in Transition Economies', *Journal of Economic Perspectives*, 16(3): 153–70.

McMullen, J. S., Bagby, D. R. and Palich, L. E. (2008) 'Economic Freedom and the Motivation to Engage in Entrepreneurial Action', *Entrepreneurship Theory and Practice*, 32(5): 875–95.

Mehlum, H., Moene, K. and Torvik, R. (2003) 'Predator or Prey? Parasitic Enterprises in Economic Development', *European Economic Review*, 47(2): 275–94.

Meijer, R. R. and Baneke, J. J. (2004) 'Analysing Psychopathology Items: A Case for Nonparametric Item Response Theory Modelling', *Psychological Methods*, 9(3): 354–86.

Metcalfe, J. S. (2004) 'The Entrepreneur and the Style of Modern Economics' in G. Corbetta, M. Huse, and D. Ravasi (eds) *Crossroads of Entrepreneurship* (Boston, New York, Dordrecht: Kluwer Academic Publishers).

Minniti, M. (2008) 'The Role of Government Policy on Entrepreneurial Activity: Productive, Unproductive, or Destructive?', *Entrepreneurship Theory and Practice*, 32(5): 779–90.

Mintzberg, H. (1978) 'Patterns of Strategy Formation', *Management Science*, 36: 934–48.

Mokken, R. J. and Lewis, C. (1982) 'A Nonparametric Approach to the Analysis of Dichotomous Item Responses', *Applied Psychological Measurement*, 6(4): 417–30.

Morgan, K. (1991) 'Competition and Collaboration in Electronics: What Are the Prospects for Britain?', *Environment and Planning A*, 23: 1459–82.

Morikawa, H. (2001) *A History of Top Management in Japan* (Oxford: Oxford University Press).

Mosey, S. and Wright, M. (2007) 'From Human Capital to Social Capital: A Longitudinal Study of Technology Based Academic Entrepreneurs', *Entrepreneurship Theory and Practice*, 31(6): 909–35.

Mukhopadhyay, H. (1999) 'Trade Liberalization in Sub-Saharan Africa: Stagnation or Growth', *Journal of International Development*, 11(6): 825–35.

Murphy, K. M., Shleifer, A. and Vishny, R. W. (1991) 'The Allocation of Talent: Implications for Growth', *Quarterly Journal of Economics*, 106(2): 502–30.

Mytelka, L. (2004) 'Catching up in New Wave Technologies', *Oxford Development Studies*, 3(3): 389–405.

National Research Council (1999) *Funding a Revolution: Government Support for Computing Research* (Washington, DC: National Academy Press).

Naudé, W. A. (2007) 'Peace, Prosperity and Pro-Growth Entrepreneurship', Discussion Paper 2007/02 (Helsinki: UNU-WIDER).

Naudé, W. A. (2008) 'Entrepreneurship in Economic Development', UNU-WIDER Research Paper 2008/20 (Helsinki: UNU-WIDER).

Naudé, W. A. (2009a) 'Entrepreneurship, Post-Conflict' in T. Addison and T. Brück (eds) *Making Peace Work: The Challenges of Social and Economic Reconstruction* (Basingstoke: Palgrave Macmillan for UNU-WIDER).

Naudé, W. A. (2009b) 'Geography, Transport and Africa's Proximity Gap', *Journal of Transport Geography*, 17(1): 1–9.

Naudé, W. A. (2009c) 'Out with the Sleaze, in with the Ease: Insufficient for Entrepreneurial Development?', Research Paper 2009/01 (Helsinki: UNU-WIDER).

Naudé, W. A. (2010) 'Entrepreneurship, Developing Countries and Development Economics: New Approaches and Insights', *Small Business Economics*, 34(1): 1–12.

Naudé, W. A., Gries, T., Wood, E. and Meintjes, A. (2008) 'Regional Determinants of Entrepreneurial Start-Ups in a Developing Country', *Entrepreneurship and Regional Development*, 20(2): 111–24.

Naudé, W. A., Oostendorp, R. and Serumaga-Zake, P. A. E. (2002) 'South African Manufacturing in an African Context: Findings from Firm-Level Surveys', *South African Journal of Economics*, 70(7): 1247–72.

Naudé, W. A., Santos-Paulino, A. and McGillivray, M. (2008) 'Fragile States', Research Brief 3 (Tokyo : UNU).

Nelson, R. R. (1991) 'Why Do Firms Differ and How Does It Matter?', *Strategic Management Journal*, 12(8): 61–74.

Nelson, R. R. and Pack, H. (1999) 'The Asian Miracle and Modern Growth Theory', *The Economic Journal*, 109(457): 416–36.

Nelson, R. R. and Winter, S. G. (1982) *An Evolutionary Theory of Economic Change* (Cambridge, MA: Harvard University Press).

Nijkamp, P. (2003) 'Entrepreneurship in a Modern Network Economy', *Regional Studies*, 37(4): 395–405.

Nijkamp, P. and Poot, J. (1997) 'Endogenous Technological Change, Long-Run Growth and Spatial Interdependence: A Survey' in C. Bertuglia, S. Lombardi and P. Nijkamp (eds) *Innovative Behaviour in Time and Space* (Heidelberg: Springer).

Nijkamp, P. and Poot, J. (1998) 'Spatial Perspectives on New Theories of Economic Growth', *Annals of Regional Science*, 32(1): 7–37.

Nijkamp, P. and Stough, R. (eds) (2002) 'Entrepreneurship and Regional Economic Development', *Annals of Regional Science*, 36(3): 369–71.

Niosi, J. (2008) 'Technology, Development and Innovation Systems: An Introduction', *Journal of Development Studies*, 44(5): 613–21.

Noorman, A. (2002) 'Flexibele Specialisatie en Virtuele Organisaties', Masters thesis (Amsterdam: VU University).

Nooteboom, B., Vanhaverbeke, W., Duysters, G., Gilsing, V. A. and van den Oord, A. (2007) 'Optimal Cognitive Distance and Absorptive Capacity', *Research Policy*, 36(7): 1016–34.

North, D. C. (1990) *Institutions, Institutional Change and Economic Performance* (Cambridge: Cambridge University Press).

North, D. C. (1991) 'Institutions', *Journal of Economic Perspective*, 5(1): 97–112.

Norton, R. D. (2001) *Creating the New Economy* (Cheltenham: Edward Elgar).

Nyström, K. (2008) 'Is Entrepreneurship the Salvation for Enhanced Economic Growth?', CESIS Electronic Working Paper Series 143 (Stockholm: Royal Institute of Technology).

Oakey, R. (ed.) (1996) *New Technology-Based Firms in the 1990s* (London: Paul Chapman).

Organization for Economic Cooperation and Development (1989) *Mechanisms for Job Creation: Lessons from the United States* (Paris: OECD).

Organization for Economic Cooperation and Development (1998) *Fostering Entrepreneurship* (Paris: OECD).

Organization for Economic Cooperation and Development (2007) *Baltic Partnerships, Integration, Growth and Local Governance in the Baltic Sea Region* (Paris: OECD).

OECD/Eurostat (2009) 'OECD/Eurostat Entrepreneurship Indicator Programme, Indicator Framework', available at: http://www.oecd.org/dataoecd/44/27/44069965.pdf

Oerlemans, L. A. G., Pretorius, M. W., Buys, A. J. and Rooks, G. (2004) *Industrial Innovation in South Africa, 1998–2000* (Pretoria: University of Pretoria).

Osiander, A. (2001) 'Sovereignty, International Relations and the Westphalian Myth', *International Organization*, 55(2): 251–87.

Parker, S. C. (2003) 'Asymmetric Information, Occupational Choice and Government Policy', *The Economic Journal*, 113: 861–82.

Parker, S. C. (2004) *The Economics of Self-Employment and Entrepreneurship* (Cambridge: Cambridge University Press).

Parker, S. C. (2006) 'Entrepreneurship, Self-Employment and the Labour Market' in M. Casson, B. Yeung, A. Basu and N. Wadeson (eds) *The Oxford Handbook of Entrepreneurship* (Oxford: Oxford University Press).

Parker, S. C. (2007) 'Law and the Economics of Entrepreneurship', *Comparative Labor Law and Policy Journal*, 28: 695–716.

Pearson, K. (1901) 'On Lines and Planes of Closestfit to Systems of Points Inspace', *The London, Edinburgh and Dublin Philosophical Magazine and Journal of Sciences*, 6: 559–72.

Penrose, E. (1959) *The Theory of the Growth of the Firm* (Oxford: Oxford University Press).

Petit, G., Salou, G., Beziz, P. and Degain, C. (1996) 'An Update of OECD Leading Indicators', paper presented at the OECD Meeting on 'Leading Indicators', October (Paris, France).

Pettigrew, A. and Whipp, R. (1991) *Managing Change for Competitive Success* (Oxford: Blackwell).

Phan, P. P., Venkataraman, S. and Velamuri, S. R. (2008) *Entrepreneurship in Emerging Regions Around the World: Theory, Evidence and Implication* (Cheltenham: Edward Elgar).

Piazza-Georgi, B. (2002) 'The Role of Human and Social Capital in Growth: Extending our Understanding', *Cambridge Journal of Economics*, 26(4): 461–79.

Pineder, M. (2001) *Entrepreneurial Competition and Industrial Location* (Cheltenham: Edward Elgar).

Piore, M. J. and Sabel, C. F. (1984) *The Second Industrial Divide: Possibilities for Prosperity* (New York: Basic Books).

Pisano, G. P. (2006) *Science Business: The Promise, the Reality and the Future of Biotech* (Boston, MA: Harvard Business School Press).

Porter, M. E. (1990) *The Competitive Advantage of Nations* (New York: The Free Press).

Porter, M. E. (2000) 'Location, Competition and Economic Development; Local Clusters in the Global Economy', *Economic Development Quarterly*, 14(1): 15–31.

Porter, M. E. (2003) 'The Economic Performance of Regions', *Regional Studies*, 37(6/7): 549–78.

Porter, M. E. (2004) 'Building the Microeconomic Foundations of Prosperity: Findings from the Business Competitiveness Index' in M. E. Porter, K. Schwab, X. Sala-i-Martin and A. Lopez-Claros (eds) *The Global Competitiveness Report 2003–2004* (New York: Oxford University Press and World Economic Forum).

Prahalad, C. K. and Ramaswamy, V. (2004) *The Future of Competition* (Boston, MA: Harvard Business School Press).

Pred, A. (1977) *City-Systems in Advanced Economies* (London: Hutchinson).

Preissl, B. and Solimene, L. (2003) *The Dynamics of Clusters and Innovation* (Berlin: Springer).

Rabellotti, R. (1997) *External Economies and Cooperation in Industrial Districts* (London: Palgrave Macmillan).

Reggiani, A. and Nijkamp, P. (eds) (2006) *Spatial Dynamics, Networks and Modelling* (Cheltenham: Edward Elgar).

Renzulli, L. A., Aldrich, H. and Moody, J. (2000) 'Family Matters: Gender, Networks and Entrepreneurial Outcomes', *Social Forces*, 79(2): 523–46.

Reynolds, P. D., Bosma, N., Autio, E., Hunt, S. De Bono, N., Servais, I., Lopez-Garcia, P. and Chin, N. (2005) 'Global Entrepreneurship Monitor: Data Collection Design and Implementation 1998–2003', *Small Business Economics*, 24(3): 205–31.

Reynolds, P. D., Bygrave, W., Autio, E., Cox, L. and Hay, M. (2002) *Global Entrepreneurship Monitor Executive Report* (Babson Park, MA: Babson College, London: London Business School and Kansas City, MO: Kauffman Foundation).

Reynolds, P. D., Hay, M. and Camp, S. M. (1999) *Global Entrepreneurship Monitor* (Babson Park, MA: Babson College, London: London Business School and Kansas City, MO: Kauffman Foundation).

Roberts, E. B. (1991) *Entrepreneurs in High Technology* (New York: Oxford University Press).

Robson, M. (2007) 'Explaining Cross-National Variations in Entrepreneurship: The Role of Social Protection and Political Culture', *Comparative Labor Law and Policy Journal*, 28: 863–75.

Rodriguez, F. and Rodrik, D. (2000) 'Trade Policy and Economic Growth: A Sceptic's Guide to the Cross-National Evidence' in B. Bernanke and K. S. Rogoff (eds) *NBER Macroeconomics Annual 2000*, Volume 15 (Cambridge, MA: MIT Press).

Rodrik, D. (2001) 'The Global Governance of Trade as if Development Really Mattered' (New York: UNDP), available at: http://www.wcfia.harvard.edu/node/587

Rodrik, D., Subramanian, A. and Trebbi, F. (2004) 'Institutions Rule: The Primacy of Institutions over Geography and Integration in Economic Development', *Journal of Economic Growth*, 9(2): 131–65.

Roller, R. and Waverman, L. (2001) 'Telecommunications Infrastructure and Economic Development: A Simultaneous Approach', *American Economic Review*, 91(4): 909–23.

Romer, P. M. (1986) 'Increasing Returns and Long-run Growth', *Journal of Political Economy*, 94(5): 1002–37.

Romer, P. M. (1990) 'Endogenous Technological Change', *Journal of Political Economy*, 98(5): S71–S102.

Rooks, G., Oerlemans, L. A. G., Buys, A. J. and Pretorius, M. W. (2005) 'Industrial Innovation in South Africa: A Comparative Study', *South African Journal of Science*, 101(3/4): 149–50.

Rooks, G., Szirmai, A. and Sserwanga A. (2009) 'The Interplay of Human and Social Capital in Entrepreneurship in Developing Countries: The Case of Uganda', Research Paper 2009/09 (Helsinki: UNU-WIDER).

Roper, S. (2001) 'Innovation, Networks and Plant Location: Some Evidence for Ireland', *Regional Studies*, 36(3): 373–86.

Rostow, W. W. (1960) *The Stages of Economic Growth: A Non-Communist Manifesto* (Cambridge: Cambridge University Press).

Roweis, S. (1998) 'EM Algorithms for PCA and SPCA', *Advances in Neural Information Processing Systems*, 10: 626–32.

Rui, H. and Yip, G. S. (2008) 'Foreign Acquisitions by Chinese Firms: A Strategic Intent Perspective', *Journal of World Business*, 43: 213–26.

Sabel, C. F. and Zeitlin, J. (1985) 'Historical Alternatives to Mass Production: Politics, Markets and Technology in Nineteenth Century Industrialization', *Past and Present*, 108: 133–76.

Sachs, D. J. and Warner, A. M. (1997) 'Fundamental Sources of Long-Run Growth', *American Economic Review*, 87: 184–8.

Sachs, J. D., Warner, A. M., Åslund, A. and Fischer, S. (1995) 'Economic Reform and the Process of Global Integration', *Brookings Papers on Economic Activity*, 1: 1–118.

Saisana, M. and Tarantola, S. (2002) *State-of-the-Art Report on Current Methodologies and Practices for Composite Indicator Development* (Paris: OECD).

Salgado-Banda, H. (2007) 'Entrepreneurship and Economic Growth: An Empirical Analysis', *Journal of Developmental Entrepreneurship*, 12(1): 3–29.

Sanders, M. (2007) 'Scientific Paradigms, Entrepreneurial Opportunities and Cycles in Economic Growth', *Small Business Economics*, 28: 339–54.

Saxenian, A. L. (2006) *The New Argonauts: Regional Advantage in a Global Economy* (Cambridge, MA: Harvard University Press).

Say, J. B. (1803) *A Treatise on Political Economy, or the Production, Distribution and Consumption of Wealth* (London).

Scarpetta, S., Hemmings, P., Tressel, T. and Woo, J. (2002) 'The Role of Policy and Institutions for Productivity and Firm Dynamics: Evidence from Micro and Industry Data', Working Paper 329 (Paris: OECD).

Schmitz, J. A. (1989) 'Imitation, Entrepreneurship and Long-Run Growth', *Journal of Political Economy*, 97(3): 721–39.

Schneider, F. and Enste, D. H. (2000) 'Shadow Economies: Size, Causes and Consequences', *Journal of Economic Literature*, 38(1): 77–114.

Schramm, C. J. (2004) 'Building Entrepreneurial Economies', *Foreign Affairs*, 83: 104–15.

Schulpen, L. and Gibbon, P. (2002) 'Private Sector Development: Policies, Practices and Problems', *World Development*, 30(1): 1–15.

Schultz, T. W. (1975) 'The Value of the Ability to Deal with Disequilibria', *Journal of Economic Literature*, 13(3): 827–46.

Schultz, T. W. (1980) 'Investment in Entrepreneurial Ability', *Scandinavian Journal of Economics*, 82: 437–48.

Schumpeter, J. A. (1911/1934) *The Theory of Economic Development: An Inquiry into Profits, Capital, Credit, Interest and the Business Cycle* (Cambridge, MA: Harvard University Press).

Schumpeter, J. A. (1933) 'The Common Sense of Econometrics', *Econometrica*, 1: 5–12.

Schumpeter, J. A. (1942) *Capitalism, Socialism and Democracy* (New York: Harper and Row).

Schumpeter, J. A. (1950) *Capitalism, Socialism and Democracy* (New York: Harper and Row).

Scott, A. J. and Storper, M. (2003) 'Regions, Globalization and Development', *Regional Studies*, 37(6/7): 579–93.

Sen, A. (2000) *Development as Freedom* (New York: Anchor Books).

Serida, J., Borda, A. and Nakamatsu, K. (2006) *Global Entrepreneurship Monitor: Peru 2006* (Lima: Universidad Esan).

Shan, J. (2005) 'Does Financial Development "Lead" Economic Growth? A Vector Auto-Regression Appraisal', *Applied Economics*, 37(12): 1353–67.

Shane, S. A. (2003) *A General Theory of Entrepreneurship: The Individual-Opportunity Nexus* (Cheltenham: Edward Elgar).

Shane, S. A. (2008) *The Illusions of Entrepreneurship. The Costly Myths that Entrepreneurs, Investors and Policy Makers Live by* (New Haven, CT and London: Yale University Press).

Shane, S. A. and Venkataraman, S. (2000) 'The Promise of Entrepreneurship as a Field of Research', *The Academy of Management Review*, 25(1): 217–26.

Shanghai Bar Association (2006) 'The Situation of Illegal Business Activities Practised by the Foreign Law Firms in Shanghai is Severe', memorandum, 17 April.

Shapero, A. (1984) 'The Entrepreneurial Event' in C. A. Kent (ed.) *The Environment for Entrepreneurship* (Lexington, MA: Lexington Books).

Siebert, H. (2007) 'China: Coming to Grips with the New Global Player', *The World Economy*, 30(6): 893–922.

Siegfried, J. J. and Evans, L. B. (1994) 'Empirical Studies of Entry and Exit', *Review of Industrial Organization*, 9(2): 121–55.

Smallbone, D. and Welter, F. (2001) 'The Distinctiveness of Entrepreneurship in Transition Economies', *Small Business Economics*, 16(4): 249–62.

Smith, M. P. (2001) *Transnational Urbanism: Locating Globalization* (Oxford: Blackwell).

Sobel, R. S. (2007) 'Entrepreneurship', entry in *The Concise Encyclopedia of Economics*, Second Edition, Indianapolis, available at: www.econlib.org/library/Enc/Entrepreneurship.html

Sobel, R. S. (2008) 'Testing Baumol: Institutional Quality and the Productivity of Entrepreneurship', *Journal of Business Venturing*, 23(6): 641–55.

Sobel, R. S., Clark, J. R. and Lee, D. R. (2007) 'Freedom, Barriers to Entry, Entrepreneurship and Economic Progress', *Review of Austrian Economics*, 20: 221–36.

Stam, E. (2003) 'Why Butterflies Don't Leave', PhD thesis (Utrecht: University of Utrecht).

Statistics Netherlands (2007) 'Figures on the Investment Climate in the Netherlands 2007' (Voorburg/Heerlen).

Stevenson, L. and Lundström, A. (2005) 'Entrepreneurship Policy for the Future: Best Practice Components' in R. van der Horst, S. King-Kauanui and S. Duffy (eds) *Keystones of Entrepreneurship Knowledge* (Oxford: Blackwell Publishing).

Stevenson, L. and Lundström, A. (2007) 'Dressing the Emperor: The Fabric of Entrepreneurship Policy' in D. B. Audretsch, I. Grilo and R. Thurik (eds) *The Handbook of Entrepreneurship Policy* (Cheltenham: Edward Elgar).

Stiglitz, J. E. (2006) 'Civil Strife and Economic and Social Policies', *The Economics of Peace and Security Journal*, 1: 5–9.

Stintchcombe, A. L., MacDill, M. S. and Walker, D. (1968) 'Demography of Organizations', *American Journal of Sociology*, 74(3): 221–9.

Storey, D. (1991) 'The Birth of New Firms: Does Unemployment Matter? A Review of the Evidence', *Small Business Economics*, 3(3): 167–78.

Storey, D. (1994) *Understanding the Small Business Sector* (London: Routledge).

Storey, D. (2005) 'Entrepreneurship, Small and Medium Sized Enterprises and Public Policies' in Z. J. Acs and D. B. Audretsch (eds) *Handbook of Entrepreneurship Research: An Interdisciplinary Survey and Introduction* (New York: Springer).

Storper, M. (1993) 'Regional "Worlds" of Production: Learning and Innovation in the Technology Districts of France, Italy and the USA', *Regional Studies*, 27: 433–55.

Stough, R. (2003) 'Strategic Management of Places and Policy', *Annals of Regional Science*, 37(2): 179–202.

Stough, R., Kukkarni, R. and Paelinck, J. (2002) 'ICT and Knowledge Challenges for Entrepreneurs in Regional Economic Development' in Z. J. Acs, H. L. F. de

Groot and P. Nijkamp (eds) *The Emergence of the Knowledge Economy: A Regional Perspective* (Berlin: Springer).

Suarez-Villa, L. (1989) *The Evolution of Regional Economies: Entrepreneurship and Macroeconomic Change* (New York: Praeger).

Suarez-Villa, L. (1996) 'Innovative Capacity, Infrastructure and Regional Policy' in D. F. Batten and C. Karlsson (eds) *Infrastructure and the Complexity of Economic Development* (Berlin: Springer).

Szirmai, A. (2008) 'Explaining Success and Failure in Development', Working Paper 2008–013 (Maastricht: UNU-MERIT).

Taslim, M. A. (1988) 'Tenancy and Interlocking Markets: Issues and Some Evidence', *World Development*, 16(6): 655–66.

Taylor, E. J. (2006) 'International Migration and Economic Development', paper presented at the 'International Symposium on International Migration and Development', UN Population Division (Turin, Italy), 28–30 June.

Teece, D. J. (1993) 'The Dynamics of Industrial Capitalism: Perspectives on Alfred Chandler's "Scale and Scope"', *Journal of Economic Literature*, 31(1): 199–225.

Teece, D. J., Pisano, G. and Shuen, A. (1997) 'Dynamic Capabilities and Strategic Management', *Strategic Management Journal*, 18(7): 509–33.

Thompson, W. R. (1968) 'Internal and External Factors in the Development of Urban Economies' in H. S. Perloff and L. Wingo (eds) *Issues in Urban Economics* (Baltimore, MD: Johns Hopkins University Press).

Thornton, J. (1996) 'Financial Deepening and Economic Growth in Developing Economies', *Applied Economics Letters*, 3: 243–46.

Thornton, P. H. (1999) 'The Sociology of Entrepreneurship', *Annual Review of Sociology*, 25: 19–46.

Thurik, A. R. (2009) 'Entreprenomics: Entrepreneurship, Economic Growth and Policy' in Z. J. Acs, D. B. Audretsch and R. Strom (eds) *Entrepreneurship, Growth and Public Policy* (Cambridge: Cambridge University Press), 219–249.

Thurik, R., Carree, M., van Stel, A. and Audretsch, D. B. (2008) 'Does Self-employment Reduce Unemployment?', *Journal of Business Venturing*, 23(16): 673–86.

Tiebout, C. (1956) 'A Pure Theory of Local Expenditures', *Journal of Political Economy*, 64(5): 416–24.

Timmons, J. A. and Spinelli, S. (2007) *New Venture Creation: Entrepreneurship for the 21st Century*, 7th Edition (New York: McGraw-Hill/Irwin).

Tipping, M. E. and Bishop, C. M. (1999) 'Mixtures of Probabilistic Principal Component Analyzers', *Neural Computation*, 11(2): 443–82.

Upton, D. M. and McAfee, A. (1996) 'The Real Virtual Factory', *Harvard Business Review*, July–August: 69–89.

van Delft, H., Gorter, C. and Nijkamp, P. (2000) 'In Search of Ethnic Entrepreneurship Opportunities in the City: A Comparative Study', *Environment and Planning C*, 18(4): 429–51.

Van der Linden and Robert, F. (2002) *Airlines and Air Mail: The Post Office and the Birth of the Commercial Aviation Industry* (Lexington, KY: University Press of Kentucky).

Van der Maaten, L. J. P. (2007) 'An Introduction to Dimensionality Reduction Using Matlab', MICC/IKAT, Report MICC 07–07 (Maastricht: University of Maastricht).

Van Geenhuizen, M. (1993) 'A Longitudinal Analysis of the Growth of Firms', PhD thesis (Rotterdam: Erasmus University).

Van Geenhuizen, M. and Nijkamp, P. (1995) 'A Demographic Approach to Firm Dynamics', Serie Research Memoranda, 25 (Amsterdam: Free University).

Van Geenhuizen, M. and Nijkamp, P. (2004) 'In Search of Urban Futures in the E-Economy' in M. Beuthe, V. Himanen, A. Reggiani and L. Zamparini (eds) *Transport, Development and Innovation in an Evolving World* (Berlin: Springer).

Van Geenhuizen, M. and Ratti, R. (eds) (2001) *Gaining Advantage from Open Borders* (Aldershot: Ashgate).

Van Geenhuizen, M. and van der Knaap, G. A. (1994) 'Dutch Textile Industry in a Global Economy', *Journal of Regional Studies*, 28(7): 695–711.

Van Oort, F. G. (2004) *Urban Growth and Innovation* (Aldershot: Ashgate).

Van Stel, A., Carree, M. and Thurik, R. (2005) 'The Effect of Entrepreneurial Activity on National Economic Growth', *Small Business Economics*, 24(3): 311–21.

Van Stel, A., Storey, D. J. and Thurik, R. (2007) 'The Effect of Business Regulations on Nascent and Young Business Entrepreneurship', *Small Business Economics*, 28(2–3): 171–86.

Van Veen, E. (2007) 'The Valuable Tool of Sovereignty: Its Use in Situations of Competition and Interdependence', Bruges Political Research Papers (Bruges: College of Europe).

Van Wissen, L. J. G. (2000) 'A Micro-Simulation Model of Firms: Applications of the Concept of the Demography of Firms', *Papers in Regional Science*, 79: 111–34.

Verheul, I., Wennekers, S., Audretsch, D. B. and Thurik, R. (2002) 'An Eclectic Theory of Entrepreneurship' in D. B. Audretsch, R. Thurik, I. Verheul and S. Wennekers (eds) *Entrepreneurship: Determinants and Policy in a European–US Comparison* (Boston/Dordrecht: Kluwer Academia Publishers), 11–81.

Vernon, R. (1970) 'Organization as a Scale Factor in the Growth of Firms' in J. W. Markham and G. F. Papanek (eds) *Industrial Organization and Economic Development* (Boston, MA: Houghton Mifflin).

Vyas, S. and Kumaranayake, L. (2006) 'Constructing Socio-Economic Status Indices: How to Use Principal Components Analysis', *Health Policy and Planning*, 21: 459–68.

Wada, K. (2006) 'The Fable of the Birth of the Japanese Automobile Industry: The Toyoda-Platt Agreement of 1929', *Business History*, 48(1): 90–118.

Waldinger, R. (1996) *Still the Promised City?* (Cambridge, MA: Harvard University Press).

Walter, T. J., Balunywa, W., Rosa, P., Sserwanga, A., Barabas, S. and Namatovu, R. (2003) *Global Entrepreneurship Monitor: Uganda Executive Report 2003* (Kampala: Makerere University Business School).

Walter, T. J., Balunywa, W., Rosa, P., Sserwanga, A., Barabas, S. and Namatovu, R. (2004) *Global Entrepreneurship Monitor: Uganda Executive Report 2004* (Kampala: Makerere University Business School).

Wennekers, S. and Thurik, R. (1999) 'Linking Entrepreneurship and Economic Growth', *Small Business Economics*, 13: 27–55.

Wennekers, S., van Stel, A., Thurik, R. and Reynolds, P. (2005) 'Nascent Entrepreneurship and the Level of Economic Development', *Small Business Economics*, 24(3): 293–309.

Westerhuis, J. A., Kourti, T. and MacGregor, J. F. (1998) 'Analysis of Multiblock and Hierarchical PCA and PLS Models', *Journal of Chemometrics*, 12: 301–21.

Whyte, W. H. (1960) *The Organization Man* (Harmondsworth: Penguin).

Wigand, R. (1997) 'Electronic Commerce', *The Information Society*, 13(1): 1–16.

Wiggens, S. N. (1995) 'Entrepreneurial Enterprises, Endogenous Ownership and Limits to Firm Size', *Economic Inquiry*, 33(1): 54–69.

Williams, C. C. (2009) 'The Motives of Off-the-books Entrepreneurs: Necessity or Opportunity-driven?', *The International Entrepreneurship and Management Journal*, 5(2): 203–17.

Williamson, O. E. (1975) *Markets and Hierarchies: Analysis and Antitrust Implications* (New York: The Free Press).

Williamson, O. E. (1985) *The Economic Institutions of Capitalism* (New York: The Free Press).

Windrum, P. and Koch, P. (eds) (2008) *Innovation in Public Sector Services* (Cheltenham: Edward Elgar).

Wold, S., Esbensen, K. and Geladi, P. (1987) 'Principal Component Analysis', *Chemometrics and Intelligent Laboratory Systems*, 2: 37–52.

Wong, P. K., Ho, Y.-P. and Autio, E. (2005) 'Entrepreneurship, Innovation and Economic Growth: Evidence from GEM Data', *Small Business Economics*, 24(3): 335–50.

Woo-Cumings, M. (ed.) (1999) *The Developmental State* (Ithaca, NY: Cornell University Press).

Woolcock, M. (1998) 'Social Capital and Economic Development: Toward a Theoretical Synthesis and Policy Framework', *Theory and Society*, 27(2): 151–208.

Wooldridge, J. M. (2002) *Econometric Analysis of Cross Section and Panel Data* (Cambridge, MA: MIT Press).

World Bank (2000) 'Anticorruption in Transition: A Contribution to the Policy Debate', available at: www.worldbank.org/ wbi/governance/pdf/contribution.pdf

World Bank (n.d.) *World Development Indicators* (Washington, DC: World Bank).

The World Bank Group Entrepreneurship Survey (WBGES) (2008), available at: www.econ.worldbank.org/wbsite/external/extdec/extresearch/0,,contentMDK:21942814~pagePK:64214825~piPK:64214943~theSitePK:469382,00.html

World Economic Forum (WEF) (2007) *Global Competitiveness Report 2007–2008* (Geneva: WEF).

Xie, W. and White, S. (2004) 'Sequential Learning in a Chinese Spin-Off: The Case of Lenovo Group Ltd.', *R&D Management*, 34(4): 407–22.

Yonekawa, S.-i. (1984) 'University Graduates in Japanese Enterprises before the Second World War', *Business History*, 26(2) 193–218.

You, J. (1995) 'Critical Survey: Small Firms in Economic Theory', *Cambridge Journal of Economics*, 20: 441–62.

Young, A. (1998) 'Growth without Scale Effects', *Journal of Political Economy*, 106(1): 41–63.

Zabala-Iturriagagoitia, J. M., Jiménez-Sáez, F., Castro-Martínez, E. and Gutiérrez-García, A. (2007) 'What Indicators Do (or Do Not) Tell Us About Regional Innovation Systems', *Scientometrics*, 70(1): 85–106.

Zacharakis, A. L., Bygrave, W. D. and Shepherd, D. A. (2000) *Global Entrepreneurship Monitor: National Entrepreneurship Assessment: United States of America* (Babson Park, MA: Babson College and Kansas City, MO: Kauffman Foundation).

Zhang, Y. (2009) 'Alliance-based Network View on Chinese Firms' Catching-up: Case Study of Huawei Technologies Co. Ltd., Working Paper 2009–039 (Maastricht: UNU-MERIT).

Zuin, V. (2004) 'Business Strategies of Informal Micro-Entrepreneurs in Lima, Peru', Discussion Paper 150/2004 (Geneva: ILO).

Index